Indigenous Cultural Centers and Museums

Indigenous Cultural Centers and Museums

An Illustrated International Survey

Anoma Pieris

ROWMAN & LITTLEFIELD
Lanham • Boulder • New York • London

This project was funded by an Australian Research Council Linkage Grant (2010–2012) titled *Indigenous Place-Making in Central Melbourne: Representations, Practices and Creative Research*; an Ian Potter Travel Grant 2009, and a seeding grant, publication grant, and Special Studies Program (SSP) funds from the Faculty of Architecture, Building and Planning at the University of Melbourne in 2009 and 2010.

Published by Rowman & Littlefield
A wholly owned subsidiary of The Rowman & Littlefield Publishing Group, Inc.
4501 Forbes Boulevard, Suite 200, Lanham, Maryland 20706
www.rowman.com

Unit A, Whitacre Mews, 26-34 Stannary Street, London SE11 4AB

British Library Cataloguing in Publication Information Available

Library of Congress Cataloging-in-Publication Data

Names: Pieris, Anoma, author.
Title: Indigenous cultural centers and museums : an illustrated international survey / Anoma Pieris.
Description: Lanham, Maryland : Rowman & Littlefield, 2016. | Includes bibliographical references and index.
Identifiers: LCCN 2016012582 (print) | LCCN 2016013538 (ebook) | ISBN 9781442264069 (cloth : alk. paper) | ISBN 9781442264076 (Electronic)
Subjects: LCSH: Arts facilities. | Museums and indigenous peoples.
Classification: LCC NA6811 .P54 2016 (print) | LCC NA6811 (ebook) | DDC 725/.8042—dc23
LC record available at http://lccn.loc.gov/2016012582

∞™ The paper used in this publication meets the minimum requirements of American National Standard for Information Sciences—Permanence of Paper for Printed Library Materials, ANSI/NISO Z39.48-1992.

Printed in the United States of America

Contents

List of Figures

List of Plates

Preface

This study is integral to a broader Australian Research Council (ARC) Linkage Project titled *Indigenous Place-Making in Central Melbourne: Representations, Practices and Creative Research*, and it involves preliminary research toward creating a Victorian Indigenous Cultural Education and Knowledge Centre in Melbourne. The ARC Project (2010–2012) was conducted by a team of researchers from the University of Melbourne's Faculty of Architecture, Building and Planning, led by Janet McGaw with Anoma Pieris and Graham Brawn, and Emily Potter from Deakin University's School of Communication and Creative Arts. Research Assistants on this project during 2010 to 2013 included Carolynne Baker, Fiona Johnson, Naomi Tootell, Tom Newman-Morris, and Rueben Berg. Our partner organizations were the Victorian Traditional Owners Land Justice Group (VTOLJG), the Melbourne City Council and Reconciliation Victoria. The VTOLJG is a community organization of traditional owner groups in Victoria. The executive members and personnel of these organizations have supported our project and its activities. The book would not have been realized without the infectious enthusiasm of Gary Murray, the current Dhudhuroa Member on the VTOLJG, and of Janina Harding, former manager of the Indigenous Arts Program at the City of Melbourne.

I largely compiled the material in this book over the ARC grant period following personal visits to many of the cultural centers featured here. Where this was not possible, research was conducted through telephone and email correspondence with architects, administrators, and stakeholders, all of whom are acknowledged in the references. They in turn reviewed and modified the text to reflect their stories. Most photographs were taken on site, but where this was not possible architects provided their own excellent images. I have also depended heavily on the Internet websites of organizations or architectural practices for material on less well-known facilities. Selections were contingent on the availability and accessibility of people and material, and the depth of analysis of any particular facility is a reflection of the degree of engagement possible at the time. Many factors, such as distance, availability of architects or administrators, and the need to seek approval from a number of stakeholders have also impacted the results.

The international content in this book was inspired by the symposium, "Practices Process and Politics of Place-Making" held at the University of Melbourne in June 2010, when academics, architects, and curators such as Lisa Findley, Emmanuel Kasaherou, Rewi Thompson,

Dillon Kombumerri, Carroll Go-Sam, Gregory Burgess, Tony Birch, and Chris Healy shared their experiences alongside Traditional Owners from around the state of Victoria.

The questions that drove our study of precedents were twofold: the lack of Indigenous cultural centers in Australian metropolitan centers, and the difficulties faced in building and sustaining them in remote locations. Our findings have been published in a book titled *Indigenous Place*, which gives a broad overview of creative place-making strategies deployed by Indigenous communities in Australia, and an academic book titled *Assembling the Centre: Architecture for Indigenous Cultures: Australia and Beyond* published in 2015.

Ten of the fourteen case studies that were embedded in our book *Assembling the Centre* have been further elaborated in this book as separate chapters devoted to physical facilities. They inform the content of the following nine chapters: chapter 1, Aboriginal Tent Embassy; chapter 2, Australian Institute of Aboriginal and Torres Strait Islander Studies and National Museum of Australia; chapter 20, Musée du Quai Branly and Universitè Wing; chapter 22, Museum of New Zealand Te Papa Tongarewa; chapter 25, National Museum of the American Indian and Cultural Resources Center; chapter 26, Needwonnee Walk; chapter 30, Reconciliation Place; chapter 33, Sámi Parliaments, Norway, Sweden, and Finland; and chapter 38, Uluru-Kata Tjuta Cultural Centre. This book offers a different kind of overview of this material, framed as a survey of multiple extrapolations of the center brief, the versatility of which best emerges through comparative study. The following chapters have been replicated from *Assembling the Centre*: chapter 17, Living Kaurna Cultural Centre, and chapter 28, Nk'Mip Desert Cultural Centre (which were published as case studies 5 and 6 in chapter 4, Land: Belonging, Law, Rights); chapter 23, Musgrave Park (which was published as case study 9 in chapter 6, (Im)materialities: Clearing, Erasure, Disguise); and chapter 24, National Centre of Indigenous Excellence (which was published as case study 13 in chapter 8, Conclusion: Re-Assembling the Indigenous Cultural Centre). The following chapters were originally published in *Architecture Australia*, the magazine of the Australian Institute of Architects, and have been reproduced with permission: chapter 29 was originally published as Elizabeth Grant, "Port Augusta Courts," *Architecture Australia* 98, no. 5 (2009): 86–90; and chapter 39 was originally published as Michael Tawa, "Wilcannia Health Service," *Architecture Australia* 19, no. 4 (2002): 70–76.

The diversity of responses featured serves to illustrate the complexity of the sociospatial environments and scenarios that are shaped by their "Indigenous" attributes. I have not attempted to theorize these responses except in the Introduction in order to gain a broader popular reception for this book and by doing so to expand its audience.

Extensive collaboration during the writing process mirrors in part the complex engagements required of these commissions. As with any project, there are many gaps and omissions that we strove hard to address. It is possible that the administrators who communicated with us, or the funding for these organizations, have altered since our discussions and visits, which is a reflection of the economic fragility of many of these ventures. I apologize for any mistakes or misrepresentations on our part. All monetary figures are given in US currency as approximate at the time of completion of the projects concerned. Photographs commissioned by the architects typically represent the current condition of the projects at the time of completion, and if provided by the author they were taken at the time of the research visit (between 2009 and 2012). Readers viewing this publication should be aware that names may be mentioned or images portrayed of people who are now deceased. Any distress this might cause is sincerely regretted.

Acknowledgments

This book is the result of many conversations at Indigenous cultural facilities or by telephone and via email, during which texts, photographic material, and web-based information was passed back and forth. This dialogic process, which has been detailed further below, involved administrators, architects, Indigenous stakeholders, and others involved in the conception, design, or management of the facilities we have studied. I am indebted to all those who generously responded to my many queries and to the architects, center or museum administrators, and photographers who generously provided the material for this book. My colleague, Janet McGaw, who framed and led the wider ARC research project, provided constant invaluable support and conducted some of the research included in this book.

The international precedents were studied with an Ian Potter Travel Grant 2009, and a seeding grant, publication grant, and Special Studies Program (SSP) funds from the Faculty of Architecture, Building and Planning at the University of Melbourne in 2009 and 2010. Elizabeth Grant and Michael Tawa generously contributed chapters on facilities with which they were familiar, and our research assistants Carolynne Baker, Fiona Johnson, and Naomi Tootell researched and wrote on specific facilities. Carolynne, in particular, wrote the original texts for chapters 4, 5, 8, 11, 13, 15, and 37. Janet McGaw conducted interviews and photographed facilities in Melbourne, New Zealand, Tasmania, and Queensland, which formed the basis for their inclusion in this study. Cait Storr assisted in editing the manuscript. Thanks also to Charles Harmon at Rowman & Littlefield for giving us this opportunity.

I have detailed the grant project surrounding this book in the preface outlining the contributing institutions, including our two universities and partner organizations, the Victorian Traditional Owners Land Justice Group and the Melbourne City Council and Reconciliation Victoria. The Victorian Traditional Owners Land Justice Group (VTOLJG) is an unincorporated organization of Traditional Owner groups in Victoria that gives equal value to every voice among its large and diverse membership. The group has undergone a number of structural and personnel changes over the course of our grant. We would like, therefore, to acknowledge the endorsement and support of Len Clarke, Bobby Nicholls, and Graham Atkinson, the cochairs in 2010 when we were awarded the ARC Linkage Grant; the current executive, which includes two co-chairs, Annette Xiberras and Bobby Nichols; and three executive members, Graham Atkinson, Geoff Clark, and Darren Perry. We note the particular support and vision of the current Dhudhuroa member on the VTOLJG, Gary Murray, who was nominated by the co-chairs and executive to manage the day-to-day running of the project. Wurundjeri Elder and member for Way Wurru, Margaret Gardiner, also offered considerable support and advice. Katie Phillis, Traditional Owner Corporation Development Advisor, and Jill Webb, Policy Officer at Native Title Services Victoria, were both pivotal in facilitating the process.

We would also like to acknowledge Janina Harding, Shona Johnson, and Elizabeth Cavanagh at Melbourne City Council, and, at Reconciliation Victoria, Frank Hytten, CEO of Reconciliation Victoria until 2010; co-chairs Keith Gove and Vicki Clark; current statewide coordinator Erin McKinnon; and Helen Bnads, who supported us during the course of our project.

Specific individuals who communicated with the author and provided feedback on the respective projects are acknowledged with each chapter. They include Michael Anderson, Ruth Gilbert, Gary Foley, and Jude Kelley for the Aboriginal Tent Embassy; Tracy Sutherland, Peter Thornley, and Marie Ferris for AIATSIS and NMA; Marlene Atkinson at the Bangerang Cultural Centre; Jeremy Clark at the Brambuk Cultural Centre; Ngemba Elder Aunty Jen (Jeanette Barker), Ian Merritt, and Carole Medcalf at the Brewarrina Business Centre for the Brewarrina Aboriginal Museum; chief executive officer Ross Farnell at the Burrinja Cultural Centre; Jennifer Rayner, Anna Cossu, Alice Livingston, and Susan Sedgewick at Sydney Living Museums for Edge of the Trees; Linc Yow Yeh from the Gunung-Willam-Balluk Learning Centre; Jennifer Joy Field and staff at the Gwoonwardu Mia Gascoyne Aboriginal Heritage and Cultural Centre; Emmanuel Kasarhérou and Jean Pipite on the Jean-Marie Tjibaou Cultural Centre; Maitland Parker and Mel Berris at the Karijini Visitor Centre; Tom Mosby and Giacomina Pradolin at the Koorie Heritage Trust; Colleen Hayward at the Kurongkurl Katitjin Centre; Leonie Cameron for the Lake Tyers Training Centre and Lake Tyers Health Centre; Craig Cooper and Gavin Malone for the Living Kaurna Cultural Centre; the Public Relations Unit of the General Affairs Section at Minpaku; Philip Newland and Marion McLeod at the Mossman Gorge Centre; Magali Melandri at the Musèe du Quai Branly; William McLennan at the Museum of Anthropology, University of British Columbia; Arapata Hakiwai, Rhonda Paku, and Ian Wedde for the Museum of New Zealand Te Papa; Scott Anderson and Carroll Go-Sam for Musgrave Park; Nancia Guivarra at the National Centre of Indigenous Excellence; Fiona Rice, Leonie Dickson, and Verna Nichols for Needwonnee Walk; Evan Maloney for the Ngarluma Yindjibarndi Cultural Complex; Clarence Louie, Charlotte Stringam, Margaret Holm, and Noreen Taylor for the Nk'Mip Desert Cultural Center; Justin Estoque, Duane Blue Spruce, Tionna Moore, Lou Stancari, Tanya Thrasher, and Michael Pahn at the NMAI; Rosanne McInnes and Paul Tanner for the Port Augusta Courts; Rob Tindal for Reconciliation Place; Clair Andersen at the Riawunna Centre; Felicia Dean, Patricia McQuinn, and Brigid Thompson for the Rumbalara Medical Clinic, Mooroopna and Rumbalara Elders Care Facility; Marie Enoksson for the Sámi Parliament, Kiruna; Anders Henriksen, for the Sami Parliament, Norway; and Anneli Länsman from Sámi Parliament, Finland; Annie Chen at the Shung Ye Museum of Formosan Aborigines; David Gough, Paul Docking, and Michelle Pearce for the Tiagarra Aboriginal Cultural Centre and Museum; Neil Anderson and Geoff Olson for the Tjapukai Aboriginal Cultural Park; Damian McLean, and councillors Lalla West, Preston Thomas, and Cyril Simms for the Tjulyuru Cultural and Civic Centre; Grace Moore at Uluru Media for the Uluru-Kata Tjuta Cultural Centre; and Ron Bradfield, Beverley Iles, Peter Farmer, Jenny Dawson, and Sandra Hill for the Yagan Memorial Park. Architects consulted on their various projects provided data and clarified details. They include Howard Raggatt, Gregory Burgess, Libby Guj, Phil Harris, Glenn Murcutt: Olga Kosterin and Peter

Poulet of the Government Architect's Office, NSW; Tony Styant-Browne, John Nichols, Carey Lyon, Jefa Greenaway, Rueben Berg, Deb Fisher, Graham Brawn, Robert Toland, Denis Harrison, Peter Elliott, Hiromi Shiraishi, Tania Dennis, Dillon Kombumerri, Ivan Mercep, Richard Kirk, Bruce Hayden, Hans Murman, Janne Laukka, and Merete Haukedal. I am grateful to the architectural practices and organizations that generously provided photographs and drawings. These include the work of both professional and amateur photographers. I would particularly like to thank John Gollings, Peter Bennetts, Simon Devitt, Andrew Pritchard, Brett Boardman, Nic Lehoux, Trevor Mein, James Horan, Adam Bruzzone, Bjarne Riesto, Jaro Hollan, Mika Huisman, Mike Gillam, Jillian Wallis, Elizabeth Grant, Andrea Damarell, Lindy Joubert, and Fred Chen.

Introduction: Architectures of *Survivance*: An Antipodean Perspective

The three decades from the 1980s to the early 2000s marked a period when programs for Indigenous cultural facilities challenged abstracted aesthetic responses and demanded culturally particular, symbolic, sensorial, and social approaches to design. These approaches evolved through consultative and collaborative processes involving informed stakeholders and client groups. They presented an alternative "cultural" worldview to the postcritical formalism that dominated late-twentieth-century design culture.[1] "Time," "dialogue," and "social concerns" were reinserted into design processes that elsewhere were servicing expedient globalization. This publication reviews the architecture of this period, using Indigenous museums and cultural centers as its main foci. The architectural projects included here demonstrate that Indigenous stakeholders represent complex living communities—remote, urban, and suburban—and that they share the same metropolitan, rural, and geographical terrain with generations of settlers. These projects can reveal that metropolitan communities are often of mixed descent and share common values. They also show how, as the client group varies across regional, national, or international geographies, each community responds uniquely to its own history of dispossession or marginalization, their desires and aspirations defining very different programmatic and aesthetic outcomes.

Whereas museums are perceived as cultural contact zones with histories of conflict over collection practices and repatriation claims,[2] and the cultural center is seen as a more inclusive gathering place for people, ideas, and artifacts, these two programs remain closely related—as evident in the examples in this book. However, the consultation for and execution of Indigenous cultural building projects, and the ways in which they are conceived, fashioned, or delivered, have not always accorded with the needs and expressions of communities. The cross-cultural reeducation of architects has been an important part of this process. More significantly, as Indigenous cultural centers are increasingly incorporated into metropolitan civic programs—sometimes as tokenistic gestures alongside other strategies of gentrification—urban Indigenous communities find themselves further marginalized, either through their relative impoverishment and civic exclusion or due to shallow appropriations of their culture. The successes and failures of three decades of professional engagement with Indigenous communities offer illuminating precedents on how Australian architects have contributed to "closing the gap."[3] This book examines these interactions, focusing on purpose-built cultural facilities, with the intention of inserting Australian examples into a broader internationally vibrant field of practice. Borrowing the neologism *survivance* from the Anishinaabe cultural theorist Gerald Vizenor, it approaches the difficult gestation, execution, and reception of Indigenous cultural facilities.[4] This connection between Vizenor's ideas and an Indigenous architectural expression was made by founding director W. Richard West at the opening of the National Museum of the American Indian in Washington, DC.[5] Drawing on these various associations, this book raises the questions:

> Can architecture, including urban place-making and landscape design responses, be used to decolonize museum practice?
> Can this architecture provide a culturally inclusive, discursive political space?
> Can it give expression to the specific requirements of previously marginalized communities?
> Do their culturally ascribed social and material practices inform contemporary aesthetic responses?
> Who is best equipped to interpret and deliver these responses?
> How are these projects received?

When applied to the relationship between an Indigenous community and a metropolitan Eurocentric profession, such questions become the bases for critical aesthetic practices around issues of "identity" and "social agency." Historic injustices and discriminatory policies deepen their impact.

Vizenor combats stereotypes of Indigenous victimization and cultural subsistence with an inspiring exploration of "active survival" through the reshaping and reinvention of cultural identities. Whereas Vizenor's "postindian simulations" take the form of resistant literary and political practices, I argue that architectural responses may be similarly deconstructive.[6] They may disrupt processes of dominance and assimilation through explicit formal and aesthetic representations or implicit spatial strategies. Where architectural praxis is politically insulated and dominated by market forces, commissions for Indigenous stakeholders present innovative alternatives. This volume interrogates that possibility of designing cultural resilience as a self-conscious and socially engaged process. However, it is also mindful of some stakeholder skepticism of architecture's reconciliatory capacities, even concerning the centers we have selected for discussion. In many instances, designs for or with Indigenous communities address culturally diverse communal expectations suspicious of secular goals. Building trust and consideration for the client group's cultural needs, and demonstrating the profession's capacity to service them, becomes a challenge. Metropolitan architects designing for remote Aboriginal communities need to develop new sensitivities and competencies. The profession's preferences have been historically shaped by societal prejudices toward Aboriginals and non-Europeans as nonprogressive. The structural asymmetries and cultural binaries of this latent colonial mindset translate into Indigenous stereotypes or assimilatory models. The pursuit of abstract formalism as the iconic signifier of contemporaneity has generalized aesthetic approaches that exclude minority cultures.

Modern architecture is closely allied to Western industrialization and measured via abstract schedules, work regimes, and material and labor productivity. Its products are commodities, bought and sold in the marketplace. Community processes, interests, and desires are highly subjective, emotive, dialogic, and local. More critically for architecture, the notion of a collective cultural brief conceived for communal ownership and self-determination challenges idealized prerogatives of individuation, institutionalization, and land tenure. Indigenous groups have experienced degrees of dispossession, displacement, and detribalization followed by assimilation and institutionalization. The alienation of their rights and lands has impoverished them, in some circumstances producing extreme levels of social dysfunction. The fragility of the knowledge and social coherence they seek to emplace makes culture production critical and political. Or to argue it differently, a culture that was violently rendered intangible is being given shape, form, and physical presence through architecture. While the effectiveness of architecture in achieving this end is debatable, it provides a visible, material means for anchoring alienated rights to ancestral lands. Architecture manifests a form of ontological security—of ways of being and of dwelling—recognizable to the broader metropolitan public as a means of staking a proprietary claim.[7] Permanent physical facilities offer new zones of contact where cultural difference and complexity might be valued.

CULTURAL DIFFERENCE

The processes that altered the profession's attitudes to cultural difference responded to two decades of civil rights activism and parallel discourses on multiculturalism in Australia.[8] Multiculturalism initially recognized non-Anglophone postwar immigrants and their potential contribution to Australian society and commerce. Although largely circulated as a depoliticized discourse, the accommodation of plurality gave visibility to those forms of cultural difference that had penetrated everyday life. Both agricultural and urban consumption were transformed through immigrant activity, producing new commodities and exports. Between the 1970s and 1980s, government policies on multiculturalism waxed and waned in the wake of the Racial Discrimination Act of 1975, moving from assimilation to integration and multiculturalism.[9] Originating in migrant settlement and welfare policy, the threat of ethnic diversity to social cohesion was the main subject of debate. An Office of Multicultural Affairs was established in 1986, and policies were developed in the ensuing decade under the Labour-led Hawke and Keating governments (1983–1991 and 1991–1996).[10]

The most significant policy of this era was the Labour government's National Agenda of 1989, which focused on cultural identity, social justice, and productive diversity.[11] But the broadening of multicultural policies to incorporate Indigenous Australians proved problematic. Although the New Agenda of 1999, under the Liberal-led Howard government, recommended the separation of Indigenous and multicultural interests, these changes were not implemented.[12] While tolerant of politically inert cultural expressions, the Howard government was reticent in public policy and intolerant of affirmative action. Multiculturalism became a contentious political terrain. A nationalist backlash toward Asian immigration during the late 1990s marked a new spirit of intolerance, during which critiques of multicultural policies were voiced. In November 2001, still under the culturally conservative Howard government, Indigenous, multicultural, and immigrant affairs were incorporated in a single department. These distinctions were subsumed by a unifying citizenship discourse after the September 2001 attacks in the United States. The term *multiculturalism*, officially dropped in 2007, was revived in 2011.[13]

The 1990s was the period during which purpose-built cultural facilities began to appear in the Australian built landscape. Facilities, largely devolving from localized community arts spaces but often disconnected from political or legal bodies, were funded by state governments, councils, and some private organizations. Architects designing for Indigenous communities during this period frequently undertook commissions for other cultural groups. The programmatic type was split between the normative civic cultural center and the community facility for a cultural minority. The depoliticized emergence of cultural facilities had implications for Indigenous communities.

INDIGENOUS SELF-DETERMINATION

For Australia's Aboriginal communities, land justice is a resilient claim that reinforces associations with "country"—of geographic belonging, custodianship, and the place of their dreaming—that were disrupted by European contact. Civil rights activism during the 1960s made Aboriginal communities visible on the basis of the politics of civil rights. Similar transformations occurred in other countries where Indigenous communities became politically vocal alongside other forms of minoritarian politics. Yet the recognition of Indigenous communities came relatively late, evidence of the prejudicial scientific and humanist positions that were rallied for hegemonic national discourses and against Indigenous recognition. In fact, the political mobility of Indigenous minorities occurred through a counter, First Nations ideology that reterritorialized national space. Such efforts culminated in and were supported by the United Nations Declaration on the Rights of Indigenous Peoples in 2007. Indigenous cultural facilities transformed into symbols of collective self-determination for a transnational Indigenous community that could place pressure on national governments.

As demonstrated by Joy Malnar and Frank Vodvarka in *New Architecture on Indigenous Lands*, there has been some progress in strengthening political rights via architectural processes, such as the evolution criteria set down by the Centre for American Indian Research and Native Studies (CAIRNS).[14] According to these criteria, built responses to Native American client needs should incorporate spatial, social, spiritual, and experiential attributes that conceptually define Native American societies. The call for inclusion of social criteria highlights the degree to which mainstream architectural practice in secular postindustrial societies has become disassociated from fundamental human needs and preoccupied with aesthetic artifice. But it also reminds us that cultural spaces of Indigenous recognition are never politically void and are increasingly measures of social equity deliverance within individual nation-states, as well as potential sites of internationalization.

THE INTERNATIONALIZATION OF INDIGENOUS CULTURES

The proliferation of Indigenous facilities throughout Australia, their internationalization, and their transnational communal reach have highlighted the diversity and political significance of Indigenous communities. For example, Australia is being internationalized through the visibility of Aboriginal aesthetic practices, as exemplified in the art commission at Musée du Quai Branly. External political influences penetrated during the 1960s and 1970s when Australian Aboriginal activism was informed and influenced by pan-African and African American civil rights movements. Similarly, museums such as the National Museum of the American Indian (NMAI) on the National Mall in Washington, DC, are internationally significant physical spaces carved out for Indigenous representation. Museums with similar representational briefs have worked hard to reconcile troubling histories of museological and anthropological practice, to concede to the repatriation of human remains, and to produce inclusive histories across international borders. Their ideological reconception has benefitted from a generation of Holocaust memorials and museums that accompanied the resurgence of such politically difficult projects at the end of the Cold War. New museology has had to translate troubling cultural legacies for diverse and erudite metropolitan and global audiences.

Richard Sandell argues that the social agency of museums is measurable beyond the signification of cultural authority and that social responsibility is achieved by disturbing established settler histories.[15] Within this rescripting of the national narrative for an emergent, globally visible, and vocal Indigenous community, museums have shifted into a different domain that frames a postcolonial living culture. At the Museum of New Zealand, Te Papa Tongarewa in Wellington, the Jean-Marie Tjibaou Cultural Centre in Nouméa, and the Sámi Parliaments in Scandinavia, the specific postcolonial inscriptions of the nation-state are exposed and renegotiated, in the latter case toward greater political empowerment of Indigenous representatives. If, as argued by Laurier Turgeon and Elise Dubuc, ethnographic museums "are places where the majority group's limits of tolerance are measured," then these national institutions have pushed those boundaries.[16]

Only one of the international museum facilities discussed here is designed by an Indigenous architect—the NMAI in Washington, DC, was designed by Métis/Blackfoot architect Douglas Cardinal. The museum is one of three noteworthy national examples from North America that clearly identify the shifting parameters of museology. It is ideologically preceded by the Canadian Museum of Civilization in Ottawa, also by Cardinal, which includes Indigenous communities in a broader narrative of Canadian history.[17] The NMAI is followed by the Canadian Museum for Human Rights (CMHR), designed by Albuquerque architect Antoine Predock, where histories of genocide and civil rights activism are on display. The latter institution is also concerned with civil rights activism among Indigenous communities.[18] The CMHR is developed in the tradition of Holocaust museums in Europe and America that have broadened their agendas to include traumatic international histories, ranging from ethnic conflicts to apartheid. Museums such as the NMAI, which symbolizes Indigenous self-determination, are bookended between more generalized teleological framings of multiple cultures and the specific focus on difficult histories.

While such ambitious international narratives are absent in Australia, the National Museum of Australia (NMA) offers a complex intermingling of progressive and genocidal pasts. Indigenous curatorial voices suggest strategies of inclusion, as does the incorporation of the Australian Institute of Aboriginal and Torres Strait Islander Studies (AIATSIS) in the master plan. The controversy surrounding the first years of the museum's operation under Indigenous female director Dawn Casey have been detailed in a lengthier account.[19] The NMA repositions Australian Aboriginality in its Gallery of First Australians, yet, unlike at the NMAI, Indigenous architects are conspicuously absent from the design process.

A more confronting reminder of the excision of Indigenous communities from national processes in the past and their marginal presence in the federal parliament is the tenacious presence of the Aboriginal Tent Embassy in Canberra, both a trace of a historic moment in land rights activism and a spatial provocation signaling ongoing injustices. Its disruption of Canberra's land axis strung between the present and provisional parliaments on one side and the Australian War Memorial on the other gives the Embassy its political power.

The Center of the Nation

The act of placing cultural difference at the center of nation-space demands recognition of the inapplicability of Eurocentric notions of law and governance across a diverse and uneven cultural landscape. It challenges the belief that settler cultures can assume the universality of their institutions. The ephemeral materiality of the Aboriginal Tent Embassy, its informal and transient occupation of land, its adaptability, and its accommodation of newcomers occur in stark contrast to the inert institutions that surround it. The physical expression of the Embassy complements the *corroboree* (the open-air gathering space) and embraces geographical features in its symbolic cultural imaginary. In contrast, an institution that is designed and purpose-built concedes to European ideas of property ownership and requires a form of political compromise. The resilience and perpetual return of the Tent Embassy reminds us of the divisiveness of cultural issues in New World colonies and their persistent legacies of poverty and discrimination.

Australia's internationally representative architectural space that was purpose-designed for an Indigenous community has no comparable political agenda. It is the Uluru-Kata Tjuta Cultural Centre in the Northern Territory, in Australia's "red center." A signature building with a zoomorphic form, hand-made tectonics, and enigmatic design process, it has won its architect Gregory Burgess international acclaim.[20] The Centre at Uluru has evolved from the largely pragmatic, low-cost facilities for remote communities typically encountered in Australia. Similar examples are evident across North America associated with Native American reserves.[21] While many of these are nondescript buildings designed for everyday use, government, private, or corporate funding combined with community resources have in some cases produced iconic "cultural" tourist facilities. The immanent flaws in such projects include their overdependence on short-term revenue streams and funding cycles. They also expose remote communities to invasive forms of international tourism that lack education in cultural protocols, the ignorance of which—as at Uluru—cause conflicts between the community and tourists. Cultural centers that are designed for tourism are essentially extensions of museum practice, except that ownership and management by the living culture is on display. Unlike their colonial predecessors, they are zones of social contact that must deal with the contemporary cultural legacy of previous racist encounters. The keeping place and the museological display may seem similar on the surface, but their cultural and political legacies and meanings are worlds apart.

There is an important distinction to be made between these new cultural keeping places and their predecessors, particularly with regard to remote cultural centers. These facilities are cultural symbols of the custodianship of larger territories such as national reserves: traditional lands of Aboriginal populations that following historic dispossession and native title legislation have been placed under joint management by state bodies and Aboriginal communities. The Indigenous cultural center frequently functions as a gateway and interpretive center to a distinctive ecological environment challenging settler histories of an already transformed landscape.[22] By educating visitors in environmental knowledge alongside Indigenous cultural protocols, such centers convincingly demonstrate how interpretations of nature are culturally inscribed.

Australasian Regionalism

Considerations of culture, local region, and ecological environment locate Indigenous cultural facilities within a broader discussion of regionalist architecture in Australia, dominated by climate-sensitive responses from the tropical north. Whereas designing across cultures was a familiar practice in the colonial period, and culturally attenuated architectural examples were introduced in many parts of Asia, the Australian case is significantly different for two reasons. Colonial architecture in Australia paid little regard to Aboriginal built traditions, while devastating strategies of dispossession ensured their subsequent erasure. Scant evidence of urban settlements or reliance on dwellings, many of which were built with temporary materials, resulted in colonial disregard for Indigenous built form. This has created cultural discontinuities and an artificial *tabula rasa* that makes space for architectural reinvention. In mainstream Australia, regional architectures inspired by agricultural buildings—typically variants of timber, tin-roofed woolshed structures—have become popular and distinctive. Many of the Indigenous facilities depicted in this book are hybrids of these early industrial structures with culturally derived symbolisms, differentiated through the application of earth tones or natural textures. Several use circular or curvilinear forms.

The difference of Australian centers from examples of Asian regionalism is instructive. The notion of a pragmatic vernacular architecture erected by the community for community use without professional involvement has been documented extensively in neighboring Indonesia, focusing largely on the houses of its Indigenous communities.[23] Such examples were politicized as regional architectures in Asia in efforts to distinguish them from colonial architecture and deploy them for identity discourse. Continued reliance on labor-intensive craftsmanship and the prevalence of agricultural communities in many Asian countries extends and legitimizes the cultural traditions that underlie these architectural expressions. Asian architects borrow, enlarge, or replicate traditional buildings quite liberally without experiencing modernist angst.

Although similar cultural considerations are evident among Australia's Aboriginal facilities, practices of "borrowing" or "replicating" is frowned upon by a highly self-conscious modernist architectural fraternity. A largely urban architectural culture examines, critiques, and awards these facilities in relative isolation from the client community, which lies outside this system of accolades. Once again, comparison with Asia is useful. Despite an early reliance on colonial architects, decolonization in Asia produced three generations of design professionals for whom operation within their own political cultures has created opportunities and commissions. Self-determination has been supported by cultural and political consensus and prestige. Community and cultural concerns have not been alienated in the quest for secular forms of governance. They have been politicized via nostalgic architectural references to precolonial cultural authenticity.

Yet another dimension of architecture in Asia resonates with the Indigenous Australian case. Asia has a large agrarian population whose culture combines preindustrial and industrial lifestyles with less dependence on literacy. Rural architecture in Asia is designed to accommodate intuitive and pragmatic spatial practices. In tropical Asia, outside affluent urban centers, buildings depend on passive environmental systems and outdoor spaces and are less reliant on mechanical temperature controls. More importantly, public buildings are designed for a range of collective social behaviors, formal and informal.

While the blurring of ethnic cultures and the everyday absorption of Aboriginal practices enriches the texture of its national cultures, the recognition of Aboriginal peoples across Asia is uneven. The construction of native indigeneity against European colonizers has suppressed demographically smaller Indigenous cultures. Asian cultures that have their basis in complex social hierarchies and urban institutionalized religious cultures are also guilty of colonial exclusions. This is evident in a survey of Indigenous cultural facilities across Asia, where museums range from broadly ethnographic or cultural museums that define culture as a "traditional" heritage to cultural theme parks linked to ecotourism populated by replica vernacular structures. The National Museum of Ethnology (Minpaku) in Osaka, Japan, is an example of the former, while examples of the latter abound. The Chinese Ethnic Cultural Park in Beijing,

China; Taman Mini "Indonesia Indah" in Jakarta, Indonesia; the Ainu museum in Shiraoi, Hokkaido, Japan; and the living cultural museum in Sarawak, East Malaysia all target both internal and external tourism. In comparison, the Shung Ye Museum of Formosan Aborigines in Taiwan is a privately owned purpose-built museum designed by veteran modernist architect Kao Erhpan. Its prominent location diagonally across from the National Palace Museum in Taipei mirrors Taiwan's political stance on its Indigenous cultures. The island nation has mobilized its Austronesian Indigenous cultures in differentiating itself from the Chinese mainland.

Australia's resistance to decolonization has delayed politicization for its Indigenous communities, limiting access and opportunity. There are few Indigenous Australian architects, and they operate at the periphery of a predominantly white metropolitan profession. Indigenous architectures that are recognized by the profession seldom bear political briefs. Although displaying many of the attributes of Australian regionalism, these facilities rarely feature in mainstream debate or discourse. If, as argued for Asia, vernacular and regional built forms offer important expressions of geographic belonging, then Australian Indigenous facilities would be convincing equivalents; yet unlike in Asia, their regional location insulates many Australian Indigenous facilities from broader national cultural visibility. They represent a depoliticized cultural space, the occurrence of which alone must be read as political. The limited metropolitan visibility of Aboriginal communities mirrors other failures of multiculturalism. Competition between socially disadvantaged new-immigrant and Indigenous groups has produced isolated strategies of assimilation or resistance within top-down scripted messages of plurality. Cultural identification produces divisive political claims between black and white, metropolitan and rural, settler, immigrant, and Aboriginal Australians, hindering cultural affiliations. Culture, if not sanitized as a universal global practice linked to class interests, is increasingly viewed as a troubling unauthorized avenue for minoritarian politics.

Cultural and Communal Spaces

For most Indigenous communities, the creation of a cultural space that respects their values is largely an issue of safety, security, and mutual benefit. Quite apart from the provision of critical community services, such as legal aid, health, education, and employment, the expectation created by these spaces is that individuals might be empowered through shared social relationships. Histories of dispossession make such spaces critical for reinvigorating values and passing down cultural practices across the community. They are by and large elaborations of settler architectural types adapted to Indigenous community needs. Characteristically local, such buildings are identified with specific geographic regions, associated language groups, and lands over which they claim custodianship. Their formalization is largely related to encounters with the broader settler community whereby particular knowledge is communicated to a broader public. Located at the intersection of settler/Indigenous relationships, such centers are frequently run collaboratively with local councils and state government bodies. Indigenous communities often struggle to maintain such centers long term.

Metropolitan cultural centers are harder to identify as they are often embedded in larger institutions or lost in the sprawl of growing cities. Frequently relegated to poorer inner-city suburbs that are being gentrified, such buildings have to be versatile and adaptable. Their function is to reinsert a marginalized community into a collective metropolitan imaginary. Yet the service provided is critical, considering the needs of urban communities and the large numbers of suburban and urban Indigenous residents in the southern states. Positioning such centers within settler society without losing visibility or agency becomes the greater challenge.

Any assertion of Indigenous presence on Australian territory must additionally engage with native title claims as important vehicles for the political mobilization of Australian Aboriginal peoples. Yet the necessary shift from a socially negotiated communal space to a static claim on property places considerable strain on the performance of Indigenous culture. Cultural visibility is gained following specific compromises to existential and ontological understandings of indigeneity. Static, monolithic spatial experiences may be historically associated with institutionalization and confinement. These issues influence the creation of purpose-built cultural centers.

THE ARCHITECTURE OF INDIGENOUS CULTURAL CENTERS

A commission for an Indigenous cultural facility demands an explicitly ethical architecture, largely atypical to market-driven responses (with the exception of civic and institutional programs). The profession is structured for competitive tendering rather than the mutual cooperation typical of preindustrial ways of life. Consequently, the contribution made by a different kind of cultural engagement and end product has been invaluable in reshaping architectural practice, changing its notions of time and property. Cultural and environmental debates within architecture have been invigorated through commissions for Indigenous cultural facilities. Many have won prestigious awards. Yet at the end of this era, when we can name both architects and commissions that are exceptional in the field, we now also recognize the problems of that visibility. Incorporated into mainstream cultural discourse, Indigenous expressions can lose their political impact. Indigenous facilities run the risk of becoming institutionalized and subsumed into the general anonymity that marks bureaucratic culture. Where these processes are resisted through cultural differentiation, there is an equivalent risk of becoming essentialized. Zoomorphic or biomimetic forms have developed into formulaic responses, equating Aboriginality with nature and environmental sustainability. Preindustrial tectonics, rough textures, and earth tones have been used to differentiate these buildings from their modern equivalents, and yet iconic or signature buildings that adopt these design approaches have been interpreted as patronizing labels of indigeneity. There have been accusations of primitivizing Aboriginal communities, of equating them to premodern societies, and of ignoring their modernity and urbanity. Both the best and the worst examples of architecture designed for Indigenous communities display these traits. Critiques and debates on representational strategies, advanced by numerous Australian scholars, including Paul Memmott, Kim Dovey, Caroll Go-Sam, and Shaneen Fantin, serve to demonstrate the diversity of Aboriginal communities and the specificity of each community's needs.

Key differences between professional representations and scholarly debates on Indigenous facilities are that the former tend to evaluate their aesthetic built outcomes while the latter scrutinize the design process and related degrees of Indigenous social agency. These debates are haunted by the familiar distinction between product and process, and frequently expose the insecurity of the profession regarding particular kinds of critique. The architectural profession maintains the autonomy of their aesthetic preferences and choices, and signature styles are held in high regard. Indigenous communities subject to similar kinds of scrutiny regarding their requirements or choices are often fearful of being overexposed. These two kinds of vulnerability—the former to the marketplace, and the latter to the culture that produces that market—determine what is said about Indigenous cultural facilities in the public domain. They have informed the representations in this book. A continuing irony is the depiction of

communal spaces for social gathering through "hero shots" of vacant buildings prior to occupation. While we have tried to balance these with more mundane images, their Indigenous
occupants are deliberately omitted due to ethical constraints. These two forces of commodification and legal protection collude to visually erase the representative Aboriginal communities
from the pages of this book.

Mindful of what is at stake for both the professional and the Indigenous communities
involved, this collection has been crafted around programmatic approaches. Indigenous facilities designed as tourist commodities have no future, it is argued, unless they can be programmatically linked to the sustainability of broader local communities. Through the infusion of
community support and participation, these facilities might develop robust manifestos that
resist tourism-led invasion and exposure. Such critical collaborations at an everyday level have
determined the success or failure of many of the facilities. They are typically supported by
other fundamental social claims, including land rights claims.

The focus of architectural discourse has also been myopic. Professional fora have over-
whelmingly focused on aesthetically compelling architectures produced for settler tourism
while ignoring pragmatic social briefs that require sustained engagement. This is partly due
to gaps in the way architecture is taught and framed. We tend to interpret culture in terms
of artistic production. Social injustices seldom penetrate our worldview. This distinction
accelerates the objectification of Aboriginal cultural facilities, reproducing them as cultural
commodities to be displayed alongside other cultural products. As signature buildings charged
with representing Aboriginal culture, these facilities insulate audiences from more pressing everyday concerns. These distinctions have increasingly drawn Aboriginal cultural centers into a
new arena of curated civic spaces in capital cities that are considered manifestations of a more
inclusive public practice. Yet they are also being scripted into the everyday visions of a new
museology on a gentrified public stage. Although they draw from the collective experiences of
a generation of predecessors, utilizing complex technologies for varied representational effects,
these buildings are largely politically void.

Designing Indigenous Cultural Facilities

As discussed above, commissions for significant cultural buildings by renowned interna-
tional architects have inserted Indigenous facilities into mainstream architectural production.
Examples from the Australasian region include the Uluru-Kata Tjuta Cultural Centre designed
by Gregory Burgess Architects; the Australian Institute of Aboriginal and Torres Strait Islander
Studies by ARM Architecture; the Jean-Marie Tjibaou Cultural Centre in Nouméa by Renzo
Piano Building Workshop; the National Museum of Ethnology in Osaka (Minpaku) by Kisho
Kurokawa; and the Museum of New Zealand, Te Papa Tongarewa in Wellington by Jasmax.
Whether cultural complexes or museums, such institutions redefine their host environments
by acknowledging their genocidal pasts. While the politics of their emergence marks various
stages in the political decolonization of their respective societies, their architectural purpose is
more nuanced. At the national level, and in the administration of such facilities, these centers
promote equity and collaboration.

Still, Indigenous architectural involvement is sparse. There are too few Indigenous architects to sustain professional collaboration: for example, this research project revealed only
thirteen in Australia. The profession must relinquish its class privilege to train previously marginalized communities. This calls for affirmative action by tertiary institutions and programs.
It also calls for a reconsideration of the postmodern/poststructuralist debates of an earlier era

that have been abandoned due to neoliberal pressures. The resultant professional discomfort with cultural difference and resort to techno-cosmopolitan solutions (favoring climate, geography, and tectonics over social questions) has been exacerbated by global economic trends. The transformation of the environmental discourse from moral economy to techno-scientific product, quite remote from environmental social praxis, is a case in point.

As outlined so far, the brief for a cultural center is inherently problematic, a legatee of troubling museum practices, and often predicated on the encounter between remote communities and tourists. The projected program frequently mimics colonial institutional practices of collection or exchange. Periodic government support via competitive funding cycles creates precarious cultures of dependence that undermine cultural confidence. Far away from the national center, even when designed to give safety and dignity to a specific local community, the cultural center faces other problems. Local community interest waxes and wanes. Remote Aboriginal communities seldom have the person-power to sustain and maintain cultural centers and their leadership. Fragmented community politics can impact the strength of their claim. The vulnerability of communities that commission metropolitan architects places specific pressures on that relationship. The struggle for survivance is reflected in the indeterminacy of these facilities.

The role of predominantly white metropolitan architects designing *for* Indigenous communities is also fraught with difficulties. As in any cross-cultural encounter where language, cultural practices, and geographical knowledge is relatively unknown, the capacity for cultural interpretation is dependent on developing mutual trust. Colonization, dispossession, and hostile civic activism have produced cultural divisions and defensiveness between clients and architects. Professionals who make this commitment are necessarily humbled by the encounter, and learn that trust takes time to develop and can break down several times in the lifetime of a project. Both client group and architect need to develop resilience in navigating their cultural differences. Indeed, a different sense of time, space, and commitment has to be learned by architects who are commissioned for such projects. Meanwhile, architects who build for Indigenous communities need to sustain their own practices during the lengthy periods of consultation and execution demanded by this process. There are several dedicated practitioners featured here who have been open to these challenges. Similarly, best-practice examples involving Australia's few Indigenous architects such as Merrima Design and Indigenous Architecture and Design Victoria (IADV) reveal the importance of a dialogic process over an end product.[24] As demonstrated in the work of Merrima Design, the process can be deployed for other forms of communal and social empowerment. Where training in construction and management is anticipated in design development, community upliftment is a persistent goal. IADV's advocacy educates both Indigenous communities and the profession in cross-cultural awareness. They are defining important new roles for Indigenous professionals based on socialization and engagement. These practices are making the spaces they want to occupy.

Since no design response will ever perfectly match the program envisioned by the client group, multiple consultations and presentations are part of the design process. Even as the architect adjusts to the needs of the community, the community has to adjust to new forms of self-representation. Their cultural translation through a static urban architecture can be simultaneously empowering and disorienting. When this architecture purposefully adapts Indigenous iconography or seeks association with symbolisms familiar to the community, it also risks essentializing that culture. Where several communities are represented through a particular project, the choice of symbolism becomes an issue; yet when a center ignores cultural particularity and designs in a metropolitan vocabulary, it may silence the community through a functionalist response. Fixing a culture through a formal design is an inherently flawed practice since culture is fluid and performative, and cultural interpretation is necessarily subjective.

FRAMING THE STUDY

This book looks at the architecture commissioned by and for Indigenous communities as an attribute of their social and cultural location, their political place in the nation, and their visibility in everyday civic space. It addresses a range of programs that are culturally inscribed. These include facilities developed specifically for tourism, keeping places, and community institutions that are reconfigured as culturally welcoming environments, such as educational institutions and purpose-built cultural facilities that combine many of these programs and services. They are viewed as means for institutionalizing ephemeral place-making practices by which Indigenous communities gain agency over and recognition for the spaces they occupy. The means by which a minority culture can become visible and relevant and how architecture can be deployed in mediating such a process is considered. Not all of the projects included here are designed as cultural facilities. Many of them—such as the health, justice, or educational facilities—have very different aims and programs, and must be viewed comparatively as supporting Indigenous communities in specific ways. The cultural centers that have been selected are regarded as experimental hybrids of an evolving typology. Our audience for this study consequently includes both Indigenous client communities engaged in transformative place-making and practitioners committed to these visions. Each case study is presented as a building review, providing a list of key consultants and discussing the background to, description of, and reception of each project in a format that facilitates comparative referencing.

In introducing this study, it is helpful to refer to previous observations on the place of cultural centers in order to address the difficult task of framing "culture" in an era of diminishing multicultural and welfare policies. Many of the centers we have visited are on the brink of closure, subject to destabilizing funding cycles, and, unless politically significant, dependent on the efforts of a small and dispersed Aboriginal community. The stories behind the founding of these centers share common threads of land rights struggles, a few committed individuals, and decades of campaigning for sites and for funding. The long-term survivance of these facilities—their management and maintenance—is impacted by the response of local settler communities, which may be hostile or supportive.

However, it is also evident that Indigenous cultural centers have responded positively to the prerogatives of new museology, and have driven a shift toward collaborative, interpretive projects and programs. They have compelled architects educated in the Euro-American tradition to take stock of their profession, and have prompted efforts at deimperializing both teaching and practice. International facilities have conveyed the salience of a broader pan-Indigenous landscape in linking previously marginalized communities across the world. In these ways, the architecture of Indigenous communities has provided platforms for reflection on and critique of mainstream practice. Evidence of the many projects described in this book suggests that there is sufficient literature to sustain further discourse and debate.

This book had its genesis in a request by members of a local Indigenous organization for a survey that might inform a proposed metropolitan cultural facility. This remains an active goal. The book looks at thirty-five projects throughout Australia, including those in remote areas and major metropolitan centers. These vary in terms of program and scale, institutional location, and audience. The thirteen centers outside Australia have been selected due to their prominence and emergence within an ongoing discourse on Indigenous museums and cultural facilities. They highlight examples from New Zealand, North America, Scandinavia, France, Taiwan, New Caledonia, and Japan. The process of selecting these facilities was guided by program rather than aesthetic, and the objective was to capture the diversity of community needs. The client groups involved in these facilities include the local Indigenous community, the urban or regional council, and the state or federal government bodies who need to concur on the program. Each perspective is slightly different, making the task of research both interesting and arduous.

The projects surveyed can be broadly defined in terms of their complexity. Cultural centers designed to advance the needs and cultural expressions of remote communities are located "on country" on traditional Indigenous lands, and sometimes act as interpretive centers for environmental reserves. They vary in the degrees to which their representations are culturally inscribed. Some of these facilities do not include explicit Indigenous cultural briefs but are focused on tourism revenue. These examples are typically recognizable as facilities specific to a particular region and language group or groups. Some facilities additionally act as keeping places whereby historic artifacts may be returned to country. Their fortunes may be dependent on tourist interest and numbers since local Aboriginal communities are small.

Indigenous group identities are frequently created by shared histories of dispossession that brought diverse communities together on a mission station, reserve, or specific urban context. In such instances, displacement onto mission lands was followed by native title claims on that territory, a process that has produced distinct community identities. Where communities have remained on those lands they are easily identifiable, but in many instances these communities became fringe dwellers in nearby urban centers. Such histories inform a second group of projects that have evolved from urban or suburban community needs related to health care, education, and legal services. Typically run by Aboriginal co-operatives in various metropolitan centers and previously accommodated in extant architectures, the desire to give these facilities distinctive expressions has arisen with aspirations of community empowerment. They reveal the impoverishment caused to the Indigenous communities by dispossession, and demonstrate community efforts at overcoming historic structural exclusions.

Urban institutional connections may or may not empower such projects. Some of the examples included here are in the process of expanding or reinventing themselves to ensure their long-term sustainability. There are also instances in which a culturally inscribed facility associated with Aboriginal identities is located within a settler community. Such facilities may not be under Indigenous ownership or management. For example, educational buildings may be linked to tertiary institutions and may either be designed as stand-alone iconic buildings or as extensions of that institution's architecture in order to target a new generation of Indigenous students. Judicial facilities maintain their core functions while being adapted to cater to Aboriginal clientele. Health care or aged-care facilities may be reconceived to accommodate Indigenous family structures and community gatherings. Some of these facilities additionally offer services to the greater urban community. Such buildings can be regarded as transition zones providing protected spaces that, while mimicking their urban counterparts, provide distinct and differentiated duties of care.

Community and cultural services may also become conflated in a direct derivation of urban institutional architecture. For example, keeping places may be associated with an earlier history of colonial museums and collection practices that were hostile to traditional Indigenous societies. Yet unlike the museums of the past, the contents and activities of new keeping places under Indigenous management address both historic and contemporary needs. They may contain libraries with audiovisual archives critical for Indigenous histories of community. They are often linked with larger national institutions that have reviewed their collection practices. While bearing the attributes of the keeping place, these new museums cater to multiple activities, drawing attention to archaeological and heritage sites and introducing heritage trails. The museum model derived from a settler metropolitan institution is undoubtedly the most extreme manifestation of the institutionalization of cultural practices and is also the hardest to reconfigure.

The museums featured in this book are mainly internationally significant national projects that were created in response to revisionist political imperatives. They required specialized knowledge and funding allocations by the state, private organizations, or donors. The clients in many of these cases were state or federal governments. The shift to more inclusive collections and the employment of Indigenous curators have transformed this museum practice, providing training opportunities for previously marginalized groups. A significant feature of these institutions is the commissioning of contemporary artworks by Indigenous artists.

The involvement of artists and incorporation of Indigenous artworks runs through all these projects, particularly in Australia where Indigenous industry dominates Australian art production. Indigenous artworks occur as permanent exhibits, temporary exhibitions, building elements inscribed on floors, ceilings, and wall surfaces, or as installation art in landscaped areas. They may bear resistant political messages while located within institutionalized space. Art or landscape installations located outside institutional space are similarly used to recover lost genocidal histories. In contrast, at the business end of art practice, cultural facilities may act as a place for the collection, display, and distribution of local artists' works. This function, which is carried out to different degrees in many of the cultural centers described here, provides secure, ethical environments from which to deal with the metropolitan marketplace. The best of these examples engage Aboriginal custodians and guides without resorting to textual representations. They can be seen as tying the notion of the civic artwork commissioned by city councils to Aboriginal sensibilities of place-making. Recognition of displaced traditional custodians adds potency to the visual and material expression of the project.

Political programs are rarely included in these cultural facilities. The parliaments of Norway, Sweden, and Finland are unique in this regard. The Finnish Parliament in particular is remarkable for its combination of many of the services described so far. While the cultural manifestation of political space in an exquisite architectural artifact signals the affluence of these European communities, the temporariness of the Aboriginal Tent Embassy—the closest equivalent in Australia—signals the Australian Aboriginal community's comparative impoverishment through dispossession.

Certain types of culturally inscribed facilities are not included in this book. These include housing, correctional facilities, secondary schools, and private institutions where ethical considerations and the scale of investigation proved to be beyond the scope of our project. Visual representation of such socially sensitive facilities in this collection would potentially have been invasive. Similarly, our focus on purpose-designed projects eliminated a large number of excellent community ventures, heritage precincts, and keeping places that have been housed in existing or refurbished facilities. Inexpensive, pragmatic structures that provide critical community facilities are more important and useful to the community than their more expensive architect-designed equivalents; as pointed out by Shaneen Fantin, identity is created "through occupation first, representation later,"[25] and these, more so than designed responses, are demonstrative of such claims. Lastly, landscape and civic place-design, although touched upon, lie beyond our immediate focus. Some of these are dealt with in an earlier book arising out of this research inquiry titled *Indigenous Place* (2014).

Cross-Cultural Encounters

This brings us to a central research question regarding the encounter between Indigenous and settler communities, the territories they share, and the problems they encounter in their collaboration or co-existence. Cultural centers are typically commissioned either when issues of representation are at stake or there is a need to capture tourist interest. Indigenous community programs that are housed in Western-style facilities retrace the historic predicament of the community that has been institutionalized, incarcerated, and dispossessed. A number of scholars have debated the formal and aesthetic choices made by architects in interpreting cultural histories and beliefs. They have suggested strategies for understanding community needs, both at a symbolic and pragmatic level. The anxieties expressed in articulating these differences expose how social complexities are polemicized through the lens of a disenchanted modernity and fraught race relations. The collision of these cultural positions and their attendant politics is scrutinized, reconciled, or rearticulated in much of these writings.

In comparison, in similar discourses in Asia where preindustrial, industrial, and postindustrial realities are largely indivisible by race relations, such questions are not posed. In Asia, Indigenous iconography and cultural values are frequently manipulated as integral to postcolonial identity politics. They are core features of Asian architecture's regionalist responses. In such examples, the social content that shapes the architecture is culturally inscribed and made politically visible as a sign of self-determination against a colonial past. Conversely, arguments that have preoccupied Australian scholars over the validity, usefulness, or reductiveness of particular cultural signs are ultimately a conversation about or against a perceived gap within a subliminal narrative of progress. Difference or assimilation is the disputed representational strategy. The response of informed scholarship has been to propose processes that enhance community self-determination, rather than focus on aesthetic or formal representations.

The architectural writers who have navigated this difficult terrain in order to debunk assumptions and expose prejudices include Shaneen Fantin, Caroll Go-Sam, Kim Dovey, Michael Austin, Paul Memmott, and Joseph Reser, among others.[26] The previous publication in this research project, *Assembling the Centre: Architecture for Indigenous Cultures*—an academic evaluation of the creative and political potential of Indigenous cultural centers, led by Janet McGaw—aspired to extend this list.[27] These authors and their publications have sifted through the politics of representation to identify other more critical injustices or flawed bureaucratic processes that determine a project's viability or success. Dovey has deconstructed popular mythologies of harmony with the land or untransformed traditional cultures by which Aboriginality is contained within a dominant discourse.[28] Contributions such as these force architects to address their own culpability in perpetuating societal stereotypes. They expose structurally embedded histories of dehumanization that have become normalized. Such arguments have been emboldened by urgent issues of resource allocation in the face of recent political shifts away from "cultural" projects.

Sustaining community empowerment in the everyday and the long term is an undisputed goal advanced by the cultural brief. Defining "Aboriginal Architecture" as an expression of Aboriginal identity through a design process, Memmott and Reser ask how this may be achieved creatively while enhancing the agency of stakeholders: in short, how might the wishes and aspirations of the community be incorporated into a building?[29] Where clients have been culturally different and from an impoverished community, colonial architects have tended to impose Western metropolitan values quite indiscriminately, thereby subscribing to colonial civilizing missions. The orientation offered by Memmott and Reser protects the needs of Indigenous clients against the exaggerated authorship assumed by many architects who have regarded cultural projects as their private aesthetic platforms. Given the limited number of precedents available for consideration, two categories of brief are identified by them: facilities designed for community use, and those representing the community to the wider public.[30] These categories operate across different funding regimes, they observe. Cultural centers of national significance are usually government funded, while regional centers depend on a combination of state government funding, private philanthropy, and community fund-raising.[31] Due to the broad reach of these projects, the accessibility of architectural meanings and symbolism across all user groups determines the viability and success of such projects.[32]

From these examples, best-practice scenarios of consultation with the Aboriginal client group or community for initial interactions onsite, essential to building trust and confidence, can be framed, argue Memmott and Reser.[33] They recommend including respected Aboriginal Elders, artists, creative intellectuals, and/or ceremonial leaders in consultation processes.[34] Relationships with local Traditional Owners must be developed so as to ensure that the site does not encroach on existing Aboriginal sites, and to strike a balance between the diverse groups involved.[35]

In discussing layers of meaning and significance, Memmott and Reser refer to the need to capture the deep structure or layered meaning systems of Indigenous thought, an approach influenced by symbolic anthropology and structuralist thinking.[36] Another approach proposed by them is a poststructural assemblage of environmental statements related to connections with country, often the only cultural material available to a radically dispossessed community.[37] Memmott and Reser also offer a series of themes that may be considered by an architect, such as connection to country; cosmology; place, country as narrative; dwelling symbolism; inside/outside, sacred/profane; history, past and present; relatedness; experience; legibility; and characteristics of traditional Aboriginal symbolic representation, which act as keywords for stimulating the creative response.[38] They propose alternative approaches such as the "organic approach" and the neutral architectural shell, complemented by symbolic features in the landscape. They also offer cautionary advice. Monumental architecture is to be avoided, and the tensions between functional briefs and aesthetic and cultural requirements must be recognized. The use of sacred symbols must also be approached with care, since many of these are specific to language groups.[39] Principles of consultation, design strategies, and postoccupancy strategies are also outlined in detail. Memmott and Reser's recommendations highlight the profession's typical oversights in dealing with human subjects.

The projects selected in this book offer diverse approaches to the architecture of cultural centers. While acknowledging Memmott and Reser's guidelines as essential tools of engagement, this book also outlines the sociopolitical circumstances of each project's genesis. In doing so, it is asserted that these are political projects, intent on occupying spaces that were extracted through violence and that the steps taken by the community to reclaim, reoccupy, or reinvent their presence emboldens associated survivance strategies. This beleaguered process, for which there is often little support from a broader settler society suspicious of land claims and defensive of private property, is shaped against contemporary histories of activism, hostility, and institutional discrimination that need to be decolonized. Framed as projects of decolonization, the creation of Indigenous cultural facilities demand a different kind of architectural engagement with an often risky or uncertain outcome that is the lived reality of marginal and minority communities in Australia. Incidences of protest, vandalism, or economic failure dog such projects because the community they serve is often small, invisible, and undervalued by settler Australians. Visibility frequently invites hostility rather than support.

There are also issues internal to the Indigenous community. The task of representation—of identifying stakeholders and gaining consensus—is often difficult due to the fragmentation of the community and the alien patterns of representation imposed by governmental bodies. The lengthy wait for land, funds, and consensus discourages many architects unused to dealing with such uncertainties. The pacification of architecture that occurs through the homogenization of community values has not occurred in Aboriginal communities, and buildings are critical tools for making diverse claims. Internal dissent can frequently occur. The experience of designing a cultural center often reveals how "identity" has an exaggerated significance for minorities, offering them forms of ontological security. The identity stakes are heightened by structural categorizations related to land claims and by assimilation policies. In an environment burdened with such a complex history, no architectural response can expect to ignore stakeholder subjectivities that are shaped by and against settler communities. By resisting the obscurity of Western architectural forms and demanding that culture be formalized in architecture, the community makes bold claims that are material, physical, and permanent.

A Modern Community

How might we represent the complex politics of Aboriginal place-making through a profession and a discipline largely reliant on Eurocentric architectural values and educated into perpetuating them? While an "Australian" architecture has certainly emerged from the colonial settler experience, and its response to geography, landscape, and materiality is celebrated, there is equal enthusiasm for maintaining alliances with Euro-American norms. Aboriginal cultural facilities occur outside these debates, or enter at their periphery just as they inhabit the peripheral spaces of metropolitan awareness. We need to ask how architectural responses to Aboriginal cultural facilities, deemed aesthetically conservative by postmodern scholars, might be transformed by self-reflexive professional reengagement.

For the community commissioning the architect, the issue is not one of appropriate architectural representation, but a need to recognize itself in the body of the building. This may occur through organizing the program in tune with specific social practices or cultural activities, or through embedding familiar artifacts and symbols into its material form. Totemic or zoomorphic representations otherwise denigrated as populist may be meaningful for communities seeking to reconstruct environmental or traditional associations that will articulate their specific identities. None of these choices need reproduce the familiar dichotomy of tradition and modernity through which mainstream culture stereotypes Aboriginal environments. Such oppositions do not necessarily enhance ownership.

The significance of a cultural center does not lie in its aesthetics, although the profession may judge it on those terms. The act of occupation, a political act associated with land ownership, supersedes all architectural concerns.[40] The community's main goal is usually collective empowerment through the provision of a safe environment familiarized through use. Healing the community so that the next generation might be trained in self-reliance is often a pressing concern. The center is typically meant to facilitate forms of sociality that are formal and informal, and not necessarily governed by institutional programs or calendars. The brief anticipates the possibility of remaking a specific culture for the perpetuation of the community—of protecting and reproducing its treasured stories and artifacts, and translating it to those who might listen. Commercial interests must follow to make such a facility viable. All these concerns, not necessarily in this order, are invested in producing self-confidence and cultural pride, and precede an Aboriginal community's desire to reach outward to the settler community in cultural exchange or recognition. In fact, the polemics through which architectural discourse debates issues of Aboriginal architecture may not impress the stakeholders whose histories of dispossession, intermarriage, and codependence have produced other complex hybrid histories. Strengths such as these must grow from within a community in order to be sustainable. They cannot be conferred upon it by architects or architecture. In framing cultural centers as conciliatory ventures, architects may be serving the settler community's political anxieties rather than serving minority needs.

Mainstream architectural discourse—intent on representation and audience—typically glosses over the sociopolitical issues at stake. Is a different perspective in order? Do the successes and failures of Indigenous cultural centers offer critical lessons for shaping architecture's social purpose? If cultural centers are understood as social rather than institutional spaces, their funding, management, and long-term sustainability could be anticipated in the architectural brief.

In the environmentally inscribed fields of landscape management and civic art, the Indigenous community makes significant contributions. Yet Australian Aboriginal peoples are severely underrepresented in both architectural practice and pedagogy. These gaps and omissions signal failures in decolonizing institutions and curricula. The architectural survivance strategies described so far are lacking in the kind of social agency envisioned by Vizenor. Their mediation by mainstream practitioners or practices dilutes the political potential of taking cultural risks. Writing in the *Oxford Companion to Aboriginal Art and Culture* published in 2000, Alison Joy Page made the following comment:

> Understanding the uniqueness of each community, and cultural sensitivity, are best achieved by more Indigenous people penetrating the system, and working with their own and other communities. This is where universities can contribute, by using their resources to educate and encourage young Aboriginal people to take control.[41]

Fifteen years later, Indigenous communities have demanded consultative and collaborative design processes, and civic projects are incorporating some Indigenous features or buildings. Yet the education system from elementary to tertiary level lacks units or pathways for Indigenous students. Within the university curriculum, the social purpose of architecture, animated in responses to Indigenous client groups, is not prioritized as an essential part of an Australian architectural education. A comprehensive pedagogical and professional strategy for Indigenous empowerment through the spatial disciplines is the obvious next step. We need creative practice approaches that anticipate Indigenous communities as potential clients, users, employees, builders, and designers.

NOTES

1. Postcritical architecture reacted against poststructural and deconstructivist critiques of cultural hegemony and instead embraced capitalism. An example of this approach would be computationally enabled parametric modeling where the variables of a given condition are calculated to generate an extraordinary aesthetic response.

2. James Clifford, *Routes: Travel and Translation in the Late Twentieth Century* (Cambridge: Harvard University Press, 1997), 192.

3. "Closing the Gap" is a reference to the policy to reduce Indigenous disadvantage adopted by the Council of Australian Governments (COAG) in 2008.

4. The French term *survivance* has been applied in art history to describe resilient architectural traditions and more recently to folkloric traditions (as distinct from elite aesthetics) in the French-Canadian context. Vizenor uses the term to distinguish strategies of self-reliance from discourses linking survival with victimhood. The term has since gained credence in Indigenous, particularly Native American, studies. See Gerald Vizenor, *Manifest Manners: Narratives on Postindian Survivance* (Lincoln: University of Nebraska Press, 1999); Gerald Vizenor, ed., *Survivance: Narratives of Native Presence* (Lincoln: University of Nebraska Press, 2008).

5. Linda Lizut Helstren, "Museum Survivance: Vizenor Before and After Repatriation," in *Gerald Vizenor: Texts and Contexts*, eds. Deborah L. Madsen and A. Robert Lee (Albuquerque, NM: University of New Mexico Press, 2010), 231–48. See W. Richard West, "A New Idea of Ourselves: The Changing Presentation of the American Indian," in W. Richard West, ed., *The Changing Presentation of the American Indian: Museums and Native Cultures* (Seattle: National Museum of the American Indian/Smithsonian Institution with University of Washington Press, 2000), 7–13, 8.

6. Vizenor describes the ways in which the oral histories and literature of contemporary Native Americans combat and undermine dominant historic stereotypes of cultural absence by asserting their continued presence. He describes them as "postindian warriors," where the battleground has shifted to a new creative terrain. Vizenor, *Manifest Manners*, 12.

7. The term *difference* is used with reference to Martin Heidegger's use of the term in *Being and Time*, trans. J. Macquarrie and E. S. Robinson (Oxford: Blackwell Publishers, 1962) and subsequent applications of the term in the social sciences, for example, by Anthony Giddens in *Modernity and Self-Identity* (Cambridge: Polity Press, 1991).

8. Perhaps the most important critique of multicultural policy in Australia is that of Ghassan Hage in *White Nation: Fantasies of White Supremacy in a Multicultural Society* (Annandale: Pluto Press, 1998).

9. Elsa Koleth, "Multiculturalism: A Review of Australian Policy Statements and Recent Debates in Australia and Overseas," Social Policy Section, Parliament of Australia, Research Paper No. 6 2010–2011, October 2010, available at http://www.aph.gov.au/About_Parliament/Parliamentary_Departments/Parliamentary_Library/ pubs/rp/rp1011/11rp06. The Racial Discrimination Act 1975 cited in Mark Lopez, *The Origins of Multiculturalism in Australian Politics 1945–1975* (Carlton South: Melbourne University Press, 2000), 452. This book is the main source for the summary of the policies mentioned here.

10. This refers to the successive Labour governments of prime ministers Bob Hawke and Paul Keating.

11. Koleth, *Multiculturalism*, 9–11, in reference to Office of Multicultural Affairs, *National Agenda for a Multicultural Australia* (Canberra: Australian Government Publishing Service, July 1989).

12. This refers to the government of Liberal prime minister John Howard. Koleth, *Multiculturalism*, 12–14, in reference to Commonwealth of Australia, *A New Agenda for Multicultural Australia*, Canberra, December 1999, available at http://www.immi.gov.au/ media/publications/multicultural/pdf_doc/agenda/agenda.pdf. The Liberal Party under John Howard was elected to the federal government for four consecutive terms from 1996 to 2007.

13. Department of Immigration and Border Protection, "A Multicultural Australia," available at https://www.dss.gov.au/our-responsibilities/settlement-and-multicultural-affairs/publications.

14. Joy Monice Malnar and Frank Vodvarka, *New Architecture on Indigenous Lands* (Minneapolis: University of Minnesota Press, 2013), 3.

15. Richard Sandell, *Museums, Society, Inequality* (London and New York: Routledge 2002), 3–23.

16. Laurier Turgeon and Elise Dubuc, "Ethnology Museums: New Challenges and New Directions," *Ethnologies* 24, no. 2 (2002), available at http://www.erudit.org/revue/ethno/2002/v24/n2/ 006637ar.pdf.

17. The museum is to be rebranded and renovated in 2017 as the Canadian Museum of History. Melissa Aronczyk and Miranda Brady, "Crowdsourcing as Consultation: Branding History at Canada's' Museum of Civilization (Part I)," *antenna*, December 18, 2012, available at http://blog.commarts.wisc.edu/2012/12/18/crowdsourcing-as-consultation-branding-history-at-canadas-museum-of-civilization-part-i/.

18. Canadian Museum of Human Rights, "Interactive Floor Plan," available at https://humanrights.ca/explore/floor-plan.

19. See chapter 2, Australian Institute of Aboriginal and Torres Strait Islander Studies and the National Museum of Australia, Canberra, Australia.

20. Lisa Findley, *Building Change: Architectural Politics and Cultural Agency* (London and New York: Routledge, 2005).

21. Malnar and Vodvarka, *New Architecture on Indigenous Lands*, chapter 9, "Cultural and Sustainable Housing," 179–201 and chapter 10, "Forming Indigenous Typologies," 203–27.

22. Richard Sandell, *Museums, Society, Inequality*, 3–23.

23. See Roxana Waterson, *The Living House: An Anthropology of Architecture in Southeast Asia* (Oxford: Oxford University Press, 1990), chapter 1, "Origins," 1–26, for a discussion of the houses of indigenous ethnic groups in the Austranesian world and in Southern China and Japan.

24. The website of Merrima Design is at http://www.spatialagency.net/database/merrima.group. The unit was founded by architect Dillon Kombumerri, later followed by architect Kevin O'Brien and interior designer Alison Page. They have practiced separately since 2000 but have formed Merrima Design as an association of Indigenous architects "committed to the struggle for self-determination through cultural expression in the built environment." Indigenous Architecture and Design Victoria, originally known as Indigenous Architecture Victoria, was formed by Reuben Berg and Jefa Greenaway in 2010.

25. Shaneen Fantin, "Aboriginal Identities in Architecture," *Architecture Australia* 92, no. 5 (2003): 84, 86.

26. For examples see Fantin, "Aboriginal Identities in Architecture," 84–87; Mike Austin, "The Tjibaou Culture Centre," *The Pander* 8 (1999), previously available at http://www.thepander.co.nz/architecture/maustin8.php#note3; Paul Memmott, *Gunyah, Goondie + Wurley: The Aboriginal Architecture of Australia* (Brisbane: University of Queensland Press, 2007); Paul Memmott and Joseph Reser, "Design Concepts and Processes for Public Aboriginal Architecture," *PaPER* 55–56 (Cairns: Aboriginal Environments Research Centre, Department of Architecture, University of Queensland and Department of Psychology, James Cook University), 69–86; Carroll Go-Sam, "Fabricating Blackness: Aboriginal Identity Constructs in the Production and Authorisation of Architecture," paper presented at the Society of Architectural Historians Australia and New Zealand Conference 2011, Brisbane, Queensland, available at http://espace.library.uq.edu.au/view/UQ:245276.

27. Janet McGaw and Anoma Pieris, *Assembling the Centre: Architecture for Indigenous Cultures, Australia and Beyond* (New York: Routledge, 2015).

28. Kim Dovey, "Architecture about Aborigines," *Architecture Australia* 85, no. 4 (1996): 98–103, 98.

29. Memmott and Reser, "Design Concepts and Processes," 70.

30. Ibid., 70.

31. Ibid.

32. Ibid., 70, 74–77.

33. Ibid., 71, 80.

34. Ibid., 71–72.

35. Ibid.

36. Ibid., 72–73.

37. Ibid., 76–77.

38. Ibid., 77–78.

39. Ibid., 70, 78.

40. Fantin, "Aboriginal Identities in Architecture," 87; Austin, "The Tjibaou Culture Centre."

41. Alison Joy Page, "19.5. Gurung Gunya: A New Dwelling," in *The Oxford Companion to Aboriginal Art and Culture*, eds. Sylvia Kleinert and Margo Neale (Oxford: Oxford University Press, 2000), 423–26.

1

Aboriginal Tent Embassy, Canberra, Australia

Location: Lawn of the Provisional Parliament
Date: 1972; 1973–1976; 1976–1977; at Mugga Way, 1992; listed on the Register of the National Estate by the Australian Heritage Council in 1995

The Aboriginal Tent Embassy is an expression of over four decades of civil rights activism by Australia's Aboriginal communities framed through demands for land rights and the expression of a never-ceded sovereignty (Plate 1).[1] Its physical location on the land axis linking parliament and war memorial in Walter Burley Griffin's plan for Canberra is politically provocative. The Embassy disrupts a specific hierarchy of power. This bold intervention of a provisional informal assemblage, the resilience of the community in all weathers and against

Plate 1. Aboriginal Tent Embassy, Sacred Fire on the Land Axis with view toward the Australian War Memorial, Canberra, Australia. Photo by author, 2010.

all efforts at their removal, and the transformation of the space into a sustained political symbol of the land rights struggle make it a unique sight in Australia's Capital Territory. The temporary physical character of the Embassy aptly conveys the insecurity of Indigenous land tenure and histories of dispossession that underlie settler institutions. The images represented here depict the configuration of the Embassy at the time it was photographed. The survival of the Embassy reflects other more complex struggles for survival elsewhere in the nation. The physical structures and their occupants have faced eviction on several occasions.

DESCRIPTION

The spatial configuration known as the Tent Embassy comprises a shipping container that acts as the main office, the sacred fire and humpy located centrally on Canberra's Land Axis, the word *Sovereignty* constructed as part of this ensemble, and the artwork on the forecourt pavers. Flagpoles, signage, and other features are added according to the event. Accompanying these key features are the tents of Embassy residents, many of whom treat this space as an important initiation into Indigenous activism. New recruits spend a period of a couple of years at the Embassy as part of this process. Their tents are located on the right-hand side of the sacred fire (when facing the Parliament) and generally number between ten to twelve tents, although numbers fluctuate depending on the occasion. Caravans, loose furniture, chicken pens, and other camping equipment accompany the permanent tents. Christopher Vernon, whose analyses of the Embassy have consistently inserted it into architectural discourse, describes it as "the national capital's most politically animated site" that best fulfills the meaning of Canberra as a meeting place.[2] He points out that this seemingly incongruous assemblage mirrors the living conditions of many Aboriginal people.[3]

Figure 1.1.   Canberra's Land Axis, viewed from Mount Ainslie. Photo by author, 2013.

BACKGROUND

Writing on the establishment of the Aboriginal Tent Embassy in the initial years of the land rights struggle, Scott Robinson describes it as "a direct response" to the Liberal–Country Party coalition policy of a "diluted assimilationism," expressed most explicitly by then prime minister William McMahon in his Australia Day address of January 26, 1972.[4] An appeal for "land title, royalties from mining operations, and rights over land appropriated for development" was rejected, and instead McMahon implemented a lease system "conditional on the ability of Indigenous people to make economic and social use of the land, and excluding rights to mineral and forestry resources."[5] Four Indigenous representatives from the outraged Redfern Aboriginal Community in Sydney—Michael Anderson, Billy Craigie, Bertie Williams, and Tony Coorey—drove to Canberra that very evening in response to McMahon's address.[6] Aboriginal activist, playwright, and author Kevin Gilbert, who was instrumental in the conception of the Tent Embassy, procured funds from the Communist Party of Australia to enable the four young men to travel to Canberra, but he was unable to attend in person.[7] Noel Hazard, the *Tribune* photographer, drove the four activists. At 1 am on January 27, 1972, they planted a beach umbrella on the lawn of old Parliament House as a symbol of Aboriginal sovereignty. They were joined by Gary Foley, Chicka Dixon, Paul Coe, and other members of the Redfern Black Caucus.

The Sydneysiders who occupied Canberra's land axis in 1972 were participants in the already heated movement for land justice that was erupting across Australian cities. Following the Gurindji people's walkoff at Wave Hill Station in protest over stolen wages in 1966, the unsuccessful outcome in the Gove Peninsula land rights case in 1971, a nationwide protest for land rights (known as *Ningla-A-Na* or "hungry for land" in the Arrernte language), saw marches through several state capitals on National Aborigines Day in 1972.[8] Aboriginal protest in Canberra had a longer history; Aboriginal elders Jimmy Clements and John Noble appeared at the opening of the provisional Parliament House in Canberra in 1927, visibly asserting their presence among the assembled crowds.[9] The erection of the Tent Embassy there almost fifty years later highlighted Aboriginal alienation and estrangement and placed the community's grievances quite literally before the Australian Parliament. In the months that followed this initial political act in January 1972, a number of structures would surround the umbrella, augmenting a fresh wave of metropolitan Aboriginal protests.[10]

The prominent location of the Embassy attracted a flood of visitors to Canberra, and from the outset non-Aboriginal support was evident.[11] Aboriginal peoples, including Yirrkala and others from Elcho, Bathurst, and Melville islands brought a pan-Aboriginal appearance to the protest, while media coverage throughout this period brought tourists from farther afield.[12] As Robinson observes,

> The floating population usually peaked at weekends, when carloads of Aboriginal people travelled from Sydney. Chicka Dixon organised much of the transport, while prominent activists such as Gary Foley, Bruce McGuinness, Paul Coe and Sam Watson arrived at the end of each week.[13]

International visitors, including Soviet diplomats, a representative from the Canadian Indian Claims Commission, and a cadre from the Irish Republican Army made symbolic visits to the Embassy, and several international publications and media providers gave it coverage, including the *Times* of London, *Time*, *Le Figaro*, *Le Monde*, and *Israel Post*.[14] The significance of tourism for national and international visibility and for disseminating the cause of Ab-

Figure 1.2.   Aboriginal Tent Embassy, office. Photo by author, 2012.

original land justice became increasingly evident. Both tents and participants increased significantly, and at one point there were two thousand protestors contributing to the Embassy's presence.[15] The Embassy adopted diplomatic strategies, identifying Michael Anderson as its High Commissioner and Bobbi Sykes as its traveling delegate. An Embassy garden party was held on February 20, 1972, with visitors asked to bring their own provisions.[16]

Quite apart from the ubiquitous presence of police outside the Parliament, the suburban spread of Canberra and lack of a concentrated built fabric made maintaining the protest and protecting the activists relatively difficult. Canberra's Aboriginal population was small and dispersed. Tents were necessary for accommodating activists during the first critical nine months. When arguing for the advantages of this temporal presence, Robinson recalls that Aboriginal poet and author Bobbi Sykes noted that "to occupy a building similar in structure to those used by the oppressive bureaucratic machine would have been to alienate the protest from the level of the people."[17] The Embassy both embodied the temporal-spatial character of Aboriginal settlement and defied institutionalization.

The issue of land rights colored the government's antipathy toward the Embassy.[18] As High Commissioner, Anderson produced a counter plan that responded to McMahon's stated aims of assimilation with plans for Aboriginal ownership of reserves and settlements, mineral rights, land in the capital cities, preservation of sacred sites, monetary compensation, and full rights of statehood for the Northern Territory.[19] According to Robinson, the Embassy's "uncompromising public relations . . . created unprecedented media attention for Aboriginal activism and its cause," and the campsite was a source of embarrassment for the government.[20]

Consequently, there were attempts at removing the Embassy in return for permanent meeting rooms, memorial plaques, and reconciliation paths at various times, as noted by Coral Dow.[21] Ralph Hunt, then Minister of the Interior with the federal government, proposed to find an alternative and permanent Canberra building or club for the Embassy. Municipal ordinances and planning guidelines were invoked against the Embassy to no avail.[22] Instead, the Embassy gained in significance through the accumulation of associated symbols and private and public events. It became a popular location for Aboriginal protests, marriages, and memorials. Various versions of the flag were flown in February and April of 1972, until the now-familiar Aboriginal flag designed by Harold Thomas—the image of a yellow setting sun against red sky and black earth—was raised in July 1972.

The provocative presence and vocal protests of the Embassy members prompted several confrontations, which peaked during an intense, ten-day period in the latter part of July 1972. On July 20, a law related to trespassing on Commonwealth lands was modified to allow the police to move in and dismantle the Embassy. Following the first eviction, the Embassy was forced into exile in student houses and university buildings.[23] Protests continued, with efforts at reinstating the Embassy leading to clashes between police and activists on July 20. Two British newspapers featured the clash.[24] Protest marches culminated in a second violent confrontation on July 30, and a third was anticipated. However, the crowd of three to four thousand offered no resistance on that occasion, and the police were invited to dismantle the tents. A group of Aboriginal protestors mischievously raised a canvas sheet above their heads and followed them out of the crowd.[25] Since this turbulent beginning when the Embassy first staked its claim, its physical form has waxed and waned, and tends to swell with each new event of political significance to the cause of Aboriginal rights, a litmus test of Aboriginal visibility in the national capital.[26]

OFFICIAL STATUS

A timeline of the Aboriginal Tent Embassy notes that it returned in 1973 after Aboriginal protestors staged a sit-in to gain an audience with McMahon's successor, Labor Prime Minister Gough Whitlam, who previously as leader of the opposition had offered his support to the cause.[27] Whitlam introduced the Aboriginal Land Rights Act in 1976, which resulted in a temporary voluntary suspension of the Embassy. For a time the Embassy retreated from view, taking up the offer to share half of retired army colonel John Maloney's house at 26 Mugga Way. From March 1976, it stood alongside eight other embassies on this exclusive Canberra street.[28] The Embassy closed down in 1977 when lack of funds thwarted community efforts at purchasing the property.[29]

By then, the climate of land rights had already begun to alter and would set the pace for legislative changes of the 1990s. The Aboriginal Land Rights Act of 1976 allowed Indigenous people in the Northern Territory to claim title to unalienated Crown land, based on evidence of traditional association. Under the Act, mining was permitted on Aboriginal lands upon agreement with Aboriginal title holders, with payments negotiated and channeled back to stakeholders through newly created land councils. The Land Rights Act set the initial precedent for the recognition of native title in Australian law. In 1992, in the famous case of Mabo, the High Court of Australia overturned the assumption of *terra nullius* and recognized native title over unalienated Crown land where not extinguished by inconsistent grant. The federal government responded with the Native Title Act of 1993. The 1990s were significant for the Embassy. In the year of the Mabo ruling, twenty years after its inception, the Embassy reappeared at its original site to take a more permanent form. A year later in 1993, Kevin

Figure 1.3.   26 Mugga Way. Photo by author, 2012.

Gilbert's ashes were scattered at the Embassy site.[30] Two years later in 1995, the Aboriginal Tent Embassy achieved official status, and was listed as part of the National Estate by the Australian Heritage Council.

Following this formal recognition, the space was articulated through a number of symbolic features. A ground mural begun during the National Sculpture Forum decorated the pavers of the forecourt terrace in an artwork described by Vernon as drawing together the totems of the Embassy mob.[31] In 1998, Arabunna Elder Kevin Buzzacott created the "Fire for Peace and Justice" next to this forecourt, and Wiradjuri Elder Paul Coe lit it.[32]

Vernon writes that when the Embassy was reestablished in the 1990s, the site was reorganized as several humpies representing a "fire-dreaming." The traditional humpy facing the sacred fire expresses the law, "the sovereign authority which has never been ceded."[33] He describes its landscaping, the array of gunyahs, and clandestine plantings of eucalyptus as the "reverse" colonization and literal occupation of the land.[34] Information sheds were donated to the Embassy by the union movement, although one of these would be later burnt in an arson attack on June 14, 2003. During the week of the National Apology to Australia's Indigenous Peoples by then prime minister Kevin Rudd in 2008, the Embassy site was filled to capacity.

RECEPTION

As a tactical strategy, the idea of a temporal protest took on political credence and greater visibility following the incidents of 1972. The strategy was repeated in several locations;

for example, in January 1972, homeless Aboriginal peoples in central Brisbane drew attention to their housing problems through a planned tent village.[35] In February 1975 when the Brisbane space was vacated by the Aboriginal peoples, a Viet Cong Embassy occupied it.[36] In October 1975, a group of approximately two hundred Maoris set up a tent camp outside the Parliament in Wellington, New Zealand.[37] Both Gary Foley and Gary Williams attended this protest. Aunty Isabel Coe set up a protest Embassy during the Sydney Olympic Games, and the Sydney Aboriginal Embassy at Victoria Park was set up in 2001.[38] Also in 2001, the Tent Embassy was replicated at Sandon Point in New South Wales against the McCauley's beach development.[39] A Nyoongar Tent Embassy was established on Heirisson Island in Perth, Western Australia, in 2012 to raise community awareness about local native title claims.

The nature and purpose of the Aboriginal Tent Embassy in Canberra has shifted over the years, and the contemporary Embassy is distinct in configuration and purpose from the original intervention on the Canberra land axis. The original Embassy marked a historic moment in civil rights activism and political emergence, and today the Embassy is a reminder of Aboriginal presence and dispossession and asserts a particular political-spatial praxis. Its physical presence continues to be provocative, periodically attracting events and media interest. In 2012, the Embassy celebrated its fortieth anniversary with a three-day "Corroboree for Sovereignty" from January 26 to January 28, a celebration that has since been repeated annually. The event included a Land Rights and Sovereignty March and several presentations on issues of governance led by Elder and High Commissioner Michael Anderson.

NOTES

1. Thanks to Ruth Gilbert and Michael Anderson for reviewing and commenting on this draft in November 2013.

2. Christopher Vernon, "The Aboriginal Tent Embassy," *Architecture Australia* 91, no. 6 (November/December 2002): 36.

3. Aboriginal Tent Embassy, "40th," http://aboriginaltentembassy40th.com/about/ (link no longer active, last accessed October 7, 2013).

4. Scott Robinson, "The Aboriginal Embassy: An Account of the Protests of 1972," *Aboriginal History* 18, no. 1 (1994): 49–63, 49.

5. Tim Leslie, "The History of the Aboriginal Tent Embassy," Australian Broadcasting Corporation, January 27, 2012, available at http://www.abc.net.au/news/2012-01-27/the-history-of-the-aboriginal -tent-embassy/3796630; Creative Spirits, "Aboriginal Tent Embassy, Canberra," available at http://www .creativespirits.info/aboriginalculture/history/aboriginal-tent-embassy-canberra#ixzz3jJz3ad77.

6. Robinson, "The Aboriginal Embassy," 50. As noted by Coral Dow, Chicka Dixon had initially proposed occupying Pinchgut Island in Sydney but was outvoted. Coral Dow, "Aboriginal Tent Embassy: Icon or Eyesore?" *Chronology*, no. 3 (1999–2000), available at http://parlinfo.aph.gov.au/parlInfo/ search/display/display.w3p;query=Id%3A%22library%2Fprspub%2FSU716%22.

7. Michael Anderson as reported in the article by Debra Jopson, "The 40-Year Protest That Changed Little," *Sydney Morning Herald*, January 21, 2012.

8. *Ningla A-Na: Hungry for Our Land*, produced and directed by Alessandro Cavadini (Melbourne: Australian Film Institute, 1972).

9. Maryrose Casey, "Disturbing Performances of Race and Nation: King Bungaree, John Noble and Jimmy Clements," *International Journal of Critical Indigenous Studies* 2, no. 2 (2009): 25–35.

10. Robinson, "The Aboriginal Embassy," 50.

11. Ibid., 52.

12. Ibid., 53.

13. Ibid., 54.

14. Ibid., 53. "Embassy Attracts Tourists," *Canberra Courier*, June 22, 1972.

15. Tim Leslie, "The History of the Aboriginal Tent Embassy."

16. "Embassy Party," *Canberra Times*, February 19, 1972.

17. Roberta Sykes, *Black Power in Australia: Bobbie Sykes versus Senator Neville T. Bonner*, ed. Ann Turner (South Yarra: Heinemann Educational Australia, 1975), 23–24.

18. See Paul Muldoon and Andrew Schaap, "Aboriginal Sovereignty and the Politics of Reconciliation: The Constituent Power of the Aboriginal Embassy in Australia," *Environment and Planning D: Society and Space* 30, no. 3 (2012): 534–50.

19. Robinson, "The Aboriginal Embassy," 52.

20. Ibid., 52.

21. Dow, "Aboriginal Tent Embassy."

22. Ibid.

23. Robinson, "The Aboriginal Embassy," 56. They were mainly in Childers Street.

24. It was reported in the *Canberra News* on July 21, 1972, that two leading British newspapers *The Times* and the *Daily Telegraph* published photos of the clash.

25. Robinson, "The Aboriginal Embassy," 62.

26. Thanks to Jude Kelly for an interview at the Embassy on April 23, 2011, and Gary Foley for comments on this account, October 2013.

27. SBS News, "Time Line, Aboriginal Tent Embassy," September 3, 2013, available at http://www .sbs.com.au/news/article/2012/07/05/timeline-aboriginal-tent-embassy.

28. "Black Power in Mugga Way," *Courier Mail*, March 12, 1976; "New Flag to Fly in Mugga Way," *Sydney Morning Herald*, March 19, 1976.

29. "Embassy Closed by High Cost," *The Age*, September 1, 1977.

30. Indigenous Australia, "Kevin Gilbert 1933–1993," available at http://www.indigenousaustralia .info/land/land-rights/kevin-gilbert.html.

31. Aboriginal Tent Embassy, "40th."

32. Ibid.

33. Vernon, "The Aboriginal Tent Embassy," 36; Aboriginal Tent Embassy, "40th."

34. Christopher Vernon, "Axial Occupation," *Architecture Australia* 91, no. 5 (September/October 2002): 84–90.

35. "Aboriginals Plan a Tent Village in City," *Sunday Mail*, January 30, 1972.

36. "Viet Cong 'Embassy,'" *Brisbane Telegraph*, February 19, 1975.

37. "Maoris Refuse to End Protest," *West Australian*, October 21, 1975.

38. Ohms Not Bombs, "The Sydney Aboriginal Tent Embassy," available at http://ohmsnotbombs .net/indigenous/the-sydney-aboriginal-tent-embassy.

39. Michael Organ, "Kuradji Aboriginal Tent Embassy," available at http://www.uow.edu.au/~mor gan/guboo.html.

2

Australian Institute of Aboriginal and Torres Strait Islander Studies and National Museum of Australia, Canberra, Australia

Location: National Museum of Australia, Acton Peninsula, Canberra, Australia
Date: 2001
Client: Commonwealth of Australia
Architects: Ashton Raggatt McDougall (partners Steve Ashton, Howard Raggatt, Ian McDougall, and Tony Allen) in association with Robert Peck von Hartel Trethowan
Landscape Architects: Room 4.1.3 (Vladimir Sitta and Richard Weller)
Project Management Team: Craddock Morton, Peter Wright, David Waldren, Garry Eggleton, and Philip Johns Structural Engineers: Ove Arup & Partners; Taylor Thomson Whiting
Funding: Commonwealth Government's Federation Fund
Cost: approximately $83.6 million

BACKGROUND

The first museum of its kind in Australia, the National Museum of Australia (NMA) in Canberra occupies an eleven-hectare site on the Acton Peninsula, a promontory with views across Lake Burley Griffin. The site was selected for its visibility from the Commonwealth Avenue Bridge that links the Canberra city center to Capital Hill. The project included urban and landscape design for a museum complex organized around a central court, now known as the Garden of Australian Dreams (Plate 2). The Australian Institute for Aboriginal and Torres Strait Islander Studies (AIATSIS) was conceptually linked to this cluster of buildings.

The museum complex was developed following the 1975 Committee of Inquiry on Museums and National Collections chaired by P. H. Pigott, which produced the Pigott Report.[1] Three themes were proposed in the Report as central to the creation of a shared history: Aboriginal Australia, Social History, and the Environment.[2] An Act to Establish a National Museum was introduced in 1980, with the museum's opening planned for the Centenary of Federation celebrations in 2001. The decision to construct the NMA was significant, because until then the most prominent museum building in the Australian capital city had been the Australian War Memorial, dedicated to military histories. An equally substantial civic institution was needed to chart autonomous historical developments beyond these imperial connections and dependencies.

Plate 2.   National Museum of Australia, Canberra, Australia, Garden of Australian Dreams. Photo by author, 2011.

PROJECT DESCRIPTION

The design team comprised Melbourne architectural firm Ashton Raggatt McDougall in association with Robert Peck von Hartel Trethowan and landscape architects Vladimir Sitta (Sydney) and Richard Weller (Perth). The interwoven axes used to organize the site referenced Walter Burley Griffin's original Plan for Canberra, basing their formal design on a precise cast of a knot. Its subtracted figure created an opportunity to introduce new lines of intellectual inquiry. The building design was projected as a negative affirmation of historical processes, the "not" of Derridean deconstruction that resists the singular progressive narrative.[3] The theme of "tangled histories" was conveyed through looping structural elements following a Boolean knot. Dimity Reed has described it as an effort to present architecture and landscape as coextensive rather than juxtaposed, constituting a departure from modernist functionalism.[4] The manipulation of straight lines to produce wandering tangled forms, observes Reed, "posits architecture as knot and landscape as fabric."[5] Landscape architect Richard Weller echoes this observation, and he sees the complex intersection of Australia's various historical legacies as conveyed through the metaphor.[6] He identifies the topography, rather than the residual spaces created by the figure of the building, as his inspiration.

Architect Howard Raggatt describes the pavilions of the NMA as pieces of a much bigger puzzle, a postmodernist assemblage.[7] Familiar architectural references, including the footprint of the Jewish Museum, Berlin, the glazing details of the Sydney Opera House, the imitation of elements from the Australian Parliament House, and Le Corbusier's Villa Savoye, were translated through features of the museum complex in an effort to connect the museum to its broader historical and architectural context.[8] Meanwhile, the main axis, the "Uluru Line," was conceived to join the Federal Parliament House with Uluru, a site sacred to Indigenous peoples of central Australia in a gesture of acknowledgment of the significance of the Indigenous presence for Australian history. The main axis is a thirty-meter-high loop that links the NMA and AIATSIS buildings.

The design of the building was closely aligned with contemporary museological critiques of the modernist box. Postmodernist sympathy for populist expressions had entered exhibition culture, provoking controversies and debates. The resultant academic discourses encouraged the deconstruction of popular myths of progressive colonial enterprise and their underlying racist legacies. They impacted the perception and reception of the museum buildings.

THE AUSTRALIAN INSTITUTE FOR ABORIGINAL AND TORRES STRAITS ISLANDER STUDIES

Conceived as a keeping place for research, publications, and audiovisual material, including oral histories, photographs, and documentaries, AIATSIS has become a nationally significant resource for Indigenous Australian scholarship. Established alongside the museum in 2001, the Institute was first conceived through the efforts of William Charles Wentworth, a member of the Commonwealth Parliament from 1949 to 1977, who argued in 1959 for a comprehensive effort by the Australian government to record the culture of Australian Indigenous peoples. The Australian Institute of Aboriginal Studies Act of 1964 established the AIATSIS, and its founding principal was Fred McCarthy. Today, AIATSIS is governed by a Council of nine members, comprising five Aboriginal or Torres Strait Islander members appointed by the minister and four elected by the Institute's membership.[9]

Figure 2.1.   AIATSIS side view with sculptures of Bogong moths. Photo by author, 2013.

A two-story institutional complex that flanks the NMA entrance, the AIATSIS building complex is clad in brown, red, black, and yellow aluminium paneling, combining the colors of the earth and the Aboriginal flag. It presents a uniform façade to the visitor along "the Uluru line," a six-meter-wide path that links AIATSIS to the NMA. The path extends alongside the façade to curl upward on a mound just beyond the building. The line has been described as a "string" heading from the museum toward Uluru that has snapped and recoiled.[10] In a deliberate spatial move, the building is positioned with its back to the NMA, creating views across to the Brindabella Range. This orientation was additionally driven by the NMA brief, which demanded that habitable space have access to windows, and emphasized the division between public and private functions. The two-story-high main reading room looks across a garden courtyard to Lake Burley Griffin. The boardroom is aligned with the courtyard trees.[11] The landscaped area between the NMA and AIATSIS contains a sizable, circular gathering space and large cast-metal sculptures of bogong moths (*agrotis infusa*) by Ngunnawal artist Jim Williams and Mathew Harding. These artworks recognize the seasonal bogong migration and related cultural traditions of the Ngunnawal people, the traditional owners of the area.

The architectural references made in the AIATSIS design have provoked some controversy. The side elevation facing the NMA is reminiscent of the entry façade of the Parliament building while the west wing is a replica of Swiss architect Le Corbusier's Villa Savoye (1929), a white, modernist project in Poissy, France, formally reproduced in black.

The appropriation and translation of familiar architectural icons is a strategy for interrogating normative meanings, a technique associated with postmodernist critiques. Le Corbusier's iconic modernist aesthetic's architectural "rescue of the noble savage" is among the positions

Figure 2.2. AIATSIS rear view showing Black Villa Savoye. Photo by author, 2013.

challenged by such techniques.[12] Raggatt appropriates the modernist "figure in the landscape" but inverts this representation, observing that "the idea of a black Savoye is an understanding of a local version; a kind of inversion, a reflection, but also a kind of shadow—all ideas also explored in the design of the museum itself."[13] Questioned whether his design method was derived collaboratively with Indigenous communities, Raggatt states his intention was to depict Indigenous occupation of a "white" architecture, following the manner in which an 1880s bank building on Gertrude Street in Fitzroy, an inner suburb of Melbourne, was literally painted over with the colors of the Aboriginal flag when occupied by the Aboriginal Health Service from 1979 to 1992.[14] Raggatt recalls that he liaised with the board and the staff of AIATSIS and responded to their desire for a contemporary building and recognition as "an ongoing culture, and as a sophisticated and integrated learning institution."[15] The AIATSIS board did not want an overtly "Aboriginal Architecture" or, in his words, "an architecture directly derived from Aboriginal beliefs or culture, nor an abstraction of their ancient building methods or perceived attitudes."[16] Raggatt resisted producing overt Indigenous cultural associations evident in the design of many remote facilities. He notes that the AIATSIS board was vivid in their worldview, but architectural representation was not their main interest. Consequently, the orientation and spatial layout were the aspects most discussed.

Raggatt's design replicates a strategy by which Aboriginal presence was inserted into metropolitan environments through the appropriation and modification of extant institutions. The manipulation of a canonical form locates AIATSIS's architecture radically in relation to mainstream architectural discourse. Aboriginality, represented through color, is relegated to the building's surface, while the appropriation of an iconic image for representing a cultural minority is highly provocative. The architect observes that the Indigenous community's difficult relationship with white hegemony was expressed more substantially by backing the museum and providing a private gathering space. A community facility that was originally planned but abandoned due to budgetary constraints would undoubtedly have strengthened the desired spatial politics.

The main concerns of AIATSIS are not architecturally framed. They are largely regarding the institution's survival and its ability to maintain and care for the material archive. Precariously positioned in terms of resource allocation and dependent on government grants, the venue falls outside the protective framework of the university sector in which such pedagogical facilities are usually situated.[17] Its focus on family history, repatriation of cultural heritage to communities, and active forums on reconciliation sustains and supports political engagement. Although clearly forged by white pedagogical research traditions, the institution is a stage for contested histories. For example, a conference held in 2011 focused on the Aboriginal Tent Embassy (see chapter 1) and involved activists Michael Anderson, Isobel Coe, Paul Coe, Pat Eatock, Gary Foley, and Sam Watson.[18]

THE NATIONAL MUSEUM OF AUSTRALIA
AND THE GARDEN OF AUSTRALIAN DREAMS

The NMA complex forms a semicircle around the Garden of Australian Dreams, a space based on a representation of central Australia around the size of a sports oval, layered by various landscapes not necessarily legible to museum visitors. Representations of the Dreaming, Aboriginal stories of origin and life, also suggest aspirations and achievements. The garden includes a water feature and a raised central mound painted over with cartographic features and segments resembling Norman Tindale's map of tribal boundaries across Australia.[19] The lines that crisscross the garden include surveyors' reference marks, road maps, a dingo fence, and Indigenous nation and language boundaries.[20] As noted on the NMA's website, the stylized map is calculated so that one step equals one hundred kilometers across the real landmass of the country, its surface painted with terms for place and country—the word *home* is repeated in one hundred different languages.[21]

Upon entering the NMA, with its 6,600 square meters of exhibition space, visitors encounter contact period histories both in the Gallery of First Australians and again in three other galleries devoted to the Australian nation (namely "Horizons: The Peopling of Australia since 1788," "Nation: Symbols of Australia," and "Eternity: Stories from the Emotional Heart of Australia"). Exhibits contain multimedia presentations of the experiences of ordinary people, thus humanizing and interpolating the official record. This interpretive view of Australian history combines postmodern attributes of relativism and populism with new museology's interactive, technology-focused pedagogical orientations and sensorial and affective content.[22] Facilities include three permanent galleries, a touring gallery, three high-definition digital theatres, workshops and unloading facilities, curatorial facilities and major public function and orientation spaces, restaurants, and retail and grand public spaces.[23]

The rhetorical and metaphorical import of the building is not immediately apparent to visitors who enter the NMA through the main hall, an expansive, light-filled space with curving walls, windows, and ceilings. The hall is an extrusion of the conceptual rope knot as seen from the inside, a metaphor for the strands that tie Australians together as a nation, weaving together the lives and stories of Australia and Australians.[24] The line of rope through the hall leads visitors to the gallery spaces located on three levels. The upper gallery features community stories and object displays representing the diversity of communities across Australia. The lower gallery includes Indigenous histories since 1788, a dedicated Torres Strait Island gallery, and an open storage display that provides the visitor with a glimpse of the NMA's Indigenous collections, the bulk of which are held in an offsite repository. The lower gallery includes a temporary exhibition space dedicated to Aboriginal and Torres Strait Islander histories and cultures.[25] Exhibition and building design are integrated.

The museum building has been described as "antimonumental," "asymmetrical," "decentralized," and "fragmented." Its bright colors and playful forms suggest a populist architecture.[26] Naomi Stead observes that it is "much louder, more gregarious, and more deliberately contentious" than other national institutions, and in its built form "participates boldly in a critical discourse about Australian history and identity."[27] The NMA departs quite radically from the somber and monolithic architecture of Canberra's other museum space, the Australian War Memorial. Yet architect Howard Raggatt maintains that such observations are inflected with pejorative interpretations of postmodernism. In contrast, he insists his spatial approach was "deadly earnest" in its pursuit of a specific line of intellectual inquiry, and of how a plural and often contentious cultural history might be given architectural form. Raggatt describes his as a rearguard approach, whereby the object constantly defers to the idea of history.

The NMA's curatorial pluralism attracted even greater controversy, drawing critique from the conservative Howard government and feeding into the Australian "history wars." The resultant debates prompted two opposing ideological positions: the so-called white blindfold and black armband views of history.[28] Curators and architects of the NMA were seen as favoring populist representations, minority histories, and acknowledgment of colonial excesses over the view of settlement as peaceful and progressive.[29] The Museum and its board sought to maintain their autonomy against the imminent politicization of museum space.[30] They were criticized by the Howard government and cultural conservatives.[31] A government-initiated review of the NMA was completed in 2003 and led to the redevelopment of the permanent exhibitions.[32] The contract of director Dawn Casey, who had advocated the exploration of contentious issues, was not renewed.[33]

The sensibility of entangled histories is represented at the NMA via a collage of themes rather than a linear progression across chronological time. Indigenous culture is represented both as integral and separate from Australia's broader narratives within this configuration. "Complexity and contradiction" in the combination of diverse exhibits, postmodern spatial planning with multiple entry and egress points, and the populist slant of representations and choices suggest the influence of new museology—the pedagogical revision of museum practice to service a wider audience of users. It is intended that as the museum develops beyond its first decade, Indigenous and settler colonial histories will be further integrated.[34] In its current configuration, however, apart from some minor references in the mainstream exhibits, they remain spatially distinct.

THE FIRST AUSTRALIANS GALLERY AT THE NMA

The Gallery of First Australians is spatially separate, which both fulfills a statutory obligation to provide a distinct space for Aboriginal histories and offers autonomy from the surrounding controversies. No effort is made to share the colonial history of the preceding gallery exhibit, titled "Landmarks: People and Places across Australia."[35] The zigzag footprint of the gallery space references architectural forms associated with dispossession: a figure evocative of the Jewish Museum in Berlin, or Rift 1 (1968), and an artwork at Jean Dry Lake, south of Las Vegas, by California artist Michael Heizer, that makes negative incisions in the earth.

This distinctive orientation is evident from the exhibit's entry point where six life-size video screens depict individuals in both traditional and modern dress performing a welcome dance. Participation in this dance potentially transforms the passive observer by inviting visitor identification with the Aboriginal dancers. This appeal to a common humanity and recognition of a living community sets the tone for the exhibit and is continued in video recordings of people and their life stories. Ongoing community contributions are used to organize and articulate an assemblage of political and historical material, heritage artifacts and practices, and environmental law. Their conflicts, adaptations, and anxieties are clearly communicated to the visitor as a collage of diverse positions with no singular story line. Although archaeological evidence is included—for example, the display of Aboriginal artifacts of the Canberra community collected by Henry Moss—there is less regard for their antiquity and greater focus on the associated narratives. The desire to counter stereotypes that objectify Indigenous cultures remains uppermost.

The 2003 government review described the First Australians Gallery as "aurally and visually [marking] the transition from the rest of the Museum into a different kind of cultural space" and balancing "classical and contemporary" themes.[36] The plural, multivalent, and overlapping narratives complemented the Museum's design. The focus also shifts within the Gallery of First Australians from regional case studies and Aboriginal technologies to social and political issues. On the upper level, a replica of a possum skin cloak, a diving suit worn by an Aboriginal diver, batik prints from Ernabella Mission, and baskets made from kelp are linked to the survival stories of particular communities. On the level below, the more difficult contact histories of massacres, betrayals, imprisonment, civic activism, and repatriation of human remains are described. These exhibits are adjusted based on visitor responses. The density of content augmented by audiovisual features anticipates multiple visits.

Although themes of land and landscape are emphasized in the NMA, the contemporary issue of land justice is represented only indirectly, with audiovisual footage of the Aboriginal Tent Embassy.[37] The resounding success of country-based temporary exhibitions such as *Yiwarri Kuju, The Canning Stock Route* (July 2010) or *Yalangbara: Art of the Djang'kawu* (July 2011), held subsequently at the NMA, highlight this omission by expressing the significance of country to communities.[38]

RECEPTION

The NMA has won several awards including the Royal Australian Institute of Architects (ACT Chapter) Award of Merit and the Blueprint International Architecture Award for Best Public Building in 2001. AIATSIS was awarded the BHP Colorbond Steel Award in 2002. An approximately 11.1 million extension of 180 square meters was announced in January 2012.

NOTES

1. Thanks to Tracy Sutherland and Peter Thornley at the NMA for an interview and for taking me through the NMA exhibit on August 2, 2011. Thanks also to Marie Ferris, director of communication and arts at AIATSIS, for clarifications. Howard Raggatt was consulted on the draft version of this text.

2. David Dean and Peter E. Rider, "Museums, Nation and Political History in the Australian National Museum and the Canadian Museum of Civilization," *Museum and Society* 3, no. 1 (March 2005): 36.

3. In reference to Jacques Derrida's deconstructivist theory related to the many interpretations of the text, see Mark Wigley, *The Architecture of Deconstruction: Derrida's Haunt* (Cambridge: MIT Press, 1993).

4. Dimity Reed, *National Museum of Australia: Tangled Destinies* (Mulgrave: Images Publishing, 2002), 129.

5. Reed, *National Museum of Australia.*

6. Richard Weller, "Weaving the Axis," *Landscape Australia* 20, no. 1 (1998): 10–17.

7. Comments by Howard Raggatt are based on a telephone conversation in July 2015.

8. Paul Walker, "Culture," in *The SAGE Handbook of Architectural Theory*, eds. Greig Crysler, Stephen Cairns, and Hilde Heynen (London: Sage, 2012), 372.

9. Based on communication with Marie Ferris, director of communication and arts, AIATSIS.

10. Naomi Stead, "The Semblance of Populism: National Museum of Australia," *Journal of Architecture* 9 (Autumn 2004): 389.

11. Australian-architects, "The Australian Institute of Aboriginal and Torres Strait Islander Studies," available at http://www.australianarchitects.com/en/arm/projects3/ the_australian_institute_of_aborigi nal_and_torres_strait_islander_studies-29979#sthash.sVLcRCXv.dpuf.

12. See Vikramaditya Prakash, *Chandigarh's Le Corbusier: The Struggle for Modernity in Postcolonial India* (Seattle: University of Washington Press; Ahmedabad, India: Mapin Publishing, 2002).

13. Howard Raggatt, "Letters and Fixes: Howard Raggatt Replies," *Architecture Australia* 90, no. 4 (July/August 2001): 96.

14. Victorian Aboriginal Health Service, "About VAHS," available at http://www.vahs.org.au/history .html. The building, at 136 Gertrude Street, was built in 1865 for the English Scottish and Australian Bank Ltd. Since 2009 the Indigenous restaurant Charcoal Lane has occupied it.

15. Raggatt, "Letters and Fixes: Howard Raggatt Replies."

16. Trevor Scott, "Letters and Fixes: NMA, AIATSIS and Consultation," *Architecture Australia* 90, no. 4 (July/August 2001): 96.

17. Based on informal conversations with AIATSIS staff regarding funding cuts in 2011.

18. Kurt Iveson, "Cities and Citizenship," blog posted July 6, 2011, available at http://citiesandciti zenship.blogspot.com/2011/07/aboriginal-tent-embassy-canberra.html.

19. Norman Tindale, "Tribal Boundaries in Aboriginal Australia," (map) (Canberra: Australian National University Press, 1974).

20. The "dingo fence" is an approximately 3,488-mile-long pest-exclusion fence that keeps dingos from agricultural areas in the southeast of Australia.

21. National Museum of Australia, "The Museum Building," available at http://www.nma.gov.au/about_us/the-building.

22. Dimity Reed, *Land, Nation, People: Stories from the National Museum of Australia* (Mulgrave: Images Publishing Group, 2002).

23. National Museum of Australia, "The Museum Building."

24. Ibid.

25. Based on communication with Tracy Sutherland at NMA in October 2013.

26. Uros Cvoro, "Monument to Anti-Monumentality: The Space of the National Museum of Australia," *Museum and Society* 4, no. 3 (November 2006): 116–17.

27. Stead, "The Semblance of Populism," 385–86.

28. Kylie Message, "Culture, Citizenship and Australian Multiculturalism: The Contest over Identity Formation at the National Museum of Australia," *Humanities Research* 15, no. 2 (2009): 25.

29. Margaret Anderson, "Oh What a Tangled Web . . . Politics, History and Museums," *Australian Historical Studies* 119 (2002): 179–85.

30. The Hon. John Howard, "The Liberal Tradition: The Beliefs and Values which Guide the Federal Government" (Melbourne: Sir Robert Menzies Lecture Trust, Monash University, 1996), 17.

31. Kylie Message, "Culture, Citizenship and Australian Multiculturalism," 25.

32. Commonwealth of Australia, *Review of the National Museum of Australia: Its Exhibitions and Public Programs—A Report to the Council of the National Museum of Australia,* 2003.

33. Dean and Rider, "Museums, Nation and Political History," 43.

34. Interview with curator Peter Thornley on August 2, 2011.

35. National Museum of Australia, "About Landmarks," available at http://www.nma.gov.au/exhibi tions/landmarks/about_landmarks/.

36. Commonwealth of Australia, *Review of the National Museum of Australia,* 21.

37. Ibid., 22.

38. *Ngurra Kuju Walyja—One Country One People: Stories from the Canning Stock Route* (Melbourne: Macmillan Art Publishing, 2011); Margie West and Art Gallery of the Northern Territory, eds., *Yalangbara: Art of the Djang'kawu* (Darwin: Museum and Art Gallery of Northern Territory, 2008).

3

Bangerang Cultural Centre, Shepparton, Victoria, Australia

Location: 1 Evergreen Way, Shepparton, Victoria
Date: 1974–1982
Client: Shepparton Aboriginal Arts Council
Community: Bangerang community comprising ten clan groups
Architect: Frederick Romberg
Construction: KG Renwick Holdings Pty. Ltd. of Deniliquin
Administrator: Marlene Atkinson
Other consultants: Conservation management plan–Vic Urban and Greater Shepparton Council
Funding: approximately $337,000 (Shepparton Council $62,000; State Government of Victoria $151,000; Australia Council and the Aboriginal Arts Board $124,000)
Listing: Victorian Heritage Register H1082

The Bangerang Cultural Centre, the first purpose-built Aboriginal cultural center and keeping place in Australia, is the primary cultural facility for the Bangerang community of northern Victoria, which consists of ten clan groups living between the Murray and Goulburn rivers.[1] The center was founded by John Sandy Atkinson of the Moidaban community of the Bangerang, born on Cummeragunja Mission.[2] Atkinson was also founder of the Rumbalara Medical Co-Operative and was active in Aboriginal Affairs.[3] Inspired by Worn Gundidj, the interpretive center at Tower Hill designed by Robin Boyd, Atkinson approached Boyd's partner Frederick Romberg with a proposal for a similar facility with a cultural brief.[4] The siting of the cultural center at the entrance to the International Village at Shepparton, a facility designed to celebrate the immigrant culture of the city (also known as Parkside Gardens), was significant.[5] The proposal was an effort by the local council to invigorate cultural tourism. The undulating topography of the island site with a surrounding moat and waterways covered twenty-one hectares. Parkside Gardens won the Victorian Government "Year of the Built Environment Award (North-East Victoria Section)" in 2004; however, as tourist interest diminished, the site was handed over by the state government and Greater Shepparton Council for housing development.[6] Friends of Parkside Gardens, a statewide coalition aimed at protecting public lands from private developers, has been agitating for retention of the site for public use since 2005. The only structures still extant are the Bangerang Cultural Centre and Philippine House.

CONSULTATION PROCESS

Launched in 1974 by Victorian Minister for Tourism Murray Byrne, the city commenced building the International Village in 1975, using labor from the associated communities wherever possible. The invitation to the Indigenous community to participate in the development of the village was an inclusive gesture on the path to self-determination.[7] John Atkinson was appointed to the Aboriginal Arts Board of the Australia Council in 1976 and set up Shepparton Aboriginal Arts Council Co-Operative with support from the local community and funding by the Arts Board.[8] The Co-Operative lobbied for the creation of a keeping place. Shepparton Council provided the land and a grant of approximately $80,325, and in July 1978 further commitment was sought from then premier Rupert Hamer and the Victorian government.[9] The government responded with approximately $195,075 toward the building, and the Australia Council and the Aboriginal Arts Board provided an additional sum of approximately $160,650. The mission statement of the proposed center was to

> provide an Aboriginal interpretive centre that will educate persons of all ages, backgrounds, physical abilities and cultures and inspire them to explore and discover Aboriginal culture in a creative, safe, environment, where learning is fun.[10]

The architect Frederick Romberg (1913–1992, originally from Hamburg) was the son of a German judge who sought exile in Switzerland and arrived in Melbourne in 1938. Romberg

Figure 3.1. Bangerang Cultural Centre, exterior view. Photo by author, 2012.

was an admirer of the Finnish architect Alvar Aalto. Unlike many of his compatriots, he was not incarcerated in Australia during the war, but in 1943 he was conscripted by the Allied Works Council, crushing stone for a time in the Northern Territory. He was naturalized in 1945, and from 1953 to 1962 he was partner in the renowned architectural firm of Grounds, Romberg and Boyd, later Romberg and Boyd.[11] Following a ten-year appointment as professor of Architecture at the University of Newcastle from 1965 to 1975, Romberg returned to Melbourne around the time when construction on the International Village commenced.

Harriet Edquist writes that the Bangerang Keeping Place can be seen as Romberg's homage to his partner, Robin Boyd, who died in 1971, expressed in a form reminiscent of Boyd's Worn Gundidj project at Tower Hill (see chapter 40).[12] Its rustic materiality is described as possibly inspired by Aalto. The building also displayed attributes of Romberg's empiricist approach and commitment to the central plan, which, Edquist observes, was the last in a long line of pavilion designs spanning twenty years.[13] She also points out that in 1959 Romberg had built a small church—a tin shed—for Pastor Albrecht at the Lutheran mission at Hermannsburg in the Northern Territory at the instigation of Enos Namatjira, son of the late prominent Aboriginal artist Albert Namatjira.[14] These links to the Aboriginal community were resumed with the Bangerang commission.

PROJECT DESCRIPTION

Located at the southeastern corner of the village in a bush land landscape, the octagonal building has a pyramidal cedar shingle roof encircled by a veranda, the whole supported on a raft foundation slab. The circular form, insisted upon by Atkins, takes its cue from Boyd's work at Tower Hill. The roof eaves that extend to cover the veranda are supported by twenty-four timber poles on a circular concrete base. The flooring of slate imported from China extends from the veranda inward into the building. The eight faces of the building are modular, with entrances on two opposite ends. Inside the building, the ground floor, lit by skylights, is designed as a reception, central office, theaterette, and display area flanked by dioramas by George Browning, best known for his work at the Australian War Memorial in Canberra.[15]

Browning's dioramas at the Bangerang Cultural Centre were created for an exhibition in London and consisted of life-size figures, animals, artifacts, and painted backdrops to fit into the curvature of the building.[16] Themes include "Bogong Moth Feast," "Riverina Economy," "Mount William Technology," and "Corroboree." An audio backdrop of environmental sounds that can be activated by the viewer is particularly exciting for young visitors. The display also includes ceramic murals by Thanaquith artist Thanakupi (also known as Thancoupie Gloria Fletcher), who combines ceramics with traditional Indigenous imagery. A mezzanine level within the building houses a number of offices that are linked by a bridge to catwalks on the outer edge. The center is in excellent condition except for windows that had to be replaced due to vandalism. Although the bush garden proposed for the facility was not realized, cumbungi reeds used for spear making and basket weaving were planted along waterways. A moat surrounding it creates an artificial boundary to the site.

RECEPTION

Operated by the Bangerang Cultural Centre Co-Operative Ltd., the cultural center holds guided tours, artifact presentations, and music and dance performances. Artists involved in the center include Kevin Atkinson, Irene Thomas, Colin Tass, Julie Bamblett, and Roland Atkinson. Special events are generally scheduled for NAIDOC (National Aboriginal and Islander Day Observance Committee) Week each July. However, the future of the cultural center is uncertain. RBA Architects is involved in a conservation management plan for the center and the surrounding parklands and is working consultatively with the traditional owners, yet the gradual encroachment of suburban housing has had a severe impact.[17] The displacement of the other Parkside Gardens pavilions—including a windmill, Chinese Garden, and paddle steamer—to prominent locations in Shepparton, Mooroopna, and Echuca, and the inactivity of the remaining Philippine House, have adversely impacted Bangerang, removing it from former circuits of tourist activity. The local community is not interested in the facility, although school groups continue to visit. The Bangerang community uses the keeping place as a church on Sundays, proving its continued significance as a living cultural center. However, as a council involved in land sales around its perimeter owns the building, the survival of the Bangerang Cultural Centre is uncertain.

NOTES

1. The Bangerang Cultural Centre website is at http://www.bangerang.org.au/home.html. Thank you to Marlene Atkinson for agreeing to an informal interview and email correspondence on July 15, 2012. Heritage Victoria, "Victorian Heritage Database Place Details: Bangerang Cultural Centre," report published October 28, 2013, available at http://vhd.heritage.vic.gov.au/reports/ report_place/13104 (link no longer active, last accessed July 2, 2013).

2. Australian Broadcasting Commission, "Mission Voices," http://www.abc.net.au/missionvoices/ cummeragunja/voices_of_cummerangunja/default.htm (link no longer active, last accessed July 2, 2012).

3. Australian Broadcasting Commission, "Mission Voices." John Atkinson was also the chairman of the Aboriginal and Torres Strait Islanders Arts Board of Australian Council (ATSIC), a commissioner for the Aboriginal Development Commission, and was the first Indigenous person to serve on a United Nations Educational, Scientific and Cultural Organization (UNESCO) committee.

4. Robin Boyd died in 1971.

5. Greater Shepparton Botanic Gardens Association Inc., http://home.vicnet.net.au/~parkside/his tory.html (link no longer active, last accessed July 2, 2012).

6. Protectors of Public Land Victoria, http://www.protectorsofpubliclandsvic.com/LINKS/ PPLVIC%20Shepparton%20Rally%201%20April.htm (link no longer active, accessed July 14, 2012).

7. Greater Shepparton Botanic Gardens Association Inc.

8. On My Doorstep, "Bangerang Cultural Centre: Heritage Listed Location," available at http:// www.onmydoorstep.com.au/heritage-listing/13104/bangerang-cultural-centre.

9. The deputation was headed by the leader of the Country Party, Peter Ross Edwards, and included the chairman of the Australia Council, Geoffrey Blainey, Sandy Atkinson, and the then mayor of Shepparton, Murray Slee.

10. Bangerang Cultural Centre, see note 1 above.

11. "Bangerang Cultural Centre, Australia's First Aboriginal Museum," http://home.vicnet.net. au/~bangercc/Architect.html (link no longer active, accessed July 2, 2012).

12. Harriet Edquist, ed., *Frederick Romberg, The Architecture of Migration, 1938–1975* (Melbourne: RMIT University Press, 2000).

13. Edquist, *Frederick Romberg*, 62.

14. Edquist refers to an account of this in the Romberg archive.

15. Bangerang Cultural Centre, note 1 above; see also Australian War Memorial, "George Browning," available at https://www.awm.gov.au/people/P65024/.

16. Bangerang Cultural Centre, note 1 above.

17. RBA Architects, "Bangerang Cultural Centre," available at http://rbaarchitects.com.au/projects/ museums/bangerang-cultural-centre/.

4

Bowali Visitor Centre, Kakadu National Park, Northern Territory, Australia

Location: Kakadu Highway, 5 kilometers west of Jabiru
Date: 1992–1994
Client: Australian Nature Conservation Agency (now Parks Australia)
Community: Gagudju people
Architect: Glenn Murcutt (Sydney) in association with Troppo Architects (Darwin)
Construction: PW Baxter & Associates Pty. Ltd.
Engineer: Meinhardt
Signage and wayfinding designer: David Lancashire Design
Cost: approximately $2.7m

Figure 4.1. Bowali Visitor Information Centre, aerial view. Photo by John Gollings, courtesy Troppo Architects.

Completed in 1994, the Bowali Visitor Information Centre is located in Kakadu National Park, five kilometers west of Jabiru and approximately two hundred kilometers east of Darwin, on the edge of Arnhem Land.[1] The building is the product of an architectural collaboration between the Darwin-based architectural practice Troppo Architects and renowned Australian architect Glenn Murcutt. It is also the product of collaboration with Kakadu's Bininj/Mungguy traditional owners.

CONSULTATION PROCESS

Designed in consultation with local Aboriginal Elders, the building draws upon Aboriginal rituals and understanding of place. The Kakadu Board of Management includes two-thirds traditional owner representation (including the Chair), so the design of the Centre was developed in active dialogue with the Bininj/Mungguy, both formally and informally. The board is comprised of ten Bininj/Mungguy representatives from clan groups in the West, South, Central, and North, and five Balanda (non-Indigenous) representatives from the Northern Territory and Commonwealth governments.[2] The traditional owners helped the architects understand their country and its magic, provided access and assistance in sourcing bush material resources (such as rammed earth, rocks, timber, and anthills) required for the building, established a plant nursery, carried out landscaping work, and further provided labor for the building works.

PROJECT DESCRIPTION

Bowali is a Gundjeihmi name for the local area, pronounced "Bor-warl-ee." The Bowali Creek flows nearby the Visitor Centre. The design for the Centre is based on a number of fundamental themes that draw upon Kakadu's landscapes, colors, elements, and moods.[3] For instance, the dramatic overhanging roof was designed to evoke the Aboriginal Rock Shelters found throughout Kakadu, as well as the "sense of protection that these rocky outcrops afford in the vastness of the landscape."[4] Despite its curves and cantilevers, the sculptural roof form serves to unify the disparate elements of the building.[5] Rather than adopting a single, monolithic form, the Bowali Visitor Information Centre is composed of a number of small pavilions that are dotted along a long, linear timber platform, conceived as an "observation verandah" (Plate 3).[6] Constructed of rammed earth and designed as "refuges," these small pavilions accommodate the various programmatic requirements of the brief, including spaces such as the reception area, the bookshop, and various exhibition areas. The overhanging roof effectively serves as a *brise-soleil* that tilts upward to open up into the surrounding landscape.[7] Sunlight is tempered by a variety of different measures, including high-level slatted screens of Tiwi timber and sections of translucent fiberglass sheet roofing that filter the glare of day.[8]

The building draws upon Aboriginal rituals and understanding of place.[9] Access to the building is via a ramp that runs tangentially to the main wooden platform, a path inspired by the way sacred natural sites in the region are approached and used by the traditional owners.[10] As Troppo Architects describe it, the building "is approached as one enters a rock art gallery site—obliquely, with opportunity to sing to announce your presence and to be seen: to approach softly and slowly."[11] The leading elder of the Gagudju clan, the late Big Bill Neidjie, had introduced the architects to various Aboriginal understandings of place: for instance, the idea of "a journey without beginning or end."[12] The building has no front door. Rather, the

Plate 3.   Bowali Visitor Centre, entry deck, Kakadu National Park, Northern Territory, Australia. Photo by John Gollings, courtesy Troppo Architects.

entry deck floats above the falling ground and a rock serves as the reception desk. Indeed, the Centre has been described as a building that "challenges European concepts of inside/outside . . . it reaches out to the environment with upward sweeping verandas, open planning and materials drawn from the land around—rammed earth walls, ironwood floors, and natural stone features . . . water, the ubiquitous wet season element, is invited into the building via a formalized billabong running through it. During rain, downpipes discharge in waterfalls down the internal rammed earth walls."[13]

Where possible, the palette of materials was selected from local sources. Rammed-earth walls, ironwood floors, and natural stone all feature in the building. Other materials, such as zincalume II and birch grey Colorbond sheeting for the roof and external walls, reference vernacular buildings. Ceilings are lined in a mixture of zincalume cladding and turpentine plywood.[14] Ironwood was used for the cabinet-joinery, steel framing for the structures, cypress pine for the joists, and naturally gray Tiwi timber for the veranda screens.[15] The rainwater that cascades down the building façades and huge central roof gutters have been likened to "Wet Season rains off the nearby Arnhem Land escarpment."[16] As Troppo Architects describe it, the "building tells stories of the land, is of the land, and one day will return to it."[17]

Murcutt's early sketches chart the evolution of the various themes that inform the final design: an open-ended itinerary ("a journey without beginning or end"), round an opaque, enclosed core ("initiation"), with a passageway between walls of rammed earth ("the material of the anthill") bounding it on one side ("refuge") and a vista onto the landscape on the other ("prospect"). All sketches reiterate the importance of two things: the presence of water, which, in Murcutt's words, "immediately translates the season, the rains, the drought," and natural ventilation, which captures the breezes as the sole means of providing the building with climatic comfort.[18] Even though some of these ideas were modified or abandoned during design development, many of the general principles can still be found in the final product.[19]

Figure 4.2.   Bowali Visitor Centre, shading devices. Photo by John Gollings, courtesy Troppo Architects.

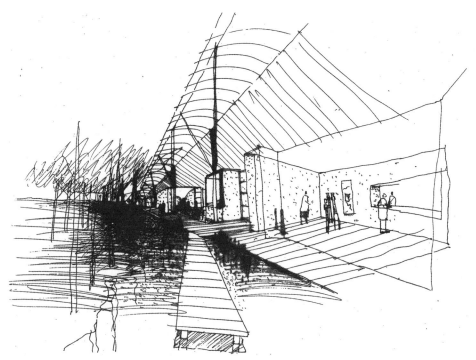

Figure 4.3.   Bowali Visitor Centre, conceptual sketch by Glenn Murcutt. Courtesy Glenn Murcutt and Troppo Architects.

The work of Murcutt and Troppo Architects at Bowali bears attributes of Australian regionalism inspired by the climate and lifestyle of Darwin and the tropical North. Representations of their work frequently allude to inspiration from Aboriginal shelters, colonial homes, and farm buildings. At Bowali, these domestic architectural inspirations are successfully expressed at an institutional scale; still, the focus of the architectural program, its orientation and spatiality is extroverted toward the splendor of Kakadu. Philip Goad has described the project as conveying an "immanent itinerary."[20] This shifting temporality characterizes the dwellings of many Aboriginal groups documented and validated in recent architectural research.[21] It equally captures the transient attributes of settler life. The now-iconic ephemeral aesthetic is likewise crafted and maintained as befits the public purpose of a permanent facility.

RECEPTION

The main objective of the Bowali Visitor Centre is to explain the park's natural and cultural features to visitors. Every half hour there is a twenty-five-minute audiovisual presentation that provides different perspectives on Kakadu and its international significance. The habitat-based display and library provides detailed information about the park. Refreshments are available from the Anmak An-me Café, while the Marrawuddi Gallery stocks Aboriginal art, crafts, books, and gifts. The park staff is available to provide information.

Awards won by the project include: RAIA (NT) Tracy Memorial Award, 1994 (in association with Glenn Murcutt); RAIA (NT) "People's Choice" Award, 1994 (in association with Glenn Murcutt); National RAIA Sir Zelman Cowen Award for Public Buildings, 1994 (in association with Glenn Murcutt); Metal Building Award, 1994–1995 (National Award by BHP/Metal Building Products Manufacturing Association).

NOTES

1. Thanks to Phil Harris at Troppo for reviewing the draft and providing photographs. Thanks to Glenn Murcutt & Associates for approvals. Chapter based on research and text by Carolynne Baker.

2. Based on communication from Tracey Diddams, Tourism and Visitor Services Manager at Kakadu National Park in consultation with colleagues in Canberra, December 2013. Information about the management of Kakadu National Park is available at http://www.environment.gov.au/ topics/national-parks/kakadu-national-park/management-and-conservation/.

3. Glenn Murcutt was brought on board at the design stage of the project.

4. Françoise Fromonot, *Glenn Murcutt: Buildings + Projects 1962–2003* (London: Thames & Hudson, 2003), 234.

5. The use of the overhanging roof in Murcutt's projects has also been described as inspired by Aboriginal bark shelters that use pieces of bark in great sheets. See Philip Drew, *Leaves of Iron: Glenn Murcutt: Pioneer of an Australian Architectural Form* (North Ryde: Angus and Robertson, 1993), 65.

6. The theme of the veranda runs through Murcutt's work and is elaborated upon in Philip Drew, *Touch the Earth Lightly: Glenn Murcutt in His Own Words* (Sydney: Duffy and Snellgrove, 1999), 117–48 and 157–58.

7. Architectural Record, "AIAA Awards Gold Medal 2009," available at http://archrecord.construction.com/features/aiaawards/09goldmedal/13.asp (link no longer active, last accessed April 1, 2010).

8. Fromonot, *Glenn Murcutt*, 234.

9. Toppo Architects website, 2010. http://www.troppoarchitects.com.au/ index.php?mode=projects &projectID=13 (link no longer active, last accessed April 1, 2010). See Philip Goad, *Troppo Architects* (Singapore: Periplus Editions, 2005): 58–65.

10. Fromonot, *Glenn Murcutt*, 234.

11. Troppo Architects website, 2010.

12. Fromonot, *Glenn Murcutt*, 234.

13. *Architectural and Interior Specifier,* "Project Review: Gone Troppo: Kakadu Information Centre," *Architectural and Interior Specifier*, no. 4 (1994): 26–29.

14. Anonymous, "News and Views: Top Award for Tourist Spot," *Building Construction Materials and Equipment (BCME)* 36, no. 43 (1995): 13.

15. Ibid., 13.

16. Troppo Architects website, 2010.

17. Ibid.

18. Fromonot, *Glenn Murcutt*, 234.

19. Ibid.

20. Philip Goad, *Troppo Architects*, 64.

21. See Paul Memmott, *Gunyah, Goondie + Wurley: The Aboriginal Architecture of Australia* (Brisbane: University of Queensland Press, 2007).

5

Brambuk Cultural Centre, Halls Gap, Grampians National Park, Victoria, Australia

Location: 277 Grampians Tourist Road, Grampians National Park, Victoria, Australia
Date: December 1989–1990
Client: Department of Conservation, Forests and Lands, Victorian State Government
Communities: Five Koori communities from South-West Victoria and the Wimmera, which together form Brambuk Incorporated. The five communities are: Framlingham Aboriginal Trust, Goolum-Goolum Aboriginal Co-Operative (Horsham), Gunditjmara Aboriginal Co-Operative (Warrnambool), Kerrup-Jmara Aboriginal Elders Co-Operative (Lake Condah) (replaced by Kirrae Whurrong Community Incorporated in the early 1990s), Portland, Hamilton, Heywood communities
Architect: Gregory Burgess Architects
Builder: Department of Conservation and Environment (Vic) using local contractors and Koori laborers
Landscape Architect: Department of Conservation, Forests and Lands
Engineer: P. J. Yttrup & Associates Pty. Ltd.
Building Area: 700m²
Cost: $780,000

The Brambuk Cultural Centre is located in the valley between Boronia Peak and the Wonderland Range, south of Halls Gap in the spectacular Gariwerd-Grampian Ranges (Grampians National Park) (Plate 4).[1] The name *Brambuk*, meaning "belonging to the Bram," references the Bram Bram Bult brothers, two figures from the local creation story. The undulant double-story building is evocative of the surrounding ranges as well as of the sweeping wings of the Djab Wurrung and Jardwadjali totemic symbol, the cockatoo.[2] Its organic form can be interpreted in any number of ways. As Roger Johnson describes it, elements hold multiple meanings: "The undulating two-tone corrugated iron roof as the feather of a bird or the carapace of a beetle; the curving ramp through the center of the building as the serpent, and the central hearth as the traditional fire."[3] Along with the Uluru-Kata Tjuta Cultural Centre at Uluru in Central Australia, Brambuk Cultural Centre has been said to be at the forefront of architecture, which uses overt zoomorphic representations of elements that derive from Aboriginal culture.

Plate 4.   Brambuk Cultural Centre, Halls Gap, Victoria, Australia, in its setting (photo: courtesy Trevor Mein)

BACKGROUND

The project had a long gestation period. A committee comprising five Aboriginal communities from the western district of Victoria and other tourism and government bodies developed it over some ten years. The product of an intense collaborative design process, Brambuk was to represent five traditional Koori communities from the Western district of Victoria with links with Gariwerd.

Prompted by the Archaeological Survey of 1976, the idea for a cultural center in the region was first formally discussed in the mid-1970s. In 1984, the idea was incorporated into the State Government's Tourism Strategy, with financial responsibility for the project devolving to the Department of Conservation, Forests and Lands (1983–1990). A Steering Committee was subsequently convened that included representatives from the five Koori communities that form Brambuk Incorporated, namely, Framlingham Aboriginal Trust, the Goolum-Goolum Aboriginal Co-Operative (Horsham), the Gunditjmara Aboriginal Co-Operative (Warrnambool), the Kerrup-Jmara Aboriginal Elders Co-Operative (Lake Condah), and the Portland, Hamilton, and Heywood communities. The Steering Committee also included representatives from the Victorian Archaeological Survey; the Department of Conservation, Forests and Lands; the Ministry for Planning and Environment; the Aboriginal Development Commission; and the Victorian Tourism Commission. The consultation process took place over a period of approximately eighteen months. Regular meetings were held and every aspect of the building came under scrutiny, from aesthetic details to budgetary constraints.

Although a body that represents five Aboriginal groups from southwest Victoria and the Wimmera regions manages it, the Brambuk building is formally owned by the State of Victoria.

CONSULTATION PROCESS

As related by the architect Gregory Burgess, the building was the result of ten years of discussion between representatives of the five Aboriginal communities and of government, environmental, cultural, and tourism bodies.[4] An intense twelve-month "hands-on" collaboration with community Elders followed. Their dormant spiritual sensitivity to the land and pride in the then recently discovered eight-thousand-year-old stone dwellings and sophisticated weir systems nearby became significant factors in guiding the evolution of the design. The community's individual totems animate and underlie this design, which incorporates the Eel (ramp), the Whale (ridge-spine), the Eagle (roof forms), Stone (base, fireplace, and floor), and Tree (posts).

PROJECT DESCRIPTION

In plan, the building is composed of five overlapping circular geometries that are centered on the vertical axis of a massive stone hearth and chimney that supports five of the axial ridge and roof beams. Each circle represents one of the five communities that form Brambuk Incorporated, while also evoking the form of eight-thousand-year-old Aboriginal stone dwellings found throughout the Lake Condah region. According to the architect's website, the design "reflects the totems of the five Koori communities who have links with Gariwerd."[5] Internally, the various spaces are radially organized by function around the central hearth. Curved

Figure 5.1. Brambuk Cultural Centre, architectural model. Photo courtesy Gregory Burgess Architects.

earthen walls, the forest of posts within, and carefully controlled lighting all combine to give the interior its dramatic character. Formed by the undulating roof, eye-shaped windows frame views of the two highest peaks in the surrounding ranges, as well as small, tantalizing glimpses out to the surrounding landscape. Access to the building is via a circuitous route—a curved "journey pathway"—through an arborium of edible and medicinal plants. A large ceremonial ground has been constructed nearby, protected by the earth berms that encircle the building.

Traditional yet innovative building techniques and a palette of local materials were used to create a responsive organic building within an extremely limited budget. Local sandstone was used to construct the plinth and the lower floors of the central area, while huge Grey Box eucalypt poles, many with bark intact, encircle the hearth, carrying the structural load of the roof as well as the curved ramp that winds its way up through the building. Australian white cypress, a highly termite- and fungus-resistant timber, was selected for the external cladding.[6] These timber boards were curved using a steam chamber so that they would fit the curved walls of the building without splitting.[7] The technique of steaming wood has been used for centuries, particularly in boat building. Steaming softens the cellular structure of the timber so that the material becomes malleable and can be bent. When the timber dries, it regains its original strength. All the curved timber elements of Brambuk, including the Victorian Ash handrails of the helical ramp, were steam bent on site.

Innovative construction solutions are often born of tight budgets. For instance, the laminated beams were simply nailed together on site to achieve large spans of fourteen or fifteen meters, and local community members made the bricks on site. A massive, undulating segmented ridge beam supporting the principal roof structure runs like a backbone between two

Figure 5.2.   Brambuk Cultural Centre, ramp. Photo courtesy Gregory Burgess Architects.

massive timber posts at the ends of the building. This beam was simply constructed from short lengths of straight material (laminated veneer lumber) lapped and nailed to follow the curve of the roof profile.[8] It was laminated on site using rings of mechanically driven nails. No effort was made to conceal these connections.

Facilities include a gathering space on the ground floor, which contains a display area, workshops for visitors and resident artists, a theater with full projection facilities, a retail shop, and managerial offices. On the first floor, a café overlooks the earth berms to the hills beyond. The spiraling ramp wraps around the central chimney, linking the two floors of the building.

As is always the case, the architectural brief can only conjecture what may be required of the building. For instance, a café was not part of the original brief for Brambuk but had to be retrofitted on the upper level, with some difficulty. Commercial activities are now accommodated in a separate building, and the original building contains only spaces for interpretative workshops, art exhibitions, and places from which to experience the landscape.

RECEPTION

According to a leaflet produced by Brambuk Incorporated, the major objectives of the cultural center are to maintain the pride of Kooris in their culture and heritage and to raise the awareness and appreciation of Koori culture, heritage, dignity, and legitimacy among Kooris.[9] The center acts as a cultural focus for the surrounding Koori communities and visitors to the area. It serves to focus attention on Aboriginal art and activities in the Grampians and encourage protection of sites and culture through greater public appreciation. As Gregory Burgess argues, "The Brambuk group stressed the need for a place for living culture rather than a museum

Figure 5.3. Brambuk Cultural Centre, entry area showing roof form. Photo courtesy Gregory Burgess Architects.

of past culture . . . a place for gathering and creation in a real sense to engender pride in Aboriginality."[10] The building remains one of the more discussed commissions for an Aboriginal community center, with scholars debating the deliberate use of rustic elements and zoomorphic forms, the relationship to the landscape, and the interpretation of Aboriginality through architecture and for heritage tourism practices.[11]

The building has won architectural prizes at both state and national levels, including the Kevin Borland Timber in Architecture Award for excellence in design and use of timber in architecture in 1995; the Kenneth F. Brown Asia Pacific Culture & Architecture Design Award for outstanding examples of contemporary architecture that reflect and enhance their Asia Pacific context in 1995; the Royal Australian Institute of Architects (Victoria) New Institutional Building Merit Award in 1990; and the Sir Zelman Cowen National Award for Most Outstanding Non-Domestic Architecture Project in 1990.[12]

ADDITION TO THE BUILDING

An entry building to the Grampians National Park was commissioned in 2006 and designed by architect Wendy Hastrich.[13] Funded by the Department of Transport and Regional Services as a partnership between Brambuk and Parks Victoria, the addition took the form of an information center for visitors to the park. Design and communications company LookEar Pty. Ltd. was asked to design the visual and written graphics both inside and outside the building. The inspiration for the form and the meandering walkways throughout this design were the story of the eel and shape of the eel net. Materials included local stone, recycled timber, and untreated copper cladding for the columns. A double roof is used to keep the building cool.

The scale and the brief, as well as the expansive use of glass, contrast sharply with the adjacent Brambuk Cultural Centre, providing an institutional interface for urban visitors. In 2007, the entry building won the Master Builders Association National Commercial/Industrial Construction Award for projects under AUD$5 million (approximately $3.9 million).

NOTES

1. Thanks to architect Gregory Burgess and Brambuk chief executive officer Jeremy Clark for clarification on this account. Chapter based on original research and drafting by Carolynne Baker.

2. Gregory Burgess Architects website at http://www.gregoryburgessarchitects.com.au. See also "Gregory Burgess: Brambuk Living Cultural Centre," *A + U: Architecture and Urbanism*, no. 320 (1997), 112–17.

3. Roger Johnson, "Brambuk Living Cultural Centre," *Architecture Australia*, no. 10 (1990), 26.

4. Based on notes of Gregory Burgess.

5. Gregory Burgess Architects website.

6. Australian white cypress is a Durability Class 1 material that is highly termite and fungus resistant. Durability Class 1 material lasts at least twenty-five years in the ground and is defined as a highly durable material.

7. They were then fixed horizontally at the lower levels and vertically on the upper levels.

8. Throughout the nineteenth century, large, curved elements in public and ecclesiastical buildings were mechanically laminated from three or more layers of timber.

9. Mathilde Lochert, "Mediating Aboriginal Architecture," *Transition*, no. 54–55 (1997): 8–19, 11.

10. As noted by Susan Ferguson, "Brambuk Cultural Centre Architectural Resource Package," available at http://www.brambuk.com.au/assets/pdf/brambukspecs.pdf.

11. Ian Clark, "Brambuk Koori Living Cultural Centre—Budja Budja, Hall's Gap, Victoria—Taking a Journey through Time," *Agora*, no. 4 (1991): 10–12; Jim Davidson, "Brambuk, Capital of Gariwerd in Victoria's Grampian Ranges," *Australian Society*, no. 12 (1991): 32–35; Kim Dovey, "Architecture about Aborigines," *Architecture Australia*, no. 4 (1996): 98–103; Ceridwen Spark, "Brambuk Living Cultural Centre: Indigenous Culture and the Production of Place," *Tourist Studies*, no. 1 (2002): 23–42; Rory Spence, "Brambuk Living Cultural Centre," *Architectural Review*, no. 1100 (1988): 88–90; and Jennifer Taylor, "A Rapport with the Setting," *Landscape Architecture*, no. 80 (August 1990): 56–57.

12. Jury Citation, "Awards 1990: Institutional New," *Architect Victoria* (September 1990): 10–12; Daryl Jackson, "The Kevin Borland Timber in Architecture Award," *Architect* (October 1995): 9–12.

13. Wendy Hastrich, "2006–New Entry Building for the National Park and Cultural Centre–Halls Gap, Victoria, Australia," available at http://wendyhastrich.com/projects_brambuk.html.

6

Brewarrina Aboriginal Museum, Brewarrina, New South Wales, Australia

Location: Bathurst Street, Brewarrina, New South Wales, Australia
Date: 1987–1988 (fit-out completed 1990; reopened August 2010)
Client: Brewarrina Aboriginal Cultural Committee
Communities: Ngemba, Muwarrari, and Yualwarri peoples
Architect: NSW Public Works Department, Lindsay Kelly Government Architect
Design and Project Architect: Olga Kosterin
Documentation Architect: David Baggs & ECA Space Design Pty. Ltd.
Structural Engineers: Painter, Merryfull, Griffiths & Associates Pty. Ltd.
Landscape Architects: Carolyn Burke & Tony Popovitch PWD
Construction: Heinz Lukas, Brewarrina
Museum Exhibition: Jenny Ferber
Fit-out: D'Arcy, Emerson, Lorimer DCP Idoland
Cost: $540,000
Funding: $391,088 (Bicentennial Funds $288,000 for building and $64,800 for fit-out; Office of Aboriginal Affairs, Department of Aboriginal Affairs and Aboriginal Development Commission $39,000 for fit-out)

Constructed for Australia's bicentenary celebrations in 1988 by the architects and consultants of the Public Works Department of New South Wales,[1] the Brewarrina Aboriginal Museum is located at an ancient Dreamtime site near one of the oldest man-made structures in the world: the Aboriginal fisheries on the Barwon River in far northern New South Wales (Plate 5).[2] Estimated to be approximately forty-thousand years old, the Brewarrina fish traps—or Baiame's Ngunnhu (pronounced "By-ah-mee's noon-oo") as they are otherwise known—are an elaborate network of stone fish traps near the confluence of the Barwon and Darling rivers with the small township of Brewarrina on the south bank of the Barwon. The site was one of the great traditional intertribal meeting places for Aboriginal people of Eastern Australia, and the place sustained thousands of Aboriginal people during tribal gatherings prior to European settlement.[3] The shire itself is home to the Ngemba, Muwarrari, and Yualwarri peoples.

Plate 5.   Brewarrina Aboriginal Museum, New South Wales, Australia, entrance. Photo courtesy NSW Government Architect's Office (GAO).

BACKGROUND

The exact meaning of the word *Brewarrina* has been lost over the years, leaving five competing interpretations, the most common being "clumps of acacias." Other interpretations include "where the gooseberry grows," "fishing," and—perhaps most plausibly—"place of gooseberries," which derives from the combination of the words *warrina* (meaning "place of") and *bre* or *burie* or *biree* (meaning "gooseberries").[4] The name is associated with the history of the local Aboriginal community both before and after colonization.

The Brewarrina fish traps—the Ngunnhu—is part of a creation myth of the local Ngemba people, who were given custodianship of the fisheries by the creator spirit Baiame.[5] Family groups were made responsible for the maintenance of specific traps, and neighboring tribes were invited for ceremonies, trade, arrangements of marriage, corroborees, retributions, and consultations among elders on tribal law. The Ngemba Billabong was the site of the Brewarrina Aboriginal Mission operative from 1886 to 1966 and was described in the Heritage Register as the first institution to be formally established by the Aboriginal Protection Board in New South Wales.[6] It was the longest running reserve station in the state, designed to segregate the Indigenous population by relocating them 16 kilometers out of Bre township.[7] The mission became home to other dispossessed Aboriginal peoples from Tibooburra, Angledool, Goodooga, and Culgoa. The mission had a reputation for harsh treatment, and segregation of the Aboriginal community proved difficult. The heritage listing states that the reserve was reduced from 4,638 acres to 638 acres in 1953. The station buildings included cottages, a school, a garage, a small treatment room, and a hall; the manager's house, office, and a small cemetery occupied a small portion of the site in 1965, but today only the cemetery remains—the last burial there being in 1971.[8] The Mission population was moved to a new location in West Brewarrina in 1965, where they began to establish political and social service organizations, including legal services and land councils.[9]

Brewarrina has also seen two traumatic incidents both in its colonial history and more recent past. The Hospital Creek Massacre saw four hundred Aboriginals massacred at a site 15 kilometers from Brewarrina along the Goodooga Road in 1849.[10] Brewarrina was also the scene of the 1987 death in custody and ensuing protests that became one of the cases for the Royal Commission into Aboriginal Deaths in Custody (1991).[11] This occurred at the time that the cultural museum was being developed.

The Brewarrina Aboriginal Cultural Museum serves an educative purpose, telling the story of the local Indigenous people, the fish traps they have cared for over thousands of years, and the troubled history of European contact. It also serves as a cultural focus for the surrounding communities and visitors to the area, offering the chance to experience Aboriginal culture

Figure 6.1. Brewarrina Fish Traps. Photo courtesy NSW Government Architect's Office (GAO).

firsthand in a historic gathering place. As stated by the chairman of the Aboriginal Cultural Committee, Mr. Les Darcy, on the project:

> The aim is to preserve, develop and promote our culture, heritage and tradition. To enlighten the broader community and most importantly our own young. To let them be aware of their ancestors, let them be proud of their descendants, and let them know how they struggled, suffered and created happiness, so that we still survive in the driest continent on earth, knowing that through different governments and policies over the last 150 years we still have our identity. This project is about Aboriginal pride.[12]

PROJECT DESCRIPTION

The project architect, Olga Kosterin, of the Public Works Department, New South Wales, observes that a rectangular site in town was rejected by the community, with Les Darcy, chairman of the Brewarrina Aboriginal Cultural Committee, observing, the "spirit doesn't move in straight lines." Other Aboriginal clients during a previous "Five Communities Project" for Aboriginal housing also expressed this preference for nonorthogonal forms. This prompted Kosterin to suggest a change of site to a location above the fish traps, despite its delaying the inception of the project. An appropriately open site with historic and continued relevance for the Aboriginal community, able to accommodate a free-form building, was procured by the committee.

The Cultural Museum was conceived as a place of introduction to the fish traps and the country around it, through Indigenous knowledge, community history, and Dreamtime stories. Visitors could also walk to the actual fish traps below. The building was dedicated to

Baiame, the creator spirit of the Ngemba people who had given them the fish traps and taught them to herd fish. Kosterin describes extensive community consultation and the efforts of Les Darcy in developing the concept, with the scheme, plans, models, and details presented to the community to seek their agreement.[13] The program included a shop, offices, fisheries display, audiovisual room, a model of the river, projection area, crafts/function room, and a ceremonial ground and paving area outside the museum.

Set into the riverbank above the fish traps, Brewarrina's Aboriginal Cultural Museum adopts an organic form intended to express the Aboriginal people's spiritual connectedness with the land. As described by David Rowe,

> The earth cover with drought resilient native planting enhanced this connection and provides a low maintenance building. This form also achieves an internal environment to house the exhibition needing minimum of openings and limiting external light and providing a very secure building for the artefacts. The building, needed to be sustainable, with low running costs in terms of energy use—the budget did not allow for air-conditioning.[14]

A pragmatic, low-maintenance, earth-covered structure was designed to "minimise internal fluctuations of temperature and relative humidity."[15] The semiarid climate at Brewarrina is characterized by hot, dry summers and relatively warm winters with a diurnal range that is capable of exceeding 20°C.[16] In 40 degree heat the temperature remains a relatively cool 27 degrees, which is maintained all year round. An earth-covered building answered many of the client's brief's requests and worked within funding limitations.

Upon entry, visitors encounter a shop where local artists sell their wares from around the region. A small office is also located at this point for management and record keeping. A photograph and model of the fish traps placed centrally in the foyer introduce visitors to the past history of the site. Progression from the foyer to the exhibition area leads visitors into a large space in semidarkness, aimed at capturing the spirit of the Dreamtime. Various shades of blue adorn the dome-shaped ceiling to represent the dark sky. This space continues the oral tradition for storytelling and hearing various indigenous languages spoken, so critical for the survival of the community. The space doubles up as an audiovisual room where multiple screenings are possible.

The theme of the river runs through the project. As expressed by Kosterin, "The river exhibition is physically central to the museum because it is culturally central to the people of this region and always has been." A model river flows from the "Dreamtime Room" to "Tribal Life" (time before European contact) and to the "Present-Day Exhibition," and the flowing water provides a pleasant, murmuring effect as visitors look at the displays. The display surfaces are designed as ledges that follow the contours of the form internally, varying in width and creating a continuous flowing effect. Modulated lighting is evocative of the Dreamtime, and stories are projected onto the wall surfaces. The atmosphere is heightened by the interior finishes in varied shades of blue. The security screens on glass are designed with patterns representing "Aboriginal Groupings." Red earth lines the exhibition displays, and the red earth is also suggested by the jarrah wood paneling used in the shop area.

The water pump and audiovisual equipment is housed in the central space. The latter is used for the projection of stories and to run the language tapes recorded by Janet Matthews in 1968. They document songs, language, cultural discussions, and oral histories from the NSW Aboriginal Communities.[17]

Figure 6.2.   Brewarrina Aboriginal Museum, interior. Photo courtesy NSW GAO.

CONSTRUCTION PROCESS

The plan is composed of a number of overlapping circles that rise up to form interlocking domes. Composite construction methods using hybrid ferro-cement and reinforced concrete were developed to build the necessary curvilinear forms, and maximum use was made of prefabricated units due to the difficulty of obtaining skilled workers in the area. The reinforcing profiles were assembled in situ to form several ferro-cement shells, further layered with an impermeable epoxy membrane, insulation, and a meter depth of soil. Saltbush plants (a species of salt-tolerant *Atriplex*) from the area were established around the structures and on their surfaces. The architect observes that the structural system was explained to the bidding companies using visual aids so as to familiarize them with the process. External wall surfaces were treated using galvanized formwork to create a rippled effect, evocative of the water.

The structure was completed in 1988, with landscaping added later in the cooler months of the year. The fit-out was completed in 1990. The architect observes that members of the community would wander through the half-finished structure with much pride and enthusiasm. The building was opened with a special ceremony of dance, with all the Elders honored and present.

Figure 6.3.   Brewarrina Aboriginal Museum, structure. Photo courtesy NSW GAO.

LATER DEVELOPMENTS

The next stage of the building reveals some of the difficulties encountered in building in regional sites and issues of management, ownership, and expertise faced by Aboriginal communities. Although paid for by the bicentennial funds, the building ownership would fall to the Aboriginal organization that was incorporated as a joint committee for commissioning later expansion. Lack of funding was a real concern. A reduction of funds by the bicentennial committee led to the omission of the craft area, which was planned for interactive learning. The remote location of Brewarrina made further supervision difficult for the DPW architects. The Aboriginal community undertook to complete the second stage a few years later, without detailed drawings.

The second building deviated from the original design. The local builder commissioned a larger base that increased its height beyond that of the original museum and reorganized the circulation detracting from the museum entry. An unplanned fence was erected to prevent vandalism, and an unplanned barbeque area was added in the entryway. Meanwhile, management issues led to the museum's closure for nearly a decade, until new management under Brewarrina Business Centre (a not-for-profit Aboriginal cooperative) took charge. The Business Centre, which offers social services and community engagement in addition to its educational and cultural brief, works in partnerships with the Murdi Paaki Regional Assembly (MPRA), which includes sixteen communities across New South Wales, and Lion, a leading food and beverage company.[18] The Business Centre provides financial management for a number of projects with the objective of addressing "a systemic lack of opportunity for Aboriginal people."[19]

The Brewarrina Aboriginal Cultural Museum was unofficially reopened in August 2010 following a refurbishment funded by the brewer, Lion Nathan.[20] Olga Kosterin was recommissioned to organize the design of the landscape through the Office of Public Works under Peter Poulet, the current government architect. Drawings and specification were prepared by the Government Architect's Office of Landscape and Urban Design Group under Barbara Schaffer and Landscape Architecture. Design and documentation was prepared by Luke Wolstencroft. The museum entry was emphasized and paved. A raised amphitheatre was created to the northwest.[21] The creation of a medicinal herbal garden of traditional Indigenous plants was an opportunity to remove various obstacles to the museum entry. The community carried out the work.

The future of the museum is by no means assured, and without additional ongoing funding, it faces imminent closure.[22] Although tours of the fish traps have been operating since the facility was reopened in 2010, tourism alone is insufficient due to the remote location of the Museum. Future plans to expand and adapt the Museum program to include a community facility, a building that can accommodate weddings and funerals, is already underway.[23] It is anticipated that a third building will house these local activities and include facilities for training Indigenous youth.

RECEPTION

Currently run by the Brewarrina Business Centre, the museum represents a symbol of hope in this tiny northern NSW town where nearly 70 percent of its 1,100 residents are Aboriginal and opportunities for employment are limited.[24] Visitors to the center include school groups, families, and individuals, and displays cover Dreamtime, tribal language, local culture, and traditional artifacts. There are guided tours of the museum.[25] The museum tells the story of "Baiame's Ngunnhu," and in addition to its displays it acts as a regional retail outlet with a range of paintings, crafts, artifacts, and books for sale.[26] Local Aboriginal artists are paid for their art works by the center, and regional companies place their products there for sale. The proceeds from these sales support the ongoing operation of the center. [27]

The design process described here suggests the ongoing necessity for architectural involvement during the lifetime of a project as changing community needs and funding shortfalls modify the original brief. Communities who take ownership of their facilities seldom have the means to recommission architects, and maintaining initial design prerogatives is a continuous challenge. More significantly, the Brewarrina Aboriginal Cultural Museum acts as a center rather than a museum, providing a space for nurturing a living community. In fact, the facility has undergone a name change and is described as the Brewarrina Aboriginal Cultural Centre on the Business Centre website.[28] The sustainability of remote facilities and the types of funding, collaboration, and public programs that might ensure and extend their longevity are highlighted by this example, where a more viable programmatic hybrid appears to have evolved.

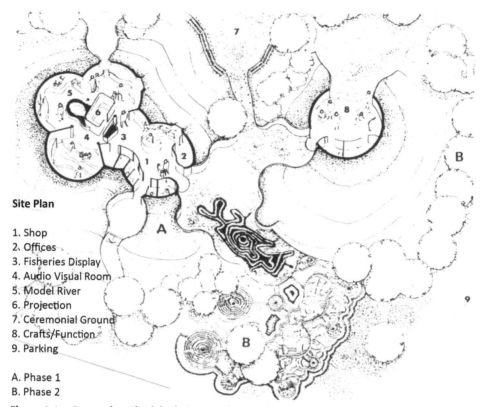

Site Plan

1. Shop
2. Offices
3. Fisheries Display
4. Audio Visual Room
5. Model River
6. Projection
7. Ceremonial Ground
8. Crafts/Function
9. Parking

A. Phase 1
B. Phase 2

Figure 6.4.   Brewarrina Aboriginal Museum, layout plan. Courtesy NSW GAO.

NOTES

1. Other consultants include: interior color scheme Kerry Gallagher (Public Works Department NSW); electrical engineer Roger Weir (Public Works Department NSW); mechanical engineer David Rowe (Public Works Department NSW); supervising construction David Walker (Public Works Department NSW, Bathurst); and senior works supervisor John Oxley (Public Works Department NSW, Dubbo). Ian Thomson was the initial government architect on the project up to 1988 and was followed by Lindsay Kelly.

2. Thanks to Ngemba Elder Aunty Jen (Jeanette Barker) of the Northern Star Aboriginal Corporation for reading our draft; to Ian Merritt and chief executive officer Carole Medcalf at the Brewarrina Business Centre for comments; and to architect Olga Kosterin for detailed feedback on the draft, additional material, and photographs. Thanks also to Peter Poulet of the PWD NSW for material and permissions.

3. Brewarrina Shire Council website is at http://www.breshire.com/.

4. Ibid.

5. Australian Government Department of Environment, "National Heritage Places, Brewarrina Aboriginal Fish Traps (Baiame's Ngunnhu)," National Heritage List available at http://www.environment.gov.au/node/19636.

6. Office of Environment and Heritage, "Brewarrina Aboriginal Mission Site," NSW Government, available at http://www.environment.nsw.gov.au/heritageapp/ ViewHeritageItemDetails.aspx?ID=5053415.

7. Saffron Howden, "Survival Story Looking for Happy Ending," *Sydney Morning Herald*, October 21, 2010.

8. Office of Environment and Heritage, "Brewarrina Aboriginal Mission Site."

9. Royal Commission into Aboriginal Deaths in Custody, "Report into the Death of Lloyd James Boney," January 24, 1991, available at http://www.austlii.edu.au/au/other/IndigLRes/rciadic/individual/brm_ljb/.

10. Brewarrina Shire Council, "Hospital Creek Massacre," available at http://www.breshire.com/tourism/visitor-information/our-history/hospital-creek-massacre.aspx.

11. Royal Commission into Aboriginal Deaths in Custody, "Report into the Death of Lloyd James Boney."

12. Australian Government Department of Environment, "National Heritage Places, Brewarrina Aboriginal Fish Traps (Baiame's Ngunnhu)."

13. Communication with Olga Kosterin, January 2014. The section on architecture above is based on her notes.

14. David Rowe, "Olga Kosterin: NSW Public Works Department: Brewarrina Aboriginal Cultural Museum," *A + U: Architecture and Urbanism* 265 (October 1992): 12–19, 12.

15. Rowe, "Olga Kosterin: NSW Public Works Department," 12.

16. David Rowe, "Olga Kosterin," 12.

17. Janet Mathews, "Language Elicitation from Bourke, NSW, and some SA Language Material," sound recorded in 1968, available via Australian Institute of Aboriginal and Torres Strait Islander Studies online collections at http://www.aiatsis.gov.au/collections/using-collection/search-collection.

18. Brewarrina Business Centre website is at http://www.brebc.com.au/.

19. Brewarrina Business Centre.

20. Saffron Howden, "Survival Story Looking for Happy Ending."

21. Brewarrina Museum, NSW Public Works, Government Architects Office, 2010, PS_Landscape_10_Brewarrina_Museum (accessed January 30, 2014).

22. Saffron Howden, "Survival Story Looking for Happy Ending."

23. Based on telephone conversation with Ian Merritt, June 2013.

24. Saffron Howden, "Survival Story Looking for Happy Ending."

25. Brewarrina Aboriginal Museum.

26. Ibid.

27. Ibid.

28. Ibid.

7

Burrinja Cultural Centre, Glenfern Road, Upwey, Victoria, Australia

Location: 351 Glenfern Road, Upwey, Victoria
Date: 1998–2011
Client: Shire of Yarra Ranges
Architect (auditorium): Gregory Burgess Architects
Construction: Procon Developments
Landscape Architects: Taylor Cullity Lethlean
Art of Place Indigenous cultural garden project: AQL with Sinatra-Murphy
Urban Planning: Hansen Partnership
Theatre and acoustics: Marshall Day Entertech and Acoustics
Theatre technical designer: David Campbell
Cost: $5,662,000
Venue Operations Manager: Tony Kirk
Yarra Ranges Council Manager of Arts, Culture and Heritage: Greg Box
Executive Officer: Ross Farnell
President (Burrinja): Louis Delacretaz

Burrinja is the operational name for the Dandenong Ranges Community Cultural Centre Incorporated, a not-for-profit arts organization incorporated in 1999.[1] An independent Committee of Management governs the center, and includes representatives of the Yarra Ranges Council and services a community of around twenty thousand in the Upwey, Belgrave, and Tecoma community areas. The primary user group is from the surrounding residential community, and activities are tailored to their needs. The Burrinja Cultural Centre provides an example of a settler community's recognition of prior Indigenous claims and the complex process by which that acknowledgment is concretized collaboratively within the broader framework of community-based cultural centers (Plate 6). In this example, Indigenous presence has been acknowledged by the renaming of the facility, by the incorporation of forms and aesthetics evocative of Indigenous culture, and by inviting and accommodating Indigenous artists and theatre groups in the center's program. The choice of Gregory Burgess Architects—with a reputation created through cultural centers at Uluru and Brambuk—for the design of the auditorium was also significant in indicat-

Plate 6. **Burrinja Cultural Centre, Olinda, Victoria, Australia, view of auditorium. Photo by An-drea Damarell, courtesy Gregory Burgess Architects.**

ing recognition of prior Indigenous claims to the area (for other designs see Uluru-Kata Tjuta Cultural Centre and Brambuk Living Cultural Centre).

The history of the Cultural centre, as outlined on its website, includes two decades of community activism aimed at saving the former brown-brick Sherbrooke Shire Offices at Upwey.[2] Sherbrooke, Lilydale, Upper Yarra, and Healesville were amalgamated as the Shire of Yarra Ranges Council during the 1990s, and these former office buildings were put up for sale. A number of community organizations, including United Neighbourhood of the Hills, Save Our Sherbrooke Association, and Save the Dandenongs League campaigned to save the buildings and retain them as a community cultural center. Lin Onus, the prominent Scottish-Aboriginal artist and activist, was among these campaigners.[3] In 1997, the newly amalgamated shire acquiesced to community demands and in 1998 released a business plan and proposal for the Dandenong Ranges Community Cultural Centre. The leasing of space for an Indigenous art gallery to local artist/art collector Neil McLeod made the running of the center cost neutral.

The gallery was named after Onus, a close friend of McLeod, who had died at age forty-seven after a protest meeting for the Cultural centre in October 1996.[4] *Burrinja*, meaning "star," was Onus's Yorta Yorta nickname. Well known for his political and surreal photorealist artworks and role in the urban Aboriginal art movement, Onus is also familiar to Aboriginal children as the creator of characters such as Captain Koori and the Aboriginal freedom fighter Mosquito.[5] He was the son of Aboriginal activist Bill Onus, a former president of the Aboriginal Advancement League. As chairman of the Aboriginal Arts Board of the Australia Council and founder of Viscopy, the artist's copyright agency, Onus brought new attention to the disproportionately large contribution made to the national art industry by Aboriginal art. Examples of his political works included the *Maralinga* series, *Political Bedrooms*, and works on the freedom fighter Mosquito. Speaking at Onus's funeral, friend and collaborator Michael Ether described him as using art as "a tool, a weapon and a shelter."[6]

The early years spent in establishing partnerships and revenue streams created a number of disparate activities at the center site, including the Dandenong Ranges Community Cultural Centre, Burrinja Gallery, and Uncle Neil's Place Café. These initiatives were combined into a common vision of "Building Community through Art" in 2001, and adopted a unifying name and goal in 2004. The choice to extend the name *Burrinja* to the entire facility combined a history of Indigenous art and local community activism.

PROJECT DESCRIPTION

Within the stated objective of "Building Community through the Arts," the Burrinja Cultural Centre focuses on four key areas of activity: arts, performance, education, and community. The facilities provide for arts activities and events; Indigenous gallery, collection, and cultural education; contemporary arts gallery; performing arts; arts incubator studios; live music, community cultural development including youth arts and seniors programs; workshops; café; and tourism. In addition to the Burrinja Gallery there is the Jarmbi Gallery, the collection gallery, the artist's space, the performance space, the meeting place, and the café and bar. In 2012, there were four tenant artists and one musician leasing studio spaces. The most important addition to the center was the four-hundred-seat auditorium built in 2011, which offers a professional venue for local groups.

The auditorium, designed by Gregory Burgess Architects, includes backstage facilities, foyer and staff amenities, and required the sensitive retrofitting of the existing building interiors and a thematic response that built on its original aesthetic.[7] The architect also needed to maintain a

Figure 7.1.   Burrinja Cultural Centre, architectural model. Photo courtesy Gregory Burgess Architects.

human scale in keeping with the residential setting. The dominant structure of the auditorium looms above the incline at the back of the site and is not visible to the visitor. Materials such as corrugated cladding and concrete panels keep the cost of the building as low as possible. The curvature of the addition softens its impact, while the colors are vibrant and distinctive and stand out from the surrounding bush landscape. The orange-painted steel of the community building is complemented with patterned earth-toned concrete tiles used for paving and façade. Both the form and the colors articulate the project as a cultural facility with reference to motifs associated with Indigenous culture.

RECEPTION

The key challenge for Burrinja was of enhancing Indigenous participation in the community center in the absence of a significant Aboriginal community in the Yarra Ranges Shire. The task thus became one of defining, claiming, or maintaining Indigenous presence within a broad and inclusive definition of culture or community against a prior colonial history of forced exclusions.

The contribution to the community is substantial. Not only is it able to expose the local residents to performances occurring at a national level but also increased involvement of schools and local artists suggest the use of the facility as a training ground for professionalization.[8] Activities staged at the center in 2012 included a range of productions such as *Moth*, *Treasure Island*, *Kapow*, *The Mikado*, *Rhinestone Rex and Miss Monica*, and *Caravan Burlesque*, and exhibitions of Australian photography. Indigenous exhibitions featured during this period included *Ngarrambel* ("White Ochre"), an exhibition by Baluk Arts, and *Jus' Drawn*, a touring exhibition by eight Indigenous artists.

Given the higher ratio of non-Indigenous to Indigenous activities, it is important to understand how indigeneity is otherwise inscribed in the Burrinja Cultural Centre. The Burrinja Gallery holds a collection of both traditional and contemporary Aboriginal art, as well as carvings and masks from Papua New Guinea. Educational tours of this collection disseminate Indigenous culture to the wider community and are supported by activities such as hands-on Aboriginal art classes with an Indigenous artist. An Indigenous cultural garden called "Art of Place" has also been planned, with the objective of creating a place for learning, reflection, gathering, creativity, reconciliation, and celebration. Reconciliation Week is celebrated with specialized activities across the center's multiple venues. Membership of Burrinja has been framed as *Jarmbi*—the Yorta Yorta term for "friend"—and the gallery shop has books, objects, and artworks, many of which follow Indigenous themes. The inscription of Indigenous identity as central to the project thus occurs internally as well as externally through the insertion of previously marginal names, spaces, and processes.

Meanwhile, in addition to the Indigenous exhibits, the participation of artists from the broader community sustains the Cultural Center. For example, the group of sculptures by Anton McMurray titled *Monuments to Nature* captures visitor attention at the entrance to Burrinja and depicts the human impact on the environment. McMurray's sculptures were selected from an exhibition called *Into the Wild* held at Burrinja Gallery in 2001.

Burrinja was awarded the Archival Survival Award for Small Museums 2010 by Museums Australia (Victoria) for its exemplary public programs.[9]

NOTES

1. Burrinja Cultural Centre website at http://www.burrinja.org.au/. Thanks to Burrinja chief executive officer Ross Farnell for comments and to Gregory Burgess Architects for architectural data.

2. Burrinja Cultural Centre, "History of Burrinja," available at http://www.burrinja.org.au/index.php/about/history. The details in this chapter are gained largely from the website and via a visit to Burrinja Cultural Centre on July 1, 2012.

3. Burrinja Cultural Centre, "Building Community through the Arts," brochure available at the facility during 2011 to 2012.

4. Margo Neale, "Lin Onus," *Artlink*, no. 1 (2000), available at https://www.artlink.com.au/articles/1394/lin-onus/.

5. Adrian Newstead, "Into Dreamtime," *The Age*, November 13, 1996.

6. Newstead, "Into Dreamtime."

7. Emily Potter, "'Structural and Poetic': Burrinja Cultural Centre by Gregory Burgess Architects," *Architecture Review Asia Pacific*, no. 125 (2012): 90–95.

8. Based on conversation with staff at Burrinja.

9. Burrinja Cultural Centre website.

8

Edge of the Trees, Museum of Sydney, New South Wales, Australia

Location: Forecourt, Museum of Sydney, corner of Phillip and Bridge streets, Sydney, Australia
Date: 1995
Communities: Eora (twenty-nine clans from the Sydney area represented in the installation)
Artists: Collaboration between Janet Laurence and Fiona Foley
Curator: Peter Emmett
Builder: various artisans and contractors contributed to the different components of the sculpture
Materials: twenty-nine pillars of sandstone, wood, steel, oxides, shells, honey, bones, hair, ash, zinc, glass, sound
Funding: Historic Houses Trust
Cost: $132,600

Rising like a forest on the edge of the forecourt to the Museum of Sydney, *Edge of the Trees* is a site-specific sculptural installation by artists Fiona Foley and Janet Laurence (Plate 7).[1] The award-winning public art installation is composed of twenty-nine pillars or totems, each of which has been designed to represent one of the twenty-nine Eora groups from around Sydney. The installation engages a variety of textual, visual, aural, spatial, and haptic means by which to chart and overlay various understandings—and perhaps misunderstandings—of place.

BACKGROUND

Located on the site of the first Government House built on the continent, *Edge of the Trees* overlays Eora memories with colonial memories to mark 1788 as a pivotal turning point in a continuous history, rather than as the singular event it is sometimes made to seem. The installation marks an interstitial space that charts various landscapes of remembrance and forgetting; for, as Peter Emmett argues, this place is "contested ground; contested then, and contested still, for the right to be in this place and the favoured version of national originals."[2]

Plate 7.   Edge of the Trees, Museum of Sydney, New South Wales, Australia. Photo by Brett Boardman, courtesy Sydney Living Museums.

The name of the installation derives from an essay by historian Rhys Jones:

> The "discoverers" struggling through the surf were met on the beaches by other people looking at them from the edge of the trees. Thus the same landscape perceived by the newcomers as alien, hostile, or having no coherent form, was to the indigenous people their home, a familiar place, the inspiration of dreams.[3]

PROJECT DESCRIPTION

The twenty-nine pillars are constructed variously from sandstone, wood, and steel as a means by which to evoke both the natural and cultural histories of the site. For instance, the wooden pillars were recycled from one of Sydney's lost industrial buildings, an old Pyrmont foundry that later became the McWilliams Winery Building. The timber for the foundry had originally been sourced from the ironbarks and tallowood that once grew around Sydney. This recycling of materials was intended to highlight how place and the structures that define it can be as ephemeral and transient as those who people the place. Notches in the pillars dating from their industrial incarnation have been reinvented as windows that house a variety of organic materials and substances—human hair, shells, bone, resin, midden ash, pipe clay, feathers, ash, and honey—the flotsam and jetsam of an earlier way of life. Certain pillars are inscribed with remnants of surviving snippets of information from earlier times. For instance, the names of botanical species found in pollen readings of the governor's garden are carved or burnt into the wooden pillars in both Latin and Aboriginal languages. Archaeological investigations of the site revealed that a grove of stone pines once grew there, and in many respects the form of the installation reflects this earlier site condition.

Sandstone was selected as "a natural ground on which to map" the work.[4] It is the stone on which Sydney is founded and the earth on which Eora camps stood, as well as being the material that characterizes much of Sydney's built heritage. Some of the sandstone pillars are inscribed with the names of the Eora who lived in Sydney between 1788 and 1850, a mapping that is countered by a list of signatures from some of those on the First Fleet that are engraved on zinc labels and mounted on one of the pillars. Place-names are inscribed on the sandstone pillars in both English and Aboriginal languages.[5]

From deep within the twenty-nine pillars emits a ghostly soundscape of Eora voices reciting traditional place-names of the Sydney region that have been all but overwritten by colonial occupation. This soundscape was originally conceived as a map on the ground engraved with the names of Eora groups in the Sydney area, as sourced from an eighteenth-century fishing map. However, the matter of creating such a map was called into question during the development of the design, and the map evolved into a soundscape in which lilting sounds chart the country in a manner reminiscent of song lines.

The steel pillars provide a link to the steel and glass construction of the museum directly to the west, thereby extending the museum architecture into the forecourt while at the same time implying that the installation is a museum exhibit that has somehow escaped the confines of the institutional imagination. Corten steel was selected to symbolize cycles of development and decay.[6]

Even as it draws on various cultural and historical aspects of the site, the installation is rich with contemporary urban allusions—its verticality a maquette for the surrounding high rise or the masts on the harbor, its materiality a play on that of the city in which it sits. In this respect, the installation illustrates how public art might be successfully integrated into the urban fabric as a fundamental part of place-making.

Figure 8.1.   Edge of Trees, Museum of Sydney, detail. Photo by James Horan, courtesy Sydney Living Museums.

RECEPTION

In 1995, the Royal Australian Institute of Architects (NSW Chapter) awarded the Lloyd Rees Award for Civic Design for the development of First Government House Place, Sydney to artists Janet Laurence and Fiona Foley and Denton Corker Marshall Architects.

NOTES

1. Thanks to Jennifer Rayner, Anna Cossu, Alice Livingston, and Susan Sedgewick at Sydney Living Museums. Original draft by Carolynne Baker.

2. Peter Emmett, "What Is This Place?" in *Edge of the Trees: A Sculptural Installation by Janet Laurence and Fiona Foley*, ed. Dinah Dysart (Sydney: Historic Houses Trust of NSW, 2000), 23.

3. Rhys Jones, "Ordering the Landscape," in *Seeing the First Australians*, ed. Ian Donaldson (Sydney: Allen & Unwin, 1985), 185.

4. Janet Laurence and Fiona Foley, "The Artists' Submission," in Dysart, *Edge of the Trees*, 49.

5. Museum of Sydney, "Edge of the Trees," http://sydneylivingmuseums.com.au/exhibitions/edge-trees.

6. Janet Laurence, "Edge of the Trees," http://www.janetlaurence.com/edge-of-the-trees.

9

Galina Beek Living Cultural Centre, Healesville, Victoria, Australia

Location: Gleneadie Avenue, Healesville, Victoria
Dates: 1992–1995
Client: Aboriginal Affairs Victoria
Community/Proprietor: Coranderrk Koori Co-Operative
Architects: Anthony Styant-Browne Architect (project team Anthony Styant-Browne, Jen Rippon, John Simmons, Carlos Lay, Ming-En Lim, and James Staughton)
Master Plan and Business Case Ratio Consultant: Jeffrey Wolinski
Civil and Structural Engineers: Ove Arup & Partners
Services Engineers: Scheme Group
Landscape Architects: Graeme Bentley
Construction Contractor: A&M Martino
Funding: Aboriginal Affairs Victoria, Aboriginal and Torres Strait Islander Commission
Cost: $702,000

Galina Beek, which means "loving the earth" in the Woi Wurrung language, was built on the site of the Coranderrk Station (1863–1924) and was perhaps the most significant purpose-built Indigenous cultural center to be located immediately outside Melbourne during the late 1990s.[1] Its position in the vicinity of the Healesville Sanctuary along the road leading from the Sanctuary entrance is indicative of the center's agenda both to renew Aboriginal claims to the area and to capture tourists and visitors. Designed as part of a larger master plan to develop a thirty-five-hectare bushland site, the Cultural centre's brief was "to nourish and service the community activities of the local Coranderrk Koori community, and to create, display and sell Aboriginal culture to visitors."[2]

BACKGROUND

To realize this brief, Ratio Consultants in association with Anthony Styant-Browne Architect (now Workshop Architecture) was commissioned by Aboriginal Affairs Victoria to prepare a master plan, conceptual design study, and business case for the project. Galina Beek was Styant-

Browne's first Australian Indigenous project. He had previously worked with local people in Papua New Guinea on community development projects for Butibum and Kamkumung villages in Lae, as well as planning and design projects for First Nation Peoples of the United States, specifically the Navajo and Salt River communities. The Ratio team submitted the study to Aboriginal Affairs Victoria with recommendations for implementation. The Living Cultural Centre was to be constructed during the first stage of the implementation. The then minister for Aboriginal affairs, Tom Roper, announced funding for the first stage shortly afterward, and Anthony Styant-Browne Architect was engaged as principal consultant. Unfortunately the funding allocated was roughly half that nominated in the business case, and the building had to be designed and documented for construction in two stages. Stage One comprised a gathering space, administration, amenities, artifacts shop, and associated site works, including parking and an outdoor performance area. Stage Two comprised a restaurant, display gallery, and workshops for the production of artifacts by Coranderrk artists and craftspeople. The expectation of both architect and client was that once Stage One was completed and operating well, Stage Two would commence construction; however, this did not eventuate. Soon after completion, the operator, the Coranderrk Koori Co-Operative, ran into financial difficulty and the operation failed. The center was subsequently leased to a commercial operator.

Galina Beek was planned to include workshops and an exhibit area, designed to enable community cultural and economic development. The gathering space, which was to be the heart of the Coranderrk community, was fitted out with a display that tells the story of Coranderrk Station. On failure of the project, these spaces were lost to the community, and the subsequent implementation of the master plan, including plans for a childcare center and conference center with accommodation and interpretation trails, was never realized.

CONSULTATION PROCESS

Although the formal client and funding body for the project was Aboriginal Affairs Victoria, the Coranderrk Koori Co-Operative were the actual clients with whom the architect engaged in a long collaborative process. Throughout the center's long gestation through the design phase, the architect and the Co-Operative met regularly, originally in the Co-Operative's space in Healesville and later in a new space on the outskirts of the town. All Co-Operative members were invited to participate in a hands-on, inclusive, and interactive workshop setting. A core of the community attended most workshops, with other members dropping in and out on occasion. A permanent display was maintained in the community space showing the current state of the design. In this way, the architect sought to achieve community ownership of the project and to ensure its cultural appropriateness. The location was selected because it was an available site in Coranderrk territory.

PROJECT DESCRIPTION

The circular building form was derived from artistic representations of the Aboriginal act of gathering (Plate 8). A double-height drumlike conference room was the form-giving element, surrounded by offices, service spaces, and an encircling gallery. The pathway from the street leads the visitor through the gallery to the conference room top-lit by clerestory windows with

Plate 8. Galina Beek Living Cultural Centre, Healesville, Victoria, Australia, exterior view. Photo by John Gollings, courtesy Workshop Architecture.

the surrounding forest of gum trees visible through the north-facing glass wall. The space has been described as having "a serene and contemplative presence."[3] The path extends to the veranda and onward, leading the visitor outdoors to a ceremonial ground and eventually a path into the forest. Stage One of the project included the design of the conference room, gallery, shop, and offices. A third layer was to be added in Stage Two forming a set of concentric spaces that would recall the recurring motifs of much Indigenous painting.[4] An ancillary wing including workshop and display space was also planned for Stage Two.

The completed building is the core of a larger composition of buildings on the site, radiating from the center and inflecting toward the forest like the outstretched fingers of a hand. The linear circulation spine extending west from the drum marks a boundary between colonial and Indigenous space, facing the parking lot and road beyond to the south and the bush to the north.

Writing on the project in 1996, Kim Dovey described the Galina Beek design as indicative of the cultural tensions surrounding "the construction of Aboriginality in Australian society."[5] He described Styant-Browne's architecture as a fusion of "the Aboriginal and the contemporary, avoiding the literal or organic."[6] His reading of this tension is based on the juxtaposition of natural materials and colors—ochres, yellows, natural timbers, and reds—with the purple-painted octagonal steel frame of the central drum. He also describes a similar "unease on the street frontage" where "wall junctions splay and crack in a manner that generates the spiral form with a certain edginess, reflecting an unfinished process of reconciliation." Dovey hastens to add that the design is neither radically deconstructive nor reduces the architecture to text. He describes it as "a finely composed building" respectful of the Aboriginal client community that "uses these tensions for aesthetic interest."[7]

Figure 9.1.   Galina Beek Living Cultural Centre, interior. Photo by John Gollings, courtesy Workshop Architecture.

Activities undertaken while the center was in use can be found in tourist literature of the late 1990s, which advertise dance performances and guided bushwalks.[8] The facility was open daily from 9 am to 6 pm with an entrance fee of AUD $7 (approximately $5), and showed regular screenings of videos on aspects of local Aboriginal culture. The art gallery sold paintings and artifacts made by local artists. The centerpiece of the facility was an exhibition about the history of Coranderrk and the Aboriginal people associated with the Station. Dovey, however, observes that the Victorian Government appropriated the conference room and subdivided it as a museum exhibition area, displacing the living culture with historic displays.[9] He argues that "the segmentation of the gathering place paradoxically damages the experience of the building, yet underlies its representation as a place of ongoing struggle."[10]

RECEPTION

Galina Beek was awarded a Royal Australian Institute of Architects (Victoria) Architecture Award in 1996. By 2011, however, the Cultural Centre was no longer operative. A visit in early 2011 found the building abandoned and showing signs of use immediately prior to closure as a mainstream operation, the Platypus Restaurant. The building closed down entirely in 2013. An information officer at the Healesville Tourist Centre recalled that the building had for a time been used as an Indigenous restaurant that sold jams and jellies but had subsequently abandoned the Indigenous theme. She also observed that while it was running as a cultural center the local non-Aboriginal community had little involvement unless there was a specific event being staged in the hall.

The questions arising from Galina Beek haunt all remote facilities purpose-built for tourism. Reliant on funding cycles and a fluctuating tourist economy, the long-term upkeep and community sustainability of such ventures cannot be supported by the relatively small Indigenous communities they represent. These communities, moreover, often struggle with their own everyday survival and lack the capacity to maintain such a facility without broad-based community participation. How such centers might engage local non-Indigenous communities as well as tourists remains a challenge.

NOTES

1. Thanks to Tony Styant-Browne from Workshop Architecture for notes and revisions of the draft chapter.

2. Kim Dovey, "Continuing Cultural Tensions Are Evident in Stage One of the Galina Beek Living Cultural Centre at Healesville, Victoria by Anthony Styant-Browne," *Architecture Australia*, no. 5 (1996), available at http://architectureau.com/articles/galina-beek/.

3. Dovey, "Continuing Cultural Tensions."

4. Ibid.

5. Ibid.

6. Ibid.

7. Ibid.

8. "Healesville," *The Age*, January 23, 2008; Pacific Island Travel, "Healesville," http://www.pacific-islandtravel.com/australia/victoria/healesville.asp (link no longer active, last accessed May 20, 2010).

9. Dovey, "Continuing Cultural Tensions."

10. Ibid.

10

Gunung-Willam-Balluk Learning Centre, Broadmeadows, Victoria, Australia

Location: Building W, Pearcedale Parade, Kangan Institute, Broadmeadows
Date: 2004
Client: Kangan Batman Institute of Technical and Further Education [TAFE]
Architect: Gregory Burgess Architects
Landscape Architect: Thompson Berrill Landscape Design
Project Manager: Peter Davies Project Management Pty. Ltd.
Structural Engineer: P. J. Yttrup & Associates Pty. Ltd.
Builder: Cockram Builders Pty. Ltd.
Cost: $975,000
Manager Indigenous Education Centre: Linc Yow Yeh

A purpose-built facility designed by Gregory Burgess Architects, the design for Stage One of the Gunung-Willam-Balluk Learning Centre aimed at merging traditional and contemporary Aboriginal culture, cutting-edge technologies, and practical learning in a pedagogical environment.[1] Located within the Kangan Batman Institute of Technical and Further Education (TAFE), the Centre provides pathways for Indigenous students to careers and to tertiary study through academic and prevocational courses. The Centre is the biggest provider of Indigenous education in Victoria, with thirty staff members and sixteen programs. It provides vocational pathways in twenty-six courses, including management, business, building and construction, Victorian Certificate of Applied Learning, community services, cultural arts, information technologies, and conservation and land management.[2] The courses are taught in a culturally appropriate way and are grounded in Indigenous knowledge systems. Teaching tools include art exhibitions, music festivals, community projects, and the use of multimedia resources. The annual Ningulabul Reconciliation Lunch held in partnership with the Hume City Council creates a dialogue regarding reconciliation with community members.[3] In 2012, Indigenous artists Kutcha Edwards and Paul Carey as well as Aboriginal music, art, culture, dance, customs, and traditions were featured at this event.[4]

There is growing community of Indigenous residents in the region served by the Institute. According to the 2011 census data, the number of Indigenous people in the Hume Council area increased from 892 in 2006 to 1,047 in 2011. Darebin, Whittlesea, and Hume councils in the north and west metropolitan regions have the largest populations of Aboriginal and Torres Strait Islanders in Melbourne.

BACKGROUND

The Indigenous Education Centre at Kangan Institute was established in 1998 within a "village" of portables that had previously been used at Melbourne's now closed Pentridge Prison and were relocated to the Broadmeadows site. Known as "G" Block, the Koori Programs Unit was managed by Terrance Kildea with three staff members. When the Unit outgrew the portables in 2004, a state-of-the-art Indigenous facility was proposed. Kildea, the manager of Koorie Programs from 1999 to 2009, was instrumental in the development of the new building for the Indigenous Education Centre. Kildea involved local Elder Norm Hunter (also known by his tribal name *Wonga*, meaning "Bronze Winged Pigeon"), the leader (or *Nurangeita*, meaning "Wise Elder") of Gunung Willam Balluk, one of the five clans of the Woiwurrung language group, traditional owners of the area around Broadmeadows and Hume. Kildea and Hunter chose the site for the building on a mound overlooking Hume to the left of the main entry to the Kangan Institute. The land belonged to the Hume City Council. The Council had inadvertently built a basketball stadium on the property of the Kangan Institute a few years earlier, so the parcel of land that Kildea and Hunter selected was traded with Kangan in its stead.

The Government of Victoria funded the building with significant sponsorship from corporate providers, and it cost approximately $1 million. Gregory Burgess Architects was selected because of its reputation in the collaborative design of cultural buildings for Indigenous communities. Following a long and elaborate consultation process, involving community meetings at Youth Central with the local Indigenous community and with Kangan management, a facility was designed based on three design stages, the first of which is complete. The brief required that the building forms express something of the local Wurundjeri culture, and was expressed in the eagle-like form of the roof and celebration of water and canoes.[5] The new building was opened in April 2004 and was endorsed by Norm Hunter and named after his clan. The business proposal for the next stage is under preparation by Linc Yow Yeh, the current manager.

PROJECT DESCRIPTION

Water is a key symbolic and material element in the architecture, designed to represent the Gunung Willam Balluk or "creek dwelling water people" associated with the area around Mount Macedon and Bacchus Marsh. The Gunung Willam Balluk are a part of the Woiwurrung clans who lived in the drainage basin along the Yarra River and its tributaries and shared the *Bunjil/Waa* moiety system of kinship and totemic class of the Kulin nation.[6] *Bunjil*, the wedge-tailed eagle creator spirit, is represented in the plan of the building: the entry foyer is *Bunjil*'s "heart," a key meeting place where important gatherings take place, and the left wing contains the administration manager's office, teachers' stations, bathrooms, and individual music tuition areas. The right wing contains four classrooms. Operable walls enable the foyer and two classrooms to open up to form one large space, which becomes a venue for significant community gatherings two to three times a year. Other key aspects of the brief were that the

Figure 10.1.   Gunung-Willam-Balluk Learning Centre, gathering space, showing skylights. Photo courtesy Gregory Burgess Architects.

building would be environmentally sustainable. A large beak spout acts as a rainwater head that funnels rainwater from the roof onto the rocks below, and inverted-canoe skylights are designed to cast pool patterns under the entrance canopy.[7] Rainwater tanks collect water for gardens and toilets, and solar collectors heat the water in the building. Bathrooms were to be fitted with showers, as a number of the students do not have access to bathing facilities or hot running water in their own homes.

RECEPTION

The aim was that the building itself—its form and fabric—could be used for teaching cultural knowledge, and that the spaces would convey a sense of freedom. The art/craft workshop areas were deliberately designed with high ceilings. The relationship to the outdoors is also critical; the building is oriented so that it opens out on to landscaped gathering spaces in the north and a public park in the south. The garden is used for teaching land conservation, and food-handling courses include the building of a fire pit in a sand-filled courtyard for traditional meat preparation. Students studying building construction have built the outdoor decks and pathways, creating a sense of ownership and collective cultural investment in the life of the facility. A series of totem poles at the entry depict *Bunjil*, followed by other animals. "Man" appears second to last. The final pole is a spear that points to the future at the entry to the building, symbolizing the importance of education and training in Western and Indigenous knowledge systems for the future of Indigenous people. Kangan Institute was the 2006 Australian Timber Design Awards Finalist for Environmental Commitment.

NOTES

1. Thanks to Linc Yow Yeh for information on the Centre and Gregory Burgess Architects for architectural data. Kangan Institute, Indigenous Education Centre, https://www.kangan.edu.au/students/departments/indigenous-education-centre. The material presented here is largely based on an informal interview of manager Linc Yow Yeh, conducted by Janet McGaw in July 2012.

2. Kangan Institute, *2012 Course Guide*, available at http://bluestudies.com.au/en/wp-content/uploads/pdf-files/kangan_2012-course-guide.pdf.

3. Kangan Institute, "7th Annual Ningulabul Reconciliation Lunch," available at http://www.kangan.edu.au/news/media-releases/2011/110601-7th-annual-ningulabul-reconciliation-lunch/ (link no longer active, last accessed July 17, 2012).

4. Stephanie Zevenbergen, "NAIDOC Week: Celebrating 40 Millennia," *Hume Weekly*, http://www.humeweekly.com.au/news/local/news/general/naidoc-week-celebrating-40-millennia/2618256.aspx (link no longer active, last accessed July 27, 2012).

5. Gregory Burgess Architects, "Gunung-Willam-Balluk Learning Centre," available at http://www.gbarch.com.au/projects/2004/gunung-willam-balluk-koorie-learning-centre--kangan-batman-tafe/.

6. Gary Presland, "Woi Wurrung," eMelbourne: The City Past and Present, available at http://www.emelbourne.net.au/biogs/EM01629b.htm.

7. Gregory Burgess Architects, "Gunung-Willam-Balluk Learning Centre."

11

Gwoonwardu Mia Gascoyne Aboriginal Heritage and Cultural Centre, Carnarvon, Western Australia, Australia

Location: 146 Robinson Street, Carnarvon, Western Australia
Date: 2004–2005
Client: Piyarli Yardi Aboriginal Corporation (Gascoyne Development Commission)
Architect: JCY Architects & Urban Designers [Jones Coulter Young]
Project Team: Libby Guj, Charles Thwin, Vince Faladi, Linda Chiew, Hean Wei Phay
Communities: Baiyungu, Inggarda, Thalanji, Thudgarri, and Malgana
Engineer: BG & E
Builder: Jaxon Construction
Cost: $4.9 million
Funding: Government of Western Australia through the Gascoyne Development Commission
Center Manager: Jennifer Joi Field

Inspired by the symbol of the cyclone, the Gwoonwardu Mia Gascoyne Aboriginal Heritage and Cultural Centre (formerly Piyarli Yardi Gascoyne Aboriginal Heritage and Cultural Centre) is located in Carnarvon, approximately 904 kilometers north of Perth.[1] Designed to serve as a home to the diverse communities known as the Yamatji peoples, the design of the building evokes one of the common features of life in the Gascoyne region, namely, the rain-giving cyclones that periodically sweep across the coast and into the arid interior of the continent. *Gwoonwardu* means "where the fresh water meets the sea water."[2]

The Centre website states that the organization is owned and operated as a not-for-profit corporation with a Board of Management, supported culturally by an Indigenous Reference Group.[3] This Group includes key Elders from each of the five language groups of the region: the Baiyungu, Inggarda, Thalanji, Thudgarri, and Malgana (also spelled Bayungu, Yinggarda, Thalanyji, and Thadgari). These language groups cover a broad area and include the communities of Carnarvon, Exmouth, Coral Bay, Denham/Shark Bay, Gascoyne Junction, and the Aboriginal community of Burringurrah in Western Australia's North West.[4] An acute challenge faced by the architects was designing a single facility that could satisfy the visions of very different regionally dispersed language groups.

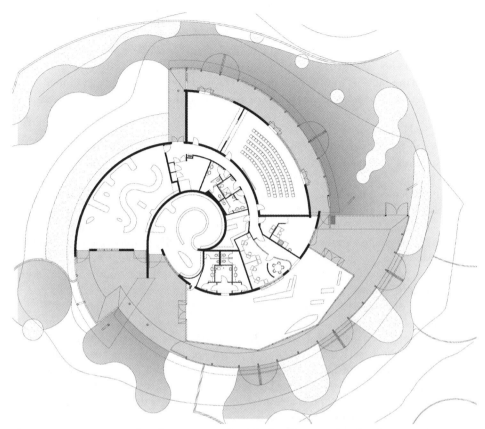

Figure 11.1. Gwoonwardu Mia Gascoyne Aboriginal Heritage and Cultural Centre, plan. Courtesy JCY Architects & Urban Designers.

BACKGROUND

Although the first recorded European sighting occurred in 1839, it was not until 1876 that European settlement occurred in the region, when approximately four thousand sheep were herded into the area. Carnarvon was gazetted in 1883 and named in honor of the Earl of Carnarvon, Secretary of State for the Colonies from 1873 to 1877. The Gwoonwardu Mia Gascoyne Aboriginal Heritage and Cultural Centre is located at the point beyond which, as recently as the mid-twentieth century, no Aboriginal person was allowed to pass unless they were planning to work in Carnarvon, a time of segregation remembered clearly by the local Aboriginal community Elders.

As a counter to this history of segregation, the Gwoonwardu Mia Gascoyne Aboriginal Heritage and Cultural Centre serve as a bridge between cultures. In this respect, the symbolism of the building is "grounded in the site."[5] The Centre is intended to become the new gateway to Carnarvon, serving as a cultural keeping place, a place for learning, and a place in which to celebrate Aboriginal culture, both future and past.[6]

As outlined by Desert Knowledge Australia, the Cultural Centre was conceived in relation to the native title claim mounted in 1994 by the Yinggarda people, traditional owners of the area for at least thirty thousand years.[7] That year, several male Elders approached the then Deputy Premier Hendy Cowan and sketched their country and stories in the sand. They wanted "a place to tell their stories." The Gnulli Native Title Working Group settled an Indigenous Land Use Agreement with the Western Australian Government in 2002. The Gnulli claim (*Gnulli* meaning "all of us") was lodged and formed the process and sought the "right to negotiate" over this area. Under the Land Use Agreement, the Shire of Carnarvon exchanged land for a proposed new waterfront estate and provided approximately $2.5 million to build an Aboriginal cultural center.

The Piyarli Yardi Aboriginal Corporation (PYAC) was a group of representatives from each of the Yinggarda, Baiyungu, Talanji, Thudgarri, and Mulgana language groups, whose cultures were to be represented by the proposed center. The PYAC responded to the government's requirement that an Aboriginal management body work with the Gascoyne Development Commission and a land management body in the development of the project by forming the Yuggoo Aboriginal Corporation, so that a land vesting management order could be made out in its favor. However, the process did not go smoothly. By 2004, concerned at their exclusion from decision making, a group of Elders approached the Gascoyne Development Commission and the then Minister for Regional Development and requested that control of the cultural center project be removed from the PYAC. Following several meetings, the Elders were given full control to determine the future direction of the facility.

In shifting ownership to the Elders, the then-Minister for Regional Development made several administrative changes. A Board of Directors comprised of three Indigenous members including the recognized Elders and three respected non-Indigenous members of the community was appointed. An Indigenous Reference Group was also formed, comprising three representatives from each of the five language groups. The Minister also committed additional funding of approximately $120,000 a year for four years to fund the employment of a manager and operator for the center.[8] The Gwoonwardu Mia Gascoyne Aboriginal Heritage and Cultural Centre opened on October 23, 2009 (Plate 9).

COMMUNITY CONSULTATION

The consultation process was complex and long. It involved many people, families, and organizations of extremely diverse backgrounds from numerous places spread across a region of Australia that spans several thousands of square kilometres. Ranging from the wild coast of Shark Bay and the Ningaloo Reef to Mount Augustus in the pastoral lands, the rich diversity and culture of the region informed the process. The consultation process focused strongly on connecting across generations by including children, teenagers, families, and elders. Language, values, respect, strong connection to past, culture, and most significantly future formed the foundation of the consultation process. One of the most powerful and significant moments during the process was the evening blessing of the site, when hundreds of people from all over the region gathered for an evening of song, food, stories, and the sharing of this piece of land.

PROJECT DESCRIPTION

The single-story building adopts a spiraling form that is emphasised by the pointed eaves of the overhanging roof. Perforated Corten steel screens wrap around the building's façades. On one

Plate 9.   Gwoonwardu Mia Gascoyne Aboriginal Heritage and Cultural Centre, Carnarvon, Western Australia, exterior view. Photo by Andrew Pritchard, courtesy JCY Architects & Urban Designers.

level, these curved screens serve simply as functional sun shades. However, closer inspection reveals that these screens "depict the spirit of youth": duplicated images of children fishing, playing basketball, and surfing have been laser cut into the sheets of weathered steel.[9] During the day, these playful images designed by local Aboriginal high school students throw ever-changing patterns of sunlight across the interior of the building, while also providing glimpses out to the surrounding landscape. At night, it is the light from the building itself that illuminates the surrounding landscape: a glowing "filigree of figures" playing and dancing upon the building façades.[10] Although aesthetically distinctive, maintenance of these curved screens has proved difficult.

The Centre includes a café, artists' residential space, retail space, conference and public meeting rooms, and two galleries with interpretive exhibitions.[11] It also includes an outdoor performance space. Training in hospitality, tourism, leadership, and business is described as a feature of the organization. An ethno-botanical garden and an interpretive exhibition with audiovisual and touch tables was opened by the Western Australian premier Colin Barnett on June 8, 2012. The exhibition includes images and artifacts, including the "Burrowing Bee" film and a thirty-two-thousand-year-old shell necklace. The center also includes a sky dome, which tells the story of the *Jungurna* or emu in the Milky Way.

RECEPTION

The Gwoonwardu Mia Gascoyne Aboriginal Heritage and Cultural Centre serves a community of approximately nine thousand. The Artist in Residence program is open to perform-

Figure 11.2. Gwoonwardu Mia Gascoyne Aboriginal Heritage and Cultural Centre, interior corridor. Photo by Andrew Pritchard, courtesy JCY Architects & Urban Designers.

ing, visual, and literary artists from regional and remote areas with a focus on community cultural development. A permanent interpretive exhibition titled *Burlganyja Wanggaya* or "old people talking" was developed over a five-year period to present the rich and vibrant history of the Gascoyne.[12] Local Elders share their stories in the exhibition space, presenting "their histories and culture" and "their stories of ancient and continuing connections to the land of the Gascoyne."[13] Developed through the active participation of the Gwoonwardu Mia Indigenous Reference Group, the exhibition won the Museum and Galleries National Award (MAGNA) for 2012.

The Gwoonwardu Mia Café is a hospitality training facility delivering training to Indigenous staff and students in partnership with the Durack Institute of Technology and local schools. Students train in the center facilities, and a catering service supplies lunches for civil work contractors in the community. The Centre is a member of the Gascoyne Food Trail showcasing the produce of the region.

NOTES

1. Thanks to Jennifer Joy Field and staff at the Centre for correspondence on the draft, and architect Libby Guj at JCY for notes and photographs. The material in this chapter is largely drawn from information included on the Centre website and material provided by JCY Architects. Draft text by Carolynne Baker.

2. Gwoonwardu Mia Gascoyne Aboriginal Heritage and Cultural Centre, "About Us," available at http://www.waitoc.com/operator-info/gwoonwardu-mia-the-gascoyne-aboriginal-heritage-and-cultural -centre-inc.

3. Gwoonwardu Mia Gascoyne Aboriginal Heritage and Cultural Centre, "About Us."

4. Ibid.

5. Anoma Pieris, *JCY: The Architecture of Jones Coulter Young* (Balmain, NSW: Pesaro Publishing, 2005), 115.

6. Anoma Pieris, *JCY*, 115.

7. Desert Knowledge Australia, "The Gascoyne Aboriginal Heritage and Cultural Centre," available at http://www.desertknowledgeaustralia.wikispaces.com/file/view/DKA+Part+1.ppt (link no longer active, last accessed December 19, 2013). The three stages outlined here are based on the text in the above presentation.

8. Desert Knowledge Australia, "The Gascoyne Aboriginal Heritage and Cultural Centre."

9. Pieris, *JCY*, 115.

10. Ibid., 115.

11. Gascoyne Development Commission, http://www.gdc.wa.gov.au/contents/projects/gascoyne -aboriginal-heritage-and-culture-centre.htm?id=207.

12. Gwoonwardu Mia Gascoyne Aboriginal Heritage and Cultural Centre, "Exhibitions."

13. Ibid.

12

Jean-Marie Tjibaou Cultural Centre, Nouméa, New Caledonia

Location: Rue des Accords de Matignon, Tinu, Nouméa, New Caledonia
Date: 1992–1998
Client: Agency for the Development of the Kanak Culture (ADCK), Marie Claud Tjibaou
Director General ADCK: Octave Togna
Inaugural Cultural Director: Emmanuel Kasarhérou (formerly anthropologist and Kanak director of the Territorial Museum in Nouméa)
Architect: Renzo Piano Building Workshop (Renzo Piano, Paul Vincent)
Contractor: Glauser International
Engineer: Ove Arup & Partners
Wood Construction: Mathis SA
Area: 8,000 square meters
Site: 10 kilometers from Nouméa on the site of cultural festival Melanesia 2000
Funding: Grand Project by François Mitterrand and the French Government
Cost: $54 million

The Jean-Marie Tjibaou Cultural Centre in Nouméa was a gift from New Caledonia's former colonial administrator, the French government, to the Kanak People of New Caledonia. The Centre was received as giving the Kanak People dignity, agency, and a territorial claim to the area.[1] The last of President François Mitterrand's seven "Grand Projects," it attracted an international profile and funding that rendered its remote island location visible and significant, and the elegant design by Pritzker Prize–winning Italian architect Renzo Piano has been celebrated in architectural circles. The creation of the Centre is frequently represented as an act of reconciliation, albeit underwritten by postcolonial patronage framed in the continuing neocolonial relationship between France and New Caledonia. Issues that require redress include not only the contemporary repercussions of a history of colonial exploitation, genocide, and human displacement but also the removal of culturally significant artifacts into museums and the discursive reduction of the diversity of cultures Indigenous to the region to the singular undifferentiated label of "Kanak/Canaque."[2] French control of New Caledonia's nickel industry prolongs this unequal relationship. The Centre represents the "Canaque" (who comprise 45 percent of New Caledonia's population), a formerly negative identification now reclaimed as the basis of a unifying Kanak political identity.

BACKGROUND

The 1988 civil war between the French and the Kanak, the most recent of many confrontations, ended with the Matignon-Oudinot Accords. The Accords were negotiated for the Kanak by politician Jean-Marie Tjibaou, who declared during the process that "culture is capital." The institutionalization of the development of Kanak culture became a political prerogative to which the government responded with the creation of a dedicated agency (the *Agence de Development de la Culture Kanak* or ADCK) and a commitment to a representative Kanak cultural center in Nouméa. The metropolitan location gave the center global visibility, which contrasts with the spectacular natural and antiurban setting on the Tinu Peninsula. This was the location for Melanesia 2000, a cultural festival gathering first held in 1975 and hosting over fifteen thousand Kanaks. The festival prefigured claims for the repossession of land and the repatriation of cultural artifacts.[3] The role of the landscape in providing spectacular opportunities for gathering and celebration was recognized through the cultural center project.

Figure 12.1. Jean-Marie Tjibaou Cultural Centre, architectural model. Courtesy ADCK, Centre Cultural Tjibaou, and Renzo Piano Building Workshop; photo courtesy Lindy Joubert.

PROJECT DESCRIPTION

Piano's design derives from Kanak building traditions that, with the contributions of anthropologist Alban Bensa, incorporates a complex relationship with elements and markers in the natural landscape.[4] A lengthy consultative process with the Kanak Elders, a desire to translate their *habitus* (both dwelling form and spatial practices) into the museum program, and the tectonic and material complexity of the aesthetic outcome suggest multiple levels of engagement. Findley identifies four elements that informed Piano's design: a ridgeline recalling the earthworks on which Kanak villages are built, the linear layout along a central walk, the verticality of the low-scale but high-roofed conical houses, and the pinelike araucaria of the landscape.[5] Piano's distribution of the buildings along the ridge of the peninsular as an *allée* (lane or path), and its composition of ten "houses" along an interpretive Kanak Path, is an innovation in culturally specific museum planning. The brief was for a cultural center and not a museum; core cultural values maintained by the architect include the celebration of the visitor as part of the building and the new rigorist approach to the building's structure.

The Centre's facilities form three clusters, described as three villages, with low volumes oriented toward the reef side and high volumes of the conical houses toward the lagoon. The first village is related to the High Place, and includes welcoming facilities, an exhibition space, cafeteria, four-hundred-seat hall, and open-air auditorium.[6] The second village houses the mediatheque, temporary exhibition space, administrative areas, and meeting rooms. The third village is for teaching, discussion, and administration. The second and third villages are linked by an underground passage. Restaurant, accommodation, and workshop spaces overhang the villages, while several conical structures located at the pit of the bay area have been designed for ritual activities. The landscaping of araucaria pines and coconut palms reinforces the informality of the scattered buildings and village sensibility. At a more intimate level, it recreates a Melanesian food garden.[7] The asymmetrical organization of spaces allows for a number of paths between facilities. The metaphor of the village is one that is hard to abstract due to its use in many themed tourist resorts and, although frequently alluded to in these terms, Piano's project is a hybrid building that draws equally from a European tradition of architecture (Plate 10).[8]

Piano was keen to invoke the frugality of natural materials.[9] The traditional materials used for the conical Kanak dwellings—coral, wood, and bark—were translated into a lath-clad dual structure in oroko wood (an imported African mahogany), with nacos for ventilation and a connecting 250-meter-long corridor in glass and wood.[10] The structure for the high-curved building volumes was tested in a prototype built in France in July 1993, and comprises pairs of glulam arches linked by horizontal steel bracing spaced at 2.25 meters and diagonally wind-braced. These are set in a grid 0.9 meters apart, where the modular internal face allows for interchangeable panels that are either glazed, include openable glazed blades, or are of perforated or solid wood. The external skin is of horizontal blade panels in oroko.[11] The cladding is designed as a weave with varying opacity, while the roofs are either opaque or glazed with sun-shield.

Low volumes use similar technologies. A major innovation is evident in the harnessing of natural ventilation for the buildings. A cross-based double cylinder shell allows air to be drawn in and circulate in the form of a chimney. Valves are used to control air circulation. This technological approach that, as with many of Piano's international projects, is complex and highly innovative, has attracted much criticism for projecting an image of an environmentally sustainable architecture while relying on the importation of materials at great cost.[12]

Plate 10. Jean-Marie Tjibaou Cultural Centre, Nouméa, New Caledonia, landscape with traditional structures. Courtesy ADCK, Centre Cultural Tjibaou, and Renzo Piano Building Workshop; photo courtesy Lindy Joubert.

Figure 12.2. Jean-Marie Tjibaou Cultural Centre, structural details of *cases*. Courtesy ADCK, Centre Cultural Tjibaou, and Renzo Piano Building Workshop; photo courtesy Lindy Joubert.

Figure 12.3.   Jean-Marie Tjibaou Cultural Centre, exterior view of *cases*. Courtesy ADCK, Centre Cultural Tjibaou, and Renzo Piano Building Workshop; photo courtesy Lindy Joubert.

RECEPTION

The Tjibaou Cultural Centre is a model for a new museology rooted in and representative of local concerns. In addition to promoting and conserving Kanak culture, it has forged interregional partnerships, outreach programs with rural Kanak communities, and "Travelling Educational Kits," including folding suitcase-style models of the cultural center easily transported to schools for educational programs.[13] The centre's library and digital catalogue perform the critical function of documenting and preserving Kanak heritage. The center also interacts with other cultural centers and museums in the Pacific region, in France and internationally. Kylie Message describes it as "an official site for testing and holding dialogue and debate" on appropriate signifiers for a renewal of cultural identity for New Caledonians.[14]

NOTES

1. Thanks to Emmanuel Kasarhérou for initial communication and J. Pipite for further correspondence and image approval. Thanks also to Lindy Joubert for providing photographs.

2. Lisa Findley, *Building Change: Architecture, Politics and Cultural Agency* (London and New York: Routledge, 2005), 45–46.

3. Findley, *Building Change*, 50, 53.

4. Findley, *Building Change*, 54.

5. Alban Bensa, "Piano Nouméa," *L'Architecture d'aujourd'hui* 308 (December 1996): 44–57.

6. Bensa, "Piano Nouméa," 51.

7. Bernice Murphy, "Centre Culturel Tjibaou: A Museum and Arts Center Redefining New Caledonia's Cultural Future," *Humanities Research* 9, no. 1 (2002): 77–90.

8. Murphy, "Centre Culturel Tjibaou," 85. Mike Austin, "The Tjibaou Culture Centre in New Caledonia," in *Re-Framing Architecture: Theory, Science and Myth*, eds. Michael J. Oswald and R. John Moore (Sydney: Archadia Press, 2000), 25–29.

9. Murphy, "Centre Culturel Tjibaou," 84.

10. Bensa, "Piano Nouméa," 45.

11. Ibid., 52.

12. *James Wines, Green Architecture* (Los Angeles: Taschen, 2000), *226–37.*

13. Kylie Message, "Contested Sites of Identity and the Cult of the New: The Centre Culturel Tjibaou and the Constitution of Culture in New Caledonia," *reCollections: Journal of the National Museum of Australia* 1, no. 1 (March 2006): 7–28.

14. Message, "Contested Sites of Identity," 11.

13

Karijini Visitor Centre, Karijini, Western Australia, Australia

Location: Karijini Visitor Centre, Banyjima Drive, Karijini National Park, Western Australia
Date: Completion April 2001
Communities: Banyjima, Yinhawangka, and Kurrama communities
Architect: Woodhead International BDH
Project Team: John Nichols, Craig Forman, Martin Neilan, and Karl Woolfitt
Structural and Civil Engineer: Connell Wagner
Builder: Wylie & Skene Pty. Ltd.
Developer: Pilbara Development Commission
Landscape Design: Department of Conservation and Land Management
Interior Design: Woodhead International BDH
Display Design: David Lancashire Design
Cost: approximately $1.6 million

The Karijini Visitor Centre is located in the Hamersley Ranges in the East Pilbara, a remote region in northwest Western Australia famed for its rugged scenery, spectacular gorges, and ancient geological formations.[1] It is composed of a number of free-standing, overlapping Corten steel walls that rise dramatically from the rust red earth, signifying the iron-rich landscape. The single-story building thereby engages with both the surrounding landscape of the Karijini National Park and the cultural history of the site (Plate 11).

CONSULTATION PROCESS

Part of the project brief was for the built form to represent the Aboriginal cultural history of a geographical area of over 627,000 hectares associated with three primary language groups. The facility is located on the land of one of these groups. The Government of Western Australia commissioned the project, and the Aboriginal stakeholders whose culture was to be on display were initially afforded no formal authority. A lengthy consultation process had to be undertaken to build trust with the community, understand their cultural frameworks, and make decisions on the kind of content to be conveyed through interpretive displays. John Nichols, the

Plate 11.   Karijini Visitor Centre, Western Australia, aerial view. Photo by John Gollings, courtesy Woodhead.

project architect who led the consultation process, has subsequently observed the importance of developing mutual trust and respect over an extended period of time; the outcomes desired by the community charged with the operation of the Centre became paramount.[2]

The challenges faced by the client group included accepting a site in the land of a particular community as representative of all three language groups, settling on a mode of combined representation that respected their differences, and working with government bodies and architects. The key challenge for the architect was of conceiving a representative aesthetic that could be accepted by all three groups. As with many designs for facilities charged with this task, the landscape became a source of inspiration. Building trust required the recognition of client concerns: as Nichols observed, "These are complex, demanding projects which are often hijacked to serve other agendas."[3] At Karijini, Nichols first established his independence from government as a practitioner so that he could develop a personal relationship with Aboriginal stakeholders. This relationship was developed over a two-year period from January 1997. Construction was completed in November 2000, and interpretive displays were installed in April 2001.

PROJECT DESCRIPTION

Accounts of Karijini tend to describe the building as a figurative interpretation, although this association is not immediately apparent to the pedestrian observer. Aboriginal stakeholders chose the *kurrumanthu* or goanna as their shared cultural symbol, the elongated form of the animal giving a distinct spatial character to the building. In plan, the freestanding steel walls are composed to provide an abstract representation of the *kurrumanthu*. The tail represents the traditional owners' history and the head their future, with both meeting in the Centre, which represents Aboriginal law.

Yet the organic form of the building can be interpreted in any number of ways. For instance, the tall, weathered steel walls of the visitor center have been seen as subverting the fundamental assumptions of architecture as a colonizing practice.[4] As Nichols observes,

> The wall is the most profoundly transfiguring innovation imposed on the Australian landscape by European settlement. In its many guises it encircles, shields, excludes and divides. The walls in this project are separated, allowing passage between them and refocusing the visitor on an unalienated landscape.[5]

Visitors enter the building by moving between sheer panels of Corten steel, an entry that is intended to evoke the experience of moving through the sheet-sided gorges for which the Karijini National Park is famed. The intention is to privilege the wall, which alludes to both the landscape and the symbolic form of the goanna, as the dominant expression and experience of the center. Every design move was conceived to maximize this effect. Tall panes of frameless glass set between the steel wall panels blur the distinction between interior and exterior by providing tantalizing glimpses out to the surrounding landscape, thereby enabling the visitor to read the irregular shape of the structure. The palette of materials is minimalist, including WR350 weathering steel plate, floors of red oxide–colored concrete, and a ceiling of expanded metal lathe under a Colorbond roof concealed between walls. Various design features—such as the choice of construction materials, minimal openings, and few places to trap debris—have been incorporated to help the building withstand the fires that periodically sweep through the area.[6] Steel plate gutters are integrated into and concealed within the wall design. While the services—selected for ease of operation, low impact, and low maintenance—are fully self-contained, the service infrastructure is located outside in the carpark area so as to not interrupt the eloquent, formal expression of the building. The rough coloration of the rusted Corten steel gives a rustic, earth-toned surface to the walls (Plate 12).

Plate 12.   Karijini Visitor Centre, Western Australia, exterior, rear view. Photo by John Gollings, courtesy Woodhead.

Figure 13.1. Karijini Visitor Centre, entrance, exterior view. Photo by John Gollings, courtesy Woodhead.

OBJECTIVES

The project brief was to create a place for the sharing of information about the Karijini National Park—its geology, flora, fauna, people, and history. A further objective of the project as stated by the architect was to

> represent through the built form respect for the objectives and preoccupations of the Aboriginal stakeholders and to stimulate interest in the reappraisal of our collective past, the land and the relationship between Aboriginal and non-Aboriginal people.[7]

The Centre both provides employment opportunities for local Aboriginal people and provides visitors with the opportunity to speak with the traditional owners of the land in order to learn about their culture and association with the land.

Inside, the visitor center provides information on the natural and cultural histories of the area. A range of static and interactive natural and cultural heritage displays serve to introduce visitors to the places and people of Karijini, both past and present.[8] The staff at the Karijini Visitor Centre is equipped to provide accurate information on gorge, walk, or road closures, information that could prove vital in the harsh, arid environment of the East Pilbara.[9] The Centre itself contains a display area, theatre, and offices on the north side, and a shop. Other facilities include telephones, a shaded seating area, toilets, and showers, including facilities for people with disabilities.

RECEPTION

The Karijini Visitor Centre was the recipient of several awards in 2001, including the RAIA BHP Colorbond Steel Award, Western Australia; the PCA WA Rider Hunt Award; and the World Architecture Awards Readers Choice Award for World Architecture in 2001 and 2002.[10] The center received a Commendation for Public Buildings from the Royal Australian

Institute of Architects, and was shortlisted for the World Architecture Awards, Berlin–Australasia Region Category Project, Public and Cultural Category in 2002.

NOTES

1. Thanks to former Centre manager Maitland Parker and architect John Nichols for reviewing the draft of this chapter, and to Assistant Manager Mel Berris for helpful correspondence. Draft text by Carolynne Baker.

2. Based on correspondence with John Nichols, September 20, 2013. On file with author.

3. Ibid.

4. John Nichols, "Karijini Architectural Design Awards Submission," available at http://www.dec .wa.gov.au/content/view/391/1270 (link no longer active, last accessed May 20, 2012).

5. John Nichols, "Karijini Architectural Design Awards Submission."

6. Ibid.

7. Ibid.

8. Woodhead International BDH, "Karijini National Park Visitor Centre," available at http://www .architecture.com.au/awards_search?option=showaward&entryno=20016001.

9. DriveWA.com, "Karijini Visitor Centre," available at http://www.drivewa.com/poi/915/karijini -visitor-centre.html.

10. Woodhead International BDH, "Visitors Centre Karijini National Park, Pilbara, Western Australia," available at http://www.woodhead.com.au/projects/visitors-centre-karijini-national-park-pilbara -western-australia (link no longer active, last accessed May 20, 2012).

14

Koorie Heritage Trust, Federation Square, Melbourne, Victoria, Australia

Location: Levels 1 and 3, The Yarra Building, Federation Square, Melbourne, Australia
Date: 2015
Client: Koorie Heritage Trust Inc.
Architect: Lyons Architecture with Indigenous Architecture and Design Victoria
Engineers: Waterman and AHW Pty. Ltd.
Structure: Hyder Consulting
Construction: Kane Constructions Pty. Ltd.
Joinery: Michael Schiavello and Earl Pinto
Funding Agency: Victorian Government
Chief Executive Officer: Tom Mosby
Cost: approximately $1.6 million

BACKGROUND

The Koorie Heritage Trust[1] was established by Gunditjmara man Jim Berg in 1985 in response to a growing awareness of the need for southeastern Australian Aboriginal cultural heritage material to be controlled, managed, and curated by Aboriginal people.[2] Berg was an inspector under the Archaeological and Aboriginal Relics Preservation Act 1972. In subsequent decades, the Trust expanded to include a permanent display, four galleries, a museum, a library, and a cultural awareness program. A ground-level shop sold books and Indigenous craft works. It became home to the Victorian Aboriginal Corporation for Languages established in 1994, and it runs a genealogy service to help connect Koorie individuals with their family and country. The Trust is overseen by a Board of Management, which includes a majority of Koorie members.[3]

The collections at the Trust began during the early 1980s with a donation of a grinding stone to Jim Berg.[4] Since then, a range of contemporary artworks and craft items have been purchased or commissioned. These include paintings by Lin Onus, Les Griggs, and Ray Thomas; wooden artifacts by Peter and Alex Mongta; basketry by Connie Hart and Emma Karpany; and jewelery by Maree Clarke and Sonja Hodge. The Trust has a substantial collection of 2,600 artifacts and over 48,000 photographs and images. Among over nine hundred paintings, drawings, collages, and digital images held in the collection are historic paintings from the nineteenth century by *ngurunggaeta* (clan leader) of the Woiwurrung/Wurundjeri people, William Barak, and by Kwatkwat artist Tommy McRae. They depict life from the "Koorie perspective."[5] Possibly the most important parts of the collection are some 1,400 audio and visual recordings collected as part of the Trust's Oral History Program. Among these, the collaborative online project "Mission Voices" features many respected Elders recounting their lives on missions and reserves.[6] This history of dispossession told from the Aboriginal perspective is unique in Victoria.

One of the many innovative ways in which the Trust interacted with its urban landscape was through the creative imagination. Walking tours in the city, including in the nearby Flagstaff Gardens and the "Walkin Birrarung" tour along the Yarra River from Enterprize Park to Federation Square, are among the most effective ways the Trust has developed to help visitors imagine the city before and during European colonization. Supported by an introduction to the Trust that includes a broader overview of the Traditional Owners of Victoria, the language groups, their cultural practices, and their traumatic dispossession, the Koorie Heritage Trust offers a revisionist history of Melbourne.

From 1985 to 1999, the Museum of Victoria provided the Koorie Heritage Trust with office and exhibition space. In 1999, the Trust was preparing to move to its new home on Lonsdale Street, designed by Gregory Burgess Architects, when the building was destroyed by fire.[7] The Trust was subsequently relocated to temporary premises on Flinders Lane in the Melbourne city grid, before moving to a location on King Street in 2003.[8]

From 2003 to 2014, the Koorie Heritage Trust occupied a three-story brick building at the top end of King Street, in the far northwest corner of the city grid. Originally a warehouse, the building was refurbished by RMIT University for use as studios, then renovated for use by

Figure 14.1.   Koorie Heritage Trust, Lonsdale Street building that was destroyed by arson. Photo courtesy Gregory Burgess Architects.

Figure 14.2.   Koorie Heritage Trust, King Street building, exterior view. Photo by author, 2012.

the Trust. Maintaining the Trust long term in the King Street location proved to be an uphill task for several reasons. King Street itself has little foot traffic by day and is renowned instead for its many seedy bars and clubs that operate mostly by night and the related alcohol-fueled violence.[9] Few tourist attractions exist in the immediate vicinity, and there is little reason for a tourist to venture further north on foot. According to Chief Executive Officer Tom Mosby, the peripheral location proved a hindrance to attracting tourists and other visitors.[10]

Despite its location, the Trust's physical structure was important in providing a base from which Koories and non-Koories could work together to create counternarratives to the dominant discourse of triumphant colonialism. However, for fiscal reasons, and in order to fulfill its reconciliatory aims, the Trust needed to attract tourists and other visitors at the same time as serving the needs of the local Koorie community. These concerns prompted plans to sell the building in 2013 so as to keep the organization solvent and to relocate the Trust to a more central location.[11]

The history of the relocation of the Koorie Heritage Trust provides a noteworthy example of the difficulties experienced in integrating Aboriginal presence within the settler city. The necessity of adapting existing facilities through transformations of surfaces, or reorganization of interiors, suggests adjustments to metropolitan architectural norms. Asserting cultural difference within this framework and maintaining interest and support has proven challenging.

According to architect Gregory Burgess, who refurbished the King Street building for the Trust, the most striking feature of this location was its "bold, robust timber post-and-beam structure [which] provided a disciplined and adaptable framework of considerable character and dignity."[12] The intention behind Burgess's redesign, which "cleaned up, exposed and enhanced the building with colour," was "to create memorable spaces of strong local Koorie character" and to give "support to the process of reconciliation."[13]

The exterior of the King Street building was painted in muted black, yellow, and red tones, while the Trust's emblem (a black hand and a white hand gripped in a handshake) was screen-printed on the sliding glass entrance doors. At each opening and closing of the doors, the hands separate and come together again, in a continual reenactment of the Trust's motto, "Give me your hand my friend and bridge the cultural gap." Inside, a large replica of a scarred eucalypt tree from Ebenezer Mission stretched up through the building's core, through a void in each of the floors, while a spiral staircase wound its way around it. The tree was replicated by creating a life-size cast of the original, which translated all its markings, including a scar used for a bark canoe, onto the replica. This was then transferred and established as the centerpiece at the Trust. At the top of the tree was a large nest filled with a stuffed wedge-tailed eagle, representing *Bunjil*, the Kulin creator spirit.

Figure 14.3.   Koorie Heritage Trust, King Street building, replica eucalypt with representation of *Bunjil*, the wedge-tailed eagle, on top. Photo by author, 2012.

During an exhibition of his photographs titled *Silent Witness* held at the Trust in 2005, Jim Berg observed that scarred trees were as significant as historic buildings, and represented the healing process of Koorie and non-Koorie people coming together.[14] The artificial insertion of the tree as an architectural feature, its replication along with its numerous markings, and its conversion into a pedestal for *Bunjil* encapsulated both the desire for authenticity and its impossibility.

PROJECT DESCRIPTION

The opportunities presented by a dedicated building for the Trust were highly compromised by the disadvantages of its King Street location, and the building was sold in 2013. Established Melbourne firm Lyons Architecture were commissioned to refurbish a new rental space for the Koorie Heritage Trust inside the Yarra Building at Melbourne's Federation Square, a celebrated urban complex on the banks of the Yarra River. Following a feasibility study on how to accommodate the expansive collection in its new location, a spatially efficient strategy was proposed.[15] The brief included designing for a visible collection and serving the aspirations of a living contemporary culture while recognizing the Trust as a community-capital building organization that seeks to place Koorie culture center stage.

Key to developing the new proposal was Lyons's collaboration with Indigenous Architecture and Design Victoria (IADV), a young team of Indigenous practitioners appointed as cultural and design consultants in September 2014. IADV advised the design team on how to incorporate Indigenous design ideas and values; however, it was not IADV's role to endorse or authorize the design on behalf of the Aboriginal community. Kalinya Communications, a Koorie owned and managed marketing and events company, independently organized community consultations.

Founded by Rueben Berg and Jefa Greenaway in 2010, IADV's manifesto encourages both greater engagement by the Indigenous community in architecture and design and greater engagement of design professionals with Indigenous culture.[16] The team builds cultural awareness through events, publications, and cultural competency training while pursuing architectural design teaching and practice. For example, Jefa Greenaway's own practice, Greenaway Architects, undertook furniture design and selection, the design of window surrounds, and other specialized features for the Koorie Heritage Trust project.

Carey Lyon sees architecture in Victoria as undergoing a significant cultural learning curve through commissions such as these. He observes that while various Indigenous communities differ greatly in their requirements, they share a powerful connection to country. The client-architect relationship is based on extensive consultation. "We were reluctant to work without IADV involvement," observes Lyon. "They are defining a new role for Indigenous professionals."[17]

The new location places the cultural facility within an existing deconstructive architectural envelope, approached across the undulating surface of the urban plaza, Nearamnew. Consequently, the location compromises some of the distinctiveness that might be achieved by a stand-alone or purpose-designed architecture that signals Aboriginal presence in the space. Conversely, the move to a central civic location adjacent to the Yarra River is an important benefit. Whereas the previous building was gridlocked in a densely built area of the city, the new location renews associations with *Birrarung* or "River of Mists," the original name of the Yarra River on the traditional lands of the Wurundjeri. Associations with the river, reminders of its presence, and oblique views of it through the windows are replete in the design. The architects, Greenaway and Berg, observe that there was a strong desire to develop a clear narrative that could be woven through and connected to the places (across the three levels). A number of key decisions developed a "river story," which spoke to proximity to the life blood of the city (Birrarung) and its cultural connection to pre-colonial history.[18]

Long relegated to the periphery of the colonial grid, the local Indigenous community have been excluded and alienated from their traditional lands by the City of Melbourne's chronic neglect of the Yarra and by land reclamation and construction projects that cover over creeks and swamplands.[19] Ecological erasure and social marginalization have accompanied urban growth. Federation Square's lack of visual connections to the Yarra inadvertently reinforces this historical disappropriation. In addressing this architectural erasure, IADV developed a renewed thematic purpose for the Trust, further reinforced by displaying specific artifacts such as Yorta Yorta/Moidaban Elder Uncle Wally Cooper's bark canoe. The canoe is encountered on the second level along the circulation axis between the ground-level gallery space and shop and the main activity spaces on the third level, which include the boardroom, display area, offices, Moogji lounge, and kitchen.

The location of the Trust at Federation Square has called for other changes in the design. For example, there was no volume capable of accommodating the replica-scarred tree that had dominated the King Street site.[20] Many possibilities were debated and explored before *Bunjil*, the wedge-tailed eagle, was perched ceremoniously on top of the escalator and stairs, which provide the main circulation axis through the building. The symbolic feature that dominates the third level, which is the main operative space of the Trust, is a seven-meter-long "making-table" in the form of a canoe (Plate 13). The table evokes the scarring formed on trees from the removal of bark for canoes, shields, and other everyday objects, thus reiterating the connections of the Trust to the river and the tree. The walking tours in the Melbourne CBD will also adopt this focus on *Birrarung*.[21]

Plate 13.   Koorie Heritage Trust at Federation Square, Melbourne, Victoria, Australia, in 2015. Photo by Peter Bennetts, courtesy Lyons Architecture and Koorie Heritage Trust.

The table is surrounded by visible storage in transparent cabinetry and easily accessible drawers that artfully display the Trust's collection and library, leaving views to the offices behind. The socialization of story-artifacts through their integration with other activity spaces is a key attribute of the new design. Coinciding with the Federation Square relaunch, the exhibition *Wominjeka: A New Beginning* ran from September to November 2015 to celebrate the Trust's thirtieth birthday.[22] Five emerging Koorie artists were paired with Indigenous mentors to create new works inspired by items from the Trust's collections.[23]

Elsewhere, symbolic motifs integral to the Koorie community and the Trust's identity are reinterpreted and incorporated in the building. The door details include the Trust's logo, and the steel trees (totem poles) from the former facility are repeated in the new layout, in addition to diamond-patterned carpeting and painted surfaces. A decal of the Manna Gum blossom is featured prominently along the building's circulation axis as a symbolic representation of the "welcome to country" ritual. Aboriginal presence in the building is further normalized through, for example, signs for the rest rooms that include the local Koorie term *Djilawa*.[24]

The new Trust premises are organized for socialization as a reflection of the values of the Trust and the community.[25] Seating around the entrance foyer and an array of informal and formal spaces create opportunities for engagement and exchange. The kitchen and the Moogji lounge are prominently located on the top floor, an encouragement to visitors to relax and socialize, quite contrary to the standard brief of a gallery or archival space. A sliding partition featuring a map of local Indigenous languages divides the combined Aunty Joyce Johnson and Uncle Stewart Murray Meeting Rooms into smaller workshop spaces. The design is challenged to maximize the limited space, restricted views, and concealment of the site behind the aesthetically dominant building façade of Federation Square. The Trust's tenacious navigation of these constraints is an apt metaphor for community resilience and adaptation.

Since its relaunch in September 2015 at the Federation Square site, the Trust has expanded its activities and programs to address the diverse needs of Koorie and non-Koorie communities.[26] These include a family history service, the ongoing collection and exhibition program, the oral history program, walking tours, and cross-cultural awareness training. The Trust also fosters strong links with regional Aboriginal cultural centers, organizations, and communities in Victoria. It employs around nineteen people. The success of the move to the new Federation Square location became evident in its first month when over 4,500 people visited the Trust, a figure twice that received at the former King Street site.[27]

Although presently limited to the first and third levels of the building, the ultimate goal is to increase the Trust's exhibiting and meeting spaces by occupying Level 2, which is currently leased by the Melbourne Festival. Under the Community Curate Program, community members are invited to tell their personal stories through engagement with the Trust's collection. They choose items from the collection and provide interpretive texts for display in the Level 3 cabinets.[28]

The Trust's greatest challenge is to make its presence visible behind the fractal geometries of Federation Square. To this end, discussion is currently taking place to create a light installation that will reinterpret the façades as the traditional Koorie shield pattern of the diamond. The idea is to overlay the shield motif directly onto the façade geometry as visible elements during the day and as public artwork by night.[29]

CEO Tom Mosby describes the Koorie Heritage Trust as "a bold and adventurous 21st century organization offering an inclusive and welcoming place for all."[30] An important attribute of this orientation is its embrace of digital technology for delivering client services, engaging with young Koorie people, and recording the memories of Koorie Elders. Mosby sees the Trust as a unique and safe space for Koorie and non-Koorie cultural exchange, a knowledge bank, and a vital community resource.[31]

NOTES

1. Thanks to CEO, Koorie Heritage Trust, Tom Mosby, for reviewing the draft and providing extensive comments, and general manager Giacomina Pradolin for offering further insights to the author during a visit in November 2015. Thanks also to Carey Lyon of Lyons Architecture, Gregory Burgess of GBA, and Jefa Greenaway and Rueben Berg of IADV for details of their design contribution for the new facility at Federation Square. Thanks to Lynda Kotze at GBA for providing relevant material on the King Street premises. This chapter has expanded the original text by Naomi Tootell on the former building.

2. Culture Victoria, "The Vision for a Trust: Interview with Jim Berg, Founder of the Koorie Heritage Trust," available at http://www.cv.vic.gov.au/stories/the-koorie-heritage-trust-collections-and-history/6306/the-vision-for-a-trust/.

3. Koorie Heritage Trust, "Board of Management and Executive," available at http://www.koorie heritagetrust.com/about_us/governance_information/board_of_management_and_executive__1.

4. Koorie Heritage Trust, "Collections," available at http://www.koorieheritagetrust.com/collections.

5. Koorie Heritage Trust, "Collections."

6. Culture Victoria, "Mission Voices," available at http://www.cv.vic.gov.au/stories/aboriginal-culture/missions/mission-voices/.

7. "Fire Damages Koori Centre," *The Age*, February 22, 1999, available at http://newsstore.theage.com.au/apps/viewDocument.ac?page=1&sy=age&kw=fire+and+lonsdale+and+koori&pb=all_ffx&dt=selectRange&dr=entire&so=relevance&sf=text&sf=headline&rc=10&rm=200&sp=nrm&clsPage=1&docID=news990222_0393_5331.

8. Carolyn Webb, "Aboriginal Cultural Centre a First for Melbourne," *The Age*, September 2, 2003.

9. Anne Wright, "Booze and Violence Make King St Strip Melbourne's Most Feared Spot," *Herald Sun*, March 30, 2012.

10. CEO Tom Mosby was reported as saying that the King Street location had been a "major constraint in attracting visitors to the Trust, particularly passing foot traffic." See Simon Johanson, "Koorie Heritage Trust Headquarters on Move," *The Age*, March 16, 2013.

11. Johanson, "Koorie Heritage Trust Headquarters on Move," Also Simon Johanson, "Trust Building Sale Sparks Optimism," *The Age*, May 8, 2013.

12. Email correspondence with architect Gregory Burgess, October 12, 2012.

13. Ibid.

14. Larry Schwartz, "Message of Healing," *The Age*, June 13, 2005. This article reviews Jim Berg's exhibition *Silent Witness*, in which more than fifty photographic images of scarred trees of the Wotjobaluk people on the banks of the Wimmera River, near Antwerp, northwest of Melbourne, were displayed.

15. Based on phone conversation between author and Carey Lyon on November 11, 2015.

16. Indigenous Architecture and Design Victoria, "About IADV," available at http://iadv.org.au/about-iadv/.

17. Based on phone conversation between author and Carey Lyon on November 11, 2015.

18. Based on email communications with Jefa Greenaway and Rueben Berg during October and November 2015. On file with author.

19. Janet McGaw and Cliff Chang, "Melbourne's Hidden Waterways: Revealing Williams Creek," *Double Dialogues*, no. 13 (Summer 2010), available at http://www.doubledialogues.com/article/melbournes-hidden-waterways-revealing-williams-creek/.

20. Based on email communications with Jefa Greenaway and Rueben Berg during October and November 2015. On file with author.

21. Based on notes provided by CEO Tom Mosby on November 10, 2015. On file with author.

22. Koorie Heritage Trust, *Wominjeka: A New Beginning* (Melbourne: The Koorie Heritage Trust, 2015).

23. Based on notes provided by Tom Mosby on November 10, 2015. On file with author.

24. Based on email communications with Jefa Greenaway and Rueben Berg during October and November 2015. On file with author.

25. Ibid. Also conversation between author and General Manager Giacomina Pradolin on November 6, 2015.

26. Based on notes provided by Tom Mosby on November 10, 2015. On file with author.

27. Ibid.

28. Ibid.

29. Ibid.

30. Ibid

31. Ibid.

15

Kurongkurl Katitjin Centre for Indigenous Australian Education and Research, Edith Cowan University, Mount Lawley, Western Australia, Australia

Location: Building 15, 2 Bradford Street, Mount Lawley, Western Australia
Date: 2002–2005
Client: Edith Cowan University
Communities: Noongar people as traditional owners, and all Australian Indigenous peoples
Architect: JCY Architects & Urban Designers
Project Team: Paul Jones, Libby Guj, Charles Thwin, Vince Faladi, Brent Aitkenhead, and Hean Wei Phay
Civil and Structural Engineer: Terpkos & Santillo Pty. Ltd.
Builder: Merym Construction
Funding: Edith Cowan University and Federal Government grant
Cost: approximately $5.6 million

Completed in 2005, the Kurongkurl Katitjin Centre for Indigenous Australian Education and Research is located on the Mount Lawley campus of Edith Cowan University in Perth.[1] Representing a deliberate departure from the tendency to use natural materials and vernacular references as architectural expressions of Aboriginality, the colorful building is composed of a number of interlocking plastic extruded forms at a variety of scales. These forms rise up to an overall height of three stories in a manner that has been described as being suggestive of "rocky outcrops in the desert plains."[2] The interplay of light and dark, object and landscape, contrast and scale produces a building that evokes the contrasting colors, elements, and forms of the ever-changing Australian outback: day, night, sky, earth, water, and vegetation. In terms of spatial organization, different color palettes identify different programs, while the mixture of different hues, textures, and finishes in the paneled façades help create a pixilated, playful quality to the elements (Plate 14). The colors of the Aboriginal and Torres Strait Islander flags are also evident in the building, although perhaps not readily apparent to a casual observer.

Figure 15.1. Kurongkurl Katitjin Centre for Indigenous Australian Education and Research, mosaic paving. Photo by Andrew Pritchard, courtesy JCY Architects & Urban Designers.

Plate 14. Kurongkurl Katitjin Centre for Indigenous Australian Education and Research, Edith Cowan University, Mount Lawley, Western Australia, exterior view taken in 2005. Photo by Andrew Pritchard, courtesy Jones Coulter Young Architects & Urban Designers.

BACKGROUND

Kurongkurl katitjin (pronounced "koor-ong-kurl cut-it-chin") is a Noongar phrase meaning "coming together to learn."[3] First established in 1993, shortly after the former Western Australian College of Advanced Education became Edith Cowan University (ECU), Kurongkurl Katitjin is now one of four component schools and centers in ECU's Faculty of Education and Arts.[4] The first Aboriginal teacher in Western Australia graduated in 1951, with fifteen others graduating in the years 1954 to 1977. These teachers completed their studies without the support of Indigenous-specific programs.[5] The beginning of Indigenous-specific programs at ECU dates back to 1975, when the Aboriginal Teacher Education Program was established on the Mount Lawley campus. In 1976, the first group of eleven Indigenous students entered the Diploma of Primary Teaching course through special entry provisions. Three achieved timely completion of the course in 1978.[6]

As well as being one of the first universities in Australia to offer special entry provisions for Indigenous students to enter degree courses in 1976, ECU was the first to offer a bridging program in external mode in 1978, and an innovator in establishing off-campus centers to serve students in rural and remote locations from 1983. Including students educated in its predecessor teachers' colleges, ECU has more than five hundred Indigenous graduates who have qualified as teachers or achieved associate degree and above qualifications.

CONSULTATION PROCESS

Consultation for the project involved discussion with the Elders representing the Noongar people, as well as representatives from numerous community groups through Perth and Western Australia as well as the community and the University. The process undertaken was facilitated through key representatives of Kurongkurl Katitjin itself, who assisted the design team by bringing together various groups at various times as well as undertaking key research on language, culture, environment, and people, which served to inform and guide design at all stages.[7]

Designed in consultation with Noongar Elders to "graphically represent Aboriginal culture and the Australian landscape," the architects focused on the narrative potential of space as a means by which to explore alternative understandings of space and time.[8] For instance, the six garden spaces surrounding the Centre have been designed to represent the six Noongar seasons.[9] These seasons are not necessarily understood as chronologically distinct entities but as parts of a process of temporal change. Several of the façades are inscribed with Noongar words about place, song, dance, community, learning, and family—"a cultural graffiti"—that were selected by the Noongar community to describe their culture and values.[10] The building can be entered from all directions, and is surrounded by landscaping that is visible from within—aspects of the building that are said to "highlight . . . the Aboriginal connection with the land."[11]

PROJECT DESCRIPTION

The center has been sited to ensure that its program and purpose integrate with the University's broader educational agenda.[12] Still, the building's exuberant explosion of color stands in sharp contrast to the reserved monochromatic buildings that characterize the surrounding ECU campus. In many respects, this contrast reflects the objectives of the Centre itself, which provides an alternative for Indigenous students, enabling them to undertake university studies within the context of their own culture.[13] The placement of the building within the campus environs heightens the opportunities for social encounter for both settler and Aboriginal communities. Through this gesture, the architect acknowledges continued Aboriginal cultural presence through a dynamic modern architecture.

Located at the crossing of four storytelling paths, an integral part of the building and landscape design was to represent this metaphorical link to the four corners of Western Australia. Five mosaic artworks were commissioned as part of the building design. Four mosaics represent the points of the compass, and the fifth represents a Noongar "Welcome to Country," located in the main entry where all story paths cross. This point is the metaphorical center of the building.[14]

Although the Centre is based at ECU's Mount Lawley campus, it supports students from further afield, including from ECU's Joondalup and South West campuses.[15] While recognizing the Whadjuk people of the Noongar nation as the traditional custodians of the country on which the building sits, the building has been designed to more broadly extend this recognition to all Aboriginal and Torres Strait Islander people, past and present.[16] The distinctive forms and materials adopted by the architect are a deliberate attempt to address the broader Indigenous community; as project architect Charles Thwin has stated, the intention was to "reflect the urban Aboriginal population as well as the Indigenous people

Figure 15.2.   Kurongkurl Katitjin Centre for Indigenous Australian Education and Research, interior corridor. Photo by Andrew Pritchard, courtesy JCY Architects & Urban Designers.

throughout Western Australia."[17] The Centre's mission is to "provide excellence in teaching, learning and research in a culturally inclusive environment that values the diversity of Indigenous Australian history and cultural heritage."[18]

RECEPTION

Today, Kurongkurl Katitjin offers a range of units for Indigenous and non-Indigenous students, and provides support to Indigenous students across the University. The Centre boasts a range of active research programs that aim to contribute to Indigenous well-being and promote the process of reconciliation.[19]

Kurongkurl Katitjin was awarded a Commendation in the Department of Housing and Works Award for Public/Institutional Architecture category in the Western Australian Architecture Awards of the Royal Australian Institute of Architects in 2006. The jury commended the building for its graphic statement and visual interest, describing it as "a very brave building . . . [that] . . . challenges traditional ideas of what architecture is."[20]

NOTES

1. Thanks to both Libby Guj at JCY Architects and Colleen Hayward, pro-vice chancellor (Equity and Indigenous) at the Kurongkurl Katitjin Centre at ECU, for reviewing the draft and providing additional information. Original draft text by Carolynne Baker.

2. Royal Institute of Architects, "2006 RAIA Western Australia Architecture Awards," Jury Citations, available at http://www.raia.com.au/i-cms?page=8115.

3. Edith Cowan University, "Kurongkurl Katitjin," http://www.ecu.edu.au/schools/kurongkurl -katitjin/overview.

4. Edith Cowan University, "Kurongkurl Katitjin: About," http://www.ecu.edu.au/schools/ kurong kurl-katitjin/about.

5. Based on communications with current Kurongkurl Katitjin staff members, 2013. On file with author.

6. Edith Cowan University, "Kurongkurl Katitjin: About."

7. Based on communications with Libby Guj, May 1, 2013. On file with author.

8. Edith Cowan University, "Kurongkurl Katitjin: About."

9. Ibid.

10. JCY Architects, "Kuronkurl Katitjin Centre for Indigenous Australian Education & Research," http://jcy.net/project/kuronkurl-katitjin-centre-for-indigenous-australian-education-research/.

11. JCY Architects, "Kuronkurl Katitjin Centre for Indigenous Australian Education & Research."

12. Ibid.

13. Anoma Pieris, *JCY: The Architecture of Jones Coulter Young* (Balmain: Pesaro Publishing, 2005).

14. Edith Cowan University, "Kurongkurl Katitjin."

15. Ibid.

16. Ibid.

17. Commercial Design Trends, "Sense of Place," *Commercial Design Trends* 21, no. 15 (2005): 82.

18. Edith Cowan University, "Kurongkurl Katitjin."

19. Ibid.

20. Royal Institute of Architects, "2006 RAIA Western Australia Architecture Awards."

16

Lake Tyers Training Centre and Lake Tyers Health Centre, Lake Tyers, Victoria, Australia

Location: Lake Tyers, Victoria
Client (Training Centre): Lake Tyers Aboriginal Trust and Bung Yarnda Housing and Infrastructure Cooperative
Client (Health Centre): Lake Tyers Health and Children's Services
Architect: Anthony Styant-Browne Architect Pty. Ltd.
Project Team: Jen Rippon (project architect), Tony Styant-Browne (design architect), Colum Colfer (architect), and Alex Duncan (student architect)
Landscape Consultant: Anthony Styant-Browne Architect Pty. Ltd.
Structural Consultant: Lambert and Rehbein (Vic) Pty. Ltd.
Civil Consultant: Lambert and Rehbein (Vic) Pty. Ltd.
Builder: East Gippsland ACDEP Co-Operative
Program Manager: Arup
Lake Tyers Trust Executive Officer: Leonie Cameron
Funding: see building-specific sections below
Cost: see building-specific sections below

LAKE TYERS TRAINING CENTRE

Date: 2000–2004
Client: Lake Tyers Aboriginal Trust and Bung Yarnda Housing and Infrastructure Cooperative
Funding: Victorian Department of Education and Training and Aboriginal Affairs Victoria
Cost: approximately $450,000

LAKE TYERS HEALTH CENTRE

Date: 2003–2006
Client: Lake Tyers Health and Childrens' Services
Funding: Office of Aboriginal and Torres Strait Islander Health
Cost: approximately $876,000

Lake Tyers is an Aboriginal community of about 140 located around 350 kilometers east of Melbourne on 1,600 hectares of land overlooking the Gippsland Lakes.[1] The nearest small towns are Nowa Nowa and Wairewa, and the nearby larger towns of Lakes Entrance, Bairnsdale, and Orbost have been important destinations for tourism since the late nineteenth century. The facilities run by the Lake Tyers Aboriginal Trust include a training center, community hall, and a church. A childcare center, health clinic, and children's services are run by Lake Tyers Health and Children's Service. Lake Tyers is the meeting point of three different historical strands of the Gunaikurnai, who were often hostile to the Kulin peoples to the west in the precolonial era. Their lands are defined by the rivers and coastal areas of Eastern Victoria, and their heritage is distributed over an expansive terrain. Lake Tyers is equally connected to a more difficult mission history of Aboriginal dispossession, containment, and display.

Built innovatively on a very low budget, Lake Tyers Training Centre and Health Centre designed by Anthony Styant-Browne Architect (now Workshop Architecture) are venues for community interaction and identity. They exemplify community facilities focused on community empowerment. The training center advances an agenda of community skills and employment, whereas the health center provides an important community service.

BACKGROUND

The land historically associated with the Gunaikurnai (Gunai/Kurnai) peoples, and later with the Lake Tyers Mission established in 1863, was handed over to mission residents in 1971 following the passage of the Aboriginal Lands Act in 1970. The displacement of large numbers of Aboriginal peoples from other areas throughout the mid to late nineteenth century brought diverse groups together at Lake Tyers Mission. With the growth of settler tourism, the Mission and its residents became objects of curiosity and display.[2] Anglican missionary John Bulmer ran the Lake Tyers Mission from 1861 until 1907 and was known for his sympathy with Aboriginal practices. Bulmer encouraged the residents to pursue everyday activities such as fishing to supplement their rations. However, these activities were on display for tourists along with Indigenous items presented as souvenirs. Such troubling enterprises can be regarded as precursors to the commodity-driven, tourism-oriented model of cultural centers, which has since become common. In contrast to this early history of mission tourism, contemporary facilities at Lake Tyers are solely for community use.

PROJECT DESCRIPTION

The commission was awarded to Melbourne-based architect Anthony Styant-Browne, who has designed number of Indigenous facilities (the largest being the award-winning Galina Beek Living Cultural Centre in Healesville—see chapter 9).[3] Styant-Browne had extensive experience working with Indigenous peoples in Papua New Guinea and the United States during the 1970s and 1980s. Other projects in Victoria designed specifically for Indigenous communities include the concept design for the Wurundjeri Cultural Centre and Keeping Place on the Burnley Circus site, and the Community Care Centre for the Dhauwurd Wurrung Aboriginal Elderly Citizens Association in Portland. Styant-Browne has also been involved in teaching at the Royal Melbourne Institute of Technology and the University of Melbourne, including the running of design studios on architecture for Indigenous communities.

Cost was a significant factor in the design of both centers, demanding inexpensive and innovative architectural responses to the needs of pragmatic community facilities not dependent on tourism income. Both centers were designed interactively with community involvement. Styant-Browne has commented that there were tensions in this process due to changes in client group personnel and internal community problems.[4] Both facilities feature in ongoing community development plans between the Nowa Nowa, Wairewa, and Lake Tyers Aboriginal Trust, the Victorian Government, and the East Gippsland Shire Council (including the plan for the Nowa Nowa District and the Lake Tyers Aboriginal Trust Conservation Management Plan).[5] Produced by the Victorian Department of Planning and Community Development via lengthy community consultation, these plans seek to meet the needs and services of the community in the foreseeable future. The two centers may be regarded as the first among many projects aimed at meeting these needs.

LAKE TYERS TRAINING CENTRE

The Training Centre designed for Lake Tyers Aboriginal Trust and Bung Yarnda Housing and Infrastructure Cooperative suffered a major setback early in its genesis. Originally granted Victorian Government funding of approximately $900,000 for the project, the Lake Tyers Community took so long to agree on a site and program that 50 percent of the funding was confiscated and given to another Indigenous Victorian community that was better organized at the time. This early setback initiated a pattern of difficulties with the project throughout its long design and construction period. The purpose of the project was to provide the youth of Lake Tyers with training in a set of disciplines appropriate for their place, local economy, and culture. The program of accommodation included a lecture room, seminar room, computer laboratory, commercial kitchen, multipurpose room, administrative offices, and associated amenities. An outdoor performance area was to be provided, along with external breakout spaces for respite and outdoor learning.[6]

Figure 16.1.   Lake Tyers Training Centre, exterior view. Photo courtesy Workshop Architecture.

Figure 16.2. Lake Tyers Training Centre, exterior view. Photo courtesy Workshop Architecture.

Figure 16.3. Lake Tyers Training Centre, interior. Photo courtesy Workshop Architecture.

An early feasibility study showed that limited funding necessitated staged development, and the community decided to relegate the woodworking shop and aquaculture facility to a second stage.[7] A long and arduous interactive design process ensued, with community absenteeism and numerous changes of personnel making it difficult to achieve a linear design trajectory. Conventional two-dimensional architectural representations were supplemented by study models, three-dimensional hand sketches, and analogies with known architectural elements.

Community consensus was finally achieved, construction documents completed, and the project tendered to several builders selected from the large number who registered interest. Included on the list was a Bairnsdale-based Indigenous construction company, East Gippsland Acdep (Aboriginal Community Development Employment Projects) Co-Operative, which drew much of its funding from the federal scheme for community development (CDEP). The Co-Operative won the tender, but due to tensions with the Lake Tyers Aboriginal Trust, the appointment of a contractor was delayed. Following months of discussion, Anthony Styant-Browne Architects persuaded the Lake Tyers Aboriginal Trust to sign the contract. As such, an Indigenous organization constructed the building for the Indigenous client, and several Indigenous apprentices (including one from Lake Tyers) received construction training. This was an important achievement. Although its completion took longer than conventional projects, the finished building achieved a qualitatively high standard of construction and was within budget.

The limited budget compelled the architect to innovate. A new wall construction method used conventional timber walls without openings other than doors.[8] Corrugated steel cladding, corrugated clear and translucent polycarbonate, flat polycarbonate, and plywood vents were fixed to the external face of the continuous stud frame, which was lined with plywood panels. The roof was constructed of exposed gang-nail trusses and flooring of exposed particle board panels on timber framing. The resulting architecture referred to the existing agricultural buildings on the Lake Tyers land and in the surrounding rural area. This construction method would be considered by many to be more appropriate to a light industrial or agricultural building rather than a place of learning, but the unconventional aesthetic made the project feasible. The design proved so cost effective that a modified version was developed for the separate Health Centre.

The final blow for the Training Centre occurred when the building was complete and ready for occupation. The Department of Education, Employment and Training, which monitored the project through the design and construction phases, refused to fund the training program. The building subsequently stood unoccupied for eighteen months, gathering spiders and dust. Finally, the Bairnsdale TAFE agreed to run programs in the building. Without consultation with the original design architects, the TAFE inserted partition walls into the building, compromising its architectural integrity. The Training Centre was defunded in 2012 and is now used as an activities space.

LAKE TYERS HEALTH CENTRE

Whereas the Training Centre was located in an undeveloped area of the Lake Tyers site, the Health Centre was sited in the Lake Tyers hamlet. It was placed opposite the historic mission administration building near the former hospital and morgue, both now vacant and dilapidated but with particular associations for the community. The building was oriented to form a mini-park and public area for the community. The client for the project was the Lake Tyers Health and Children's Services under the auspices of Gippsland Lakes Community Health. Funded by the Office for Aboriginal and Torres Strait Islander Health, the range of health services offered included a visiting doctor, social and psychological counseling, paramedic care, health education, and a planned dialysis room.

The Health Centre went through a long and difficult design and documentation process prior to tender. Designed as a rotated T-shape plan that subdivided the site into three zones, the single-story building enclosed a mini-park in its northwest quadrant around two magnificent palm trees, a parking lot, and ambulance pickup zone on the east side, and a porte co-chère at the west end (Plate 15). A playground and garden was included on the south between the Health Centre and old hospital and morgue. The simple floor plan was organized as rooms leading off two cross-axial, single-loaded corridors.

The building design was developed through consultative workshops held over a long period of time with the Health Centre Board of Management, the core of which became the "Four Aunts"—Josie Mullett, Lorraine Sellings, Joan Saunders, and the late Ivy Marks—who had been working toward the establishment of a health center for over twenty years.[9] The Board additionally included community members and health care professionals. Together they evolved a collective vision for the facility. However, this process was compromised by three events in the community as described by the architect.[10] First, there was violence on the site, necessitating the temporary relocation of the clinic off site; then a coup within the organization radically changed the composition of the Board; and finally, a key advocate for the predominantly female Elders of the Board resigned.

Plate 15.   Lake Tyers Health Centre, Lake Tyers, Victoria, Australia, exterior view. Photo by John Gollings, courtesy Workshop Architecture.

Figure 16.4.   Lake Tyers Health Centre, exterior view. Photo by John Gollings, courtesy Workshop Architecture.

The design of the Health Centre aims at familiarizing the facility for its clients by reinforcing the sense of community ownership. This is achieved by the use of informal architectural language and the incorporation of community art. Painted plywood mural panels and mosaic-tiled animal motifs in the veranda and children's play area were incorporated into the building design, and carved and painted poles are to be placed in the mini-park in future. All of these works by Lake Tyers community artists were funded by the project budget. Given that the Health Centre faced the same cost restrictions as the Training Centre, the structure is designed similarly, with a concrete floor slab and timber stud frame on a 600-millimeter-high masonry plinth. The single pitch roof with highlight windows enables the design of operable ventilation on the high side, maximizing light and ventilation in the interior. Like the Training Centre, glass was not used because of the high incidence of vandalism in the community. The architect introduced natural lighting into the building through two sources: tinted corrugated polycarbonate and a combination of clear and translucent flat polycarbonate sheet. Plywood vents provide natural ventilation. A vandal-resistant reinforced concrete plinth, poured in situ, encircles the external walls at their base.

The Lake Tyers Training Centre and Health Centre are representative of the vast number of pragmatic facilities designed within Aboriginal community lands. Although not regarded as cultural centers and separated from the settler community, their genesis was in meeting the needs for basic services required in many remote regional communities. The Lake Tyers examples demonstrate the difficulty of creating and sustaining such facilities. Complex negotiations and prolonged consultative and reconciliatory strategies affected their creation and impact their future sustainability.

NOTES

1. Thanks to Leonie Cameron, Lake Tyers Trust, Executive Officer, for comments on this account. Text based on notes, revisions, and presentations given by architect Tony Styant-Browne. On file with author.

2. Australian Institute of Architects, "Lake Tyers Health Centre," http://www.architecture.com.au/ awards_search?option=showawardandentryno=2007030243 (website no longer active, last accessed June 27, 2012).

3. Tony Styant-Browne, "Work for Aboriginal Communities," *Architect Victoria* (Winter 2001): 8.

4. Based on communications with Tony Styant-Browne, June 25, 2013.

5. East Gippsland Shire Council, *Nowa Nowa District 5 Year Community Plan 2004–2009*; East Gippsland Shire Council, *Nowa Nowa Community Plan 2012–2016*, available at http://www.east gippsland.vic.gov.au/Plans_and_Projects/Community_Planning/Nowa_Nowa_and_District. Lake Tyers Aboriginal Trust, *Lake Tyers Aboriginal Trust Conservation Management Plan*, available at http://www .laketyersaboriginaltrust.com.au/ index.php?option=com_content&view=article&id=12&Itemid=19.

6. Based on communications with Tony Styant-Browne, June 25, 2013.

7. Based on communications with Tony Styant-Browne, June 25, 2013.

8. Victorian Aboriginal Community Controlled Health Organisation, "Communities Working for Health and Well-Being: Success Stories from the Aboriginal Community Controlled Health Sector in Victoria," July 2007, available at www.lowitja.org.au/.../ VACCHO-Successes-Booklet-hi-res-screen.pdf.

9. Based on communications with Tony Styant-Browne, June 25, 2013.

10. Ibid.

17

Living Kaurna Cultural Centre, Bedford Park, South Australia, Australia[1]

Location: Warriparinga Way, Bedford Park, South Australia
Date: 1998–2002
Community: Initiated by the Kaurna community
Architect: Phillips/Pilkington Architects Pty. Ltd. in association with Habitable Places
Project Team: Richard Woods and Susan Phillips
Landscape Consultant: Viesturs Cielens, Cielens & Partners
Project Manager: Campbell Mackie, SAVANT
Structural Consultant: John Bowley, John Bowley Consulting Engineer
Civil Consultant: Steve Clarke, MCE Consulting Engineers
Builder: Martin Tobin, GC&J Constructions
Kaurna Consultant: Georgina Williams
Artists and Exhibition Design: Georgina Williams, David Kerr, Gavin Malone (Interpretive Gallery); Christine Williams (Kaurna), Tony Williams (Kaurna), and Gavin Malone (function area), Martin Corbin (architectural detail)
Other Team Members: Amy Hallett, Alex James, Nigel Miller, and John Gallagher
Cultural Centre Coordinator: Craig Cooper
Funding: Commonwealth Centenary of Federation Grant
Cost: approximately $510,000

Located at Warriparinga (meaning "windy place by the river"), a nature reserve comprising 3.5 hectares in Bedford Park, Marion, a metropolitan suburb ten kilometers south of Adelaide, the Living Kaurna Cultural Centre (LKCC) is conceived for the Kaurna people of the Adelaide plains.[2] It is framed as a joint "conciliation" place between the City of Marion and the Kaurna people, and a gateway to the story of the creation ancestor, Tjilbruke (also spelt Tjirbruki) and the Tjilbruke Dreaming. The LKCC was developed collaboratively in 2001 as a federal government-funded reconciliation project between the City and the Kaurna community's Dixon and William clans; however, its framing as a "conciliation" project promotes an equal partnership, distinct from reconciliation. Phillips/Pilkington Architects Pty. Ltd. in association with Habitable Places Architects designed the project. The LKCC has also become the gateway and starting point for cultural tours along the dreaming track.

BACKGROUND

The LKCC is located in a growing ethos of civic art projects that brought attention to Adelaide's Indigenous past and reclaimed state-owned or commercial properties for affirmations of lost heritage. The commemorative rehabilitation of the triangular site as a wetland, polemically juxtaposed to its suburban metropolitan setting, animated both Kaurna and settler histories.[3] The site selected for the development lies within the grounds of the Warriparinga wetland and the Sturt River, a ceremonial and camp site for the Kaurna and place of early European settlement in South Australia also known as Fairford, Laffer's Triangle, and Sturt Triangle. Both commercial and government interests, including the consideration for major developments, saw a series of transformations into a holiday park, a restaurant, a call center, a science park, a failed Multifunction Polis project, and the Sturt police station.[4] Environmental issues related to the site became prominent in 1991 when the site was impacted by reconstruction of the south bridge of the Sturt River and the Southern Expressway. Construction of the Ansett Australia Call Centre, commissioned in 2000, proceeded in spite of activist opposition.[5] The lobby group Friends of Laffer's Triangle was formed to agitate for the site's protection, and environmental lobbyists and artists Paul and Naomi Dixon appealed to the Marion Council on this issue in 1992.[6] They proposed the creation of a "Warriparinga Interpretive Centre" based on the Ngurlongga Nunga Community Services Centre where an interactive environmental history was first developed.[7] The name *Warriparinga* derived from a number of prior Kaurna names for the site noted in colonial records, and the Friends of Laffer's Triangle renamed their group "Friends of Warriparinga."

PROJECT DESCRIPTION

A major part of the development involves the recreation of the wetlands by diverting a portion of the Sturt River into the site. An approximately $1.1 million grant from the state government to the Marion Council, the Patawalonga Catchment Water Management Board, and the Land Management Corporation enabled the recreation of the wetlands as a means of filtering the water.[8] BC Tonkin and Associates (a civil and environmental engineering firm) designed four ponds fed by the Sturt River to be stocked with fish native to the area. These were surrounded by native vegetation historically used for food or fiber by the area's Indigenous population. The whole scheme was completed between June and December 1998.

The filtering of the river and recreation of the wetlands was a critical step in establishing the claims of the Kaurna. It was the starting point for the Tjilbruke Dreaming, a story describing the creation of seven freshwater springs along the coastline of the Fleurieu Peninsula from Kingston Park to Rosetta Head at Victor Harbour.[9] The story covers four councils along the southern Adelaide coastline, including the City of Holdfast Bay, City of Marion, City of Onkaparinga, and the District Council of Yankalilla, which are incorporated in Kaurna native title claims. The track believed to be created by the tears of Tjilbruke as he carried his dead nephew's body for burial cuts across their boundaries.[10] These multiple sites were marked by cairns and plaques during South Australia's "Jubilee 150" celebrations in 1986, a project funded by the Tjilbruke Track Committee (consisting predominantly of Aboriginal members) and the Jubilee 150 Committee.[11] The most significant among these is the Tjilbruke monument, a rock sculpture by South Australian sculptor John Dowie at Kingston Park erected in 1972 and commissioned by *The Sunday Mail*.[12] The Tjilbruke

Figure 17.1.   Tjilbruke monument by John Dowie. Photo by author, 2013.

Dreaming Track established in conjunction with the South Australian Tourism Commission is part of a broader plan for cultural heritage management.

The initial proposal for the LKCC in 1992 by Paul and Naomi Dixon envisioned an interpretive center for the education of visitors. Following several years of negotiation, AUD 1.45 million was granted from the federal Cultural and Heritage Program. The development of the project encountered several difficulties, such as the need to reach a consensus among stakeholders, the selection of the site, and relationship to the existing 1920s colonial building.[13] Several individuals and organizations collaborated. Georgina Williams (Kaurna) was the lead Kaurna consultant supported by others from the Kaurna Aboriginal Community Heritage Association (KACHA), Joan Lamont, Rosalyn Weetra, Paul Dixon, Rose Dixon, and the Warriparinga Interpretive Committee.[14] George Bilney was the fire keeper. Don Chapman was the Cultural Planner from the Council.[15] Phillips/Pilkington Architects in association with Habitable Places Architects, both Adelaide practices, were commissioned for the project. Phillips/Pilkington Architects would design a major new cultural center for the City of Marion with Melbourne firm Ashton Raggatt McDougall, which approximately spanned the same time frame as the LKCC (from around 1998 to 2000).[16] The LKCC officially opened in 2002.

The built facilities consist of an interpretive gallery, described as focusing on the past, present, and future of the Kaurna people; a gallery space for displaying Kaurna artworks intended as a retail outlet for Kaurna-made artifacts and souvenirs; and a commercial kitchen and café space.[17] The main foci of the center are education and the creation of economic opportunities for the Kaurna people. The structure is inspired by the Kaurna story in which Tjilbruke takes the form of a glossy ibis. A "winged," corrugated steel roof supported by curved and tapered steel trusses that are fixed to a central boxed steel truss column represent the body of the ibis.[18] This structure allows the roof to hover clear of the walls and deliver water into a central box-gutter. The water cascades along the gutter into a well, said to evoke "the creation of the life-supporting springs which are the legacy of Tjilbruke to the Kaurna people."[19]

Figure 17.2. Living Kaurna Cultural Centre, exterior view. Photo by author, 2012.

Plate 16. Living Kaurna Cultural Centre, Bedford Park, South Australia, Tjilbruke Gateway by artists Margaret Worth and Gavin Malone with Kaurna artist Sherry Rankine and Kaurna senior Georgina Williams. Photo by author, 2012.

The architects have also incorporated other environmental strategies such as natural ventilation and shading and evaporative air conditioning, and have used naturally resilient timbers such as ironbark and cyprus pine. The programs organized by the LKCC include group tours of the Warriparinga area with Kaurna cultural guides, educational programs for schools, and Kaurna arts and cultural workshops, performances, and events. The facility is also available for private use.

An important part of the design was the *Tjilbruke narna arra, Tjilbruke Gateway* (1997) by artists Margaret Worth and Gavin Malone with Kaurna artist Sherry Rankine and Kaurna senior Georgina Williams (Plate 16).[20]

The outdoor art installation of a forest of dead tree trunks was designed to tell a layered story of Tjilbruke, colonization, and reconciliation, and became the starting point for the heritage track. Salvaged stringbark from plantation timber and gum trees, felled for the Southern Expressway, and colored sands from the Red Ochre Cove area were used in its design. Patterns around the base of the trunks symbolize the flow of the river and the gully winds, representing the life force. The work was commissioned by the City of Marion as part of the Local Councils Remember Program, a partnership between the Council for Aboriginal Reconciliation and the Australian Local Government Association.[21]

The site includes the LKCC, the state-heritage-listed Fairfield House, and its coach, gardens, and vineyards and associated facilities.[22] It became central to Kaurna-related activities in the area. Georgina Williams initiated friendship fires lit on each full moon in 1999, and a similar fire was lit in May 2004 during National Reconciliation Week. Other recorded events include a farewell ceremony for outgoing mayor Colin Haines in 2004, a protest against the building of the Ansett Call Centre, and, in 2009, the launch of the first new bark canoe since European settlement.[23] The political protests and conciliatory negotiations that marked the creation of the facility continued under its auspices. The LKCC and Tjilbruke Dreaming Track are also at the nexus of initiatives for management of cultural tourism sites, training of rangers, and developing collaborations between heritage culture and business. These aims were reiterated in a later regional agreement between the councils and Kaurna Heritage Board from 2005 to 2008.[24]

RECEPTION

The wetlands project was awarded a State CASE Earth Award by the Civil Contractors Federation and Case Construction Equipment in 1999, and a commendation in the South Australian Engineering Excellence Awards in 2000.[25] The LKCC won a Colourbond Steel Award of Merit from the Royal Australian Institute of Architects (South Australian chapter) and an Australian Timber Design Award in 2003.

NOTES

1. Published previously as "Case Study 5: The Living Kaurna Cultural Centre, Bedfork Park, South Australia," in Janet McGaw and Anoma Pieris, *Assembling the Centre: Architecture for Indigenous Cultures, Australia and Beyond* (Abingdon, Oxon: New York: Routledge, 2015), 81–86.

2. Thanks to Craig Cooper, coordinator of the Living Kaurna Cultural Centre, for correspondence on the text, and Gavin Malone for clarifying details.

3. Gavin Malone, "Ways of Belonging: Reconciliation and Adelaide's Public Space Indigenous Cultural Markers," *Geographical Research* 45, no. 2 (2007): 65.

4. "A Step Back in Time at Warriparinga," *Guardian Messenger*, June 13, 2001; Lauren Ahwan, "Little Sign of Science," *Guardian Messenger*, September 5, 2001.

5. "Call Centre a Threat to River: Group," *Guardian Messenger*, October 4, 2000; "Call Centre Opened," *Guardian Messenger*, July 25, 2001; Scott Cowham, "Marion's Culture Clash," *Guardian Messenger*, June 13, 2001; Tim Lloyd, "Suburban Designs Place Historical Perspectives Under the Spotlight," *The Advertiser*, June 16, 2001; and Emily Osborne, "New Home for Cultural Centre," *The Advertiser*, March 31, 2001.

6. Rob Amery and Georgina Yambo Williams, "Reclaiming through Renaming: The Reinstatement of Kaurna Toponyms in Adelaide and the Adelaide Plains," in *The Land Is a Map: Place-Names of Indigenous Origin in Australia*, eds. L. Hercus, F. Hodges, and J. Simpson (Canberra: Pandanus Books, 2002), 255–76.

7. Georgina Williams Yambo Kartanya, "Sustainable Cultures and Creating New Cultures for Sustainability," paper given at the Regional Institute Conference on Sustaining our Communities, Adelaide, March 3–6, 2002, available at http://www.regional.org.au/au/ soc/2002/5/williams.htm.

8. Local Government Association of South Australia and Government of South Australia, *Examples of Working Together in South Australia*, Government of South Australia, 5, available at https://www .lga.sa.gov.au/webdata/resources/files/ Examples_of_Working_Together_in_SA___Page_1_9___LGA_OLG___Nov_2000_pdf1.pdf.;Huw Morgan, "New Wetland to Filter Water to Patawalonga," *The Advertiser*, December 17, 1999; City of Marion, "Warriparinga Wetlands," available at http://www.marion .sa.gov.au/site/page.cfm?u=204.

9. In the story, Tjilbruke's nephew, Kulultuwi, killed a *kari* (emu) that was rightfully Tjilbruke's. While he forgave him for this mistake, Kulultuwi was killed by his two part-brothers, Jurawi and Tetjawi, for breaking the law. Tjilbruke determined that their act was unlawful, amounting to willful murder, and he avenged Kulultuwi's death by spearing and burning them in the vicinity of Warriparinga. Tjilbruke partly performed the smoking preparation for Kulultuwi's body and then carried it to Tulukudank (a freshwater spring at Kingston Park) to complete the smoking and then to Patparno (Rapid Bay) for burial in a *perki* (cave). The tears that he wept when resting during this journey formed the freshwater springs along the coast at Ka'reildun (Hallett Cove), Tainba'rang (Port Noarlunga), Potartang (Red Ochre Cove), Ruwarung (Port Willunga), Witawali (Sellicks Beach), and Kongaratinga (near Wirrina Cove). Following this, Tjilbruke chose to give up his human life, and his spirit became a bird, the Tjilbruke (Glossy Ibis), and his body a *martowalan* (memorial) in the form of the *baruke* (iron pyrites) outcrop at Barrukungga, described as the place of hidden fire (Brukunga, north of Nairne in the Adelaide Hills). City of Holdfast Bay, "Tjilbruke Heritage & the Kaurna People," available at http://www.holdfast.sa.gov .au/page.aspx?u=1248.

10. City of Holdfast Bay, "Tjilbruke Heritage & the Kaurna People."

11. City of Onkaparinga, "Walking Trails," available at www.onkaparingacity.com/custom/files/docs/walking_trails.pdf.

12. Gavin Malone, "Ways of Belonging," 161. Dowie, as mentioned previously, is well known for his sculpture of *The Three Rivers* in Victoria Square.

13. Emily Osborne, "New Home for Cultural Centre," *The Advertiser*, March 31, 2001; Scott Cowham, "Marion's Cultural Clash," *Guardian Messenger*, June 13, 2001.

14. Communication from Gavin Malone, November 13, 2015. On file with author.

15. Ibid.

16. Phillips Pilkington Architects, "Living Kaurna Cultural Centre," available at http://phillipspilkington.com.au/projects/cultural/living-kaurna-cultural-centre.html.

17. Australian Institute of Architects, "Living Kaurna Centre," available at http://www.architecture .com.au/awards_search?option=showaward&entryno=20035034.

18. Colourbond, "Wings of Steel Reflect Aboriginal Dreaming," available at http://www.colorbond.com/case-studies/wings-of-steel-reflect-aboriginal-dreaming (link no longer active, last accessed June 27, 2012).

19. Ibid.

20. Margaret Worth, "Tjilbruke Gateway," available at http://margaretworth.com.au/project/tjirbruke-gateway-%C2%A9-sturt,-sa/6.

21. City of Marion, "Public Art," available at http://www.marion.sa.gov.au/page.aspx?u=212.

22. City of Marion, "Living Kaurna Cultural Centre," available at http://www.marion.sa.gov.au/page.aspx?u=513.

23. "Reconciliation Burns Bright in Warriparinga," *Guardian Messenger*, May 24, 2000; Tim Lloyd, "Launch of Traditional Tree Canoe," *The Advertiser*, June 6, 2009. The canoe was carved by Paul Dixon using traditional techniques from a tree found in nearby Mitchell Park.

24. Kaurna Tappa Iri Reconciliation Working Group, "KITRA Kaurna Tappa Iri Regional Agreement, Heritage Culture and Business Development 2005–2008," University of Adelaide, 2005.

25. "Environment Award for Wetland Project," *The Advertiser*, June 19, 1999; Lauren Ahwan, "Diverse Reasons for Wetlands Award," *Guardian Messenger*, September 20, 2000.

18

Minpaku (National Museum of Ethnology), Osaka, Japan

Location: 10-1 Senribanpakukoen, Suita City, Osaka
Dates: 1974–1977 (original design and construction; additions 1979, 1981, 1983, 1989, 1993, and 1996)
Director General: Sudo Ken'ichi
Architect: Kisho Kurokawa Architect & Associates
General Contractor: Takenaka Corporation
Engineers: Gengo Matsui and ORS (structural) Inuzuka Engineering Consultants (mechanical)
Consultants: Kiyoshi Awazu
Site Area: 40,821 square meters
Building Area: 18,177 square meters
Total Floor Area: 52,648 square meters
Funding: Ministry of Education
Cost: approximately $23 million

Located in Senri Osaka Environmental Park, *Kokuritsu Minzokugaku Hakubutsukan* (National Museum of Ethnology)—or "Minpaku" as it is commonly known—is closely linked to Japan's economic recovery and internationalization after World War II, which was architecturally manifested in the 1964 Tokyo Olympics stadia and the pavilions and infrastructure for EXPO 1970.[1] These constructions were the symbolic stages for Japan's industrial reemergence on the international stage and its shedding of postwar dependencies. They opened up the country through media and tourism, exposing Japanese citizens to other cultures. In architectural terms, EXPO 70 was a global showcase for the futuristic technologies of Japan's famed Metabolist movement, in which architect Kenzo Tange played a leading role. Kisho Kurokawa (1934–2007), one of the founding members of the Metabolist movement and architect of Minpaku, tenaciously pursued the group's core theory of technology's metabolic or cyclical growth in his work. The Museum's modular design was a postmodern translation of Metabolist principles, and the ambitious scope of its ethnographic collection testified to the institution's global orientation evident in its motto "to the ends of the earth, to the depths of knowledge."

Figure 18.1. Minpaku, museum entrance. Photo by author, 2014.

BACKGROUND

The Japanese ethnographic tradition is attributed to the Togukawa period (1600–1868), a period before European influence when, according to Margaret Winkel, Japanese folk culture, customs, and manners became objects of study.[2] Japanese ethnography developed further with the influence of European early twentieth-century anthropology, which coincided with rising nationalist consciousness and inspired a search for national origins.[3] In Winkel's view, Japanese ethnography was influenced by the racial ideologies of the European colonial tradition of the late nineteenth century, and employed the civilizational hierarchies of Social Darwinism to both confirm the ethnogenesis of the Japanese race as a whole and to produce internally differentiated ethnographic subjects.[4]

The practice of ethnography hardened into a discipline following the annexation of Hokkaido under the *Kaitakushi* (Development Commission) in 1869, one year following the *Meiji* restoration.[5] The Ainu of northern Japan became the subject of sustained and invasive scientific study. Categorized as "commoners" in the Family Registration Law of 1871, the Ainu were expected to assimilate into mainstream Japanese culture.[6] To experiences of poverty and discrimination was added forced modernization, accompanied by invasive and ethnographic study of skeletal remains. Although there was nascent Ainu resistance during the 1940s, organized politicization followed much later in the 1970s when the Ainu Liberation League protested against such research practices and demanded the repatriation of human remains.[7] This activism prompted the establishment of dedicated cultural institutions, such as the Ainu Museum at Lake Poroto in 1976, known as *Poroto-kotan*. An ethnographic village built in an urban setting was relocated for this project, which accumulated numerous cultural facilities over the years.[8]

At the same time, an externally oriented ethnographic practice was shaped by Japan's imperial ambitions in the early twentieth century, which anticipated the colonization of Southeast Asia and the Pacific. Okinawans, Taiwanese, Koreans, and peoples of Japan's Southeast Asian colonies became subjects of Japanese ethnographic study. This scholarship reflected the political desire underpinning the imperial project to know and master the cultures and the territories Japan planned to occupy. The *Minzoku-kenkyûsho* Museum (National Institute of Ethnic Studies) was established in 1942 during World War II as part of the political project to design policy in the Japanese-occupied territories.[9]

Although the plan for a museum of ethnology was conceived as early as 1935, the official request was submitted much later, in 1964. By then, Japanese ethnographic practice had undergone significant transformation, reflecting the collapse of Japan's imperial aspirations after World War II. Japan's economic development in the early 1960s fostered a more international and progressive outlook on ethnographic practice. A research council was formed to conduct a feasibility study, and it submitted a concept plan to the Ministry of Education in 1972. Japanese anthropologist Tadao Umesao (1920–2010), who had been involved during the initial planning stages, headed the preparatory office. His books *An Ecological View of History: Japanese Civilization in the World Context* (1967) and *The Art of Intellectual Production* (1969) informed the articulation of civilizations on an ecological basis, eschewing the familiar divisions of East and West.[10] His interest in Central Asian nomads and commitment to museology determined the scope and organization of the collection. Junji Koizumi describes Umesao as a public intellectual, popular among academics, bureaucrats, businessmen, and mass media.[11] Umesao was awarded the Order of Culture (*Bunka Kunsho*) in 1994.

Minpaku was established in 1974, and was conceived as an interuniversity research institute with an administration department, an information and documentation center, and five research departments.[12] Its proposed functions were firstly to disseminate knowledge of different cultures among the general public, and secondly to act as a pedagogical center for cultural and social anthropology.[13] The temporary administrative office and laboratories were located at the Expo Memorial Building as the full design was developed between 1974 and 1975. As head of Minpaku's preparatory office and later as Director General, Tadao Umesao supervised assembly and documentation. This included the transfer of a collection of folklore reference materials of approximately twenty-one thousand items, owned by the former Ministry of Education Archive and previously held at the National Institute of Japanese Literature.[14] Collections were also drawn from Expo 70, the imperial household, and the University of Tokyo.[15] Umesao also initiated international expeditions for developing the collection, starting with Papua New Guinea.[16]

Minpaku commissioned a number of large-scale displays of boats and of houses that, while in some respects emulating the diorama, were focused on structural and material authenticity (Plate 17). This followed a practice described as *Modernologio* (Modernology) used by architect and designer Wajiro Kon, whose work was an inspiration of Umesao's.[17] Following the method used by Kon and the *Hakuboukai* or "White Grass Roof Society" led by Kunio Yanagita, a leader in Japanese folklore studies, the 1/10 scale models of traditional Japanese houses or *Minka* were constructed based on detailed observation and research by TEM (Tool and Technology, Environment, Man) Institute. In 2000, Kyoto writer Shige Omura donated the complete contents of his home to the Museum, including some forty thousand items. This practice of documenting and reproducing large-scale artifacts had been used at *Meiji Mura*, a museum showcasing Meiji-period buildings established in 1965 in Inuyama. This same strategy was reproduced at "Little World: Museum of Man," a theme park of world cultures sur-

Plate 17. Minpaku (National Museum of Ethnology), Osaka, Japan, full-scale display model of Mongolian Ger, interior. Photo by author, 2014.

veying international vernacular architectures established in 1983, also in Inuyama. Minpaku thus combined the *Jomon* and *Yayoyi* period traditions in its contents and its design, a cultural opposition of the dynamic and plebeian against sophisticated elite traditions that was popular in Japanese architectural circles from around 1956.[18] This dualism was emphasized by artist Taro Okamoto in his design for the EXPO Tower of the Sun, as an antithesis to Kenzo Tange's high-tech Metabolist entrance structure. This search for and imagination of alternative origins for Japanese identity were symptoms of the postwar evasion of explicitly nationalistic forms.

Koizumi observes that Minpaku has promoted "a relativistic sense of the variability of world cultures" but has also fed the popular appetite for exoticism."[19] He suggests that "these interests in exotic customs and extraordinary beliefs may perhaps be an antonym of the supposedly uniform and centripetal nature of Japanese culture."[20] More significantly, Koizumi argues that Minpaku has created "a very visual and tangible image of what ethnology and anthropology is."[21] Architecture has played a significant role in that representation.

PROJECT DESCRIPTION

The young architect Kisho Kurokawa included Umesao in the group of intellectual consultants that formed the Institute for Social Engineering, a corporate-backed think tank established in 1969.[22] This Institute would become a major resource for the Japanese government's national planning strategies. As the youngest and most tenacious member of Japan's unique

Metabolist movement, Kurokawa's major contribution to the movement had been the iconic *Nakagin* capsule building of 1972, which adopted a form of aggregated prefabricated capsule components treated as separate cells. At Minpaku, a planar interpretation of Metabolism produced the design of a lattice-like structure for a highly flexible grid.[23] The form was designed for phased development, which occurred between 1979 and 1996. The project thus embodied the Metabolist ideal of "an architecture of growth," based on a fundamental relationship between architecture, or the city, and nature.[24]

The Minpaku building is described as "a complex of diverse, interpenetrating boundaries," which serves as a metaphor for the cultural content on display.[25] The formal organization is as a series of ten volumetric blocks, designed with internal courtyard spaces clustered around a larger central patio, which serves as the information hub of the building. The patio is located behind the entrance and can be viewed while ascending a grand baroque staircase. The central courtyard, which displays "Relics of the Future," is a stepped hard scape, highly evocative of the Dutch artist M. C. Escher's lithographs of impossible architectures.[26] The classical symmetry of the formal entrance, the aesthetic associations of the central patio, and "ambivalent" austerity of smaller internal courtyards produce the semiotic stimuli of a postmodern aesthetic.

The four-story building structure above the basement has a steel frame partly encased in concrete and a reinforced concrete structure, visually expressed as post and beam construction. The circular posts emerge as turrets above the flat roof plane. The *Rikyu* gray color and horizontal aluminum tubular borders evoke associations with the familiar low-rise horizontal roofscapes of Japan. The circular form of the special exhibition hall emerges as a large cylinder from this architectural topography, its dome structure a reference to classicism. Despite the formal articulation of the separate blocks, the structure is connected across these spaces with storage located on the first floor, exhibition spaces on the second floor, an information and documentation center on the third floor, and research spaces on the fourth floor.[27]

Minpaku's exhibition areas are black-box display galleries with dedicated regional displays to Oceana, the Americas, Europe, Africa, West Asia, South Asia, Southeast Asia, and Central and North Asia. They also include an elaborate section on East Asia, including Korea, China, Ainu, and Japan displays. The exhibitions additionally accommodate sections on music and language that emphasize the importance of a cross-cultural view of the world. Minpaku's galleries are supported by a diverse program of administrative and processing facilities, storage, research rooms, administration offices, and a restaurant. The videotheque pods, where visitors can browse short documentary videos (including, for example, on the construction of a domestic house in a region of choice) are Metabolist capsules arranged on the second floor overlooking the courtyard. Displays are highly tactile and well supported by innovative digital technologies. The theme of vernacular architectures pervasive throughout the Museum and admirably executed in full-scale models emplaces the material exhibits, combining the phenomenological attributes of open-air ethnographic museums with the research focus of the academy.

As emphasized by Caroline Turner, Minpaku follows its own internal logic in its representation of global cultures, reversing the Orientalist gaze.[28] Although offering a preindustrial and largely agrarian focus, themes of European industrialization, political unification, and immigrant cultures are included. Turner argues that Minpaku examines and projects progressive ethnographic approaches ahead of policy change, as in the case of the Ainu who were first included in a separate exhibit in 1979.[29] This has occurred over time in response to Ainu activism, multiculturalism, and political change. Additional displays on Cultures of the Korean Peninsula and Regional Cultures of China were opened in 1983. Successive exhibitions,

Figure 18.2. Minpaku, entrance hall. Photo by author, 2014.

Figure 18.3.   Minpaku, central patio. Photo by author, 2014.

Figure 18.4.   Minpaku, videotheque booths. Photo by author, 2014.

research and training programs, collection and conservation, symposia, and publications have contributed to the Minpaku collection's continuous reinvention, reflective of global developments in ethnographic philosophy and practice. The infusion of the research culture through institutional collaboration and visiting scholars maintains its critical edge.

While it is possible to view Minpaku as a European colonial ethnographic model, there are features peculiar to the Japanese context. Both Japanese and European culture are included as equivalent in a narrative on the transition from Aboriginal to agrarian to preindustrial European/Christian bourgeois cultures. At the same time, the influence of Africa, the Caribbean, and Middle East on the Japanese popular cultural imagination is highlighted, as is the penetration of Japanese culture elsewhere. Finally, Okinawan culture is represented as an example of Japan's multicultural (in this case Christian) minorities.

RECEPTION

Minpaku has an impressive collection of 339,548 artifacts, 70,588 audiovisual materials, and several hundred thousand books, journals, and Human Relations Area Files (HRAF), in addition to digitized databases.[30] The Museum recorded 192,241 visitors in 2013, reaching an estimated total of ten million visitors in September that year. Its website, networks, outreach programs, and training and educational programs extend beyond its pedagogical framework to the general public. It is feted as a trailblazer in ethnographic research. Minpaku's Center for Research Development and Graduate University for Advanced Studies engages over sixty academics. The museum has an approximately $26,682 annual budget as of 2014.[31]

Minpaku's revisionist museology enabled by its Metabolist design template reciprocates Japan's own journey toward Ainu recognition, through reparation of grievances. At the Japanese Society Ethnology conference in 1988, the Ainu were invited to directly engage scholars on issues of research practice.[32] The Hokkaido University created a Center for Ainu and Indigenous Studies in 2005. Professor Kazuyoshi Ohtsuka, Minpaku's expert on Ainu culture responsible for its display, assisted in the development of Hokkaido's new Ainu museums.[33] Shigeru Kayano, an Ainu activist and Member of Parliament, also involved in the Hokkaido museums, is Minpaku's advisor on Ainu culture. Following the United Nations Declaration on the Rights of Indigenous Peoples in 2007, which laid an important precedent for political recognition, the legacy of Ainu activism finally bore fruit. On July 7, 2008, the Japanese government unanimously passed a resolution that recognized "that the Ainu are indigenous people who have their own language, religion and culture."[34] The Council for Ainu Policy Promotion was subsequently established in 2009.[35]

Minpaku's active involvement in this reparation process foregrounds its increasingly progressive approach to inserting contemporary artworks of extant communities into museological practice. As part of its research focus on Japan's minorities, minority cultures, and communities, a range of Indigenous agents have been brought on board. Since the Museum's thirtieth anniversary in 2007, ten of its exhibits have undergone renovation, and the South Asia and Southeast Asia sections are currently under review. This demonstrates the Museum's desire to revise ethnographic approaches on a more inclusive and equitable footing. Caroline Turner describes this as a significant shift from earlier practices of static ethnography to an emphasis on "living" cultures, now typically associated with Indigenous cultural centers.[36]

Koizumi suggests that this new focus is additionally linked to sectoral changes brought about by the privatization of national universities in 2004.[37] Although Minpaku is still funded by the Ministry of Education, Culture, Sports, Science and Technology (formerly the Ministry of Education), the funding atmosphere is much more competitive, reflecting the global shift toward neoliberal economics. Minpaku has subsequently been incorporated into a new umbrella organization called the National Institute for the Humanities, and has partially lost its original autonomy.[38]

More recently, Minpaku has focused on the impact of globalization. The resultant transformation of traditional societies and drastic changes to living environments has become an explicit concern. Following the devastating earthquake and tsunami in Japan in 2011, the Museum has registered a new cultural disillusionment with technology and desire to emphasize relationships with nature, an approach that actually complements the original ecological framing of the building.

Minpaku has received several architectural awards, including the Mainichi Art Award (1978), the Building Contractors Society Award (1979), the Public Architecture Award (1990), and The 6th JIA 25-Year Award (2006).[39] A *Thirty-Year History of the National Museum of Ethnology* was published in Japanese in 2006. Although English-language publications are relatively few, information on Minpaku can be found in self-published, architectural monographs.[40] Architect Kurokawa has subsequently designed several museum buildings, published extensively, and gained numerous international accolades. However, none of these publications seem to make the critical connection between the ecological approach to civilization and the Metabolist embrace of the same principle embodied in its architecture.

NOTES

1. Thanks to the Public Relations Unit of the General Affairs Section of Minpaku for comments on this account.

2. Margarita Winkel, "Academic Traditions, Urban Dynamics, and Colonial Threat: The Rise of Ethnography in Early Modern Japan," in *Anthropology and Colonialism in Asia and Oceania*, eds. Jan van Bremen and Akitoshi Shimizu (United Kingdom: Curzon Press, 1999), 40–64.

3. Junji Koizumi, "Transformation of the Public Image of Anthropology: The Case of Japan," paper presented at the European Association of Social Anthropologists (EASA) 9th Biennial Conference, University of Bristol, United Kingdom, September 21, 2006, available at http://www.ram-wan.net/documents/05_e_Journal/journal-3/8-koizumi.pdf.

4. Jennifer Robertson, *Politics and Pitfalls of Japan Ethnography: Reflexivity, Responsibility, and Anthropological Ethics* (Oxford and New York: Routledge, 2013), 6.

5. Winkel mentions the contributions of Mogami Tokunai (1754–1836), who spent two years in northern Japan and wrote a description of the Ainu; Mamiya Rinzo, who studied the inhabitants of Manchuria; and Ino Kanori, who studied Taiwanese society; and Torii Ryuzo, who conducted ethnographic research throughout the Japanese empire. Winkel, "Academic Traditions."

6. Ito Masami, "Diet Officially Declares Ainu Indigenous," *Japan Times*, June 7, 2008, available at http://www.japantimes.co.jp/news/2008/06/07/national/diet-officially-declares-ainu-indigenous/.

7. Richard M. Siddle, *Race, Resistance and the Ainu of Japan* (Oxford and New York: Routledge, 2012).

8. Ainu Museum website available at http://www.ainu-museum.or.jp/en/.

9. Nelson Graburn, "Multiculturalism, Museums and Tourism in Japan," in *Multiculturalism in the New Japan: Crossing the Boundaries Within*, eds. Nelson H. Graburn, John Ertl, and R. Kenji Tierney (Oxford and New York: Berghahn Books, 2008), 218–40, 220, 235.

10. Tadao Umesao, *An Ecological View of History: Japanese Civilization in the World Context* (trans. Beth Cary) (Rosanna: Trans Pacific Press, 2003) (originally published in 1967); Tadao Umesao, *The Art of Intellectual Production* (originally published in 1969; not translated into English).

11. Junji Koizumi, "Transformation of the Public Image of Anthropology," 188.

12. National Museum of Ethnology, "About Minpaku, Japan," available at http://www.minpaku.ac.jp/english/aboutus. The National Museum of Ethnology was founded under the Law to Amend Part of the National School Establishment Law (No. 81 of 1974).

13. Institutions, "The National Museum of Ethnology," *Current Anthropology* 16, no. 2 (June 1975): 182.

14. National Museum of Ethnology, "Museum Survey and Guide 2014," available at http://www.minpaku.ac.jp/sites/default/files/english/aboutus/youran/pdf/youran2014_en03.pdf.

15. Graburn, "Multiculturalism, Museums and Tourism in Japan."

16. National Museum of Ethnology, "Museum Survey and Guide 2014."

17. National Museum of Ethnology, "'Modernologio' Now: Kon Wajiro's Science of the Present," available at http://www.minpaku.ac.jp/english/museum/exhibition/special/20120426kon/ exhibition.

18. Zongjie Lin, *Kenzo Tange and the Metabolist Movement: Urban Utopias of Modern Japan* (Oxford and New York: Routledge, 2010), 39–40. The debate was based on writings by architectural critic Noboru Kawazoe.

19. Junji Koizumi, "Transformation of the Public Image of Anthropology."

20. Ibid.

21. Ibid.

22. Rem Koolhaas and Hans Ulrich Obrist, *Project Japan: Metabolism Talks* (Cologne: Taschen, 2011), 393–94.

23. Kisho Kurokawa Architect and Associates, "Works and Projects, National Museum of Ethnology," available at http://www.kisho.co.jp/page.php/203.

24. Zongjie Lin, *Kenzo Tange and the Metabolist Movement*, 44.

25. Kisho Kurokawa Architect and Associates, "Works and Projects, National Museum of Ethnology."

26. For example, see lithographs titled "Convex and Concave" (1955) and "Relativity" (1951).

27. National Museum of Ethnology, "About Minpaku."

28. Caroline Turner, "Linking the Past and Future: Cultural Exchanges and Cross-Cultural Engagements in Four Asian Museums," *Humanities Research* 9, no. 1 (2002): 13–28.

29. Ibid.

30. National Museum of Ethnology, "Museum Survey and Guide 2014."

31. Koizumi, "Transformation of the Public Image of Anthropology."

32. Robertson, *Politics and Pitfalls of Japan Ethnography*, 9.

33. Turner, "Linking the Past and Future."

34. Masami, "Diet Officially Declares Ainu Indigenous."

35. Council for Ainu Policy Promotion, "About the Council," available at http://www.kantei.go.jp/jp/singi/ainusuishin/index_e.html.

36. Turner, "Linking the Past and Future."

37. National University Corporation Law (No. 112 of 2003).

38. Koizumi, "Transformation of the Public Image of Anthropology."

39. Kisho Kurokawa Architect and Associates, "Works and Projects, National Museum of Ethnology."

40. Books about Kurokawa include *Kisho Kurokawa: Abstract Symbolism* (Milano: L'Arcaedizioni, 1996); *Kisho Kurokawa Architect and Associates: Selected and Current Works* (Mulgrave: Images Publishing Group, 2000); and *Kisho Kurokawa: From Metabolism to Symbiosis* (New York: St. Martin's Press, 1992).

19

Mossman Gorge Centre, Mossman, Queensland, Australia

Location: Mossman, Queensland
Date: 2013
Client: Indigenous Land Corporation
Community: Residents of the Mossman Gorge community
Governing body: Bamanga Bubu Ngadimunku Incorporated, Indigenous Land Corporation
Chair: Roy Gibson
Business Plan and Management: Voyages Indigenous Tourism Australia
Architects: Fisher Buttrose Architects
Landscape Architect: Taylor Cullity Lethlean
Structural Engineer: Lambert & Rehbein
Civil Engineer: Aecom Cairns
Construction: F. K. Gardner & Sons
Project Manager: Ridgemill Project Management
Wayfinding: Dot Dash
Town Planner: Arup
Cost: approximately $20.8 million

The Mossman Gorge Centre opened in June 2012 seventy-seven kilometers north of Cairns, and it is the most recent innovative Indigenous facility built for ecotourism in tropical North Queensland.[1] It serves as a visitor center for the Mossman Gorge World Heritage site in the Daintree Rainforest, an area of 120,000 hectares. The Gorge is reported to be the oldest, continuously surviving rain forest on earth, with just one hectare containing over thirty thousand species of plants and animals. It is believed to have survived 135 million years. It is the largest portion of rain forest in Australia and has the wettest climate. The Mossman Gorge Centre is designed as the gateway to this World Heritage site.

BACKGROUND

The concept for the Mossman Gorge Center was initiated by the local Aboriginal community, the Kuku Yalanji people, led by Elder Roy Gibson, who first envisioned a cultural hub on the site in 1992.[2] At the time Gibson was employed by Barry Murday in the local sugarcane fields and had "many a yarn under the Milky Pine tree" with the Bama Rangers to discuss ways of creating jobs and education for his people.[3] The Murday family agreed to sell the property now occupied by the Centre if Gibson and the Indigenous Land Corporation could raise the necessary funds. With the primary aim to alleviate endemic unemployment in the local Indigenous community, the model for the Centre capitalizes on the growing market for "ecotourism." The main attraction for tourists is the World Heritage–listed rain forest. The Centre is owned by the Indigenous Land Corporation, who engaged Voyage Indigenous Tourism Australia, the tourism arm of the Corporation, to develop the business plan.[4] Cairns-based Fisher Buttrose Architects were engaged as the architects, and Taylor Cullity Lethlean were engaged as landscape designers. Both firms worked with the Kuku Yalanji people and with local, state, and federal governments on the project.

Architect Deborah Fisher of Fisher Buttrose Architects began work on the design around seven years prior to construction, with extensive research into precedents. Cape York Partnerships provided support with economic studies and planning. One of the findings of the research was that many of the regional cultural centers in Australia that have adopted a museum model have struggled to become economically viable and attract repeat visits.[5] The region already had a steady stream of tourists, with 350,000 people visiting Mossman Gorge each year. The challenge was to develop a model to intercept and divert these tourists to a Centre that could provide a hub for Indigenous employment and training. The master stroke was to convince the Council to stop private vehicles entering the only road into the gorge. Given the planning sensitivities related to the rain forest area, the planning permit application process was complicated and protracted, according to Fisher, but the argument for removing traffic from the region on environmental grounds had broad support.[6] The concept developed by Gibson was to locate the Centre, with parking for two hundred and fifty cars and seventeen tour buses, at the point of the new road closure, and to provide low-emission electric "eco-shuttles" for a fee as the only means of transport to the Gorge. Instead of functioning as an interpretation center, which offers knowledge to tourists prior to visiting the Gorge, tourists are encouraged to engage a local Kuku Yalanji guide for an "on-country" "Dreamtime Legend Walk" or "Dreamtime Gorge Walk" along an old water supply route, which the Centre leases from surrounding landowners. This tour concept builds on a tradition of Indigenous heritage trails, where personal storytelling by Indigenous guides is preferred over static interpretive signage. Through such practices, traditional custodians of sites or environments held sacred to the community can educate tourists into the appropriate Indigenous protocols. They can also monitor tourist use and treatment of the site. At Mossman Gorge, this practice is institutionalized in an excellent example of cultural influence and exchange. According to the Centre's Annual Report for 2009 to 2010, the Department of Education, Employment and Workplace Relations funded Bamanga Bubu Ngadimunku Incorporated to create jobs and traineeships to construct four kilometers of walking track at Mossman Gorge.[7]

PROJECT DESCRIPTION

The design of an elongated and low-hung facility under a continuous roof is simple and unobtrusive, with a color scheme that reflects the surrounding environment (Plate 18).[8] This kind of simplicity is also evident in a previous design by Fisher Buttrose Architects for the Yarrabah Art Centre (2001), which adopted a relaxed, informal approach. The architects in-

Plate 18. Mossman Gorge Centre, Mossman, Queensland, Australia, exterior view. Photo by Adam Bruzzone 2012, Voyages Indigenous Tourism Australia image archive, courtesy Mossman Gorge Centre.

terpret their design for the Mossman Gorge Centre as responding to the natural landscape, which is of fundamental importance to the Indigenous community.[9] As described by the architects, a seed and pod sculpted in timber and featured in the Centre's breezeway, and an art gallery/gift shop is intended "to symbolize the core and opportunity for growth."[10] The roof is designed to allow rainwater to cascade down its slope into a sparkling spoon drain. Leaf cutouts in the ceiling cast a dappled light onto the timber deck breezeway. Some seventeen thousand plants have been cultivated at the site. These subtle design moves are an effort to blend the building with its context.[11]

The landscape design by Taylor Cullity Lethlean complements this approach. The firm's practice is well known for interpretive landscapes related to Indigenous cultural facilities, most famously at Uluru-Kata Tjuta Cultural Centre in the Northern Territory and Birrarung Marr in Melbourne, Victoria. The aim at Mossman Gorge is to provide a welcoming entry to visitors. According to Taylor Cullity Lethlean, tree canopies and understory planting grown from seed collected by the local community and propagated for this purpose are carefully designed to screen utility buildings and reduce the project's visual impact. Similarly, drainage swales are lined with rocks and interplanted with reeds to help aerate and purify storm water.[12]

The Centre includes the Mayi restaurant, which offers Indigenous bush foods, and a gift shop stocked with pieces designed and made by local Indigenous artists and craftspeople. Adjacent is a large residential training facility that offers courses in Indigenous tourism, hospitality, landscaping, and administration.[13] In addition to incorporating two small businesses already in operation (the guided walks program and a shop that sells Indigenous art and crafts), a number of new employment opportunities have been generated by the Centre, including in administration, hospitality, and landscape gardening. A major focus in the leadup to opening the Centre was to get local Indigenous staff "job ready" and keep them engaged with work after years of unemployment. Training and recruitment programs are underway to generate forty-five low-season jobs in retail, hospitality, guiding, and interpretation for tourism, administration, and support during the low season and up to seventy jobs in the high season.[14] In addition to the training facility, a work exchange program has been set up with another of Voyages Indigenous Tourism Australia's ventures in Alice Springs. One year after opening, the Centre appears to be achieving these aims. Of its sixty-six employees, fifty-nine are Indigenous, comprising around 90 percent of its workforce. The latest group of eleven trainees has graduated, and there is accommodation for eighteen students. These trainees either work at the Centre or seek employment at one of Voyages Indigenous Tourism Australia's other centers.[15] However, visitor numbers in 2013 were around 230,000 lower than anticipated, partly due to a difficult climate for domestic tourism. Still, at peak times the Centre receives around one thousand visitors per day.

NOTES

1. Thanks to Philip Newland, former director of sales at the Mossman Gorge Centre, for providing information; Marion McLeod, development manager, for providing the photograph; and to Deb Fisher at Fisher Buttrose Architects for conversations about the Centre. This text originates in an interview with Deb Fisher conducted by Janet McGaw in 2013. See also Mossman Gorge Centre, "The Environment," available at http://www.mossmangorge.com.au/The-Environment/The-Environment.

2. Anne Majumdar, "Mossman Gorge Fires Up for Next Phase," *Travel Weekly*, April 10, 2013, available at http://www.travelweekly.com.au/news/mossman-gorge-fires-up-for-phase-two.

3. Mossman Gorge Centre and Roy Gibson, http://deadlystories.yodelservices.com/entry/226 (link no longer active, last accessed October 29, 2013).

4. Voyages Travel Centre, "Mossman Gorge Centre Opens in North Queensland," July 26, 2012, available at http://www.voyages.com.au/media/360/.

5. Interview with Deb Fisher, July 29, 2013.

6. Interview with Deb Fisher, July 29, 2013.

7. Minister for Local Government and Aboriginal and Torres Strait Islander Partnerships, *Annual Highlights Report for Queensland's Discrete Indigenous Communities July 2009–June 2010*, 141–44, available at http://www.cabinet.qld.gov.au/documents/2010/nov/ highlight%20report%20for%20qld%20indigenous%20communities/Attachments/full-report.pdf.

8. Fisher Buttrose Architects, "Mossman Gorge Centre," available at http://www.fabarchitects.com.au/index.php?option=com_content&view=article&id=25&Itemid=28.

9. Ibid.

10. Ibid.

11. Ibid.

12. Taylor Cullity Lethlean, "Mossman Gorge Visitor and Training Centre," available at http://www.tcl.net.au/news/work-in-progress/mossman-gorge-visitor-and-training-centre--mossman--queensland.

13. Mossman Gorge Centre, "Training and Education," available at http://www.mossmangorge.com.au/About-Us/Training-and-Education.

14. Mossman Gorge Centre, "Training and Education."

15. Anne Majumdar, "Mossman Gorge Fires Up for Next Phase."

20

Musée du Quai Branly and Universitè Wing, Paris, France

Location: 37 Quai Branly, Paris, France
Date: 1995–2006
Architect: Jean Nouvel, France
Landscape: Gilles Clément and Patrick Blanc
Contractor: Etablissement Public Musée du Quai Branly, France
Engineering Teams: Jacques Faure and Florent Millot
Cost: approximately $273 million

UNIVERSITÉ WING

Curators: Brenda Croft (National Gallery of Australia), Hetti Perkins (Art Gallery of New South Wales), and Philippe Peltier (MQB)
Australian Aboriginal Artists: Paddy Bedford, John Mawurndjul (Kunwinjku), Ningura Napurrula (Pintupi), Lena Nyadbi (Kija), Michael Riley (Wiradjuri/Kamilaroi), Judy Watson (Waanji), Tommy Watson (artist) (Pitjantjatjara), and Gulumbu Yunupingu (Gumatj)
Installation Management: Cracknell & Lonergan Architects (Australia)

The Musée du Quai Branly (MQB) opened on June 23, 2006, on a site near the River Seine, one hundred meters from the Tour Eiffel in Paris's prestigious Seventh *Arrondissement* (Plate 19). The MQB was a grand project of President Jacques Chirac following the French presidential tradition of creating a specific cultural legacy during the presidential term.[1] The facility, dedicated to non-European cultures—in Chirac's view, those peoples to whom history has "done violence"—precipitated the dissolution of two former institutions: the Musée National des arts d'Afrique et d'Océanie (1931) and the ethnographic department of the French natural history museum, the Musée de l'Homme (1937). These institutions were replaced by an aesthetically controversial new facility designed by celebrated French architect Jean Nouvel. The MQB advanced an international trend to decolonize museums created through imperial enterprise.

Plate 19.   Musée du Quai Branly, Paris, France, exterior view. Photo by author, 2010.

The initial impetus for the Museum came from a significant 1990 manifesto to include non-Western material in the Louvre, headed by art dealer and collector Jacques Kerchache and 150 others. Yet the politics of the replacement of previous facilities and the processes of decolonizing public opinion would prove contentious on many fronts.[2] For this reason the MQB is an interesting site of new debates surrounding museology, changing public opinion, and postmodern attitudes toward interpreting culture. A new approach in which ceremonial and practical objects never intentioned as art would be displayed as spectacular aesthetic objects was subject to critique.[3] Such concerns were shared by museum directors, curators, anthropologists, and art historians and directed against the architect's desire to choreograph the museum experience, a growing trend in architectural design culture at the time. Tension between the highly curated, affective spatial experience of the building and the focused attention to the artifacts desired by curators persisted.[4]

PROJECT DESCRIPTION

The Museum's steel structure is designed to form a bridge supported on randomly placed, pendular columns and envisioned by the architect to symbolize trees of a sacred wood. This thematic is continued in the building's interior. The structure achieves spans of up to thirty-four meters and cantilevers extending to fifteen meters. The floor is supported by an irregular frame of reticulated beams and joists, supported by articulated tubular posts.[5] The structural ensemble supports the Museum and three administrative buildings, one of these being the Université building, with ceiling murals designed by Australian Aboriginal artists.[6] The environmental theme extends to the landscaping around the building's exterior, whereby a wilderness is simulated in the pristine Parisian neighborhood. A muddy pond has attracted a brood

Figure 20.1.   Musée du Quai Branly, *jardin planetaire*—world garden. Photo by author, 2010.

of ducks that have taken up summer residence. This juxtaposition bears some of the attributes of the wilderness gardens of Washington, DC's, NMAI (see chapter 25).

The *jardin planetaire* or world garden, designed by *paysagiste* Gilles Clément, is conceived as a *jardin en mouvement* or moving garden that reinforces the wall-less sanctuary envisioned by Nouvel. It combines plants from different biomes such as maple from North America, oak from Europe, and *miscanthus* from Asia, producing a sense of genius loci distinct from the surrounding nineteenth-century fabric.[7] A glass wall preserves the microclimate necessary for some of these species. A vertical living garden (*le mur végétal*) designed by Patrick Blanc, which runs two hundred meters long by twelve meters high along one face of the administrative building, reinforces this approach.

The contrast between the building and its surroundings is also reiterated in its materiality. Bright, earthy colors appear vibrantly against the white and gray surrounds and the industrial aesthetic of the iconic Tour Eiffel in the backdrop. Nouvel's conceit of a sacred wood, where visitors discover objects, manifests as a dark passage into the building and among the exhibits: "It is a place marked by the symbols of the forest, the river and the obsessions of death and oblivion."[8] In addition to the exhibition spaces, a screening room, a reading room, and several classrooms, the program includes the five-hundred-seat Claude Lévi Strauss Theatre and a multimedia library with highly valuable collections.[9] Only 3,500 items from the Museum's vast collection of 267,000 objects are on display. There is also a shop, a restaurant, and a café.

A sinuous, white, dimly illuminated entry ramp, comparable to a journey into a dark womb, winds upward from the reception, its immaculate surface sporadically lit by fragments of moving video images. This sensation continues into the interior spaces of the building, where light continues to be deliberately muted for maximum effect. Visitors circle around a cylindrical glass silo holding a spectacular array of musical instruments. The central path continues between thick, mud-colored, leather-clad walls conveying the plasticity and density of adobe construction, with the floor plane color-coded to identify different continents. Exhibits from Africa, Asia, the Americas, and Oceana are clustered by geography, with the taller pieces like totem poles in full view. The northern flank of the building has been designed as a series of rectangular protrusions that form a row of alcoves off the display floor. Sacred objects or valuable works of contemporary art are highlighted through these specialized displays. Interactive and noninteractive media is found throughout the permanent collections, either included directly in the display cases or embedded in the leather furniture and walls.

This reliance on interactive media, clustered in mezzanine levels overlooking the main gallery, is a much criticized attribute of the new museology being tested in this building. The dramatic and interpretive aesthetic context is a radical departure from the neutral environments associated with modern museums and a subject of an evolving debate between art historical and anthropological approaches to the same artifacts.[10]

UNIVERSITÉ WING

Attached to the main building through a series of bridges, the administrative wing of the Museum at 222 rue de l'Université, known as the Université wing, is a source of great pride for its administrators, not least because of its featuring spectacular modern artworks by Australian Aboriginal artists. At Nouvel's instigation, a series of ceiling paintings following the French tradition were commissioned for this building in 1999. Contemporary Aboriginal artists were invited to decorate the building's ceilings, and the cost of approximately $184,000 was divided between the Australian Ministry for Immigration and Multicultural and Indigenous Affairs, the Ministry for Foreign Affairs and Trade, and the Australia Council for the Arts.[11] The Harold Mitchell Foundation provided additional funding. The Aboriginal curators Brenda Croft (National Gallery of Australia) and Hetti Perkins (Art Gallery of New South Wales) worked with MQB's Philippe Peltier in what has been described as the most important permanent installation of contemporary Australian Indigenous art outside Australia.[12] Australian firm Cracknell & Lonergan Architects managed the installation for the Australia Council for the Arts.

The artwork decorates the walls and ceilings of different floors, its effect enhanced by mirrors attached to window reveals, in total covering 2,500 square meters of wall. The artists who were commissioned include Gulumbu Yunupingu, from Yothu Yindi; John Mawurndjul, from Maningrida; Ningura Napurrula, from Watulka; Pitjantjatjara artist Tommy Watson; Warlpiri artist Judy Watson Napangardi; and Gija artist Lena Nyadbi. Included also are the late Michael Riley's photographs. The scale of the international commission proved challenging, as observed by Donald Richardson:

> The bark-painter, Mawurndjul, was the only artist to work personally on the massive pieces: the others were all executed by artisans under the direction of the artists. All were created face-up on huge pieces of canvas on the floor then turned over and stuck to the ceilings or walls. Tommy Watson's contribution was transferred to baked enamel on stainless-steel tiles in Australia and freighted to Paris. Paddy Nyunkuny Bedford's minimalist sculptural installation was also translated in Australia.[13]

While these commissioned works decorate quotidian spaces, the Aboriginal artworks displayed within the Museum comprise bark painting collected at the instigation of Karel Kupka,

Figure 20.2. Musée du Quai Branly, Université building, interior. Photo by author, 2011.

along with acrylic paintings acquired since the 1970s. Both these art forms are collected for their artistic rather than ethnographic value, an approach that can be interpreted as elevating them into equivalence with other artworks. The ceiling paintings can be argued in a similar light, although they are reduced to visual patterns. These questions service the opposite side of the debate between art and ethnography. Art in this interpretation elevates the ethnographic object while ethnography gives art added layers of meaning.

RECEPTION

The jury citation for the Pritzker Architecture Prize 2008, awarded to Jean Nouvel, describes the Musée du Quai Branly as "a bold, unorthodox building with unusual spaces in which objects are displayed—and understood—in new ways."[14] The Museum's director, Stéphane Martin, is quoted as describing the space as a theater.[15] The decontextualization of the artifacts has been much criticized. A review of several debates on postcolonial museum practice included in the book *Paris Primitive* provides insights into the underlying politics: the postcolonial museum evolves from problematic colonial collection practices, which are often suppressed when historical objects are represented as art.[16] The museum landscape is largely oriented toward a bourgeois European public, and the task of the postcolonial museum, critics argue, is to expose the stories of imperial history and its resilient politics of difference, and to engage with culturally diverse audiences nationally and internationally.[17]

The Musée du Quai Branly has developed extensive pedagogical and public outreach programs, including conferences, workshops, exhibitions, performances, and publications, with the intention of facilitating "dialogues between cultures."[18] It has launched programs and exhibitions featuring transnational Indigenous communities, many of them from former colonies. More recently, extramural programs framed as *Les Ateliers Nomades* (nomadic or transient workshops) diversifies its metropolitan reach. The program for 2014 and 2015 includes collaborative activities in the economically marginal, "immigrant" Paris suburbs of Clichy-sous-Bois and Montfermeil.[19]

NOTES

1. Thanks to curator Magali Melandri for an interview held in September 2010. Image use permissions via Scala, London.

2. Alexandra Sauvage, "Narratives of Colonisation: The Musée du Quai Branly in Context," *reCollections: Journal of the National Museum of Australia* 2, no. 2 (September 2007), available at http://recollections.nma.gov.au/issues/vol_2_no2/papers/ narratives_of_colonisation/.

3. Michael Kimmelman, "A Heart of Darkness in the City of Light," *New York Times*, July 2, 2006.

4. Kimmelman, "A Heart of Darkness in the City of Light."

5. Summary of description from Pierre Engel, Case Studies: Quai Branly Museum.

6. Pierre Engel, "Quai Branly Museum," Arcellor Mittal, available at http://www.constructalia.com/english/case_studies/france/quai_branly_museum#.VjsL_64rKRs.

7. Fi's Growing Gardening and Design, "Musee du Quai Branly," available at http://growingardeningdesign.blogspot.com/2010/08/musee-du-quai-branly.html.

8. Pierre Engel, "Quai Branly Museum."

9. France Diplomatie, "Dossiers: Official Statement–The Quai Branly Museum: A New Institution Engaged in the Dialogue of Cultures and Civilizations," available at http://www.diplomatie.gouv.fr/en/france_159/discovering-france_2005/france-from-to-z_1978/culture_1979/the-musee-du-quai-branly_5035.html.

10. Agnès Blasselle and Anna Guarneri, "The Opening of the Musée du Quai Branly: Valuing/Displaying the 'Other' in Post-Colonial France," Humanity in Action, available at http://www.humanityinaction.org/knowledgebase/200-the-opening-of-the-musee-du-quai-branly-valuing-displaying-the-other-in-post-colonial-france.

11. Sauvage, "Narratives of Colonisation."

12. Australian Indigenous Art Commission, "Musée du Quai Branly: Where Cultures Meet in Dialogue," available at http://www.quaibranly.fr/uploads/media/ Australian_Indigenous_Art_Commission.pdf.

13. Donald Richardson, "The Dilemma of Aboriginal Art," available at http://www.donaldart.com.au/Writings/dilemma.html (link no longer active).

14. Jury Citation, Pritzker Architecture Prize, 2008, available at http://www.pritzkerprize.com/2008/jury.

15. Peter Naumann, "Naturally in Paris," *Architecture Australia* 95, no. 5 (September 2006): 88–95.

16. Sally Price, *Paris Primitive: Jacques Chirac's Museum on the Quai Branly* (Chicago: University of Chicago Press, 2007).

17. Blasselle and Guarneri, "The Opening of the Musée du Quai Branly."

18. Musée du Quai Branly, "Exhibitions," available at http://www.quaibranly.fr/ en/programmation.html.

19. Musée du Quai Branly, "Exhibitions." Civil unrest in these two suburbs during October and November 2005 was attributed to the cultural maginalization, impoverishment, and high levels of unemployment of Muslim, North African, and sub-Saharan immigrants in this area. See Gilles Kepel, *Banlieu de la Republique: Société, politique et religion à Clichy-sous-Bois et Montfermeil* ("Suburbs of the Republic: Society, Politics and Religion in Clichy-sous-Bois and Montfermeil") (Paris: Gallimard Editions, 2012).

21

Museum of Anthropology, University of British Columbia, Vancouver, Canada

Location: N. W. Marine Drive, University of British Columbia, Vancouver
Date: 1973–1976
Director: Dr. Michael M. Ames
Architect: Arthur Erickson
Landscape Architect: Kenneth Morris
Engineering: Bogue Babicki and Associates
Functional Program: Graham Brawn and Associates
Area: 58,000 square feet (later expanded to 72,000 square feet)
Funding: Government of Canada, National Museums of Canada, and University of British Columbia
Construction cost: approximately $4.2 million
Expansion: 1990
Architect: Arthur Erickson
Area: 6,500 square feet
Funding: The Odlum family, Walter C. Koerner, and University of British Columbia
Expansion and renovation: 2010
Director: Dr. Anthony Shelton
Architect: Arthur Erickson with Stantec Architecture
Landscape Architect: Cornelia Oberlander
Functional Program: Michael Lundholm Architects
Construction Management: Stuart Olson Construction
Area added: 43,000 square feet
Funding: Canada Foundation for Innovation, British Columbia Knowledge Development Fund, University of British Columbia, and private donors
Construction and renovation cost: approximately $52.2 million

An early example of a purpose-built museum designed specifically for Indigenous cultural artifacts, the award-winning Museum of Anthropology (the MOA) of 1976 extends the pedagogical framing of its host environment, the University of British Columbia.[1] Designed by the Canadian architect Arthur Erickson and situated on the cliffs of Point Grey overlooking the

Figure 21.1. Museum of Anthropology, University of British Columbia, view facing lake. Photo by author, 2009.

ocean, the MOA building occupies the former site of three gun emplacements built to protect the Vancouver harbor during World War II. Arthur Erickson (1924–2009), a modernist Canadian architect renowned for his concrete architecture, based his design of successive portal frames on the Northwest Coast post-and-beam structures used in Indigenous "bighouses" or lineage houses from the central and northern coast of British Columbia. Indeed, the MOA building's architecture was conceived to accommodate the tall totem poles created by First Nations groups, including the Haida, Gitxsan, Nisga'a, and Kwakwaka'wakw. The translation of these forms into a contemporary material with fifteen-meter-high panes of glass inserted between concrete structural elements produces a remarkable interior flooded with natural light.

A pond was constructed for the opening of the building in 1976 but was not filled with water because of maintenance and engineering concerns. Prior to 2010, heavy rain would temporarily gather in the pond depression, and it was intentionally filled for three special occasions but emptied afterward. As of September 2010, the pond has been permanently filled. The association with water was important to the predominantly coastal Indigenous artifacts displayed in the building.

Edith Iglauer recalls Erickson as saying:

> When I was designing the museum, I remembered a photograph of an early Indian village between the edge of the forest and the sea. The inhabitants had carved the trees with the animals they hunted and the fish they netted, and arranged these marvelous totems that gave special powers to the families who owned them in a legend of natural survival, following the crescent of the beach.[2]

The driving force behind establishing the new museum was Harry Hawthorn, the director and founder of the Anthropology Department at the University of British Columbia, together with his wife, Audrey, the first curator of the collection. A grant of approximately $2,538,258 and the gift of the Walter and Marianne Koerner Collection were awarded to the MOA as part of British Columbia's centennial celebrations.[3] Harry Hawthorn worked closely with Erickson in developing the design. The functional program was developed by Graham Brawn Associates.

BACKGROUND

The MOA must be regarded as a metropolitan institution, which in its sensitivity to Indigenous issues differentiates itself from the activities and displays of European and American collectors. The totem poles in the MOA's collection were purchased during the 1950s with the permission of either the families who held ownership rights or the elected band councils that were responsible for the reserve where the poles were standing. The MOA's largest Northwest Coast Aboriginal collection is the Kwakwaka'wakw collection of masks, poles, feast dishes, and other items. Native families largely sold this collection directly to the MOA in the early 1950s, and the museum maintains connections with these families.

Previous patterns of displacement provoked political demands for remote facilities and keeping places in Indigenous reserves. The Haida have an award-winning Haida Heritage Centre at Kay Llnagaay on Haida Gwaii (Queen Charlotte Islands) on British Columbia's Northwest Coast.[4] Such centers may be constructed in part to create a source of tourism revenue and to serve as a cultural learning center and gathering place for the community. Kay Llnagaay draws heavily from the local Band Council funding. The MOA in contrast may be considered an exemplary pedagogical model that reconceptualizes the purpose of the Museum.

PROJECT DESCRIPTION

Due to the siting of the MOA on one side of an incline, its entrance is unassuming and at a human scale. The building is flanked by a number of courtyards that connect it to the surrounding landscape, designed by landscape architect Cornelia Oberlander. Indigenous plants and grasses comprise a key part of the landscape scheme. Two outdoor Haida Houses, two carved house posts, a welcome figure, and ten totem poles (one of them a house post inside a Haida house) are located in the museum grounds. The entrance to the Museum was originally through a set of massive doors carved in 1976 by four master Gitxsan artists, Walter Harris, Earl Muldoe, Art Sterritt, and Vernon Stephens. These doors now frame the opening to the Museum shop. Beyond the entrance and reception, a long, dark passageway flanked by monumental sculptures creates the sensation of entering a womb or tunnel, drawing the visitor inward and toward the naturally lit and vast space of the Great Hall. The sense of drama achieved by this contrast is deliberate. As described by curator Bill McLennan, some bands do have reservations about the display of artifacts in a museum setting due to negative associations with institutions in the past.[5] When First Nations community members visit Vancouver and out to the MOA, they want their artifacts (their history) to be respectfully shown and represented. The Museum has had compliments from community members who feel that the MOA represents their heritage well, and curators continue to work with community members through research, displays, and other programs in order to build strong relationships.[6]

The MOA was founded as a teaching museum for housing the spectacular collection, which had from 1949 been located in the basement of the main university library, built in 1925. Its objective was to enable access to all artifacts in the collection, necessitating specialist display

Figure 21.2. Museum of Anthropology, University of British Columbia, Great Hall. Photo by author, 2009.

areas for some ten thousand objects. The entire collection comprises 36,000 ethnographic objects and 535,000 archaeological objects, many of which originate from the Northwest Coast of British Columbia. In addition to totem poles, carved boxes, bowls, and feast dishes, which are featured in the Museum's Great Hall, smaller and everyday artifacts of gold, silver, argillite, wood, ceramic, reed, cane, and other materials are exhibited in the interior Multiversity Galleries. The new Audain Gallery, a 5,800-square-foot exhibition hall for temporary exhibitions, showcases traveling and temporary exhibitions.

The objective of the Museum is pedagogical. The First Nations House of Learning located on the University of British Columbia campus extends this goal by creating a comfortable space for Indigenous scholars and visitors, run by First Nations scholars and professors. The MOA incorporates contemporary First Nations art, images, and commentary into its exhibit spaces, making it clear to the public that First Nations communities change, grow, and continue their traditions in modern and historic form.

Curator Bill McLennan observes that First Nations visitors are often apprehensive about museums and anthropology and how their history is portrayed. Many people have suggested that MOA is a very different type of museum and perhaps should have a different name. The moribund nature of exhibits can make visitors apprehensive, as does the association of museums with death. McLennan describes a joke among artists and the community—"Don't get too near that empty case, or you might get stuck in there!"[7]

The MOA's determination to represent a living culture involves combining old and new artifacts and artworks. Among these, the most prominent are the works of the inspirational Haida artist Bill Reid.[8] Described as a "superb craftsman," his monumental interpretation of the Haida creation story, *The Raven and the First Men*—a figure of the Raven carved out of yellow cedar, with the first humans coming out of a clam underfoot—takes pride of place in a sky-lit rotunda

Figure 21.3. Museum of Anthropology, University of British Columbia, sculpture by Bill Reid, *Raven and the First Men*. Photo by author, 2009.

Figure 21.4. Museum of Anthropology, University of British Columbia, sculpture by Bill Reid, *Haida Bear*. Photo by author, 2009.

in the MOA. Reid's large bronze casting of a canoe filled with supernatural creatures, titled *The Spirit of Haida Gwaii*, is on display at Vancouver International Airport.[9] Contemporary interpretations of Indigenous themes take the form of stylized artworks in steel and ceramic.

RECEPTION

Subsequent expansion and renovation of the MOA in 1990 and again in 2010 testify to its continuing relevance as a teaching museum. The Koerner Ceramics Gallery, which opened in 1990, features six hundred European ceramic pieces collected and donated by the late Dr. Walter Koerner. A new wing was added in 2010, effectively doubling the Museum's size, and includes a resource library, teaching laboratory, office, and exhibition gallery. Spaces were also designed for academic functions such as classrooms, labs, archival storage, and offices, and additional exhibition and performance spaces, visible storage galleries, a shop, and rental facilities were added. Among these are spaces inaccessible to the public, such as rooms containing secret regalia and objects sacred to particular communities.

Recent commissions at the Museum include two outdoor sculptures by Musqueam artists, one by Joe Becker and the other by Susan Point. Additionally on May 27, 2011, as part of the Festival of Architecture in Vancouver, the building was awarded the 2011 *Prix du XXe siècle*, which "recognizes the enduring excellence of nationally significant buildings in the historical context of Canadian architecture."[10] The award reaffirms the conviction that Erickson's building captures the "Spirit of Canadian Architecture."

NOTES

1. Museum of Anthropology, "Director's Welcome Message," available at http://moa.ubc.ca/welcome/. Thanks to William (Bill) McLennan, Curator (Pacific Northwest) at MOA for interview on November 7, 2009.

2. Edith Iglauer, *Seven Stones: A Portrait of Arthur Erickson, Architect* (Vancouver: Museum of Anthropology, University of British Columbia, 1972), 116.

3. Audrey Hawthorn, *A Labour of Love: The Making of the Museum of Anthropology, UBC, The First Three Decades, 1947–76* (Vancouver: UBC, Museum of Anthropology, 1993), 78–81.

4. The Haida Heritage Centre includes a magnificent 53,000-square-foot cedar multicomplex consisting of five contemporary monumental timber longhouses. It houses the expanded Haida Gwaii Museum, additional temporary exhibition space, two meeting rooms/classrooms, a Performing House, Canoe House, Bill Reid Teaching Centre, the Carving Shed, a gift shop, and a small restaurant/café. The official Grand Opening Ceremony took place on August 23, 2008. See Haida Heritage Centre, "The Centre," available at http://www.haidaheritagecentre.com/.

5. Communication by Bill McLennon during interview on November 7, 2009.

6. Ibid.

7. Ibid.

8. Bill Reid, formerly a popular presenter on Canadian national radio, discovered his Indigenous roots as an adult and gave up his career in broadcasting to become a craftsman and artist.

9. Also known as the "Black Canoe," the original bronze cast of 1991 is located in front of the Canadian Embassy in Washington, DC. There are two castings of the sculpture, the black casting and the green casting.

10. Royal Architectural Institute of Canada, "*Prix du XXe siècle* 2011 Recipient: the Museum of Anthropology at UBC," http://www.raic.org/honours_and_awards/awards_xxe/2011 /museum_e.htm (link no longer active, accessed July 20, 2012).

22

Museum of New Zealand Te Papa Tongarewa, Wellington, New Zealand

Location: 55 Cable Street, Wellington, New Zealand
Date: 1994–1998
Client: Museum of New Zealand Te Papa Tongarewa
Architect: Jasmax Architects (principal architect Ivan Mercep)
Landscape Architect: Boffa Miskell
Contractor: Fletcher Construction
Structural Engineer: Holmes Consulting Group
Project Manager: Carson Group
Cost: approximately $187 million

The design for the Museum of New Zealand Te Papa Tongarewa (known as "Te Papa") in Wellington gave material form to a national policy of biculturalism following renewed commitment to this policy through the 1975 Treaty of Waitangi Act.[1] Framed as a "partnership between two founding peoples, neither of whom are superior but are autonomous over their respective spheres," the model is distinctive, differentiating New Zealand from Australia where Aboriginal groups remain minorities.[2] Three institutions—Museum of New Zealand Te Papa Tongarewa, Tairawhiti Museum, and Whanganui Regional Museum—adopted new collaborative governance strategies thereafter, with Te Papa replacing the former National Art Gallery and Dominion Museum in Wellington.[3]

Changes in national governance followed, whereby the consultation process between the client group and the architect broadened to include a national constituency of iwi (Māori tribes). It informed the collaborative model implemented at Te Papa. The building served as a precedent for institutional best practice recognizing "the right of Māori to determine the ways in which their treasures . . . are managed and interpreted."[4]

BACKGROUND

The mandate for the museum commission was to represent "the bicultural nature of the country . . . and provide the means for each [group] to contribute effectively to a statement of the nation's identity."[5] The initial proposition of three large independent museums was replaced with a proposal for a single museum in 1989. This was conceived according to five corporate principles: biculturalism, scholarship and Māori knowledge and learning, customer focus, being commercially positive, and being both "an entryway to New Zealand" and "a catalyst for New Zealanders to reflect on their cultural identity and natural heritage."[6] Three Māori, one Pacific Islander, and three *Pākehā* (or non-Indigenous New Zealanders) were appointed to the Project Development Team in 1985. Māori were included in staffing and management as a feature of the bicultural partnership. Cheryll Sotheran was appointed *kaihautu* (a title meaning *steersman* in Māori) alongside CEO Cliff Whiting in 1995.[7] A *marae* (communal or sacred place) was designed and integrated with the permanent structure, and Māori treasures were included as part of the shared national heritage.[8]

PROJECT DESCRIPTION

The design commission for Te Papa was won in an international competition by local practice Jasmax Architects, led by Ivan Mercep. Mercep's philosophy of community consultation, developed from the 1980s, informed his approach to the building, as did the separation of customary from contemporary spaces.[9] The architect was involved in designs for several *marae*.[10] The largest among these was the national museum (Plate 20). The design articulated a threefold distinction between the land, the Māori, and settlers in its spatial organization. It was conceived as a free museum required to fund 25 percent of operating costs, and included thirty-six thousand square meters of public floor space.[11] It would take a further nine years to realize the project.

The site was reclaimed from the Wellington waterfront and had spectacular views to the ocean, but it needed to be built on 150 shock absorbers to protect against seismic activity.[12] The 14,500 gray and yellow stone panels used to clad the building surface reinforced its urban institutional presence, while New Zealand–grown timbers naturalized its interior finishes (including mataī for wall panels, *Eucalyptus pilularis* for some of the floors, macrocarpa for ceilings, tawa for handrails, and rewarewa for elevator linings).[13]

Plate 20.   Museum of New Zealand Te Papa Tongarewa, Wellington, New Zealand, exterior view. Photo by Simon Devitt, courtesy Jasmax Architects.

Figure 22.1. Museum of New Zealand Te Papa Tongarewa, interior. Photo by Simon Devitt, courtesy Jasmax Architects.

The three key thematic distinctions were delineated by the Project Development Board as follows: *Paptuanuku*, representing the earth on which we live, which focused on the natural environment of Aotearoa-New Zealand; *Tangata Whenua*, representing those who belong to the land by right of first discovery, a section focusing on the culture, history, science, society, and technology of the Māori and their relationship with the land; and *Tangata Tiriti*, representing those who belong to the land by right of treaty, a section devoted to the subsequent settlers and migrants and their culture, science, and technology.[14] The partnership anticipated by the original 1840 Waitangi Treaty—New Zealand's founding treaty between Māori and Pākehā—underscored the orientation of the building's major spaces. Its seaward, north-facing Māori face designed for the *marae* is named Rongomaraeroa, and it is placed there as a welcome to visitors across the ocean; the south facing Pākehā (European face) was turned toward the colonial grid, the pattern of which influenced the placement of exhibits on that side.[15]

A wedge-shaped, high-ceilinged space was created between the Māori and Pākehā sections for *an exhibit on the Waitangi Treaty, titled Signs of a Nation or Ngā Tohu Kotahitanga.* The words of the original treaty are inscribed on an eight-meter sheet of glass in this space. English and Māori versions are reproduced on the two walls of the gallery. *Taonga*, cultural treasures belonging to the Māori chiefs who signed the treaty (namely, the Pūmuka, Mohi Tāwhai, Patuone, and Wāka Nene) are also exhibited. Alongside these precious and political objects, opinions on the treaty of ordinary New Zealanders are conveyed through audio recordings, activated as visitors weave through a cluster of poles installed in the space.[16]

The duality expressed in the building design evokes both natural and urban and Māori and Pākehā, and reflects those tensions within New Zealand history and landscape tradition as an acknowledged and dynamic social reality. At Te Papa, the juxtaposition of these two traditions informs the architectural orientation, the spatial planning, and the exhibition content. *Signs of a Nation (Ngā Tohu Kotahitanga)* is flanked to the left side by *Mana Whenua*, an effort at conveying Māori sociocultural heterogeneity by combining more permanent displays with rotating tribal exhibits.[17] To the right of the treaty gallery, the display *Passports* represents British and other immigrant experiences. The museum simultaneously becomes a *waharoa* or gateway, a welcoming point and a threshold where these diverse cultures meet. Physical *waharoa* designed to honor "the various peoples who have settled in New Zealand" are located on the *marae* and in the building's Wellington Foyer.[18] These settlers include "the great Māori ancestor Kupe, and the many ocean-going people who followed him across the Pacific"; "Abel Tasman, James Cook, and other European navigators"; and "other ethnic groups who subsequently arrived here."[19] The themes of travel, ocean, and island geographies underscore these persistent dualities reconstituting all New Zealanders as visitors or travelers.

RECEPTION

Te Papa offers an example of consumer-led, entertainment-centered museology that combines government policy, audience expectations, and a highly desirable ethical shift toward bicultural values. The Museum was pivotal in the transformation of Wellington into a tourist, leisure, and working destination as part of what Lorna Kaino describes as a "creative industry."[20] Kaino observes that by 2001, 48 percent of all New Zealanders had visited the Museum and that Te Papa had the highest visitation rate in Australasia (1.34 million) in 2002 to 2003.[21] The postmodern character of the Museum, the accessibility of the exhibits, and their interpretive and interactive character are among the attributes deemed responsible for this popularity.

However, the reinvention of the Museum in a populist guise attracted much debate and criticism both prior and subsequent to its opening.[22] Nevertheless, as a consumption-driven model, Te Papa has proved to be a success both in marketing itself as a site of cultural production and in augmenting the reputation of its host city. The Museum also works hard to establish institutional contacts with schools, universities, and other museums, thus enriching and expanding its audience. The policy of biculturalism has likewise created a more inclusive model of governance that extends to employing Māori, Pacific Islander, and other minorities at the reception and galleries, thereby increasing social contact and training creative workers.

NOTES

1. Thanks to the following for interviews conducted in 2011 by Janet McGaw: Arapata Hakiwai, Māori Scholar at Te Papa; Rhonda Paku, Senior Māori curator at Te Papa; Ivan Mercep, architect at Jasmax Architects; Ian Wedde, a New Zealand novelist and cultural commentator and one of five involved in the team that developed the Museum conceptually and curatorially. Thanks also to the architects for the provision of data. See David Butts, "Māori and Museums: The Politics of Indigenous Recognition," in *Museums, Society, Inequality*, ed. Richard Sandell (London and New York: Routledge, 2002), 225; and Nigel Cook and John Hunt, "Nationalistic Expression," *Architecture New Zealand* (November/December 1990): 21.

2. Butts, "Māori and Museums," 225, in reference to Augie Fleras, "Politicizing Identity: Ethno-Politics in White Settler Dominions," in *Indigenising Peoples' Rights in Australia, Canada and New Zealand*, ed. Paul Havemann (Auckland: Oxford University Press, 1999), 207.

3. Butts, "Māori and Museums," 225.

4. Ibid., 227.

5. Design Brief for Te Papa Tongarewa 1989 as cited in Laura Hourston, *Museum Builders II* (Hoboken, NJ: Wiley Academy, 2004), 38.

6. Butts, "Māori and Museums," 230.

7. Ann French, "Setting Standards: Te Papa Kaihautu,"*Architecture New Zealand* (February 1998): 72.

8. Ibid.

9. Deidre Brown, "Respecting Experience," in *Jasmax*, ed. Stephen Stratford (Auckland: New Zealand Architectural Publications Trust, 2007), 171.

10. Brown, "Respecting Experience," 171.

11. William Tramposch, "Te Papa: An Invitation for Redefinition," *Museum International* 50, no. 3 (1998): 28–32. See also Te Papa Tongarewa, "Our Building," available at http://www.tepapa.govt.nz/aboutus/pages/ourbuilding.aspx#design.

12. According to the Museum's website, the 2.3019 hectares on which it stands is owned by the museum, while a 5,689 square-meter block including access ways is leased.

13. Te Papa Tongarewa, "Our Building."

14. Senka Bozic-Vrbancic, "One Nation, Two Peoples, Many Cultures: Exhibiting Identity at Te Papa Tongerewa," *Journal of the Polynesian Society* 112, no. 3 (2003): 297.

15. Te Papa Tongarewa, "Our Building."

16. Ibid.

17. Bozic-Vrbancic, "One Nation, Two Peoples," 298–99.

18. Te Papa Tongarewa, "Our Building."

19. Te Papa Museum website.

20. Lorna Kaino, "What Difference Does a Museum Make? Te Papa's Contribution to the New Zealand Economy," *Media International Australia*, no. 117 (November 2005): 31–42. Kaino defines "creative industries" after the Creative Industries Mapping Document, prepared by the United Kingdom Department of Culture, Media and Sport in 1998, as "those activities which have their origin in individual creativity, skill and talent and which have the potential for wealth and job creation through the generation and exploitation of intellectual property" (as cited in Terry Flew, "Beyond Ad-Hockery: Defining Creative Industries," paper presented at the Second International Conference on Cultural Policy Research, Wellington, 2002, 181–92).

21. Kaino, "What Difference Does a Museum Make?" 33.

22. Initially there was a debate under the incumbent Prime Minister Helen Clark as to whether Te Papa should be built in Auckland or Wellington. It eventually opened under the National Government led by Jenny Shipley.

23

Musgrave Park, South Brisbane, Queensland, Australia[1]

Location: 121 Cordelia Street, South Brisbane, Queensland
Date: proposed 1998–2005 (unrealized)
Client: Musgrave Park Community Centre and Arts Queensland
Council: Brisbane City Council
Architect: Richard Kirk Architect and Innovarchi Architects
Landscape Architect: Splat
Structural and Civil Engineers: Cardno
Area: 2,500m²

Musgrave Park, a 9.3-hectare parcel of parkland bordered by Russell, Cordelia, Vulture, and Edmondstone streets in South Brisbane and situated within the Kurilpa region of the city, is an important meeting point for the Aboriginal community. Gazetted as the "South Brisbane Recreation Reserve" in 1865, the area is believed to have been traditionally used prior to colonization as a place of neutral gathering for local Aboriginal communities.[2] Its history is marked by demographic shifts indicative of the colonial history of South Brisbane, including the forced removal of Aboriginal populations by the Aboriginals Protection Act of 1897, the colonial conversion of the park into a recreational and horticultural venue, and its use for cosmopolitan events following the influx of Mediterranean migrants after World War II. The Jagera Community Arts Resource Centre was established at the former Bowls Club clubhouse in 1988 and was used by Aboriginal residents returning and reconnecting with their communities in the city.

The story of the Musgrave Park Cultural Centre illustrates the multiple ways in which public space is claimed, used, and imagined by Aboriginal communities, and what is at stake in the incorporation of these processes into mainstream cultural production. The park has at least since colonization been an important place for informal gathering and protest by the Aboriginal community, predicated on social activities rather than by civic design. During the Brisbane Commonwealth Games in 1982, Aborigines and Torres Strait Islanders established a camp in Musgrave Park as part of a broad agenda of protests and political actions.[3] With Musgrave Park becoming the focal point, a stage and speakers were erected.[4] Celebrations for the bicentenary of the landing of the First Fleet and fear of gentrification due to the proximate

Figure 23.1.   Musgrave Park Cultural Centre's temporary home in the historic Jagera Arts Centre Community Hall is marked with graffiti on an embankment on Cordelia Street. Photo by Janet McGaw 2013.

siting of the World Expo '88 site invited further public protests. The Park was used for both Aboriginal and non-Aboriginal protests.

Today, Musgrave Park is the location of the Panyiri Greek Festival, as well as serving as the NAIDOC Week gathering space for the Aboriginal communities of Brisbane.[5] The design for a cultural center in the Park, while strengthening the Indigenous claim on the space, invariably formalizes this more spontaneous, unscripted sociality. Tensions surrounding the use of the Park and the list of prohibited activities suggest that formal claims have become essential. Such claims enable and legitimize continued Indigenous occupation of urban places.

BACKGROUND

The first formal proposal for a cultural center in Musgrave Park dates back to 1985.[6] According to Aboriginal architectural graduate Carroll Go-Sam, this date coincides closely with assertions that Musgrave Park was a sacred site.[7] Anthony Brown states that European settlers had cleared sacred sites known as Bora rings from the Kurilpa region, and so Aborigines established a makeshift Bora ring in Musgrave Park at that time.[8] However, Go-Sam suggests that this reference can be traced to a European researcher named Kerkhove, and despite its uncertain origin has become "embedded into urban place mythology," and that the number of claimed sacred sites in the area had increased by 2008 to number between two and three sacred men's sites.[9] Go-Sam observes that such invented traditions are reflective of the "disempowered position occupied by minority groups outside mainstream power and economic structures."[10] It demonstrates both the need for and desire to substantiate cultural claims in terms recognized by the white mainstream.

The timeline of the history of the cultural center project is summarized on the Musgrave Park Cultural Center's website as follows.[11] Discussion of the Centre was initiated in the 1960s, and individual advocates including Pat Murdoch, former administrator for the Musgrave Park Aboriginal Corporation, and Selwyn Johnson Senior, former chairperson of the Musgrave Park Cultural Centre, Inc., played significant roles. Murdoch made the first formal proposal in 1985, and the Brisbane City Council recommended it in 1988. Community consultations followed between 1990 and 1994, led by the Musgrave Park Aboriginal Corporation and later by the Council as part of a conservation study into the Park's future use. This study supported the development of the Centre, and a lease was granted by the Council, however the state government refused to endorse the decision. In 1996, the Musgrave Park Cultural Centre Steering Committee was established as a subcommittee of the Musgrave Park Aboriginal Corporation. Musgrave Park Cultural Centre, Inc., was incorporated in 1997. The difficulties faced in implementing the proposal were discussed at the National Community Cultural Development Conference that same year, and the proposal won community support.

The allocation of land for the cultural center was delayed until 1998 when the southeastern section of the park, including the tennis courts and Jagera Centre, was designated for Indigenous purposes. The land was to be held in trust by the Brisbane City Council and leased out to Musgrave Park Cultural Centre, Inc. Between 1999 and 2002, the project seemed to gather momentum. The site was surveyed, leases were signed, and architects were selected for the project. Architectural consultant Carroll Go-Sam was retained to provide support for the development proposal for Musgrave Park Cultural Centre. The plan and tender process commenced in 2004 with a view to completion by 2005, envisioned as part of Arts Queensland's Millennium Arts precinct.

PROJECT DESCRIPTION

Go-Sam has detailed the difficult history of the cultural center project between 1999 and 2005.[12] Originally the center was imagined as a mixed-use Aboriginal facility incorporating gallery space, a performances space, café, retail, a keeping place, and a meeting place. A design proposed by Brisbane-based Richard Kirk Architect and Sydney-based firm Innovarchi Architects was developed between 1999 and 2004. This design differed greatly from contemporaneous architectural trends for iconic buildings.[13] It deliberately rejected an overt architectural expression of identity through the incorporation of symbolic cultural elements, which was typical of Indigenous cultural facilities at that time.[14] In a restrained response, with only a solitary flagpole flying the Aboriginal flag, the unbuilt design did not reference Aboriginal culture and appeared "to passively reinforce the building's neutral stance on identity ideology," Go-Sam has argued.[15] The design raised the much-debated topic on what kind of architecture is suited to metropolitan Indigenous facilities.

The Musgrave Park Cultural Centre was subsequently absorbed into the $208.4 million Millennium Arts Project, which saw the development of an impressive cultural precinct that included the Judith Wright Centre of Contemporary Arts, the Queensland Gallery of Modern Art, and the State Library of Queensland Redevelopment (also known as the Millennium Library Project).[16] The Musgrave Park brief sat within this expanded metropolitan civic cultural program. The design included a covered open area, exhibition space, flexible

Figure 23.2. Musgrave Park, design by Richard Kirk Architect and Innovarchi Architects. Photo courtesy Richard Kirk Architect.

meeting rooms, outdoor amphitheatre, and the office rooms expected of a cultural facility. It incorporated ecologically sustainable design principles that were by then mainstream in institutional architectural projects.[17] The architects proposed an aesthetic that was "overtly contemporary and urbane."[18]

Underlying these representational debates were other more pressing questions regarding the role of a cultural center in translating place associations into built form. The history of Musgrave Park, and the very different perceptions of the place held by Indigenous and non-Indigenous communities, may be partly responsible for the various difficulties encountered. For example, the meaning of the park for the Indigenous community is shaped through particular forms of occupation over the decades, and Musgrave Park has an established significance as both a meeting and gathering place. Gloria Beckett, interviewed by Aird, recalls that Musgrave Park in the 1960s was an important social meeting place in Brisbane, where social networks and connections were formed. According to Beckett, "(a)ll us Murris would get together and all yarn and just be together."[19] She describes a typical journey through the area, "from Musgrave Park to Manhattan Walk to Manhattan Hotel, to the Pie Man, back to the Adelaide Hotel, to the Ship Inn, to the Palace Hotel and to OPAL House and then back over to Musgrave Park, then back to where a few Murris lived in flats at South Brisbane."[20]

The hotels in South Brisbane are points of social contact but are also linked to the prevalence of alcoholism in the community. Phyllis Coolwell, also interviewed by Aird, recalls the presence of a community of Aboriginal men who occupied the park in 1948: "They would all be there—old Snowy Long, and all them old fellas, and Old Uncle Jack Oliver, he was another returned soldier."[21] In Phyllis's recollections of her experience of the park as a teenager, the consumption of alcohol is acknowledged but not overt: "(t)hey would all be there of a Sunday morning sitting in Musgrave, they might have had a coffee bottle full of rum, but we never saw no grog."[22] Pastor Brady, a reformed alcoholic, acquired a reputation as the "Punching Parson" due to his ability to handle homeless alcoholics frequenting Musgrave Park.[23] Go-Sam suggests that "the sustained presence of 'parkies' or Aboriginal public place-dwellers engaging in drinking undermines any positive narrative of place attachment, by their resistance to alcohol consumption laws."[24] The gentrification of white public space and laws prohibiting alcohol consumption in public spaces produces a parallel discourse on parkies, poverty, and homelessness. These characterizations are frequently racialized and associated with violence.

According to Go-Sam, the contested nature of the place of Musgrave Park has contributed to the difficulties faced by the Musgrave Park Cultural Centre project, which has been subject to "heightened and exaggerated claims about its purpose and intent to those within and outside its Aboriginal constituency."[25] Go-Sam relates that a funding shortfall scuttled the project in part due to a protracted native title claim as well as escalating construction and infrastructure costs. She observes that ultimately the project fell outside of the objectives of the Millennium Arts Project, and was excluded from funding adjustments.[26]

RECEPTION

As at 2013, the Musgrave Park Cultural Centre is located within the Jagera Arts Centre, a heritage-listed hall adjacent to Musgrave Park. Markwell Consulting, an Aboriginal owned and operated cultural consultancy, is currently engaged by Arts Queensland to review the planning work originally undertaken between 1997 and 2005.[27]

In the meantime, the park continues to function as a significant center for Aboriginal gathering and protest. A Sovereign Tent Embassy was established at Musgrave Park and remained there for a two-month period in response to the fortieth anniversary of the Aboriginal Tent Embassy in Canberra (see chapter 1).[28] This camp was forcibly evicted from the park on May 16, 2012, and was subsequently reestablished at a different location within the park close to the Jagera Arts Hall.[29] A meeting between Lord Mayor Graham Quirk and Brisbane's Indigenous leaders on May 22, 2012, to discuss the future of the camp was used as an opportunity to open a new public discussion around the Musgrave Park Cultural Centre proposal.[30] However, state funding for the project was withdrawn in September 2013.[31]

NOTES

1. Published previously as "Case Study 9: Musgrave Park Cultural Centre, Brisbane," in Janet McGaw and Anoma Pieris, *Assembling the Centre: Architecture for Indigenous Cultures, Australia and Beyond* (Abingdon and New York: Routledge, 2015), 135–39.

2. Musgrave Park, "Brisbane City Council Heritage Citation," available at http://workersbushtele graph.com.au/2013/02/18/musgrave-park-heritage-register/. Thanks to Scott Anderson, chairman and event manager at Musgrave Park Family Fun Day, for seeking permission from the Elders to publish this account.

3. Michael Aird, *Brisbane Blacks* (Southport, Queensland: Keeaira Press, 2001), 116.

4. Aird, *Brisbane Blacks*, 116.

5. Ibid., 92. *NAIDOC* is the acronym of *National Aborigines and Islanders Day Observance Committee*.

6. Musgrave Park Cultural Centre, Inc., "History of the Musgrave Park Cultural Centre," available at http://www.musgravepark.org.au/14.html.

7. Carroll Go-Sam, "Fabricating Blackness: Aboriginal Identity Constructs in the Production and Authorisation of Architecture," in Antony Moulis and Deborah van der Plaat, eds., *SAHANZ 2011: Audience–XXVIIIth International Conference of the Society of Architectural Historians, Australia and New Zealand*, proceedings of the conference held in Brisbane from July 7–10, 2011, 17.

8. Anthony Brown, "The History of Musgrave Park," *Green Left Weekly*, no. 212 (November 21, 1995) available at http://www.greenleft.org.au/node/10288; and Anthony Brown, "The Struggle for Musgrave Park," *Green Left Weekly*, no. 212 (November 21, 1995) available at http://www.greenleft.org.au/node/10308.

9. Go-Sam, "Fabricating Blackness," 16.

10. Ibid., 17.

11. Musgrave Park Cultural Centre, Inc., "History of the Musgrave Park Cultural Centre," available at http://www.musgravepark.org.au/.

12. Go-Sam, "Fabricating Blackness," 3.

13. Ibid., 2–3.

14. Ibid., 3.

15. Ibid., 3.

16. Ibid., 7–8.

17. Richard Kirk Architect, "Musgrave Park Cultural Centre," available at http://www.richardkirkarchitect.com/en/projects/cultural-public/musgrave-park-cultural-centre.

18. Ibid.

19. Aird, *Brisbane Blacks*, 40.

20. Ibid., 40.

21. Ibid., 48.

22. Ibid., 48.

23. Ysola Best, "Brady, Donald (Don) (1927–1984)," *Australian Dictionary of Biography*, available at http://adb.anu.edu.au/biography/brady-donald-don-12246.

24. Go-Sam, "Fabricating Blackness," 17.

25. Ibid., 18.

26. Ibid., 17.

27. Markwell Consulting, "Musgrave Park Cultural Centre," available at http://www.markwellconsulting.com.au/musgrave.html#%60.

28. Amy Remeikis, "Pitching Camp for a Cultural Cause," *Sydney Morning Herald*, April 1, 2012.

29. Amy Simmons, "What Is the Brisbane Sovereign Embassy?" ABC News, available at http://www.abc.net.au/news/2012-05-18/what-is-the-brisbane-sovereign-embassy3f/4016942.

30. Tony Moore, "Musgrave Park Cultural Centre Hopes Revived," *Brisbane Times*, May 22, 2012.

31. Belinda Seeney, "State Backflip on Murri Multicultural Centre Funding Angers Community," *Courier Mail*, September 19, 2013.

24

National Centre of Indigenous Excellence, Redfern, New South Wales, Australia[1]

Location: 166–180 George Street, Redfern, Sydney, New South Wales
Date: 2006–2010
Client: Indigenous Land Corporation
Architects: Tonkin Zulaikha Greer Architects
Landscape Architects: 360 Degrees Landscape Architects
Heritage Architect: Tonkin Zulaikha Greer
Project Manager: Incoll Management
Structural/Civil Engineer: Simpson Design Associates
Builder: St. Hilliers
Construction Manager: Coffey Projects
Environmental Graphic Design: TZG Signage
Funding: Indigenous Land Council
Cost: approximately 28.8 million
NCIE Chief Executive Officer: Jason Glanville

The National Centre of Indigenous Excellence (NCIE) is part of a broader program for the redevelopment of the Redfern area, which reflects a shift toward the revitalization of the suburb in Sydney's inner south.[2] Beginning with a grant from the Whitlam Government in 1973 to purchase and renovate a group of terrace houses known as "The Block" and the creation of a cohesive community network around the Aboriginal Housing Corporation (AHC), Redfern has been the locus of two types of developmental tensions: the first, to protect and provide a safe environment for Aboriginal residents, and the second, to prevent their eviction via the predatory market forces of gentrification. Underlying these often conflicted aims is Redfern's past history of public dysfunction related to drugs and crime, its association with degraded social housing, and the historic marginalization of the Aboriginal community. Since the "Redfern Riots" of 2004—a protracted conflict between the Aboriginal community and local police—drew excessive media attention to the area, successive improvement projects have sought to gentrify the neighborhood, often to the dismay of long-time residents. The projects conceived by and for the Aboriginal community need to be evaluated within this historical trajectory as both advancing and resisting change.

They display strong urban characteristics and commitment to a civic precinct approach, indicative of the Aboriginal community's longevity in the area.

BACKGROUND

Recognized as the birthplace of the land and civil rights movement in Australia, Redfern is described by Dean as "simultaneously a space of timeless importance and of continual challenge and contest."[3] It remains an important exemplar of an urban place inscribed by Aboriginal displacement into the city during the recessions and industrial change of the 1930s, 1950s, and 1970s, and is indicative of the efforts to produce a coherent communal identity of traditional country.[4] Over the twentieth century, Redfern developed a reputation as a friendly center for an Aboriginal transient population seeking employment and inexpensive housing.[5] As such, it offers place-making strategies on a neighborhood scale within lands belonging to the Gadigal people of the Eora nation who were dispossessed by settler colonization. Over the years, Redfern has been subject to many changing public policies toward Aboriginal residents, who have responded by consolidating their rights in the face of governmental intervention. These claims have been both spatially and legally defended, developing in tandem with a broader civil rights discourse.

The Aboriginal civil rights movement flourished in Redfern during the 1960s and 1970s in the wake of the 1967 referendum, and on the back of the election of the socially progressive Whitlam Government, with its platform of improving relations between Aboriginal peoples and white Australia.[6] Urbanized members of the Stolen Generations were united with those coming from country New South Wales to seek work in Sydney. Redfern's hotels served as the meeting ground of a new generation of Aboriginal rights activists.[7] The Redfern Black Caucus erected the Tent Embassy in Canberra in 1972 (see chapter 1). This timeline of activism has been incorporated as an artwork on the glass doors to the NCIE EORA Fitness Centre by architects Tonkin Zulaikha Greer.

Although Redfern became a thriving community, living conditions were poor.[8] There was an undersupply of affordable housing, with reports of racial discrimination in the real estate market and poor nutrition in the community.[9] This situation reached a crisis point, with squatters taking refuge in the vacant houses of "The Block," an area bounded by Eveleigh, Caroline, Vine, and Louis streets in Redfern.

These spaces received disproportionate attention from the police.[10] The hotels in Redfern were progressively closed down in an effort to disrupt centers of activism.[11] Nevertheless, the push toward Aboriginal self-determination persisted through the establishment of self-determined social services within the Aboriginal community. Redfern became the locus over the years for numerous progressive Aboriginal organizations and services, beginning with the Aboriginal Legal Service. These services now include: the Aboriginal radio station 93.7 FM Koori Radio; the National Congress of Australia's First Peoples; Wyanga Aboriginal Community Aged Care and Cultural Services; Aboriginal Native Title Services; and the Aboriginal Medical Service. The creation of the Aboriginal Housing Service in the 1970s saw the first Aboriginal urban land rights secured in Australia.[12]

Redfern has also developed a reputation for creative arts resulting in new Aboriginal institutions. For example, the black theatre movement, which formerly occupied a warehouse in Redfern, is now housed in a multiuse development by the Indigenous Land Corporation (2005). It includes the Aboriginal Dance Theatre, Gadigal Information Services (including

Koori Radio), and the National Congress of Australia's First Peoples. Architects Tonkin Zu-laikha Greer (TGZ) designed the three-story former National Black Theatre Site.[13] They were additionally responsible for the design and restoration of the Carriageworks Arts complex on the edge of Redfern, which hosted the 2009 exhibition *There Goes the Neighbourhood*.[14] The exhibition focused on ideas of gentrification and urban politics in the Redfern area.

The success of these recent, place-making efforts needs to be contextualized in this lengthy and contested history of place-claims both within and by the Redfern Aboriginal and Tor-res Strait Islander community. The process of change has been arduous and frequently met with both internal and external hostility. They are indicative of the varied struggles for self-determination of marginal communities alongside market forces. Similarly, the architecture of the area has gradually shifted from surface alterations signaling Aboriginal ownership to extant buildings and to commissions for purpose-built facilities.

PROJECT DESCRIPTION

The development of the National Centre of Indigenous Excellence on the site of the former Redfern Primary School is an example of this process. The NCIE evolved from a land acqui-sition program of the Indigenous Land Corporation, and it is a prominent example of Ab-original stakeholder self-determination. It is an urban facility that provides social and cultural services and acts as a community hub (Plate 21).

Plate 21. National Centre of Indigenous Excellence, Redfern, New South Wales, Australia, en-trance and street façade. Photo by Brett Boardman, courtesy Tonkin Zulaikha Greer Architects.

The NCIE is one of several prominent commissions proposed for Redfern's revitalization, including the Pemulwy Project, a redevelopment of "The Block."[15] This project includes sixty-two affordable housing units and a forty-two-unit student facility to be managed by the AHC, a gymnasium, a childcare facility, a community gallery, and a public meeting place. The Redfern Park and Oval Upgrade is redeveloping a site well known as a gathering point for Aboriginal people and supporters, including during the 1988 "Survival Day" rally that protested Australia's bicentennial celebration of the arrival of the First Fleet. Redfern Park was the venue for Prime Minister Paul Keating's 1992 Redfern Address, which formally acknowledged the history of the Stolen Generations and adopted the language of reconciliation.[16]

Developed on the land and property of the former Redfern Primary School, the NCIE includes a sports complex with a heated swimming pool, gymnasium, basketball stadium, oval, outdoor basketball court, outdoor gymnasium, accommodation, conference facilities, and a digital innovation center. On its grounds are the Tribal Warrior Association, AIME (Australian Indigenous Mentoring Experience), National Indigenous Sporting Chance Academy, and Exodus Tutorial Centre.[17] The Indigenous Land Corporation envisioned the Centre in 2006 as a National Indigenous Development Centre.[18] In 2009, it was named the National Centre of Indigenous Excellence under CEO Jason Glanville. The NCIE's stated aim is to build "capabilities and creates opportunities by delivering life-changing programs and promoting progressive thought leadership through its enterprises and facilities."[19] Leadership and excellence are its foundational values. Since its opening, over twenty thousand Aboriginal and Torres Strait Islander people have participated in its programs.

In addition to providing programs and services for Aboriginal peoples, an important function of the NCIE is in influencing the relationship of Indigenous and non-Indigenous Australians in the community through the provision of common facilities and services. Among twenty or more programs run by the Centre are those geared toward employment and training, many targeting schoolchildren and youth. While many of these programs make use of the sporting facilities, others include media and digital storytelling, lifestyle innovation, and conferences. The EORA Campus is geared to house visiting groups who can participate in extended programs.

The Indigenous Land Corporation purchased the primary school site and commenced the development of the project in 2006, engaging the architectural practice TZG. The site

Figure 24.1. National Centre of Indigenous Excellence, sports field. Photo by Brett Boardman, courtesy Tonkin Zulaikha Greer Architects.

included a group of heritage-listed buildings dating from 1958. Both these and vacant areas on the site were integrated and developed into the NCIE plan through strategies for their adaptive reuse focused on several major activities. A full heritage assessment and impact study was followed by extensive consultation involving a number of stakeholders.[20] The proposed brief was for "a multi-use residential, training and education facility catering for both the local community and rural interstate groups." The design needed to satisfy the NCIE's objectives to facilitate programs for local and national Indigenous youth, in pathways of arts and culture, health and wellness, learning and innovation, and sport and recreation. This ambitious project envisioned an Indigenous civic center and urban campus organized around welcoming outdoor spaces, contained within secure boundaries given the NCIE's duty of care toward its young clientèle.

The EORA Campus was created through the refurbishment of three of the four heritage-listed school buildings. These were developed as dormitory accommodation for up to 120 people, in anticipation of visiting educational and sporting groups from the country or interstate. This facility included sleeping, dining, and recreation areas and a football training field. The EORA Fitness and EORA Aquatic Centre are contained in a three-story, multiuse complex with a naturally ventilated sports hall, gymnasium, weights room, kiosk, and adjacent twenty-five-meter indoor swimming pool open to the wider community. It provides an important point of interaction and an inner-city community service.

This strategy is reinforced by Gadigal House, the fourth former school building, which leases out office spaces in addition to housing the various administrative facilities. The Exodus Foundation, an Indigenous educational group, is also housed in the complex. In addition to their sensitive treatment of heritage buildings, TZG have applied a simple palette of steel, glass, timber, and concrete, with the bold application of color to the façade, which playfully responds to the urban context.[21]

The NCIE project reflects the challenges facing Redfern, with its tradition as a gathering place for the Aboriginal and Torres Strait Islander Community, as it transitions to meet the demands of the escalating property market. TZG advances an ideal of "urban pleasures," which is central to their interpretation of urbanity.[22] While achievable and achieved in many of its excellent civic projects, the architects have skillfully manipulated the extensive boundaries around the site to soften their public interface. The public domain is instead internalized. Local landscape architecture firm 360 Degrees has converted the former school playground into a multilevel public forum across the changing levels of the site.[23] A mix of asphalt and a circle-patterned rubber softfall ground plane, designed to follow the graphic logo of the Centre, is applied across the site, sealing the environmentally degraded soil beneath it, while hardy bush tucker planting is introduced throughout. Central vistas draw us in a carefully choreographed movement through a series of individually secured facilities. The ubiquitous steel fences, hard building edges, and planter boxes are ingeniously deployed tactics of containment that maintain the urban sensibility of a highly protected place.

RECEPTION

The NCIE has received several awards, including the National Architecture Awards—National Commendation for Urban Design in 2011 and the Lloyd Rees Award for Urban Design and the Commendation for Public Architecture at the New South Wales Architecture Awards in 2011.

NOTES

1. Published previously as "Case Study 13: Redfern and the National Centre for Indigenous Excellence," in Janet McGaw and Anoma Pieris, *Assembling the Centre: Architecture for Indigenous Cultures, Australia and Beyond* (Abingdon and New York: Routledge, 2015), 189–95. Fiona Johnson researched and drafted some of the content on Redfern and the NCIE, which is referred to in this chapter.

2. Thanks to the National Centre of Indigenous Excellence for comments on this text in February 2014. The design team at TZG included Peter Tonkin, Bettina Siegmund, Jeremy Hughes, Julie Mackenzie, Roger O'Sullivan, Elizabeth Muir, Vanessa Van Schalkwyk, Wolfgang Ripberger, Christian Williams, Tamara Frangelli, Regina Meyer, Brian Zulaikha, Paul Rolfe, Toby Ware, Simon Rochowski, Julin Ang, Antonia Bromhead, Ruth Leiminer, and Ben Daly. Representatives of NCIE include Divisional Manager, Ashley Martens; Project Manager, Richard Larkins; and Client Representative, Kate Alderton. Representatives of ILC include: David Galvin, CEO, and David Baffsky, Board Member.

3. Bec Dean, "Where Goes the Neighbourhood?" in *There Goes the Neighbourhood: Redfern and the Politics of Urban Space*, eds. Zanny Begg and Keg De Souza (Sydney: Breakdown Press, 2009), 8–9.

4. Melinda Hinkson, *Aboriginal Sydney: A Guide to Important Places of the Past and Present* (Canberra: Aboriginal Studies Press, 2001), 74.

5. Hinkson, *Aboriginal Sydney*, 74.

6. Ibid., 78.

7. Gary Foley, "Black Power in Redfern," in Begg and De Souza, eds., *There Goes the Neighbourhood*, 5. The term *Stolen Generations* refers to Aboriginal and Torres Strait Islander children who were forcibly removed from their families under Acts of Parliament from 1869 to 1969.

8. Hinkson, *Aboriginal Sydney*, 78.

9. Ibid., 78.

10. Ibid., 77.

11. Ibid., 77.

12. Angela Pitts, "Dreaming the Block," *Architecture Australia* 97, no. 5 (September/October 2008): 105.

13. Tonkin Zulaikha Greer Architects, "Black Theatre Site," available at http://www.tzg.com.au/projects/black-theatre-site.

14. Begg and De Souza, eds., *There Goes the Neighbourhood*.

15. Developed through the combined efforts of the AHC, Aboriginal architect Dillion Kombumerri of the NSW State Government Architect's Office, and Cracknell and Lonergan Architects (2004).

16. Hinkson, *Aboriginal Sydney*, 75. Designed by landscape architects Spackman Mossop Michaels.

17. National Centre of Indigenous Excellence, "Our Story," available at http://ncie.org.au/home/our-impact#-/home/our-story.

18. Ibid.

19. Ibid.

20. Tonkin Zulaikha Greer Architects, "National Centre of Indigenous Excellence," available at http://www.tzg.com.au/projects/ncie-redfern.

21. Australian Institute of Architects, "2011 NSW Architecture Awards: Jury Citations 1–Public Architecture," available at http://www.architecture.com.au/i-cms?page=15800.

22. Tonkin Zulaikha Greer Architects, "The TZG Office: Atmosphere and Urbanity," available at http://www.tzg.com.au/about/.

23. Mark Tyrrell, "National Centre for Indigenous Excellence," *Landscape Architecture Australia* 127 (August 2010): 42–46, available at http://architectureau.com/articles/national-centre-for-indigenous-excellence/.

25

National Museum of the American Indian, New York and Washington, DC, and Cultural Resources Center, Maryland, United States of America

NMAI NEW YORK

Location: Alexander Hamilton Custom House, Bowling Green, New York
Date: 1994
Refurbishment: Ehrenkrantz and Eckstut Architects, working with the Federal General Services Administration
Architect: Denis Kuhn
Area: 520,000 square feet
Cost: approximately $60 million

NMAI WASHINGTON, DC

Date: 2004
Location: National Mall, Washington, DC
Architect and Project Designer: Douglas Cardinal (Blackfoot), Ottawa, Canada
Design Architects: GBQC Architects of Philadelphia, and architect Johnpaul Jones (Cherokee/Choctaw)
Project Architects: Jones & Jones Architects and Landscape Architects Ltd., Seattle, and SmithGroup, Washington, DC, in association with Lou Weller (Caddo), the Native American Design Collaborative, and Polshek Partnership Architects, New York
Design Consultants: Ramona Sakiestewa (Hopi) and Donna House (Navajo/Oneida)
Landscape Architects: Jones & Jones Architects and Landscape Architects Ltd., Seattle and EDAW Inc. of Alexandria, Virginia
Construction: Clark Construction Company and Table Mountain Rancheria Enterprises, Inc.
Cost: approximately $199 million (plus $20 million for exhibits)

CULTURAL RESOURCE CENTER, MARYLAND

Location: Suitland, Maryland
Date: 1998–1999
Architectural and Engineering Services: Polshek Partnership of New York, Tobey + Davis of Virginia, and the Native American Design Collaborative
Area: 145,000 square feet

Indigenous museums in the United States are largely focused on collecting from within the continent rather than from a vast colonial empire, thus giving these museums a different orientation and purpose.[1] However, by identifying as "national" and seeking metropolitan visibility, they tend to compromise the distinctive politics of First Nations identity. Cultural identity is reproduced within accepted institutional frameworks in institutions such as national museums and through the renegotiation of representational practices.

The debate over representational practices takes place against a colonial history of private collections and their institutionalization during the early twentieth century, and the review of these practices following political pressure from the Red Power movement of the 1960s and 1970s.[2] The National Museum of the American Indian was the response to the need to accommodate the private collection of George Gustav Heye (1874–1957), the largest collection of Indigenous artifacts in the United States.[3] Heye, a wealthy engineer and financier, had previously housed his collection in a private facility known as the Research Branch in the Bronx, New York City. This location became financially unsustainable following the city's reorganization under Mayor Rudy Guiliani. As interest in the Heye collection dwindled, in 1989 a decision was made to relocate it, and over eight hundred thousand objects were transferred to the Smithsonian Institution.[4]

In 1988, the NMAI was established by legislation in the US Congress introduced by Senator Ben Nighthorse Campbell and congressman and senator Daniel Inouye. They insisted that Native Americans should hold more than half the seats on the NMAI's governing Board of Trustees.[5] The Smithsonian appointed a Southern Cheyenne, W. Richard West Jr., as founding director. The Museum's founding legislation stipulated that three institutions would comprise the Museum: the New York Wing, maintained to acknowledge the Museum's origins and significance for the Native American community in New York; the Washington Museum, built on the last available piece of site on the National Mall; and the Cultural Resource Center in Suitland, Maryland, where collections would be stored and cared for. Private funds would account for over half of the $219 million budget.[6] The relationship to Heye's colonial collection in New York was maintained via the New York wing.

NMAI NEW YORK

A part of the George Gustav Heye Collection is housed in the former Customs House, a spectacular work of architecture in the Beaux Arts aesthetic, designed by Cass Gilbert in 1907. The building is shared with the New York City Bankruptcy Court. The Museum entrance is flanked by four sculptures of seated female figures by Daniel Chester French, famed sculptor of Lincoln's statue for the Lincoln Memorial. The figures represent four continents: Europe reigns proudly in all her glory, an Indigenous warrior crouches at America's shoulder, a slave is attached to Asia, and Africa is asleep. A reflection of early twentieth-

Figure 25.1.   National Museum of the American Indian, Smithsonian Institution, New York City, exterior view. Photo by author, 2009, courtesy NMAI.

century racial prejudices, the sculptures provide an ironic preface to the resilience of native populations on display within. The building interior includes an elliptical rotunda painted with murals by New York painter Reginald Marsh. The murals depict vignettes of early explorers and of a ship entering New York Harbor, embodying the spirit of Manifest Destiny.[7] Inside the Museum, artifacts from the larger collection, since removed to Washington, are displayed in rotation through curated exhibitions.

The New York wing of the NMAI is an expression of an earlier era when Indigenous institutions were accommodated in culturally incongruous institutional buildings adapted temporarily for community use. It reminds us that clandestine occupations of imperial and colonial institutions were the only recourse for the Native American community in the past, and that purpose-built facilities are a recent phenomenon. Within sight of the Museum, further down the street, is the American Indian Community House, located on the second floor of an office building, which offers a place of refuge and a meeting place for many among the twenty-seven-thousand-strong American Indian population of New York.[8] The annual feast at the Community House has served as an inspiration for the restaurant at the new NMAI.

NMAI WASHINGTON, DC

The political decision to establish a National Museum of the American Indian under the umbrella of the Smithsonian Institute in Washington, DC, on the National Mall was passed by Congress in 1988. An arduous consultation process followed, with twenty-five to thirty consultations over three years, during which the Museum's team invited twenty-four representative community-curators to Washington.[9] The themes of "Our Universe," "Our Peoples," and

"Our Lives" were proposed and discussed dialogically with consultation on the objects, displays, and design strategies to be employed. A lengthy design brief titled "The Way of the People" compiled by the architectural firm Venturi Scott Brown Associates was completed in 1993 and documented this collaborative process.[10] The political discourse on genocide and colonization was accompanied with the discourse of "survivance (strategies for survival over time), self-determination and sovereignty."[11] The commission, completed in 2004, was awarded to a team comprising a number of Indigenous architects, including Blackfoot architect Douglas Cardinal, who designed Canada's Museum of Civilization in Ottawa. The team included two Indigenous women, ethno-botanist Donna House and artist Ramona Sakiestewa, and two Indigenous men, architects Douglas Cardinal and Johnpaul Jones.[12] Although Cardinal was replaced midway by the Native American Design Collaborative with Polshek Partnership (designers of Washington's Holocaust Memorial Museum), the building was essentially his design.

Project Description

Said to invoke the mesas of Arizona, shaped by the forces of wind and water, the building rises on a 4.25-acre site like a monolithic geological mass in an avenue of cubic boxes, confronting and reminding the US Capitol of its colonial responsibility (Plate 22). The landscaping around the building comprises rough grasses, indigenous plants, and various types of corn, a strategy repeated at Musée du Quai Branly in Paris and elsewhere. The landscaping evokes wetland, forest, meadow, and cropland habitats, and inserts 150 different species and 33,000 plants into the highly manicured metropolitan environs.[13]

Plate 22. National Museum of the American Indian, Smithsonian Institution, Washington, DC, exterior view. Photo by author, 2015, courtesy NMAI.

Figure 25.2. National Museum of the American Indian, Smithsonian Institution, Washington, DC, Potomac Atrium. Photo by author, courtesy NMAI.

The materiality of the building similarly contrasts with those around it. It is clad in Kasota limestone of a yellowish color, rough-hewn at the base and smoother on the building's surface. The circular/curvilinear forms and geomorphic associations, now increasingly identified with Cardinal's aesthetic, appear in stark contrast to the modernist boxes arraigned orthogonally along the Mall. The entrance faces eastward to the capital and leads the visitor into the internalized sky-lit Potomac space, a circular trading place around which shops and a restaurant are arranged. The circle is associated with gathering and ritual dances, and articulated using cardinal directions, planetary configurations, and the angles of solstices and equinoxes. The connection between the earth and the sky is maintained through an oculus over the Potomac, and the importation of forty "grandfather rocks" from New Brunswick. Attempts are made to anchor the design both through scientific discourses and geomantic traditions.[14]

The theme of circular forms pervades the interior exhibition spaces. The exhibits reproduce this organic circular theme of gathering and storytelling using circular partitioned cubicles. The exhibits are sensitive to Indigenous politics, and carefully balance histories of colonization and resistance. The continuing story of modern, urban Indigenous populations, racial mixing, and the contemporary criminalization of Indigenous peoples are examined. A highlight of the Museum is the restaurant Mitsitam, where the New York feast is reproduced in a hawker-style arrangement with communal eating.

CULTURAL RESOURCE CENTER, MARYLAND

The remainder of the Heye collection that feeds the rotating displays of the NMAI is housed in a separate "home for artifacts" at the Cultural Resource Center (CRC) in Suitland, Maryland, where the Smithsonian warehouses its vast collection. Unlike the storage spaces that surround it, the CRC is designed as a home for artifacts, with the training of Indigenous curators in mind. The website describes it as providing "state-of-the-art resources and facilities for the proper conservation, protection, handling, cataloguing, research, and study of the museum's collections, library holdings, and photo and paper archives."[15] The Centre is a hub for the NMAI's community services, educational outreach, technology and Web development, and information resources, and is the production center of the NMAI's public facilities. The design follows a nautilus shape, perceived as a form from nature, with landscape features that reinforce this association, including ritual spaces for blessing and dedicating artifacts (Plate 23). Light penetration and storage on the building's different levels are designed to respect the sacred hierarchy of living artifacts. When compared with the surrounding buildings that warehouse the Smithsonian's other collections, the CRC's strategy attempts to preserve the sacrality of Indigenous artifacts against their commodification for tourism elsewhere.

The NMAI has asserted its metropolitan presence by deploying a purpose-built facility designed in a distinctive geomorphic form. It serves multiple national and international audiences and links Indigenous communities globally. Still, the NMAI buildings offer a complicated response to the Indigenous community's need for political visibility by using an equivalent scale and mass to the institutions that surround it. The physical manifestation and concretization of a tradition that has always occupied the land minimally and respectfully exposes one of the main contradictions faced in responding to a commission for a metropolitan Indigenous center such as this one. Difficulties typically arise from the complexity of the brief, the diverse cosmologies of the peoples represented, and their varied materiality that cannot be given singular representation without resorting to cultural reductiveness.[16] There are

Plate 23.   National Museum of the American Indian, Smithsonian Institution (S16118), Cultural Resources Center, Maryland, aerial view. Photo by NMAI Photo Services.

also contradictory needs underlying the building's representation; namely, creating visibility with largely non-Aboriginal audiences while at the same time providing neglected Indigenous communities with a community facility and keeping place. The NMAI's target is its metropolitan audience of around four million annual visitors, 99 percent of whom are not Native American.[17] The scarcity of funds means that the essential collaborative research process that must precede design is underresourced or, as in the case of the NMAI, expended before the architect can begin design development.[18] Finally, the pedagogical objectives of such a metropolitan institution, however laudable, may reflect metropolitan and therefore non-Indigenous interests. The balance between these positions of self-determination and assimilation unsettle the certainties of museum practice.

Whereas the validity of the formal response is subjective and open to debate, the sociality conveyed by the contrived forms suggest a different dimension rooted in the Museum's dialogic origins. The NMAI intends to humanize the colonial institution through what was termed the "Fourth Museum"; namely, the outreach programs run for communities, students, and professionals. The NMAI also trains Indigenous curators so they might gain ownership over their resources, artifacts, and processes of care. Yet this training process also involves unavoidable levels of institutionalization, and the reliance on fixity and visibility in conferring cultural authority. The unique design of the Cultural Resource Center with its innovative approaches to collection and custodianship remains hidden away in suburban Maryland.

The NMAI also adopts established methods for disseminating its knowledge. The initial flurry of promotional literature has been replaced by academic publications, anthologies, and journals that cast a wider net. For example, anthologies produced in 2005 and 2006 on Indigenous museums elsewhere reposition the NMAI centrally in an intellectual Indigenous universe.[19] The Museum also publishes the *American Indian*, a quarterly magazine and publications on temporary exhibitions. Among the products on offer are DVDs documenting the inaugural procession of twenty-five thousand or more Native Americans advancing along the National Mall from the Washington Monument toward the Capitol Building. Celebrations and speeches at the Museum's opening are featured.[20] The claim made by this particular dynamic act of occupation, whereby Indigenous presence and ownership is inscribed within the capital, animates the more static claims of an institutional architecture.

RECEPTION

The architecture of the NMAI on the Washington Mall has been awarded a Leeds Silver rating. In 2000, the NMAI's Cultural Resources Center won the *Buildings Magazine* Construction Award in the category of New Public/Government Construction and an Award of Excellence in Commercial Architecture from the Northern Virginia Chapter of the American Institute of Architects.[21]

NOTES

1. Thanks to Duane Blue Spruce of NMAI, New York, and Justin Estoque of NMAI, Washington, DC, for interviews in November 2009. Thanks also to Tionna Moore for arranging these meetings, and to Lou Stancari, Tanya Thrasher, and Michael Pahn from the photo archives. Duane Blue Spruce, ed., *Spirit of a Native Place: Building the National Museum of the American Indian* (Washington, DC:

Smithsonian, National Museum of the American Indian, 2004); Ira Jacknis, "A New Thing?: The NMAI in Historical and Institutional Perspective," *American Indian Quarterly* 30, nos. 3 and 4 (Summer and Fall 2006): 529.

2. Ira Jacknis, "A New Thing?" 514–25.

3. Blue Spruce, *Spirit of a Native Place*.

4. James Lujan, "A Museum of the Indian, Not for the Indian," *American Indian Quarterly* 29, nos. 3 and 4 (Summer and Fall 2005): 511.

5. W. Richard West Jr., "As Long as We Keep Dancing: A Brief Personal History," in Blue Spruce, *Spirit of a Native Place*, 54.

6. The three biggest Indigenous donors were the Oneida of New York, the Mashantucket Pequot, and the Mohegan. Amanda Cobb, "Interview with W. Richard West, Director, National Museum of the American Indian," *American Indian Quarterly*, *American Indian Quarterly* 29, nos. 3 and 4 (Summer and Fall 2005): 534.

7. National Museum of the American Indian, "Architecture and History," available at http://nmai .si.edu/visit/newyork/architecture-history/#.

8. The American Indian Community House, *Community Bulletin* 24, no. 1 (Summer 2009).

9. Cobb, "Interview with W. Richard West," 526.

10. Interview with Justin Estoque of NMAI Washington, conducted on November 10, 2009.

11. Lisa King, "Speaking Sovereignty and Communicating Change: Rhetorical Sovereignty and the Inaugural Exhibits at the NMAI," *American Indian Quarterly* 35, no. 1 (Winter 2011): 75–103. *Survivance* is a term used by Native American author and scholar Gerald Vizenor and elaborated in his recent edited book, *Survivance: Narratives of Native Presence* (Lincoln and London: University of Nebraska Press, 2008).

12. Duane Blue Spruce, "Carved by Wind and Water," in Blue Spruce, *Spirit of a Native Place*, 67–69.

13. Duane Blue Spruce and Tanya Thrasher, eds., *The Land Has Memory* (Washington, DC: Smithsonian, National Museum of the American Indian, 2008).

14. Amanda Cobb, "The National Museum of the American Indian: Sharing the Gift," *American Indian Quarterly*, *American Indian Quarterly* 29, nos. 3 and 4 (Summer and Fall 2005): 369–71.

15. National Museum of the American Indian, "Cultural Resource Center," available at http://nmai .si.edu/explore/collections/crc/.

16. Thanks to Lisa Findley for an interview conducted at Berkeley on April 27, 2010.

17. Cobb, "Interview with W. Richard West," 522.

18. Interview with Lisa Findley conducted at Berkeley on April 27, 2010.

19. Karen Coody Cooper and Nicolasa I. Sandova, eds., *Living Homes for Cultural Expression: North American Native Perspectives on Creating Community Museums* (Washington, DC: Smithsonian Institution, 2006); National Museum of the American Indian, *The Native Universe and Museums in the Twenty-First Century: The Significance of the Museum of the American Indian* (Washington, DC: Smithsonian Institution, 2005).

20. Cobb, "Interview with W. Richard West," 532.

21. National Museum of the American Indian, "National Museum of the American Indian," available at http://www.nmai.si.edu/.

26

Needwonnee Walk, Melaleuca, Tasmania, Australia

Location: Melaleuca, Tasmania
Date: 2010–2011
Collaboration: Tasmanian Aboriginal Land and Sea Council and Parks Wildlife Service Tasmania
Project Manager: Michael Garner
Interpretation Consultant: Fiona Rice
Interpretation Advisors: Tony Brown, Kylie Dickson, and Peter Grant
Installation Artists: Verna Nichols, Leonie Dickson and Kylie Dickson, Anthony Dillon, Kye Langdon, Jamie Langdon, Sam Lennox, Sheldon Thomas, Jay-Dee Jackson, Sky Maynard, and Nathan Maynard
Graphic Design: Dixie Makro
Sign Production: Graham Saunders at Saunders Signs
Trackwork: Craig Saunders, Sam Lennox, Matthew Smith, Holger Brinker, Geoffrey Lea, Phil Duggan, Daral Peterson, Damion Smith, Anthony Dillon, Jamie Green, Chris Green, Tim Chappell, and Roger Ling
Advisors: Tony Brown, Kylie Dickson, John Dickson, Janet Fenton, Steve Gall, Colin Hughes, Qug King, Peter Mooney, Fiona Newson, Caleb Pedder, Ashley Rushton, Theresa Sainty
Funded: Australian Government Jobs Fund—Tasmanian Wilderness World Heritage Area Aboriginal Heritage Management Partnership
Cost: approximately $392,700

The result of a partnership between Tasmania Parks and Wildlife Service and the Tasmanian Aboriginal Land and Sea Council, the Needwonnee Walk in remote southwest Tasmania is located in the former homelands of the Needwonnee Aboriginal people.[1] There are no living descendants of the Needwonnee kinship group, whose country extended from Port Davey to New River Lagoon and inland to Bathurst Harbour. The Needwonnee were one of four bands of the South West nation, whose contemporary members comprise around eighty.[2] The Needwonnee's story helped the Tasmanian southwest wilderness area secure a World Heritage listing.[3] The site falls within the Tasmanian Wilderness World Heritage Area, first listed in 1982 to cover 15,800 square kilometers of temperate wilderness, and extended in

1989, 2010, 2012, and 2013.[4] The World Heritage Area has repeatedly been challenged by logging and mining concerns.

The interpretive walk is a retrospective effort by local Aboriginal groups to reconnect with Needwonnee history and tell their story.[5] The Needwonnee Walk revives the intangible heritage of a lost kinship group through contemporary creative art practices. The notion of a trail that is imaginatively derived from temporal spatial practices of storytelling is articulated by a series of ephemeral installations, which capture the fragility of the trace. Apart from an introductory panel and end panel, the remaining experience is purely sculptural and devoid of textual interpretation, demonstrating how Aboriginal practices might inform settler heritage strategies. Interpretation consultant Fiona Rice describes the value of using natural materials that will return to the landscape, and temporary structures that will need to be refurbished or reinterpreted as they deteriorate. She describes this ephemerality as "a fitting tribute to the Needwonnee people who lived a transient lifestyle with homes and tools that were mobile, not permanent."[6] The changing seasons add an additional dimension of temporality to the project. Yet the Walk is also a stark reminder of the genocide of Tasmanian Aborigines, and a vehicle through which displaced and dispossessed descendants of local communities may reunite and relearn past traditions. The project exemplifies a valuable approach whereby the departure from traditional museum practice prevents the pitfalls encountered in formalizing fragile histories.

BACKGROUND

The history of the Needwonnee, and indeed of Tasmania's Aboriginal inhabitants, is that of series of violent encounters with European colonists from 1804 to 1830. These include the Black War of 1824 to 1830 and the Black Line campaign of 1830, ordered by Lieutenant-Governor George Arthur and aimed at capturing and containing the Aboriginal population on island reservations. The resulting annihilation of a large part of the Tasmanian Aboriginal population opened up the land for European pastoralists. In contrast to Arthur's brutality, George Augustus Robinson is regarded more sympathetically due to his appointment in 1829 as a "Conciliator" who would lead the remaining two hundred Aboriginals to Wybalenna on Flinders Island from 1830 to 1834, where they were interned.[7] Those who were not located by Robinson were believed to have died from European diseases or to have gone into hiding.

These historic events and the extent of the Tasmanian genocide fostered a widely held belief that Tasmanian Aboriginal peoples were rendered extinct in the mid-nineteenth century. Since the 1970s, however, research by Patsy Cameron and others from the Tasmanian Aboriginal community have highlighted the histories of descendants of sealers and sailors who took Aboriginal wives.[8] Details of their island culture have provided counter histories of survival and created a resurgence of interest in the Tasmanian Aboriginal community, currently estimated at 19,625.[9]

Recreated against this history of dispossession and historical erasure, the Needwonnee project demonstrates how Tasmania's Aboriginal communities use creative art and place-making practices as potential means of cultural reparation. The stated purpose of the project was "to develop an Aboriginal interpretation loop walk at Melaleuca and to work towards establishing greater involvement of the Aboriginal community in management of the area."[10] Surveys and strategies developed during the late 1990s identified the Aboriginal heritage on site, tracing its cultural significance, creation stories, and interpretive themes.[11] Aboriginal organizations and government representatives visited the site at that time; however, it took a further ten years to produce an Interpretation Action Plan and procure funding. In 2010, a project team was established and a collaborative partnership forged between the Tasmanian Aboriginal Land and Sea Council and the Tasmanian Parks and Wildlife Service.

Once the site was selected and the track, viewing platforms, and interpretive nodes were determined, interpretive research was discussed with potential key stakeholders based on Robinson's journal and the 1997 Aboriginal Heritage Assessment. A complex Interpretive Site Plan identified the objectives, audience, context, values, and established the theme of "Sharing Our Story . . . Practicing our Traditions." Next, the interpretive media was selected, and installations, methods for engaging artists and Aboriginal community members, and the project's implementation and maintenance were determined. Opportunities for the ongoing participation of the Aboriginal community with the Parks and Wildlife Service were discussed. The interpretation was developed in a consultative manner with maximum participation of Aboriginal community members (including Steve Gall, manager of Aboriginal Heritage Tasmania; Janet Fenton and Qug King of Friends of Melaleuca and leaseholders; Greg Wells of Par Avion; a botanist and zoologist from the Department of Primary Industries, Parks Water and Environment; and the Tasmanian Wilderness World Heritage Area Advisory Committee and National Parks and Wildlife Advisory Committee [through the Parks and Reservations Manager South and/or General Manager Peter Mooney]).[12]

As documented in the Parks and Wildlife Service media package titled "Needwonnee: Connecting and Sharing," the Walk was created by a team of twenty Aboriginal community members, including Elders and artists, Parks and Wildlife Service rangers, and track workers and Aboriginal trainee rangers and field officers.[13] Members of the Aboriginal community, including artists Verna Nichols and Leonie Dickson, designed and created the interpretive artworks.[14] Nichols designed the creation panels. Aboriginal artist Sheldon Thomas constructed the paperbark canoe with two rangers. The on-site audio-visual clip states that the Walk "demonstrates what can be achieved when time is taken to develop relationships, understand the potential of the interpretive space and explore possibilities courageously."[15] The collaborative process offered potential for developing a range of relationships that render the Walk more than a tourism-oriented product. Since the Walk was opened on December 6, 2011, members of the local Aboriginal community have returned to repair and refurbish the artworks on several occasions.[16]

PROJECT DESCRIPTION

The Needwonnee Walk is a 1.2-kilometer boardwalk through moorland and forest and along the edge of the lagoon that loops through the Tasmanian Wilderness Heritage Area. Visitors to the Needwonnee Walk arrive by air with Par Avion Wilderness Tours to a white gravel airstrip and pristine environment. The only manmade structures in the area are the Parks and Wildlife Service facilities, including a jetty for tour boats, toilets, a bird hide, and the boardwalk itself.[17] The remote location limits visitor numbers to around six thousand informed visitors each year.[18] The Walk responds to "a significant unmet desire for more information to be provided about Aboriginal culture and the relationship of Aborigines with specific areas."[19]

However, knowledge of the Aboriginal community is dependent on archival data—primarily on the journals of George Augustus Robinson, who in the 1830s searched unsuccessfully for the Needwonnee in his role as "Conciliator."[20] Traveling across southwest Tasmania over

Figure 26.1.   Needwonnee Walk, interpretive panel at the start of the walk. Photo courtesy Fiona Rice.

a month in 1830, he saw several huts, which he thought abandoned by inhabitants who may have fled or gone into hiding. The Walk takes up this narrative with Robinson's words on the introductory panel at the commencement of the boardwalk.

Robinson's journals are full of observations on the flora and fauna of Melaleuca Creek and the Louisa River and Bay. He notes that there are black swans and ducks, and identifies the flowers and berries eaten by natives. As he moves across the territory he notes regional particularities, such as the baskets and tools used on Bruny Island and the yellow and red *marle* (ochre) body paint used by Aboriginal people at Cox Bight.[21] At Port Davey he notes,

> The native track difficult to find . . . discovered it almost as if by instinct, as in many places there was not the least appearance of a path. But there were other marks and signs: burnt pieces of wood, fire sticks of the natives, which they had dropped, pieces of shell of crawfish which they had been eating as they went on their way, burned places in the bush, mutton-fish shells and small shrubs broken down. (Robinson, 11 April 1830, Port Davey)[22]

Equipped with these textual fragments, the Walk attempts to recapture the spirit of that journey by gradually introducing visitors to lost cultural signs and artifacts. The most significant constructions are of a traditional campsite with a dome-shaped hut built of native laurel and paperbark and thatched with roperush, a reference to the abandoned huts observed by Robinson on his journey. An open hearth contains a meal of swans' egg and shellfish and stone tools. A traditional paperbark canoe floats near the bank of Melaleuca Lagoon (Plate 24). These constructions are fashioned using local plants such as coast paperbark, native laurel, purple appleberry (a natural rope), scented paperbark and roperush (for thatching), and moss for the floor.[23] Smaller items are crafted based on the flora and fauna identified by Robinson. Bushcraft including traditional baskets, shell necklaces, and a spear, digging stick, and waddy

Plate 24. Needwonnee Walk, Melaleuca, Tasmania, Australia, paperbark canoe. Photo courtesy Jillian Walliss.

Figure 26.2.   Needwonnee Walk, finished campsite. Photo courtesy Fiona Rice.

(an offensive weapon) are replicated based on notes in his journal. The reinvention of these artifacts as material registers of a lost tradition communicates the deeper human tragedy to visitors while educating them on the Needwonnee habitat.[24] The spiritual dimension has not been neglected in the recreation of the Needwonnee story. Aboriginal artists Leonie Dickson and Verna Nichols have constructed contemporary creation figures of Moihernee and Moihernee's "wife" out of natural materials along the track.

These ephemeral installations are likely to deteriorate or change in form or color, providing ongoing opportunities for future collaboration and training. There transience is their strongest attribute, a stark contrast to the static meanings conveyed through civic exhibits.

The only permanent piece on the Walk is the creation story that was relayed to Robinson by Truganini's "husband," Wooraddy. In telling the story of the first Tasmanian Aboriginal, Parlevar, Wooraddy identifies a site at Cox Bight as the center of the Needwonnee homelands.[25] Panels fixed at one point along the Walk convey this story.

RECEPTION

The Needwonnee Walk was the recipient of the Interpretation Australia Award for Excellence—Judges Choice Award and Gold Award in 2012; the Parks Forum–Excellence in Parks Award–Cultural Category, also in 2012; and the 2013 Tourism Tasmania Award–Indigenous Tourism (Silver). Visitor satisfaction with the Walk is evident in feedback. According to the Parks and Wildlife Service, several factors—including fifteen years of prior planning, a flexible time frame, and the extension of the project to avoid the breeding season of the endangered orange-bellied parrot—have contributed to the Walk's success.[26] Long-term trust has been built with Aboriginal community members by incorporating community input to gain stakeholder support. Such strategies have been enhanced by favoring hands-on participatory collaboration and by limiting bureaucratic processes. The Parks and Wildlife Service considers the Needwonnee Walk project to be "a model for future cooperative management projects."[27] It is a means for building respect by educating visitors in the region's Aboriginal culture and ecology.

NOTES

1. Thanks to Fiona Rice for consultation on this account, and to Aboriginal artists Leonie Dickson and Verna Nichols. The project team included: at the Parks and Wildlife Service: Peter Mooney (General Manager); Mike Garner (Senior Ranger and Project Manager–Trackwork, Planning, Logistics and Operations); Peter Grant (Manager, Interpretation & Education). At the Tasmanian Aboriginal Land and Sea Council: Colin Hughes (Senior Aboriginal Heritage Officer and key contact); John Dickson (Working on Country Ranger Coordinator); Fiona Rice (Consultant for Interpretation Development and Communications); Tony Brown (board member and Curator of Indigenous Cultures); and Kylie Dickson (Chair).

2. Fiona Rice, Tony Brown, and Kylie Dickson, eds., "Needwonnee: Connecting and Sharing: The Needwonnee Walk, Melaleuca, South-West Tasmania" (Hobart: Parks and Wildlife Service, 2011), 10–11.

3. Brand Tasmania, "Melaleuca's Promise Is Over-Delivered," available at http://www.brandtasmania .com/newsletter.php?ACT=story&issue=125&story=7 (link no longer active, last accessed November 13, 2013).

4. Australian Government, Department of Environment, "World Heritage Places: Tasmanian Wilderness," available at http://www.environment.gov.au/node/19816.

5. Rice, Brown, and Dickson, "Needwonnee: Connecting and Sharing."

6. Parks and Wildlife Service Tasmania, "A Living Interpretive Experience at Melaleuca," *Buttongrass* (June 2012), available at http://www.parks.tas.gov.au/file.aspx?id=27810.

7. Lyndall Ryan, *The Aboriginal Tasmanians* (Brisbane: University of Queensland Press, 1981), 5.

8. Patsy Cameron, *Grease and Ochre: The Blending of Two Cultures at the Colonial Sea Frontier* (Launceston: Fuller Bookshop, 2011).

9. Australian Bureau of Statistics, "2011 Census Quickstats: Tasmania," available at http://www.cen susdata.abs.gov.au/census_services/getproduct/census/2011/quickstat/6?opendocument&navpos=220.

10. Parks and Wildlife Service Tasmania, "Evaluation Report 2013: Needwonnee Aboriginal Walk, Melaleuca," available at http://www.parks.tas.gov.au/file.aspx?id=31714.

11. C. Green and R. Painter, *A Survey for Aboriginal Values at Cox Bight and Melaleuca in the Southwest Conservation Area*, unpublished report prepared for the Parks and Wildlife Service and the Tasmanian Aboriginal Land Council, 1997; and Greg Lehman, *Aboriginal Interpretation of the Tasmanian Wilderness World Heritage Area: Report to the Parks and Wildlife Service, Tasmania* (Hobart: Tasmanian Aboriginal Land Council, 1995).

12. Parks and Wildlife Service Tasmania, "Evaluation Report 2013."

13. Rice, Brown, and Dickson, "Needwonnee: Connecting and Sharing"; Tasmania Parks and Wildlife Service, "A Living Interpretive Experience at Melaleuca."

14. Parks and Wildlife Service Tasmania, "Evaluation Report 2013."

15. Parks and Wildlife Service Tasmania, "Needwonnee Walk: Booklet and DVD," available at https://shop.parks.tas.gov.au/ProductInfo.aspx?id=202.

16. Parks and Wildlife Service Tasmania, "Needwonnee Walk."

17. Brand Tasmania, "Melaleuca's Promise Is Over-Delivered."

18. Parks and Wildlife Service Tasmania, "Evaluation Report 2013."

19. Based on Parks and Wildlife Service Visitor Survey Program 1999, cited in Parks and Wildlife Service Tasmania, "Evaluation Report 2013."

20. N. J. B. Plomley, ed., *Friendly Mission: The Tasmanian Journals and Papers of George Augustus Robinson, 1829–1834* (2nd ed.) (Launceston: Tasmanian Historical Research Association, 2008).

21. Rice, Brown, and Dickson, "Needwonnee: Connecting and Sharing," 14–15.

22. Ibid., 16.

23. Ibid., 18.

24. Parks and Wildlife Service Tasmania, "Aboriginal Interpretive Experience at Melaleuca," available at http://www.parks.tas.gov.au/index.aspx?sys=News%20Article&intID=2466.

25. Rice, Brown, and Dickson, "Needwonnee: Connecting and Sharing," 17.

26. Parks and Wildlife Service Tasmania, "Evaluation Report 2013."

27. Ibid.

27

Ngarluma Yindjibarndi Cultural Complex, Roebourne, Western Australia, Australia

Location: Roebourne (Ieramugadu), Western Australia
Dates: 2010–2015
Client: Ngarluma & Yindjibarndi Foundation Ltd.
Architect: Robert Toland, Toland Pty. Ltd.
Design Team: Robert Toland, Steve Thomas, Isabelle Toland, and Robert Bruce
Engineer: Simpson Design Associates/Northrop Consulting Engineers Pty. Ltd.
Contractor: NYFL Housing & Construction/Joint Venture with John Barman Constructions
Area: 2,200 square meters (gross floor area over 1.2 hectares)
Funding: approximately $197,500 from the Pilbara Regional Grants Scheme for Stage 1
Cost: approximately $20 million

The Ngarluma Yindjibarndi Cultural Complex (formerly the Roebourne Cultural Complex) was designed for the Ngarluma and Yindjibarndi peoples of the Pilbara by Toland architects in a design that evolved through lengthy consultation related both to site selection and development of the brief. As is typical of similar facilities in Western Australia, it is an example of a center conceived to cover vast geographic areas and diverse cultural groups. More importantly, both the creation and programmatic objectives of the facility are aimed at community upliftment in a majority Aboriginal township, where around 90 percent of its one thousand inhabitants are Indigenous.

BACKGROUND

Located 60 kilometers from Karratha and 1,600 kilometers north of Perth, Roebourne was founded by pastoralists who prospered there during the late nineteenth century. The economy of the area altered significantly with the commencement of large-scale iron ore mining in the Pilbara during the 1960s.[1] Both the pastoral and mining industries dispossessed the Aboriginal peoples of the region, including the Ngarluma and Yindjibarndi peoples. Ngarluma country covers much of the coastal region, including the land around Roebourne, Wickham, Point Samson, Cossack, and surrounding areas. Yindjibarndi country covers the tableland area lead-

190

ing into the Hamersley Range Plateau, along the Fortescue River, and east to the Yule River.[2] This vast expanse of territory includes the Millstream National Park. Community survival in the region has been impacted and transformed by the mining industry. Negotiations with government and mining companies over compensation and access to traditional lands have proven to be a source of both conflict and opportunity for Aboriginal communities.

The town of Roebourne has been historically marked by social dysfunction linked to the shift from a pastoral to a mining economy and the resultant lack of employment for Aboriginal peoples, who have been excluded from the mining economy. Until the 1960s, there were strict controls on the movement of Indigenous peoples in the area, and Roebourne functioned as a non-Indigenous town with Aboriginal populations living in separate missions and reserves.[3] With changes in legislation in the 1960s, Roebourne became a majority Aboriginal township with the increasing Aboriginal influx attended by a history of oppression and dispossession, welfare dependency, and high unemployment.[4] As new towns rapidly developed in the region to cater to those employed by or servicing the mining industry, Roebourne came to be seen as racially distinct and welfare dependent. Through the institutions of welfare provision, the town was subject to non-Aboriginal institutional processes, influences, and demands.[5] In response, Aboriginal community groups developed autonomous social services as means of fostering social inclusion, emplacement, and employment.

The first official Aboriginal organization, Ieramugadu, was established in 1974 to alleviate the unemployment of Aboriginal peoples in the face of economic exclusion. The organization became the principal shareholder of the Mount Welcome Pastoral Company and purchased the pastoral stations Mount Welcome and Chirritha, later purchasing Woodbrook. Living outside of Roebourne had come to be seen as desirable for Aboriginal peoples, a way to avoid urban problems and influences. Living conditions deteriorated significantly in the town. When Cyclone Chloe destroyed the Roebourne Reserve in 1975, the Western Australian Government developed the Village State Housing Commission or "Homeswest" project at the margins of Roebourne to accommodate those displaced. Continuing unemployment and social conflict in the town exacerbated the community's social problems.[6] These escalating issues led to a number of initiatives through a range of organizations to create safe environments and appropriate services away from the town.[7] A camp incorporated in 1981 as the Ngurawaana Group was established 150 kilometers from Roebourne on Yindjibarndi land.

The communities in the Roebourne area today include Mingullatharndo/5-Mile, a small community just north of Roebourne supporting an alcohol-free and positive lifestyle environment; Ngurrawaana, a community founded in 1983, some 150 kilometers southwest of Roebourne near Millstream-Chichester National Park in Yindjibarndi country; and Cheeditha and Chirritha, reserves three kilometers and forty kilometers, respectively, from Roebourne.[8] In 2007, the Ngarluma and Yindjibarndi peoples succeeded in establishing native title over their traditional lands. Ngarluma country covers the area of Roebourne.

The Ngarluma Yindjibarndi Cultural Complex has a brief to provide "the cultural, linguistic, artistic, social and environmental needs, wants and desires of Roebourne's local Aboriginal community, whilst economically sustaining itself through encouraging custom from visitors and tourists."[9] It was conceived by the Ngarluma Yindjibarndi Foundation Limited (NYFL), which was formed following a 1998 native title agreement with Woodside Energy and their North West Shelf Gas Project joint venture partners for land use on the Burrup Peninsula and areas of the Shire of Roebourne.[10] Incorporated in 2000, the NYFL was established to receive native title payments and manage funds, and is dedicated to providing training, employment, and business opportunities for its members. Governed by a ten-member board, the NYFL runs the Warrgamugardi Yirdiyabura employment program, owns the Roebourne General Store, and developed the proposal for the Ngarluma Yindjibarndi Cultural Complex, which is currently under construction.[11] The NYFL is involved in community programs that support the social, cultural, economic, educational, health, and well-being of the Ngarluma and Yindjibarndi people, and also assists in developing local art groups.[12] Membership of the NYFL in 2014 was around 1,700 members. The objective of the NYFL is to develop additional revenue streams to sustain and rejuvenate the community and its heritage. Training, employment, and business opportunities are fundamental to this aim.

CONSULTATION PROCESS

Sydney-based architect firm Toland Pty. Ltd. has been involved with a number of projects with Aboriginal communities in Western Australia, northwest New South Wales, and far north Queensland. Robert Toland observes that although each project differs, one factor common to all is the "buying-in" by the Indigenous communities. Toland's approach is to present an initial concept that enables the communities to take ownership of the project.[13] The Ngarluma Yindjibarndi Cultural Complex project was consequently developed following a lengthy, seven-year consultation process that included fund-raising and planning stages.

Toland began working with the client community in 2001, traveling and working with community members so as to gain an understanding of their "approach to and respect for one another's territories, dreaming and cultures."[14] This is particularly important in a region of vast territories and numerous language groups. The early phase of the project included a two-week community consultation tour conducted in three stages in 2003. The architects, led by two Elders, covered vast areas of the Pilbara and Kimberley regions, which together cover some 5,000 kilometers, and engaged with the communities who would potentially participate in the center's activities.[15] The objective was to present site selection, a concept master plan and design, and to seek the endorsement of communities for the program and activities planned. This first phase was largely dialogic and exploratory, focused around an effort to understand the capacity and audience for the facility. Possible affiliations with arts and performance groups, and the acquisition of artifacts and associations with other Indigenous groups beyond the Ngarluma and Yindjibarndi groups, were canvassed. Particularly important during this phase was the provision of activities for broadening the Indigenous community's skill base and providing mentorship programs.

Toland observes that there was great enthusiasm for the project during this phase, with a number of local teachers offering to lead workshops and a proposal made to train local community members in construction through the local TAFE. The latter proposal was emphasized as means for creating ownership in the project through involvement of local skills and labor and through use of local materials. From its very inception, the project was conceived as a means to engage and support the community. Ideas sourced from the local communities during this consultation process were incorporated into the design.

PROJECT DESCRIPTION

The master plan was developed around the interpretation and translation of two central ideas: the artistic representation of site, land, nature, place, and journey found in local Aboriginal

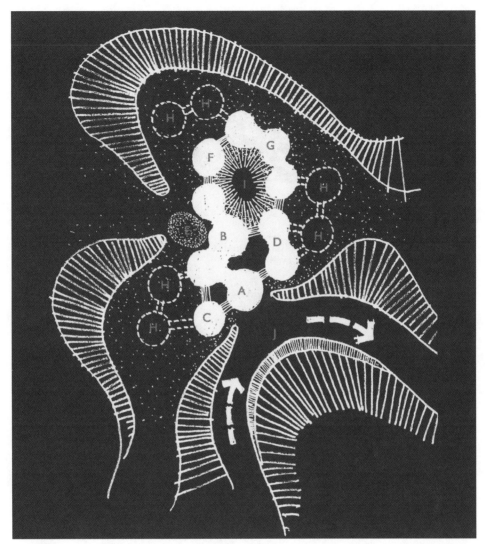

Figure 27.1.   Ngarluma Yindjibarndi Cultural Complex, conceptual master plan. Courtesy Toland Architects.

art, and formal features in the landscape such as the prominent termite mounds.[16] The cultural center was structured along a timeline, including past and present histories and future aspirations of the Aboriginal communities of the area. The master plan was presented using motifs from Aboriginal art rather than the rigid geometries of the western planning tradition.

The architects conceived of a distinctive and sculptural architecture, formally and materially derived from the surrounding environment and incorporating artworks by local artists (Plate 25). According to the design, the entire complex is to be integrated through an aesthetic that uses the rich, red Pilbara stone. The design also uses a vocabulary of screens and walls to connect the various functional spaces with the landscape and included environmentally sustainable features. The architects' website states that "the aim of the complex is to educate both the younger generation and the tourists in the ways of the people, their

Plate 25. Ngarluma Yindjibarndi Cultural Complex, Roebourne, Western Australia, entry–elevational drawing. Courtesy Toland Architects.

traditions, history and culture, whilst providing employment opportunities in the areas of tourism, hospitality and administration."[17]

The spaces proposed for the program were organized around the central idea of an amphitheatre, which would host varied cultural events including film, dance, music, theatre, and corroborees. This performative theme was extended to a range of social activity spaces including a museum, café/restaurant, rest/recreation area, and walking trail run by locals, and commercial spaces including an art gallery, artists' studios, tourist bureau, music and film production studios, communal meeting space, and kitchen and conference facilities for up to 150 people.[18] The complexity of the project was in interweaving what may be seen as traditional and modern programs so that generational needs and gender specificities could be addressed. Specialized spaces include separate men's and women's traditional meeting spaces and an Elders' teaching and workshop space designed as a social gathering space. Traditional gardens and heritage displays are complemented by private community spaces and gardens, a museum, and library. The brief also included the NYFL offices and a genealogical records department.[19] The program anticipated multifaceted needs.

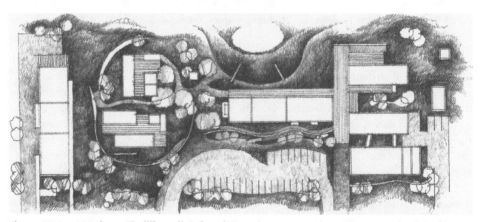

Figure 27.2. Ngarluma Yindjibarndi Cultural Complex, master plan. Courtesy Toland Architects.

Stage One of the construction commenced in 2011 with an approximately $200,897 grant from the Pilbara Regional Grants Scheme.[20] The total anticipated project cost was approximately $401,795. Six blocks of riverfront property in central Roebourne were purchased after community consultation in 2006.[21] A steering committee was appointed to oversee the process. As described in 2006 by Evan Maloney, chief executive officer of the NYFL, the objectives were to create a museum and a place for Elders, to attract local tourism, and to "become an icon for the Pilbarra located on the northwest coastal highway."[22] The center would be owned and operated by NYFL and would generate sufficient revenue to ensure its long-term sustainability as a cultural facility.

The resultant hybrid design of keeping place, cultural center, and community facility expanded the program into a major complex at a civic scale. However, the social complexity of user demands suggested a very different vision of the civic, fashioned by the relationships most critical for the community, and the spaces that might accommodate these over time. Although urban in its configuration, the amphitheater and gardens introduced regional associations to the project. Planning was staged to allow for future growth, and the building was designed to be flexible for different scales of occupation. Spaces were organized to provide breezeways, shaded areas, and breakout areas to enhance passive environmental controls.[23] The center was further integrated into the Harding River Roebourne Enhancement Scheme Precinct through guided tours along the walking trails. As the project developed into the construction phase, cyclone-resistant construction had to be incorporated to withstand wind speeds of 125 to 170 kilometers an hour. The intention that the building create employment and training, both during construction and after in running the facility, has thus far been carried through.[24]

The amphitheater has been completed, and the next stages of the complex; namely, the men's and women's private spaces and the multipurpose building that includes an Elder's area, commenced construction in mid-2013. The emerging vision is of a contemporary architecture fashioned for a dynamic Aboriginal community, aesthetically integrated through design.

NOTES

1. Thanks to Robert Toland, at Toland Pty. Ltd., Evan Maloney at Ngarluma & Yindjibarndi Foundation Ltd. for information on this project, and Mary Ashton for assisting us with clarifications.

2. Royal Commission into Aboriginal Deaths in Custody, "Report of the Inquiry into the Death of John Peter Pat: Introduction," April 1991, available at http://www.austlii.edu.au/au/other/IndigLRes/rciadic/individual/brm_jpp/2.html. The Royal Commission examined all Aboriginal deaths in custody in each State and Territory that occurred between January 1, 1980, and May 31, 1989, and the actions taken in respect of each death. See Royal Commission into Aboriginal Deaths in Custody, "Fact Sheet 112," available at http://www.naa.gov.au/collection/fact-sheets/fs112.aspx.

3. Department of Indigenous Affairs, "Roebourne Report: Issues, Current Responses and Strategies for Consideration," July 2009, available at http://www.daa.wa.gov.au/Documents/ ReportsPublications/Roebourne%20Report%202009%20(FINAL)%20-%20Department%20of%20Indigenous%20Affairs.pdf (link no longer active, last accessed November 27, 2013).

4. Royal Commission into Aboriginal Deaths in Custody, "Report of the Inquiry into the Death of John Peter Pat: Introduction."

5. Mary Edmunds, *A Good Life: Human Rights and Encounters with Modernity* (Canberra: Australian National University Press, 2013), 174.

6. Edmunds, *A Good Life*, 174.

7. These included the Ngurin Resource Centre, Mawarnkarra Aboriginal Health Service, Yaandina Family Centre, and the Gurra Bunjya Cultural Camp for Young People.

8. Department of Indigenous Affairs, "Roebourne Report: Issues, Current Responses and Strategies for Consideration."

9. Ngarluma and Yindjibarndi Foundation, "Roebourne Cultural Complex," available at http://nyfl.org.au/nyfl-businesses/roebourne-cultural-complex/.

10. Ngarluma and Yindjibarndi Foundation, "Roebourne Cultural Complex."

11. Ngarluma and Yindjibarndi Foundation, "NYFL Governance," available at http://nyfl.org.au/about/our-governance/. The Board comprises four Ngarluma and four Yindjibarndi directors who are elected by ballot of the NYFL members for terms of four years. In addition, the Board includes one Woodside-appointed director and one Board-appointed finance director.

12. Indigenous Stock Exchange, "Ngarluma and Yindjibarndi Foundation," available at https://www.isx.org.au/projects/ngarluma-and-yindjibarndi-foundation.

13. Conversation with Robert Toland, February 2014.

14. Toland Architectural Design Partners, "Ngarluma Yindjibarndi Cultural Centre," available at http://toland.com.au/pdf/Architecture_English/Archi_proj_09%20Pilbara.pdf.

15. Toland Williams Pty. Ltd., "Community Consultation Report," March–April 2003. On file with author.

16. Toland Williams Pty. Ltd., "Concept Design and Brief," March 2003. On file with author.

17. Toland Architectural Design Partners, "Ngarluma Yindjibarndi Cultural Centre."

18. Ngarluma and Yindjibarndi Foundation, "Roebourne Cultural Complex."

19. Toland Architectural Design Partners, "Ngarluma Yindjibarndi Cultural Centre."

20. The Nationals for Regional WA, "Royalties for Regions: Roebourne Cultural Complex Stage 1," available at http://www.nationalswa.com/ Default.aspx?TabId=66&postcode=6710&pid=966.

21. Indigenous Stock Exchange, "Ngarluma and Yindjibarndi Foundation."

22. Maloney speaks in a video produced by Goolarri Media Enterprises sponsored by Ngarda Civil & Mining uploaded on the Indigenous Stock Exchange website. See Indigenous Stock Exchange, "Ngarluma and Yindjibarndi Foundation."

23. Toland Williams Pty. Ltd., "Community Consultation, Ideas and Brief Development," June 2005. On file with author.

24. Toland Williams Pty. Ltd., "Master Plan Version 5, Return Brief plus Building Complex," March 2007. On file with author.

28

Nk'Mip Desert Cultural Centre, Osoyoos, Canada[1]

Date: 2006
Location: Osoyoos, British Columbia, Canada
Client: Osoyoos Indian Band, Okanagan Nation
Architect: Hotson Bakker Boniface Haden architects + urbanistes[2] (principal architect in charge: Bruce Haden)
Project Architect: Brady Dunlop
Project Team: Norm Hotson, Stephanie Forsythe, Tina Hubert, Julie Bogdnowicza
Exhibition Design: Phil Aldrich, AldrichPears Associates
Landscape Architects: PFS Studio
Structural Engineering: Equilibrium Consulting Inc.
Contractor: Greyback Construction
Subcontractor: Terra Firma Builders Ltd.
Manager, Cultural Centre: Charlotte Stringam
Marketer: Derek Bryson
Cost: approximately $7.7 million (including building improvements and interim facilities

The Nk'Mip Desert Cultural Centre in Osoyoos near Vancouver is owned and run by the Osoyoos Indian Band and has acquired a reputation for Aboriginal tourism.[3] The Centre has attracted international recognition along two avenues: the publication of compelling visual images of the Centre itself, and the reputation of its business-minded chief Clarence Louie. While the former invokes a popular ethos of vernacular and therefore sustainable architecture, the latter introduces a dynamic and self-motivated personality into a discourse weighed down by political battles. In this regard, this tiny and remote project is of critical significance as a model of cultural facilities that open Aboriginal reserves to global tourism.

BACKGROUND

The Osoyoos are part of the Okanagan Nation, which comprises eight bands sharing the Syilx language, albeit with slight dialect variations, in and around southern British Co-

197

Figure 28.1. Nk'Mip Desert Cultural Centre, plan of building. Courtesy DIALOG.

lumbia (seven bands fall within Canada and one within the United States).[4] Located on a 32,000-acre reservation in an area geographically renowned as the "last Canadian desert," the Osoyoos Band is a group of 520 individuals—including many children—led by Chief Clarence Louie. The economic basis for the current Chief's success is due to his predecessor, Chief Louie Louie's, decision to turn part of the reservation over to vineyards, thus providing employment for both Band members and the wider community. The resulting expansion of the enterprise, including Osoyoos Indian Band Holdings and eight additional businesses that followed, have transformed the Osoyoos Band from a group troubled by histories of unemployment and substance abuse during the 1950s into "Economic Warriors" featured in the *Economist*.[5] Nk'Mip comprises the Cultural Centre, the winery Spirit Ridge, and a luxury resort development in which the Band has 25 percent ownership, which includes a hotel, RV park, conference center, and golf course aimed at attracting large numbers of summer tourists.[6] A joint venture between the Band and Constellation Brands, an Ontario-based wine firm that has been leasing vineyards from the Band since 1979, has seen an expansion of business and profits since 2002.[7] The Band also owns a gas station, a construction company, a cement batching plant, a school, a health center, and a forestry program, which together generate substantial dividends for Band members. The Band has built the Senkulmen Business Park to provide jobs for the next generation on the reservation. Of these various businesses, the winery, Cultural Centre, golf course, and resort are specifically geared toward tourism. The Centre is a very small building that asserts a symbolic cultural claim on its geography and educates tourists on the culture of the Osoyoos Band.

PROJECT DESCRIPTION

Designed by Vancouver architect Bruce Haden (formerly of DIALOG), the Centre takes the form of a rammed-earth wall inserted into the hillside, behind which a series of spaces are con-

Plate 26. **Nk'Mip Desert Cultural Centre, Osoyoos, Canada, wall in the landscape. Photo by Nic Lehoux, courtesy DIALOG.**

cealed (Plate 26). The design of a handmade architecture alludes to the geological sedimentation of the surrounding mountains, although the architecture of the wall has no precedents in either the tipis of the Osoyoos or the long houses of the Haida. The wall is visible throughout the various spaces of the complex, including the offices, shops, gallery, and auditorium. It has been described as challenging the fake adobe styles that are becoming more common in the South Okanagan region.[8] By partially burying the structure in the incline of the hillside, the extremes in temperatures (approximately 0°F to 104°F) are countered, while the building's solid westward face optimizes passive solar performance.

The program for the project was generated by exhibition design firm AldrichPears Associates via a series of workshops, which initially focused on the representation of desert ecologies.[9] Site tours in Arizona to the Pueblo Grande Museum in Phoenix and the Botanical Gardens in Tucson shaped an ambitious project that recognized Osoyoos as a continuation of the Great Sonora Desert, stretching from Mexico to Canada.[10] Since the budget was not sufficient to realize this grand idea, the architects designed a rammed-earth wall, behind which facilities could grow or contract according to the availability of funds. Haden stresses the importance of the gift shop, the auditorium, and the exhibition space, and regrets the lack of sufficient teaching places, a shortcoming that was felt later on. On funding, he observes that they designed an approximately $10.3 million, $6.8 million, $3.4 million, and $214,000 building and ended up with a $3.6 million building, which took five years from design to completion. Capital operation cost and financial feasibility were primary concerns.

Funding for the project occurred in three phases. The first phase focused on capital and planning of the temporary interpretive center and outdoor trails; the second phase focused on design and capital for the permanent building, theater, and exhibits; and the third phase focused on design and capital for trails, outdoor village upgrades, and exhibits. Funding was sourced from a number of institutions. As outlined by Centre manager Charlotte Stringam, these included the Osoyoos Indian Band, government organizations focused on Indigenous heritage, including Aboriginal Business Canada; Indian and Northern Affairs Canada (now called Aboriginal Affairs and Northern Development Canada); and Canadian Heritage. Private industrial and corporate bodies, including the Softwood Industry Community Economic Adjustment Initiative, also contributed.[11] The diversity of sources demonstrates the tenacity of the Band members involved in fund-raising and their commitment to the project.

Haden observes that a fully integrated client relationship and sense of ownership of the process was important for such a project and cannot, in his view, be achieved through competitions. He observes that the Band members he dealt with were smart and very attentive. They saw the project as their own private concern, and the general public of Osoyoos, a working-class resort town, was not consulted. Instead, consultation was essentially an internal process whereby the architect and exhibition consultant worked closely with a few Band leaders and select members. Haden recalls that this approach involved establishing a degree of trust and taking care to demonstrate early on in the project that the architects were willing to work hard. Reflecting on design challenges, Haden describes the evolution of facilities for Indigenous communities from what he calls the earlier warehouse model toward a preference for figurative design, with the latter approach often proving quite reductive. In regard to the Cultural Centre, he observes:

> We thought about it a long time, to find an architectural language that was not directly figural but had to have, firstly, visual longevity [to] reflect the fact that in my view they had been there a long time and were going to be there a long time. I felt that the landscape had to tell a story—the building had to have contrast, so the building had to have a very simple formal language with a very complex tonal language. The shapes are simple, the tones are complex. It also had to be a direct reflection of the landscape—in terms of the light because it gets very hot in summer so we couldn't use glass even if we wanted. So these kind of things were really important to us. . . . We wanted it to represent long tenure—the future and the past.

The desired complexity was achieved with a low slump concrete rammed earth: a dry mix that is tamped into place (Plate 27). Additives and chemicals were used to create the color.[12]

Haden's unobtrusive cut into the landscape, although architecturally minimalist, is interpreted differently by the Osoyoos Band. An intervention in the land, once made, disturbs the land. The decision to encourage tourism demands difficult decisions regarding intervention in the landscape and sustaining tourist interest. The tourist condominiums that have been commissioned subsequently by the Band, without the involvement of Haden, are an urban archetype found elsewhere in America, with amenities for tourists. The Centre receives around eighteen thousand visitors per year.

The subsequent expansion of the Osoyoos tourist complex to include a resort and condominiums raises important questions for Indigenous tourism. The balance between maintaining the pristine landscape and leasing it for development has had to be managed quite carefully against the pressures of suburbanization. The architecture used for such resort facilities needs to be complementary, and the diverse archetypes on offer are rarely sympathetic to the natural environment. Another issue faced in the adoption of agricultural development, as with the winery at Osoyoos, is the encroachment on natural reserves and resources. As with wineries elsewhere, the extent of land cultivated and choice of water sources becomes critical for sustained ecological conservation, particularly in desert areas. Both these issues pose challenges for the further development of Aboriginal tourism. Finally, the choice of a vineyard in a community that was

Plate 27. Nk'Mip Desert Cultural Centre, Osoyoos, Canada, rammed-earth wall. Photo by Nic Lehoux, courtesy DIALOG.

once troubled by alcoholism may raise a few eyebrows, but one might argue that the common alternative, namely, casinos supported by the government, presents an even greater irony.

The content of the Cultural Centre posed an additional problem. The exhibits available for the Osoyoos, as with many inland communities, are not as impressive as those of the coastal Indian Bands, such as the totems and canoes found at the Museum of Anthropology at University of British Columbia (see chapter 21). The Band's wealth is in their surroundings and in contemporary interpretations of their history. In an effort to cultivate interest in their past, the Aboriginal collection in the museum includes a video developed by the Osoyoos on a contemporary child's return to the reservation, information on rattlesnakes, which are abundant in the desert, and children's paintings from the 1930s to the 1940s, which was a formative time for the present generation of leaders.[13] At the center of this exhibit is the story of Andrew Walsh, a teacher of white descent who taught the children on the reservation to draw, dance, and act their *chaptik* stories, nurturing in them a sense of cultural pride and respect for their beliefs.[14] The drawings were sent to the Red Cross and to Europe during the 1940s, and the children were taken to Victoria to perform in Thunderbird Park.

It is evident that the Cultural Centre aims at educating Band members in the region as much as tourists. The forced dissolution of Native American communities in the 1950s and 1960s profoundly damaged Indigenous knowledges and relationships. The annual canoe trip involving the various Indian Bands in the area has inaugurated a spatio-cultural practice that seeks to mend these broken links. Based on a dream of water by an Indigenous female Elder, the ritual involves canoe building and storytelling along the canoe track, teaching the Indigenous children of the coyote, the bear, and the creation story through oral tradition.[15]

Several strategies adopted by the Osoyoos Band have strengthened their longevity and the success of their business model. While many Bands have become entangled in protracted battles over treaties, Clarence Louie is clearly focused on self-development and particularly, on employment. The processes introduced under his leadership, moreover, are egalitarian and unimpeded by cultural stratification. The Chief is elected democratically for two-year terms and heads the corporation. Although Band members are related, nepotism is frowned upon, and young people are encouraged to participate; Louie himself was first elected at the age of twenty-four. The success of what is essentially a sound management model lies in the fact that land granted as reservation is then leased out for tourist activities, creating a flow of profit back to the corporation. The dividends gained from the various ventures finance individual Band members. Among the greatest successes of the Osoyoos Indian Band has been the positive relationship fostered with the local population, who regard the Band as a benefit to the area and as a source of employment. The Band have been the primary economic engine in the South Okanagan area and may be responsible for developments worth up to half a billion Canadian dollars.

While the Nk'Mip Desert Cultural Centre is owned and run by the Osoyoos Indian Band and generates income from retail sales, events, and admissions to the Cultural Centre, it remains dependent on annual supplementary funding from the Band.[16] The Centre is open year round, but staff is limited to two persons during the winter months. According to manager Charlotte Stringam, the Centre is working on a five-year and a ten-year strategic plan to make itself cash neutral. The strategies adopted by the management illustrate the very significant point that remote cultural centers like museums are not built for profit, and therefore creative strategies have to be employed to ensure their sustainability. Such places cannot depend on sustaining tourist interest in a very specific and narrow form of cultural education, and neither can they be assured of continuous government funding. The Nk'Mip Desert Cultural Centre is to a large extent dependent on the already robust tourist economy in the valley.

RECEPTION

The Nk'Mip Desert Cultural Centre was honored at the 2008 Canadian Governor General's Medals in Architecture, and at the inaugural World Architecture Festival. The project has been featured in *Canadian Architect*, *Architectural Record*, and most recently in the book *New Architecture on Indigenous Lands*, which includes the Centre within a broad range of facilities built on Native American reserves throughout Canada and the United States.[17]

NOTES

1. Published previously as "Case Study 6: Nk'Mip Desert Cultural Centre Osoyoos," in Janet McGaw and Anoma Pieris, *Assembling the Centre: Architecture for Indigenous Cultures, Australia and Beyond* (Abingdon and New York: Routledge, 2015), 86–93.

2. Hotson Bakker Boniface Haden architects + urbanistes subsequently collaborated with several other firms to form DIALOG Architects.

3. Thanks to Charlotte Stringam, manager at Nk'Mip Cultural Centre, for an interview and tour conducted on November 8, 2009, at Osoyoos and for facilitating clearance from the organization. Thanks also to architect Bruce Haden for an interview conducted on November 6, 2009. Photos provided by Noreen Taylor at DIALOG Architects. The text was reviewed by Charlotte Stringam, Chief Clarence Louie, consultant Margaret Holm, CFO Katherine Mac Neill, CMA, consultant Mel Woolley, and marketer Derek Bryson.

4. Syilx Okanagan Nation Alliance, "The Syilx People," available at http://www.syilx.org/who-we -are/the-syilx-people/. *Soyoos* is an Okanagan name meaning "where two lakes meet."

5. "Canada's Native Peoples: From Whine to Wine—The New Generation Means Business," *The Economist*, October 17, 2002, available at http://www.economist.com/node /1392569.

6. Indigenous and Northern Affairs Canada, "Osoyoos Indian Band Raises the Bar in Aboriginal Tourism," Winter 2009, available at http://www.ainc-inac.gc.ca/ai/scr/bc/fnbc/sucsty/arhve/2009/ wn09oibtr-eng.asp.

7. "Canada's Native Peoples."

8. Canadian Architect, "Nk'Mip Desert Cultural Centre: Governor General's Medal Winner," *Canadian Architect*, May 2008, available at http://www.canadianarchitect.com/news/nk-mip-desert-cul-tural-centre/1000222881/?type=Print%20Archives. Also see Peeroj Thakre, "Earth and Sky," *Canadian Architect* 52, no. 3 (March 2007): 27–30.

9. Interview with architect Bruce Haden conducted in Vancouver on November 6, 2009.

10. According to Haden, "(t)he tour was important because it included key Band members . . . [such as] one of the Elders, Modesta Betterton—she was a speaker of the Okanagan language—these were representatives of the Okanagan people. First we had a two-day workshop, a disciplined exercise to draw out values and interests, exhibition strategies, pragmatics . . . should the building be visibly sustainable? . . . An early version was produced as a model. We did think of rammed earth—like a large retaining wall. One of the problems was that it was essentially windowless. It wasn't an inhabited facility." From interview with Bruce Haden, November 6, 2009.

11. Charlotte Stringam provided detail of the funding breakdown in Candian dollars across the three phases as follows. Phase 1: $2,000,000 Capital Program: Osoyoos Indian Band $800,000; Aboriginal Business Canada $800,000; Indian and Northern Affairs Canada $380,000. Phase 2: Canadian Heritage $1,500,000; Osoyoos Indian Band $500,000; Infrastructure Canada $1,712,000; Softwood industry Community Economic Adjustment Initiative $487,000; Province of British Columbia $1,500,000; other corporate foundations $291,000. Phase 3: Softwood industry Community Economic Adjustment Initiative $260,000.

12. Meror Krayenoff and Terra Firma Builders executed the rammed-earth wall, working with the contractors Greyback Construction under site engineer Ray Eichberger.

13. Andrea N. Walsh, *Nk'Mip Chronicles: Art from the Inkameep Day School* (Ossoyoos, British Co-lumbia: Osoyoos Museum Society and Osoyoos Indian Band, 2005).

14. Andrea Walsh from the University of Victoria helped to put together the artwork from the period 1932 to 1942 as part of an exhibit.

15. The canoe builder was the Elder Gordy Marchand.

16. Courtesy Charlotte Stringam.

17. Russell Fortmeyer, "In Canada, A Rammed-Earth Wall for the Ages," *Architectural Record*, March 2008, available at http://archrecord.construction.com/tech/technicalities/ 0803technicalities.asp. Also Peeroj Thakre, "Earth and Sky," 27–30; and Joy Monice Malnar and Frank Vodvarka, *New Architecture on Indigenous Lands* (Minneapolis: University of Minnesota Press, 2013).

29

Port Augusta Courts, Port Augusta, South Australia, Australia

Location: 4 Flinders Terrace, Port Augusta, South Australia
Date: completed 2007
Client: Courts Administration Authority
Architect: Department for Transport, Energy and Infrastructure
Project Architect: Denis Harrison
Project Team: Paul Drabsch, Ian Abbott, and Brian Carr
Artists: Cath Cantlon and John Turpie (facilitators), Donald McKenzie, Regina McKenzie, Lavene Ngatokorua, and Deb Williams
Landscape Designer: Viesturs Cielens Design
Interior Designer: Design Inc.
Structural and Civil Engineer: Wallbridge and Gilbert
Services Engineer: BESTEC
Acoustics Engineer: VIPAC
Project Manager and Cost Manager: Department for Transport, Energy and Infrastructure (DTEI)
Contractor: Candetti Constructions
Cost: approximately $9.8 million

The Port Augusta Courts complex attempts to respond to the needs of Aboriginal peoples in the justice system, recognizing the social and legal issues that face Aboriginal communities by striving to remove some of the barriers associated with the Western justice system.[1] The complex integrates an Aboriginal Court, a concept that originated in South Australia to address the mistrust Aboriginal peoples have commonly held toward the criminal justice system. The Aboriginal Court provides an offender with opportunities for direct and meaningful engagement with the judiciary, Elders, family, and community, and connects action and consequence through intense focus. The Port Augusta Courts Complex is a significant and unique courts building, which has attempted to articulate the accessibility, accountability, and transparency of the judicial process while responding to and respecting the cultural attitudes, socio-spatial needs, and beliefs of Aboriginal peoples. Rather than alienating Aboriginal users, it presents a design that reinforces the viability of Aboriginal cultures.

Port Augusta balances on the tip of Spencer Gulf, a geographic meeting place of the ranges, gulf, desert, and plain. The massive scale of the Flinders Ranges frames the stark beauty and expansiveness of the unrelenting landscape. Port Augusta is an important transient point and settlement area for European Australians and a meeting place for Indigenous Australia.

Aboriginal people constitute between 20 to 25 percent of the population of Port Augusta and represent over twenty different language groups. Alongside the permanent Aboriginal population, a fluctuating population of Aboriginal people from the north and west of South Australia and beyond travel through Port Augusta. This mobility occurs according to a number of "lines" or "paths" reflecting attachments to place by birth, kinship ties, and traditional ownership of country. Aboriginal peoples also travel to Port Augusta to access a multitude of services not available in remote areas, including the justice system. Aboriginal people in the area face a range of familiar issues and challenges including poverty, housing, and health challenges, and tensions between Aboriginal and Western cultures. Unfortunately, Aboriginal people are disproportionately represented in statistics on incomplete education and training, low levels of qualification, high unemployment, reliance on the welfare system, involvement in the courts and prison, chronic health problems, and low-income levels.

BACKGROUND

As noted by Phillip James Kirke, the development of the concept of the Aboriginal court dates from the 1990s when South Australian magistrate Chris Vass proposed an "Aboriginal Court Day," a day when the magistrate would come down from the elevated bench to sit at eye level not only with offenders but also with their families and Elders.[2] The practice was successfully implemented in South Australia at Murray Bridge in 2001, Port Augusta in 2002, and in Ceduna in 2003. A purpose-built Aboriginal Court was introduced to Adelaide in 2005. Kirke observes that initially, innovations took the form of furniture arrangements, such as the introduction of round or elliptical tables, but it gradually extended to providing environments that were less institutional in design. He argues that the isolation of justice issues from other social rituals is peculiar to the Western justice system, and that "traditionally the Aboriginal law ground was—and in remote traditional communities still very much is—a single place in which instruction, initiation, celebration, ceremonial, religious experience and debate might all take place."[3] The Courts complex designed for Port Augusta in 2007 also provided for an outdoor court room, although this space has since not been used for that purpose.[4]

The Port Augusta Courts complex was designed to replace the outdated courthouse located in the center of the town. The old Victorian courthouse, which fronted the street, had space limitations and no capacity to integrate innovations such as the Aboriginal court concept. On court sitting days, Aboriginal people would gather on the street and in the nearby Gladstone Square. Altercations and conflict in the external areas would arise, often leading to police intervention.

From the outset, it was obvious that the design of a new court complex for the region needed to take into account the need for positive outcomes for Aboriginal people, the capacity to service a large number of matters across a wide range of jurisdictions, the socio-spatial needs of different client groups and organizations, and the necessity to incorporate the complexities and importance of place. With many court users identifying with Aboriginal cultures, there was an opportunity to move beyond traditional court architecture to integrate the traditions and needs of various Aboriginal peoples into the design. In order to achieve this, the Courts Authority set up a consultative committee, and the design team (including architects, artists, and landscape designers) consulted closely with Aboriginal and non-Aboriginal stakeholders over a four-year period. The site for the complex, which was selected by court administrators, was sectioned from the neighboring railway yards. It lies adjacent to the main business center of Port Augusta and commands distant views of the Flinders Ranges, with shorter views of the Minburie Ranges and Spencer Gulf.

PROJECT DESCRIPTION

The two-story complex is constructed of a combination of lightweight materials such as corrugated iron in natural and pre-colored finishes, fiber sheet and copper cladding against precast concrete, and texture-rendered walls. To develop open and nonintimidating architecture, large areas of glass were used to allow visual connection with the outdoors. In some areas, timber-louvered sections and artwork were used to provide shading or privacy screening. The color palette for the building's exterior was chosen by matching the colors of various Flinders Ranges ochres. A hierarchical order was then given to these choices; for example, colors reminiscent of important ceremonial ochres were chosen for imposing sections of the exterior. The building thus reflects the adjacent landscapes, with alternating colors taking the viewer's attention as the sun moves through the course of the day (Plate 28).

The complex sits along the long axis to the street frontage, with a series of long, low sand mounds planted with spinifex mirroring Port Augusta's landscape. Between the mounds, mass plantings of indigenous plants soften the building and keep the visitor on pathways while allowing privacy and views under the canopy zones. Visitors arriving at the street frontage are

Plate 28. Port Augusta Courts, Port Augusta, South Australia, exterior view. Photo by Elizabeth Grant.

Figure 29.1.   Port Augusta Courts, outdoor shelter. Photo by Elizabeth Grant.

led along the main pathway, which is colored gray, and represents Aboriginal contact with the European criminal justice system. The path intersects with another path where a depiction of *Arkurra*, the powerful and feared bearded Spirit Serpent of the Flinders Ranges Dreaming, is laid out. The presence of *Arkurra* acts as a symbol and as a way-finding mechanism leading people to the main entrance. At the entrance, another path allows diversion. This allows people an important deviation should they sense conflict in the public or entrance areas and wish to collect their thoughts or wait outside. The secondary path leads to an outdoor shelter.

The outdoor shelter is a simple, open shade structure repeating the roof lines of the court complex. The shelter commands magnificent sweeping views over the nearby Minburie Ranges and Spencer Gulf. A multifunctional structure, it is used for a range of consultations where privacy is necessary, and includes an external waiting and reflection area. The ability to seek relief from court processes by leaving the building and feeling the sun and wind on your face is central to reducing stress among Aboriginal users. The shelter has been designed to accommodate outdoor courts (although it has not been used for this purpose at this stage). Seats within the outdoor shelter and around the exterior of the site are three-dimensional translations of Aboriginal depictions of people sitting. The seats allow two or three people to sit as a group, but they are situated such that direct eye contact can be avoided between people seated in different seats, an avoidance that is necessary in many Aboriginal cultures.

Once at the entrance to the complex, the visitor notes *Arkurra*'s head sitting under the front veranda, with his beard protruding as geometric shapes from under the veranda screens. His elliptical eye appears as a pattern in the cement, and nearby a high cone shape symbolizes his tail breaking the ground outside the building. Looking into the building, people are able to directly view the layout and key destinations, and can orient themselves in the open and readable organizational system. There is a common registry with separate and discreet reception for the Youth Court, with its own foyer, conference area, interview room, and amenities.

The entrance leads into a double-height circular foyer. The area employs extensive glazing to offer views of the Ranges and the Gulf, continuing the strong relationship between the interior and exterior of the building. Just below the ceiling, elements of local history are represented in a frieze using a series of simply etched wooden panels. The panels illustrate pre-European life and historical events such as the arrival of Captain Matthew Flinders and the establishment of Port Augusta as an industrial hub. Moveable organic-shaped seating both fulfills its intended purpose and provides children with diversion, as they can move the seats to form new shapes. *Arkurra*'s path continues, denoted by the leaves of mangrove stems pointing to the doors of each of the courtrooms.

The complex has three courtrooms opening from the circular foyer: a jury court, a Magistrates' Court, and a multipurpose court. Each court has a courtyard to provide visual relief and to continue connections with the external environment. The Magistrates' Court also doubles as an Aboriginal sentencing or conferencing court. The design of the Aboriginal court at Port Augusta departs from the traditional rectangular courtroom layout, with a round table and an organic space to administer traditional sittings. Space is compressed by the use of retractable screens, which accentuate the focus on the significant circle of participants. The need for light, and for short and long views, is acknowledged in the use of large areas of glazing that offers views of internal courtyards and of the Ranges and the Gulf. Five slump glass panels frame one of the views and depict the story of Seven Sisters Dreaming. This narrative exists in many forms throughout Aboriginal Australia and is shared by Aboriginal communities as far north as the Kimberley in Western Australia right down to Port Augusta. The story reveals Aboriginal knowledge of the night sky as well as the strict moral and social codes.

RECEPTION

Discussing the nature of Aboriginal courts, South Australian magistrate Rosanne McInnes observes that they are typically used as a normal Magistrates' Court.[5] Their use for Aboriginal sentencing conferences depends on the discretion of the magistrates and judges presiding over each case. The advantage of sentencing conferences is that there is community involvement, which provides better information about a case to the magistrate. Describing her involvement at Port Augusta Courts, McInnes comments that "it was a tremendous privilege, and very rewarding, to have the opportunity to work with Aboriginal people solving their problems themselves."[6] She recollects that when dealing with young offenders, she was able to use the facility in conjunction with officers of the Department of Education and Child Services, and the facility made it possible to involve offenders' families in the process.

The three main concerns in Aboriginal sentencing conferences as highlighted by McInnes are the degree of community agency, the participation of kin, and the democratic organization of authority in the spatial arrangement. All three are socially determined attributes of a successful legal process. She points out that during community consultation for the Port Augusta Courts, there was considerable anxiety about the kind of table designed. The designer had provided an oval table with a void in the center surrounded by wooden barriers, while the community wanted a simple round table. She observes that the Anangu Pitjantjatjara Yankunytjatjara Land Courts are the best places for holding Aboriginal sentencing conferences as they are held in multipurpose meeting rooms in rural transaction centers known as *PyKu* buildings. In this setting, everyone is at one table, without barriers. She further observes that as the Aboriginal sentencing processes became more common, "unasked, Yankunytjatjara elders began working with us on their own volition."[7]

The Royal Australian Institute of Architects awarded the Department for Transport, Energy and Infrastructure's design team a Collaborative Design Commendation for its work on the approximately $9.8 million Port Augusta Courts. It was an award well deserved; the unique court complex has provided new insights and a precedent for the design of courts for Aboriginal peoples. The court building has been received well by the Aboriginal community and has set a standard for similar projects nationally and internationally.

Text by Dr. Elizabeth Grant, Architectural Anthropologist and Senior Lecturer at the Office of the Deputy Vice Chancellor and Vice President (Academic) at the University of Adelaide. Published previously as "Port Augusta Courts," *Architecture Australia* (September/October 2009), 86–90. Available at architectureau.com.

NOTES

1. Thanks to Rosanne McInnes, Paul Tanner (Aboriginal Justice Officer, Port Augusta), and Denis Harrison.

2. Phillip James Kirke, *The Shelter of the Law: Designing with Communities for a Culture of Natural Justice* (West Shelley, WA: Friend Books, 2009), 42–44.

3. Kirke, *The Shelter of the Law*, 48.

4. Ibid., 44.

5. Communication between Elizabeth Grant and Rosanne McInnes, December 30, 2013.

6. Ibid.

7. Ibid.

30

Reconciliation Place, Canberra, Australia

Location: Parkes, Canberra, Australia

Date: 2002

Client: Department of Reconciliation and Aboriginal and Torres Strait Islander Affairs, Commonwealth of Australia

Main Design Team: Simon Kringas (Canberra Architect), Sharon Payne (Aboriginal Cultural Adviser), Alan Vogt (Exhibition Design Consultant), and Amy Leenders, Agi Calka, and Cath Elliot (Architectural Assistants); Marcus Bree and Benita Tunks (Concept Designers);

Consultants: Kevin O'Brien, Graham Scott-Bohana, Andrew Smith; Paul Barnett (Architects); Jennifer Marchant, Cate Riley, Karen Casey, Belinda Smith, Rob Tindal, and Cia Flannery (Graphic Design); Michael Hewes (Sound Design)

Artists: Darryl Cowie, the Djerrkura family, Jenuarrie, Vic McGrath, Michael Hewes, Alice Mitchell Marrakorlorlo, Munnari (John Hammond), Jonathan Nadji, Violet Petyarre, Mervyn Rubuntja, Wenten Rubuntja, Jerko Starcevic, Paddy Japaljarri Stewart Thanakupi, and Judy Watson

Aboriginal Cultural Advisors: Matilda House (Ngambri), Joseph Elu

BACKGROUND

A civic landscape conceived as part of the national reconciliation policy to represent a shared history of settler and Aboriginal populations, Reconciliation Place is a pedestrian promenade in the parliamentary zone in the capital, Canberra. The promenade articulated by sculptural art installations links the High Court to the National Library of Australia and is designed to be perpendicular to Canberra's land axis, which extends from Parliament House to the Australian War Memorial.[1] Two open competitions for the design of Reconciliation Place and Commonwealth Place were announced to coincide with the centenary celebrations of the Australian Federation in 2001. The projects were completed in 2002. While Commonwealth Place reiterated the civic purpose of the parliamentary axis by introducing a multipurpose recreational space, a Speakers Square, and a ceremonial crescent at the edge of Lake Burley Griffin, Reconciliation Place crossed this axis in a reconciliatory gesture

Figure 30.1.   Reconciliation Place, eastern promenade artworks. Photo by author, 2011.

toward Australian Aboriginal peoples. The proximity and shared occupation of space by these intersecting axes was a bid to remedy political evasions of such issues in the past. The commission faced the challenge of being the first authorized expression of civic Aboriginal presence in the Australian capital.

PROJECT DESCRIPTION

The competition for Reconciliation Place took place within the context of ongoing government strategies to address the predicament of Indigenous people in Australia, including the Keating Labour government's 1990 report *Blue Print for the Future*, and the report of the Council for Aboriginal Reconciliation in 2000. The 1990 report raised several critical issues, including the lack of a historic treaty between Aboriginal groups and white settlers, the need for healing in relation to the violent histories of colonization, and the need for a national apology to the generation of Aboriginals who were forcibly removed from their communities. The conservative Liberal government elected in 1996 under then prime minister John Howard notoriously rejected the need for a national apology.[2] The Howard government opted instead to create an Aboriginal history archive and set aside money for an oral history project to be managed by the National Library of Australia. The issue of a national apology and the need for reconciliation continued to be contentious issues on which the Labour and Liberal parties took opposing positions. Both Fiona Harrison and Christopher Vernon observe that efforts by the Howard government to remove the Aboriginal Tent Embassy (see chapter 1) occurred in tandem with the launching of these new projects.[3] From this perspective, Reconciliation Place was designed to deflect demands for a national apology. A formal apology to the Stolen Generations was nevertheless made several years later in 2008, after the Labour Party had returned to power under Prime Minister Kevin Rudd.

Simon Kringas and colleagues won the competition for Reconciliation Place. The winning design advanced a thorough collaborative process, essential to the legitimacy of the project. The design required consultation with a panel, including members of the Aboriginal community, and an Aboriginal member had to be included in the design team (Sharon Payne fulfilled this role).[4] The pedestrian promenade across the land axis links the National Library and the High Court, and was designed as a series of sculptural slivers on either side of a central mound; the winning design made no recommendation of their content.[5] The slivers, designed by both Indigenous and non-Indigenous artists and documenting incidents related to Indigenous culture, leadership, women, separation, and civil rights, were authorized by the National Capital Authority with approval from Parliament.[6] The design was open-ended, with multiple entry points and open to multiple readings with the expectation that it would evolve over time, and this multiplicity reflected collaboration with participants from a number of language groups and proved to be both the project's weakness and its strength.

At Reconciliation Place, historical moments, episodes, and orientations are tackled thematically through artistic interpretations. While each individual project is collaborative, the representative politics is relatively diffused. The seventeen art installations vary from technologically sophisticated and highly curated exhibits with embedded textual, photographic, and audiovisual data to interpretive and figurative sculptures and landscape features by Indigenous artists.[7] As an early example of the kind of curated civic space that draws new museology into the public sphere—quite literally onto a public promenade—Reconciliation Place is an experiment for future urban precincts.

Artwork One, *Fire and Water* by Indigenous artist Judy Watson, and Artwork Seven, *Ngunnawal* by Kringas, Payne, Bree, Tunks, and Vogt, are specifically linked to the Canberra area. *Fire and Water* is designed as a reed bower with a gathering stone, the latter based on the Yuriarra Moth Stone used for cooking bogong moths (*Agrotis infusa)*, which is placed at the artwork's center (Plate 29). The piece includes a sound design by Michael Hughes of whirring wings or far-off chatter, suggesting gathering. Artwork Seven, which features stone from a local quarry, has a pattern of bogong moths overlaid on a map of Australia. Bogong moths migrate annually through the Canberra area, and their annual migration has long been incorporated into the ceremonial gathering and feasting traditions of the local Ngambri people. The installation also has an image of a wedge-tailed eagle, signifying the high country of the Ngunnawal people. The words *Ngunna yerrabi yanggu*, meaning "(you may) walk on this country now," extend a welcome to visitors.

Several artworks represent everyday associations and activities, quite independent of settler influences. Artwork Two, *Methalu Tharri* (Smooth Sailing) by Vic McGrath, takes its form from the sails of traditional Torres Straits Islander canoes; Artwork Five by Thanakupi (Thanacoupie Gloria Fletcher), *Kwiith, Man and Woman Yam*—or "the long yam and the cheeky yam"—consists of textured bronze sculptures derived from familiar organic forms. Artwork Seventeen, *Wati Jarra Jukurrpa* (Two Men Dreaming), is based on a painting by Warlpiri man Paddy Japaljarri Stewart, from the Northern Territory. Its translation into a pavement landscape was designed by Cia Flannery and Rob Tindal.

Artworks depicting settler institutions or processes take on a different character, typically employing industrial materials with planar surfaces and hard edges. Kringas and his team have

Plate 29. Reconciliation Place, Canberra, Australia, *Fire and Water* by artist Judy Watson with Michael Hewes and Matilda House. Photo by author, 2011.

purposefully curated them to convey specific historic encounters, using text, photographs, and captions to explain their content. The involvement of Indigenous peoples in the army, or in particular sports, such as cricket, is commemorated in Artwork Six, *Strength, Service and Sacrifice* by Simon Kringas. There are others that are associated with specific individuals such as Artwork Eight, *Leadership* by Sharon Payne, architect Paul Barnett, and the rest of the team. The installation commemorates two key figures in the civil rights story—Jagera man Neville Bonner, who in 1971 became the first Indigenous senator in the Australian Parliament, and Gurindji man Vincent Lingiari, who led the walkoff at Wave Hill Station in the Northern Territory in 1966. This exhibit also features the popular Australian song "From Little Things Big Things Grow" by Paul Kelly and Kev Carmody, which relates the story of Lingiari and the Wave Hill walkoff in protest at stolen wages. Artwork Nine, *Referendum* and Artwork Fourteen, *Land Rights* are similarly curated by Kringas and his team.

It is inevitable that the content of such exhibits once placed in the public domain are the subject of debate and controversy; this is particularly true of the core ensemble of Artworks Three and Four, *Separation*. Dedicated to the Stolen Generations, the first of these artworks was conceived to represent Aboriginal and Torres Strait Islander children forcibly removed from their families to be institutionalized or adopted by white families, a policy maintained from 1869 to at least 1969 (a policy which some advocates insist has not ceased in practice).[8] Dissatisfied with the manner in which their stories were represented, Indigenous groups created the second artwork on the experience of child removal, Artwork Four (by architects Graham Scott-Bohanna and Andrew Smith, sculptor Darryl Cowie, designer Karen Casey, and graphic designer Cate Riley). Artwork Four includes a two-thousand-word-account and

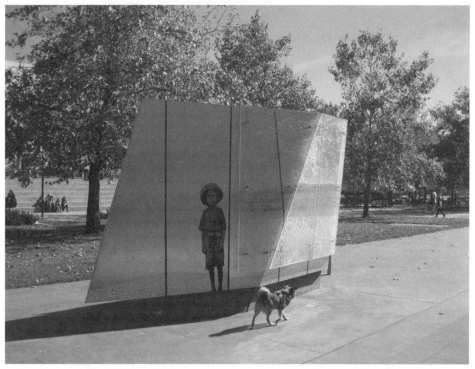

Figure 30.2.   Reconciliation Place: Artwork Three, *Separation* by Kringas and team. Photo by author, 2011.

a perforated panel in which those affected by this practice could leave messages.[9] The representation and revision of the theme of separation is indicative of the differences between the interpretation and presentation of traumatic historic events and the emotive responses evoked by the discourse of reconciliation.

Elizabeth Strakosch argues that the debate over the representation of experiences of child removal "suggests that perpetrating nation states and victimized social groups are different types of political actors with different memorial needs, and that these needs do not easily coexist in a single memorial site."[10] In fact, the jagged industrial character of those slivers that outline politically contentious issues seem to anticipate such debates. In contrast, a number of biographical artworks are dedicated to prominent individuals, such as Artwork Ten, *Women*, by artists Jenuarrie, Thanakupi, and Violet Petyarre, representing Dr. Faith Bandler, Lady Jessie Mary Street, and Dr. Evelyn Scott. Other biographical works have organic forms and textured surfaces that are suggestive of an unmediated materiality, including Artwork Eleven, representing Ruby Florence Hammond PSM; Artwork Twelve, representing Robert Lee; Artwork Thirteen, representing Wenten Rubuntja AM; Artwork Fifteen, representing Bill Neidjie OAM; and Artwork Sixteen, representing Gatjil Djerrkura OAM. These works commemorate the lives and stories of Aboriginal Elders and civil rights activists, many of which are designed by family or clan members (for example, Artwork Eleven was designed by Hammond's son Munnari (John Hammond); Artwork Twelve was designed by Alice Mitchell Marrakorlorlo, a traditional owner of Nitmiluk; Artwork Thirteen was designed by Rubuntja's son Mervyn

Figure 30.3. Reconciliation Place, Artwork Four, *Separation* by Graham Scott-Bohanna, Darryl Cowie, Andrew Smith, Karen Casey, and Cate Riley. Photo by author, 2011.

Rubuntja; Artwork Fifteen was designed by Neidjie's son Jonathan Nadji; and Artwork Sixteen was designed by the Djerrkura family).

RECEPTION

The formal nature of the intervention in the landscape at Reconciliation Place, its deployment of a ritual pathway, and its episodic character drew from existing precedents for heritage walking trails. The institutionalization of a typically informal spatial praxis, overlaid by explanatory textual annotations, illustrates its location within a broader public discourse. The necessity of incorporating Indigenous stories within settler modes of communication and their resultant depoliticization has invited considerable critique. By such strategies, Elizabeth Strakosch argues, government responsibility for past atrocities is disavowed.[11] In Strakosch's view, the sophisticated material and visual techniques used by artists, including stone or steel slivers, their polished surfaces etched with words or images, represent ambivalent readings of the issues at stake. According to Strakosch's argument, "countermonumental" representational strategies where victim and perpetrator share the same space are inherently problematic. Where the process of reconciliation is not archived or is open to interpretation and subsequent adjustment, and where viewers are relieved of the responsibility of interpreting this history, such representation often works to silence dissent.[12]

Providing a poignant contrast to the Tent Embassy's refusal to be institutionalized, Reconciliation Place thus strikes at the heart of the issues of cultural representation and the Indigenous cultural center's precarious position in Australian civic space. Postmodern forms of representation that have their basis in an inclusive plurality can be interpreted as noncommittal or comprising multiple unresolved subjectivities. It is possible that Reconciliation Place has inherited some of the critique that was directed toward the retrogressive Indigenous policies of the Howard government; in any event, it functions as an important reminder of the potential costs of civic visibility and institutional recognition.

NOTES

1. Thanks to director, estate development and renewal national capital authority Rob Tindal for clarification on copyrights.

2. Peter Read, "The Truth which Will Set Us All Free: National Reconciliation, Oral History and the Conspiracy of Silence," *Oral History* 35, no. 1 (Spring 2007): 98–106.

3. Fiona Harrison, "Not Nothing: Shades of Public Space," *Journal of Australian Studies* 27, no. 76 (2003): 42; Christopher Vernon, "Axial Occupation," *Architecture Australia* 91, no. 5 (September/October 2002): 84–90; SueAnne Ware, "Radar Competition, Section 2, Reconciling This Place," *Architecture Australia* 90, no. 5 (September/October 2001): 40; and Mark Harris, "Mapping Australian Postcolonial Landscapes: From Resistance to Reconciliation," *Law Text Culture* 7 (2003): 89.

4. The brief was developed by the National Capital Authority and a steering committee of local Ngunnawal and national Aboriginal representatives. There were seven commendations from thirty-six entries.

5. Christopher Vernon, "Canberra: Where Landscape Is Pre-Eminent," in David Gordon, ed., *Planning Twentieth-Century Capital Cities* (London and New York: Routledge, 2006), 130–49.

6. SueAnne Ware, "Radar Competition."

7. National Capital Authority, "Reconciliation Place," available at https://www.nationalcapital .gov.au/index.php/attractions-managed-by-the-nca/reconciliation-place. Information on the artworks is based on the information provided on this website.

8. Elizabeth Strakosch, "Counter Monuments and Nation-Building in Australia," *Peace Review: A Journal of Social Justice* 22 (2010): 274.

9. Strakosch, "Counter Monuments," 274.

10. Elizabeth Strakosch, "The Political Complexities of 'New Memorials': Victims and Perpetrators Sharing Space in the Australian Capital," paper presented at the "Memorials and Museums" workshop, Berlin, October 21–26, 2009.

11. Strakosch, "The Political Complexities of 'New Memorials,'" 6.

12. Ibid., 4, in reference to National Capital Authority, "Reconciliation Place," *Landscape Australia* 3 (2002): 40–41.

31

Riawunna Centre, University of Tasmania, Launceston, Tasmania, Australia

Location: Faculty of Arts Precinct, Newnham Campus, University of Tasmania, Launceston
Date: 1999–2002
Client: University of Tasmania and members of the Riawunna Community
Architect: Peter Elliott Pty. Ltd.
Project Architect: Rob Trinca, Robert Troup
Design Architect: Peter Elliott
Project Manager: John Lewis
Structural, Civil, Electrical, Mechanical and Hydraulic Consultant: Ove Arup + Partners
Builder: Fairbrother Building Contractors
Other Team Members: Helen Day, Simon Scillio, and Sarah Drofenik
Landscape Consultants: Urban Initiatives Pty. Ltd., and Sinatra Murphy, Art of Landscape
    Architecture
Concept Design: Sinatra Murphy and members of the Riawunna Aboriginal Studies Centre
Design Development: Sinatra Murphy and Urban Initiatives Pty. Ltd.
Documentation and Contract Administration: Urban Initiatives Pty. Ltd.
Rock Placement: Calverley Landscaping and Sinatra Murphy
On-Site Design of Seating Wall and Firepit: Calverley Landscaping and members of Ri-
    awunna Aboriginal Studies Centre
Cost: approximately $255,000
Centre Director: Clair Andersen

The Riawunna Centre at the University of Tasmania has a commitment "to the advancement of knowledge about Aboriginal and Torres Strait Islander cultures and societies and to the promotion of cross-cultural understandings, as well as to providing a prominent place within the University for Indigenous Australian values, traditions and discourses."[1] It has two locations within the University of Tasmania campuses, at Hobart and at Newnham in Launceston, and has support staff at the Cradle Coast Campus. The Centre hosts subject major and elective units in Aboriginal Studies within the Bachelor of Arts at the University.[2] Only the Launceston facility, discussed here, is purpose-built.

217

Proposed alongside plans for a new Faculty of Arts building, the purpose-built facility was an effort at creating a visible Aboriginal presence on campus. The former Centre for Aboriginal Research and Education (CARE), established within the University in the late 1980s, had been housed in a building at Brooks where, apart from an Aboriginal flag and an outdoor fireplace, the facility's identity was subsumed within the existing characterless buildings.[3] The Riawunna project was conceived in collaboration with the local Indigenous community with a desire to assert that Indigenous culture was not extinct in Tasmania, as is commonly believed.[4] The project brief called for "a building with its own address point, separate identity and an 'Aboriginal Native Garden.'"[5]

An important decision made earlier on in its development emphasized the need to deal with both architecture and landscape as inseparable and integral to the design of an Aboriginal facility. The building was one component in a landscape comprised of multiple features, and its design seeks to invoke the landscape of Launceston's Cataract Gorge (Plate 30).

Plate 30.   Riawunna Centre, University of Tasmania, Launceston, Tasmania, Australia, northern courtyard. Photo by John Gollings, courtesy Peter Elliott Architects.

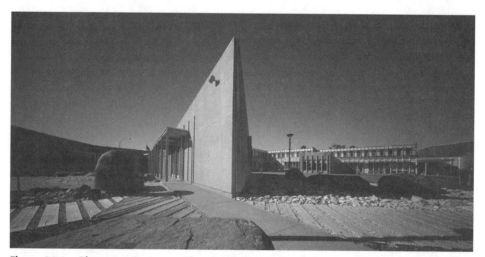

Figure 31.1.   Riawunna Centre, north-pointed tip courtyard showing Faculty of Arts precinct. Photo by John Gollings, courtesy Peter Elliott Architects.

PROJECT DESCRIPTION

The design by Melbourne architectural firm Peter Elliott Pty. Ltd. takes its curvaceous form from seedpods and crustacean shells, and has been compared with an abalone shell.[6] The introverted form achieves a sense of containment where a landscaped "native garden" or "cultural landscape" (designed by Melbourne's Urban Initiatives Pty. Ltd. in conjunction with Sinatra Murphy) completes it as a circle of gathering. *Riawunna* means "circle" in the language of the Bruny Island People, and the form complements this association.[7] The form accommodates a resource room, student computer lab, two teaching rooms, a community room with kitchen, office and reception, and six offices for permanent staff members. A glass cabinet at the entrance displays Indigenous artifacts donated to the center.

Peter Elliott Pty. Ltd. are well known for their civic projects (including North Terrace, Adelaide with Taylor Cullity Lethlean and Paul Carter). The Riawunna Centre is part of the University of Tasmania's Faculty of Arts precinct developed by the architect with academic facilities for the social sciences and humanities disciplines, a public lecture theatre and Riawunna. The two facilities are entered via a diagonal path that leads to a shared entry forecourt to both buildings. The Riawunna Centre is designed so that all internal spaces open into a courtyard encircled by the form. This courtyard, and the native garden leading from it, gives the building a protective character quite different from the orthogonal layout of the surrounding buildings. The building form, cultural landscape, Aboriginal flag, and colorful interiors give it a distinctive presence that inserts Indigenous spatialities into a colonized landscape. The stones lend a sense of permanence and longevity to the project, and the internal courtyard with its fire pit and flat, granite fieldstones recreates an Aboriginal gathering place and "connection to country."[8]

Figure 31.2.   Launceston Gorge. Photo courtesy Dean Mundey.

The metal- and timber-clad structure sits on a concrete slab with a warped skillion roof form of varying pitches sloping toward the internal courtyard.[9] The roof structure is a repetitive radial rafter system that is exposed in the interior and painted black. A pergola on the north-facing side of the courtyard forms an external corridor along one edge of the building. Timbers used include Tasmanian oak, radiated pine, and celery top pine. The curvature of the building can be read in the interior spaces, which are painted in bright oranges and reds, while the external wall of the courtyard is an ochre hue.

CONSULTATION PROCESS

Reporting on the project for the Australian Institute of Landscape Architects (AILA), Murphy and Hart stress the centrality of community-based consultation to ensure that the design outcomes were "an expression of their landscapes and their culture."[10] The key individuals behind the creation of the facility were Aboriginal Elder Patsy Cameron from the Riawunna Indigenous community and Vicki Maikutena Matson-Green of the Palawa people. Both Cameron and Matson-Green grew up on Flinders Island and have been active members of numerous Indigenous organizations and Aboriginal higher-education initiatives. Patsy Cameron describes the Riawunna Centre as "a comfortable haven for the Aboriginal community, students and staff" and "an opportunity to embrace the outside community in our own place, the way we want to."[11]

Eight members of the Riawunna people worked with the consultants at different stages of the design process in 1998, firstly to conceptualize "the living cultural landscape," and then as participants in a design workshop where a scale model was worked on by the team.[12] The resultant focus was on two objectives: "to develop a garden design that reflected the local Indigenous culture, the Tasmanian landscape and cultural connection to the land through the 'stories' of the indigenous people"; and "to establish the functional role of the garden in relation to the Centre's special needs and resources in providing educational and cultural services for its client group."[13] The focus on geology and inclusion of large, vertical dolerite stones invokes similar formations in Launceston's Gorge.

BUILDING AS LANDSCAPE

The Gorge is believed to have particular significance for Aboriginal peoples of Tasmania and, as observed by Patsy Cameron, the nine boulders in the garden represent the nine Aboriginal tribes of Tasmania as "sentinels looking over that place."[14] Prior to colonization, the Gorge was a ceremonial place and a mens' place for the Letteremairrener people of the area, but it also has strong associations for subsequent generations as a troubled place, a swimming pool used in the summer, and on its northern side, a place of peace.[15]

The lead landscape consultants, Urban Initiatives, were engaged for the design, documentation, and contract administration on the landscape of the new Faculty of Arts precinct within which Riawunna is located. Sinatra Murphy ran a consultative workshop for stakeholders in the Riawunna Centre.[16] The design development, documentation, and contract administration phases were carried out jointly. Urban Initiatives and its director, Bruce Echberg, have been involved in many civic landscape projects, including the 2010 central mall project for the University of Tasmania at Sandy Bay. Sinatra Murphy has a reputation for working in remote areas and with Indigenous communities. The design workshop led to design development and rock selection drawings, with each stone individually chosen by consultants and approved by the client group. Materials used were sourced within Tasmania. The dolerite stones came from a spoil heap at a large warehouse development in Kings Meadows, Launceston, and the quartzite gravel mulch used around the building was sourced from quarry waste.[17] Consequently, the landscape project cost under approximately $30,600 to create.

The use of Indigenous plants from coastal areas of Tasmania made the landscape less reliant on irrigation, which was only used for the lawns. Species of yakka (*Xanthorrhoea*) and native tussock grasses planted in a bed of quartzite with shell grit evoke Tasmania's coastal landscapes.[18] The palette of materials is thus indicative of different geological and geographical regions representative of the diversity of the community.

RECEPTION

Activities held at Riawunna involving the local community include events during NAIDOC Week and the involvement of Elders in Welcome to Country ceremonies. The Centre also holds barbecues and a communal lunch every Thursday, cooked on a voluntary basis by one of the staff. A shared cross-cultural ceremony was held in March 2011 with a group of Ainu people of Hokkaido, Japan, at the culmination of a five-day visit to Tasmania.[19] Traditional ceremonial dances and songs were performed at the Centre.[20] As part of its broader community education role, Riawunna hosts a number of public events throughout each year, including seminars, workshops, film evenings, and art exhibitions.

From 2013, the focus has been on enhancing Indigenous participation and employment at the University of Tasmania, as well as delivering a dedicated bridging program, which caters to around thirty Indigenous students and is designed to induct mature-age students into the University. Riawunna thus provides a safe environment where those who want to enter mainstream university studies can learn writing and computer skills. The Centre also conducts tutoring programs for Indigenous students already enrolled in the university. Important services provided include assisting students to find jobs by liaising with job agencies, providing counseling for mental health or social issues, and providing a safe environment that builds confidence in the students before they enter mainstream university life. The duty of care assumed by the Centre is particularly important for Indigenous students who are often insulated from mainstream urban society.[21]

In 2000, Riawunna was awarded the AILA Victoria and Tasmania Award in Landscape Architecture, Landscape Excellence and Building Settings, and the AILA National Project Award in Landscape Architecture, Design (Building Context). In 2001 the Faculty of Arts Precinct received a commendation in the Sir Zelman Cowen Award for Public Buildings (National) and a Public Buildings Award (Tasmanian Chapter), and in 2002 the project received a commendation from the Australian Timber Design Awards.

The Riawunna Centre makes a concern typically marginalized in Australian institutions a visible and central focus. The deployment of architecture to achieve this objective and the value of purpose-built cultural facilities combine in a new proposition of building as landscape.

Figure 31.3.   Riawunna Centre, model of structure. Photo courtesy Peter Elliott Architects.

NOTES

1. University of Tasmania, "Riawunna Centre: About Us," available at http://www.utas.edu.au/riawunna/ about-us. Thanks to Clair Andersen for correspondence and to the architects for providing data.

2. University of Tasmania, "Riawunna Centre: About Us."

3. Shayne Breen and Dyan Summers, eds., *Aboriginal Connections with Launceston* (Launceston: Launceston City Council, 2006), 120.

4. Edwina Richardson, "Riawunna Aboriginal Studies Centre, University of Tasmania, Launceston," Australian Institute of Landscape Architects, available at http://www.aila.org.au/projects/tas/Riawunna/Riawunna2.htm.

5. Phin Murphy and Tim Hart, "Riawunna: The Living Landscape Expressed through the Living Culture—Full Project Report," The Australian Institute of Landscape Architects, available at http://www.aila.org.au/projects/tas/Riawunna/Riawunna3.htm. A large part of this chapter on the facility is indebted to this detailed report.

6. Peter Elliott P/L Architects, "University of Tasmania Faculty of Arts Precinct," available at http://www.architecture.com.au/awards_search?option=showaward&entryno=20017011.

7. Murphy and Hart, "Riawunna: The Living Landscape."

8. Ibid.

9. John Gollings, Riawunna Aboriginal Education Centre, Tasmanian Timber, http://www.tastimber .tas.gov.au/Project_Detail.aspx?projectid=479 (accessed July 12, 2012).

10. Murphy and Hart, "Riawunna: The Living Landscape."

11. Breen and Summers, *Aboriginal Connections with Launceston*, 120.

12. Murphy and Hart, "Riawunna: The Living Landscape."

13. Ibid.

14. Breen and Summers, *Aboriginal Connections with Launceston*, 120.

15. Ibid., 126–27.

16. Urban Initiatives, "Riawunna Aboriginal Studies Centre," available at http://urbaninitiatives .com.au/explore-our-work/project/riawunna-aboriginal-studies-centre/.

17. Richardson, "Riawunna Aboriginal Studies Centre."

18. Ibid.

19. "Spiritual Sympathy Sparked," *Hobart Mercury*, March 3, 2011.

20. Brett Stubbs, "Sharing Struggle to Shake Cultural Shackles," *Hobart Mercury*, February 18, 2003.

21. Based on conversation with staff at Riawunna during visit on July 5, 2012.

32

Rumbalara Medical Clinic, Mooroopna and Rumbalara Elders Care Facility, Shepparton, Victoria, Australia

Date: completed 2012
Client: Rumbalara Aboriginal Co-Operative
Architecture and Interior Design: Baldasso Cortese
Landscape (Site/Master Plan): Sinatra Murphy
Civil Engineers (Site Infrastructure/Master Plan): Chris Smith Associates
Environmentally Sustainable Design (Independent Living Units): William Sales Partnership (WSP) Built Ecology
Services Engineers (Independent Living Units): WSP Group
Structural Engineers (Independent Living Units): John Mullen & Partners
Services Engineers (Elder Care Facility): CI Consulting Industries
Structural Engineers (Elder Care Facility): Intrax

RUMBALARA MEDICAL CLINIC, MOOROOPNA

Architecture and Interior Design: Baldasso Cortese
Landscape: Land Design Partnership
Civil Engineers (Site Infrastructure): Chris Smith Associates
Environmentally Sustainable Design: William Sales Partnership (WSP) Built Ecology
Services Engineers: WSP Group
Structural & Civil Engineers: VDM Consulting
Cost: approximately $6 million

RUMBALARA ELDERS CARE FACILITY, SHEPPARTON

Architecture and Interior Design: Baldasso Cortese
Landscape (Site/Master Plan): Sinatra Murphy
Civil Engineers (Site Infrastructure/Master Plan): Chris Smith Associates
ESD (Independent Living Units): WSP Built Ecology

Services Engineers (Independent Living Units): WSP Group
Structural Engineers (Independent Living Units): John Mullen & Partners
Services Engineers (Elders Care Facility): CI Consulting Industries
Structural Engineers (Elders Care Facility): Intrax
Cost: Elders Care Facility approximately $9 million; Independent Living Units approximately
   $6 million

The Rumbalara Aboriginal Co-Operative (RAC) has had two complexes designed by architects Baldasso Cortese: Rumbalara Elders Facility in Shepparton, and Rumbalara Health Services in Mooroopna.[1] The RAC provides a broad range of community services to local Aboriginal people, including primary and allied health, dental, justice, family, housing, and aged care services. The projects described here were designed to satisfy these specific programs.

BACKGROUND

The history of Rumbalara provides the backdrop to this community-centered approach. Settled initially by residents from the Cummeragunja Mission Station in New South Wales, the river flats in Mooroopna were home to around three hundred people by the 1950s.[2] Whenever the river flooded, the community would move to higher ground, to an area known as Daish's Paddock. This environment proved unhealthy to the community, and in 1958, the Aboriginal Welfare Board of Victoria erected ten prefabricated concrete houses on the Mooroopna site. No services were provided. The housing project was named *Rumbalara*, meaning "rainbow." Amenities were introduced nine years later. The project was in fact intended as an interim stage in a broader rehousing program for ex-mission residents, which proceeded with residents being rehoused in the towns of Shepparton and Mooroopna. The Rumbalara site was closed in 1969 and remained unused for five years. During the 1970s, the Goulburn Murray Aboriginal Co-Operative opposed the sale of the site, and following sustained pressure on both the Victorian and federal governments, it purchased it for a nominal sum. The community-centered approach advanced by the RAC builds on the history associated with the site. The area has the second largest Aboriginal community next to Melbourne.

   The architect selected by the RAC, Melbourne firm Baldasso Cortese, is known for aged care, childcare, and community and school buildings in Victoria, and it responded to the community vision with facilities tailored to client requirements.[3] The examples outlined here were conceptualized following consultation and Aboriginal cultural training by the architects. The stated vision for the Rumbalara projects was to educate, empower, and foster confidence in the Aboriginal community to take charge of their lives. Aboriginal employment and apprenticeship initiatives were also developed in coordination with the head contractor and KEE (Koorie Employment Enterprises). The RAC chairperson at the time, Justin Mohamed, asked for the new health facility to "look like an Aboriginal health facility without relying on signage to indicate what it is." The design response was generated from the Yorta Yorta people's affinity with the Barmah Forest and their "connection to the earth."[4]

   The challenge was to design facilities that could formally and spatially convey socially significant programs. They would also link the identity of the RAC to the creation of a healthy Aboriginal community for the Shepparton and Mooroopna area. The program was for a community facility with a specific cultural brief. More importantly, these facilities are not isolated buildings but are integrated with other community facilities. The Medical Clinic is located adjacent to the main administration complex at Mooroopna, while the Elder Care Facility is part of a broader master plan. In each case, residential and community services coexist.

RUMBALARA MEDICAL CLINIC, MOOROOPNA

The project, which is located on a flood plain, included master planning and the configuration of buildings on-site, in relationship to the surrounding environment. Neil Christensen was project leader.[5] The center was to provide health and dental care services to the Aboriginal communities of the Goulburn Valley, and with this goal in mind, the natural history of the valley, the dry riverbed pattern, and overhead canopy was drawn into the design. The architects broke up the formal organization of the facility into a number of fractured elements under cover of the connecting roof structure. Views to the forest reserve were provided to the east. The staged program of construction for the completion of the medical clinic and refurbishment of adjacent existing buildings was achieved without interruption to health and community services. Material used for the facility included timber-boarded concrete panels with a natural red ochre stain. The earth tones and gum-leaf design, a healing motif by local Aboriginal artist Lyn Thorpe, was sandblasted on the panels as a relief pattern with an applied stain finish. The pattern was also integrated into the Wathaurong Glass, feature window panels located adjacent to the entry. A number of sustainable features, such as rainwater-harvesting bladder tanks within the floor and vertical timber sunscreen blades along the western façade, complement the design approach. Health, sustainability, and connectivity to nature are driving ideas in the design. The Medical Clinic was also conceived as providing a bold new "front entry" and identity for the RAC facilities in Mooroopna.

RUMBALARA ELDERS CARE FACILITY, SHEPPARTON

Rumbalara Elders Care Facility, completed in 2012, comprises a thirty-bed aged-care facility, nineteen independent living units, and a community center. The Facility is the first stage in a comprehensive master plan for a multigenerational, communal, aged-care facility for the Aboriginal community of the Goulburn Valley.[6] The generational interaction conceived in the plan maintains the cultural value of passing down cultural knowledge. The site, formerly a disused orchard, is surrounded by housing subdivisions that require careful attention to the relative scale and the need for integration with the wider local community.

The Elders Care Facility caters for low, high, and dementia care for Aboriginal Elders. It includes a commercial café and dining spaces for residents and external users, in-house laundry facilities, activities areas, lounge area, hairdressing and podiatry, and a palliative care unit.[7] A second stage of development of a further thirty beds is anticipated.

The eight-hectare project located north of Shepparton was partnered with the Department of Human Services and Rural Housing Network Ltd., and future plans include an additional nineteen independent living units to be built in three stages. The master plan also includes training and accommodation facilities for nursing staff, a "Men's Shed," hot houses, a respite home, and home for children with disabilities.

The landscape master plan integrates cultural and sustainability approaches by using water-sensitive urban design. It is based on the Aboriginal concept of six to eight annual seasons and resultant changes in flora and fauna. A local Aboriginal nursery has propagated native

Figure 32.1.   Rumbalara Elders Care Facility, community space. Photo courtesy Baldasso Cortese.

Figure 32.2.   Rumbalara Elders Care Facility, independent living units. Photo courtesy Baldasso Cortese.

Plate 31. Rumbalara Elders Care Facility, Shepparton, Victoria, Australia, exterior view. Photo courtesy Baldasso Cortese.

seeds for the project, and the landscape will be created and maintained using Aboriginal labor procured through Koorie Employment Enterprises (KEE). In addition to employing Passive Solar Design approaches in the orientation of buildings, the master plan has incorporated a range of sustainable practices with regard to using sustainable products and materials, rainwater storage, and retention on site and drought tolerance. The aesthetic character of the design, its repetitive use of timber, stone, and corrugated-iron finishes, allows for the formal articulation of units as individual shelters while maintaining their coherence as a collective (Plate 31). Outdoor areas adjacent to units are carefully planned for collective social gathering. The architecture, which is stylistically contemporary, is drawn from domestic vocabularies rather than institutional templates.

RECEPTION

When the project was first publicized in 2009, it met with considerable objections from Shepparton residents in the immediate vicinity of the proposed project. The RAC, troubled by this response, conducted a series of informal briefings to address their concerns. It was observed that much of the opposition was due to entrenched racial stereotypes activated by the prospect of a large-scale Aboriginal facility in the neighborhood.[8] There were pejorative assumptions made regarding the nature of the facility and the community. In contrast, the purpose-designed facility, with its contemporary aesthetics and innovative program, has proved to be a leader in the provision of aged care. Its community-centered focus, including the deliberate incorporation of a community space within the complex, exposes the problems of institutionalized and individuated aged-care provision elsewhere. The capacity for community cohesion facilitated by this approach is epitomized by the community lunch hosted at the facility during NAIDOC Week.[9]

The community is mindful of their difficult beginnings and proud of its achievements. This was evident in an interview with Yorta Yorta man Leon Saunders, who lived on the site in 1958 when the government first built concrete shelters on the Rumbalara site.[10] Saunders reported that a doctor would come out fortnightly from Melbourne and practice out of one of the shelters. A few shelters have been saved as reminders of this earlier period, one of them right beside the new medical service. A museum comprising community photographs has been set up in another. The inference given is that community identity and community health have an interrelated history.

An important facet of the project was the Aboriginal employment program supported by the Waterson Building Company.[11] The expansion of the medical service created thirty jobs for Aboriginal workers, including apprentice builders, bricklayers, landscape gardeners and painters, and developed new trade-based skills in the community. High unemployment levels among local Aboriginal residents mean that opportunities to learn with Aboriginal mentorship are highly valued, particularly for young Aboriginal trainees. Still, the Rumbalara project's main contribution is in addressing the health of the local Aboriginal community and their comparably low life expectancy caused by prolonged histories of structural impoverishment.

The Medical Clinic has its own medical drivers who pick up patients from their homes and deliver them to the front door. By enabling Elders to remain in the same locality (rather than removing them to institutions elsewhere), the Elders Care Facility prevents community dissolution. Such socially responsible programs respond to and invigilate against traumatic histories of Aboriginal dispossession, and provide a protected and socially connected place for "a dignified end to life."[12]

NOTES

1. Thanks to Felicia Dean for comments on this account. Architectural data based on architect's notes. Thanks to Patricia McQuinn and Brigid Thompson at Baldasso Cortese for proving additional material on the project.

2. This history is summarized from the account given by Rumbalara Aboriginal Co-Operative, "About Us," available at http://www.rumbalara.org.au/about-us.php.

3. Based on architect's notes.

4. Based on architect's notes.

5. Baldasso Cortese, "Rumbalara Health Services," available at http://www.bcarch.net/index.php?nodeId=34.

6. Based on architect's notes.

7. Baldasso Cortese, "Rumbalara Elders Care," available at http://www.bcarch.net/index.php?nodeId=76.

8. Darren Linton, "Stereotypes Blamed," *Shepparton News*, October 7, 2009.

9. Right Now, "Aboriginal Architecture: The Rumbalara Health Facility," podcast dated July 19, 2012, available at http://rightnow.org.au/podcasts/aboriginal-architecture-the-rumbalara-health-facility-the-thursday-podcast/.

10. Ibid.

11. Mary Gearin, "Aged Care Facility Brings Together Young and Old," Australian Broadcasting Corporation, broadcast October 18, 2011, available at http://www.abc.net.au/news/2011-10-18/aged-care-facility-brings-together-young-and-old/3577850.

12. Ibid.

33

Sámi Parliaments, Norway, Sweden, and Finland

SÁMEDIGGI: SÁMI PARLIAMENT BUILDING AT KARASJOK, FINNMARK, NORWAY

Location: Karasjok, Finnmark, Norway
Date: 1998–2000 (completed 1996)
Client: Directorate of Public Construction and Property (Statsbygg)
Architect: Stein Halvorsen Ltd. and Christian Sundby Architects, Oslo
Project Team: Stein Halvorsen Ltd., Christian Sundby, and Magnus Rynning-Tønnesen
Interior Design: Beate Ellingsen, Rannveig Getz, and Heide Tjøm
Landscape Architect: Grindaker Ltd. (Lars Flugsrud)
Structural Engineer: Fredriksen Ltd.
Contractor: Bjørn Bygg Ltd.
Builder: Statsbygg
Cost: approximately $25 million

NEW SÁMI PARLIAMENT BUILDING, BADJÁNEAMPI, KIRUNA, SWEDEN

Location: Adolf Hedinsvägen, Kiruna, Sweden
Client: Statens Fastighetsverk (the Swedish National Property Board)
Architect: Murman Arkitekter Ltd. (Hans Murman)
Head of Project Team: Helena Andersson
Landscape Architect: Ulf Nordfjell, Ramboll Stockholm
Engineer: Konkret, Stockholm
Stuctural Engineer: Olle Norrman

SÁMI CULTURAL CENTRE, SAJOS, INARI, FINLAND

Location: Sajos, Inari, Finland
Client: Senaatti-kiinteistöt (Senate Properties)
Architects: HALO Architects Ltd., Oulu, Finland
Head Designer: Architects m3 Ltd. (Janne Pihlajaniemi)
Structural Engineering: Ramboll Finland Ltd., Timo Turunen, Ismo Kovalainen
Special Design: ISS Proko Ltd.
Contractor: Keskisuomen Betonirakenne Ltd.
Cost: approximately $22 million

BACKGROUND

Autonomous cultural authorities that are transnational in configuration, being representative bodies for the Sámi people in Finland, Sweden, and Norway, the Sámi Parliaments exist independently of national parliaments and are overt political translations of the cultural center program. The Sámi Parliament as an institution is repeated in Norway, Sweden, and Finland.[1] However, these political bodies are financially dependent on annual funding allocations from state governments and contained by the national legislation of each respective country. Their struggle for autonomy is received differently in each separate nation, although their collective regional identity has done much to advance the Sámi cause. Sámi Parliaments have publicly elected representatives and hold plenary assemblies several times a year.

The Sámi are Indigenous Finno-Ugric people inhabiting the Arctic area of Sápmi, which falls across parts of contemporary Scandinavia and Russia.[2] As with other Indigenous communities the world over, the traditionally nomadic Sámi were exposed to assimilatory policies that persisted until well after World War II. The diffusion of the Sámi population across the Scandinavian nation-states was regarded as a governance problem. Their distinct identity gained recognition in the latter half of the twentieth century, following increasing acceptance for cultural differences within the nation-state and growing contestation over Sámi rights. Issues of Sámi land use rights gained international attention in the context of conflicts of interest between Sámi herdsmen, environmentalists, local non-Sámi populations, and mining operatives. The Sámi have been reported as regarding mining as a form of colonization, an extension of Lutheran proselytization and related assimilatory processes that have historically impacted their communities.[3]

The Sámi Parliaments are platforms for minority self-determination within a representative democracy, empowered by electoral processes. Although subject to public law, the Sámi Parliament in Norway, Sweden, and Finland each has its own governing body that adjudicates and oversees matters concerning the community and their lands, distribution of revenue earned by the Sámi, and issues of language, culture, and legal status. This structural relationship of minority to majority is very different from the plural or multicultural models that depoliticize Aboriginal groups elsewhere. International legislation has played a critical role in gaining recognition for the Sámi. The International Covenant of 1966 on Civil and Political Rights protects the rights of individuals, while the International Labour Organization Convention concerning Indigenous and Tribal Peoples protects the right to practice culture, language, and religion. Moreover, due to their transnational connections, the Sámi have contributed to the international discourse on Indigenous rights, their location in wealthy nations being relatively advantageous when compared to that of Indigenous peoples globally. Nevertheless, they too won representation only following protracted struggles for their recognition within the framework of the Nordic Council, and recognition and rights vary at the national level.[4] Whereas the cultural identity of the Sámi may not conform to national boundaries, relationships between Indigenous parliaments and national parliaments govern issues of ancestral and customary land rights, titling of territories and communities, and election of representatives. A Nordic Sámi Convention proposed in 2005 is under debate.

The Finnish Sámi Parliament, *Saamelaiskäräjät*, located in Sajos, Inari, was established by an Act of Parliament in 1973, making Finland the most progressive of the three nations in its recognition of Sámi statutory rights. This was followed two years later by subsequent legislation ensuring the cultural autonomy of the Sámi. The Finnish Sámi Parliament functions as an independent legal body while remaining a branch of the Ministry of Justice. It took a further sixteen years for a second parliament to be established: the Sámi Parliament of Norway, *Sametinget*, which opened in 1989. Located in the village of Karasjok in Finnmark, the Norwegian Sámi Parliament evolved from the Sámi Council set up in 1964, and it was formally established by the Sámi Act of 1987. The Sámi of Norway played an active role in the United Nations working groups on the Declaration of Indigenous Rights, which was formally adopted in 2007. The latest entry into the parliamentary process was the Swedish Sámi Parliament *Sametinget*, established in 1993. The Swedish Sámi Parliament is a state administrative agency answerable to the Swedish *Riksdag* and government and as such bears responsibilities both to the Sámi people and the state.[5] Negotiating between these obligations is often quite difficult. The Parliament's head office has been located in office premises at the former Östermalm School at Adolf Hedinsvägen 58 in central Kiruna since 2004. The Swedish *Riksdag* recognized the Sámi as the Indigenous people of Sweden in 1977. A new building is being designed following a competition held in 2005.

Architect Joar Nango has expressed skepticism regarding these formal responses to the transnational issue of Sámi recognition, arguing that a unified Sámi building tradition is difficult to achieve due to the diversity of topography and climate and varied regional building traditions.[6] He maintains that in the Norwegian context there is an overemphasis on symbols such as reindeer herders from "indre Finnmark" and on the *lávvu* or Sámi tent, and that such reductive representations ignore regional differences and historical forces. Critiquing the giant *lávvu* typology of the North, Nango suggests that Sámi architecture is "a way of thinking"; as he writes,

> It is easy to spot a tradition of "Saami attitude," one that brings forth a pragmatic, composite and complex vernacular architecture often bearing the quintessential elements of recycling and spontaneous use of materials such as local wood, plastic and fiber cloths, folded-out oil barrels, cardboard, isolation-foam, etc. and whatever else might be available on site. This demonstrates a specific Saami ability to adapt and improvise according to context, surroundings and landscape.[7]

Although adaptations of circular forms reconstruct a stereotype, the circle also represents the aspiration of civic assembly embodied in the parliament form. Many museums and Indigenous cultural centers have adopted circular designs as equivalent to traditional Aboriginal space, more usually as a rotunda or public entry. The circular form has a long and complex history in many cultures and is historically associated with architectures as varied as huts, fortifications, stupas, domes, and amphitheaters. Its meanings are multiple and range from quotidian to spiritual associations. Similarly, the equation of circular forms to, or their derivation from, Indigenous vernacular architecture has been extensively reviewed and critiqued. However, the adoption of circular forms and timber finishes in the architecture of the Sámi

Parliaments is hardly formulaic. The abstraction of circular forms into elegant and materially considered architectural responses offers sophisticated rather than populist representations. Location in the far north where there is limited light for two months of the year adds a level of complexity to the Scandinavian projects, particularly in Norway. Light penetration becomes an important feature. While both formal and environmental concerns are features of mainstream architectural practice, their translation in the Scandinavian examples is significant. The parliamentary program is designed for the contentious civic engagement typically denied in museums and cultural centers. The proposed collective use of the buildings exceeds the symbolic limits of aesthetic formalism.

SÁMI PARLIAMENT BUILDING AT KARASJOK, FINNMARK, NORWAY

Located on a ridge above the Karasjok town center, the *Sámediggi/Sametinget* or *Sámi Parliament by Oslo-based architects* Stein Halvorsen and Christian Sundby serves a predominantly Indigenous population (Plate 32). Eighty percent of the townspeople are Sámi. The architectural manifestation of the Parliament spatializes a political history of self-determination stipulated in the Sámi Act of 1987, implemented in 1989. The first session of Parliament was convened that same year.

The town of Karasjok has been described as lacking urban coherence, a configuration of prefabricated structures scattered among the trees on the riverbank.[8] The *Samelandssenter*, a community and tourist center by Bjerk and Bjorge Architects, is the only community building in the town, and it originally housed the Parliament. Following the construction of the new Parliament, this complex has reverted to an exclusively tourist facility.

The architects won the project in a competition held in 1996, sponsored by the *Statsbygg* (the Norwegian government).[9] The program requirement was that "the Sámi Parliament appears in a dignified way" and "reflects Sámi architecture"; in short, that Sámi traditions be directly applied to the creation of a monumental building.[10] This overt strategy of indigenization of a European democratic institution led to a deliberately symbolic translation of Indigenous architectural form. The building was awarded the Northern Norway Architecture Prize in 2001.

Plate 32. Sámi Parliament, Karasjok, Norway, exterior view. Photo by Bjarne Riesto, courtesy Stein Halvorson Ltd.

The plenary assembly hall for the thirty-nine-member Parliament is shaped like a *lávvu,* the oblique conical form of a Sámi tent.[11] It sits within a green public space partially encircled by a two-story arc that contains supporting facilities. The concrete building, clad in gray-color larch wood paneling, easily blends with the pine trees that surround it and is oriented toward the view.[12] Related buildings of the complex, which include an auditorium, display hall, around fifty-five offices, five conference rooms, rooms for the Sámi Special Library, and facilities for the *Sámediggi* archives, are contained in the half-circle form. The use of the form of the *lávvu,* which as a popular representation of the Sámi might be regarded as predictable, is well executed; as Henry observes, while the strategy of blowing up a vernacular form to a monumental scale can produce ridiculous effects, "at Karasjok, the form is so simple, and handled with such careful abstraction that there is no question of kitsch."[13] Henry further observes that abstraction is emphasized through the bisection of the Euclidean figure by a thin, wedge-shaped glass bridge that divides the chamber from the anteroom while bringing in natural light. A further degree of abstraction is achieved through an unassuming entrance through an austere and reserved external façade. Henry describes this as an abstraction of the experience of the *lávvu* as penetrating an impassive exterior envelope to move into a complex interior environment.[14]

Other design features that strengthen the communal sensibility of this project, such as the circular, double-height gallery that defines the inside of the arc, connect the various spaces in the semicircular block. The conical form of the chamber brings the public and press gallery to the middle of the volume.[15] Each individual desk is articulated. The use of timber finishes ranging from a rough external cladding on the main building to a refined finish within the chamber similarly constructs a hierarchy of use. These design moves are deliberate and give meaning to the various elements of the project far beyond formal concerns. However, the

Figure 33.1. Sámi Parliament, Norway, exterior view. Photo by Jaro Hollan, courtesy Stein Halvorson Ltd.

Figure 33.2. Sámi Parliament, Norway, assembly chamber. Photo by Jaro Hollan, courtesy Stein Halvorson Ltd.

maintenance of the Siberian *lerke* wood siding in certain parts of the building has recently posed problems, and its preservation has called for additional measures.[16]

NEW SÁMI PARLIAMENT BUILDING, BADJÁNEAMPI, KIRUNA, SWEDEN

The proliferation of Sámi Parliament buildings suggests the resilience of the type and form. The proposal for the new Sámi Parliament in Kiruna, Sweden, won by Murman Arkitekter in 2006, concretizes Sweden's recognition of Indigenous rights (Plate 33).[17] The project was won in a competition run by the National Property Board, in which there were 111 participants. According to Prime Minister Göran Persson's promise to the Sámi, the building is to be constructed of wood.[18] Here too the inspiration is the *lávvu* (or *Tältkåta* in Swedish), albeit stretched into a ridge-shaped crescent. The form creates a semienclosed space with an open-air fireplace in its forecourt, conveying the notion of gathering around the hearth. The building is called *Badjáneapmi* (awakening). Its structure is comprised of triangular wooden frames with beams and decks built between them. The southern façade has a double layer of glazing and wood while the northern façade will be covered with cross-laminated pinewood shingles.[19]

The original site selected for the project had to be abandoned due to ground deformation caused by mining in the area. An alternative site was selected and is the cause for the delay of the project. As of 2013, discussion regarding the location of the new city center is underway, and the architects hope the project will resume. The project was awarded the World Architecture Festival Entry for Sweden in 2010.

Plate 33. Sámi Parliament, Adolf Hedinsvägen, Kiruna, Sweden, digital rendering of proposed project. Courtesy Murman Arkitekter.

SÁMI CULTURAL CENTRE, SAJOS, INARI, FINLAND

Located in the Sajos Sámi Cultural Centre in Inari at a spectacular site along the bank of the river Juutuanjoki, the Finnish Sámi Parliament is unusual for combining both political and cultural programs in a unified architecture (Plate 34).[20] The design by the Oulu practice HALO Architects employs a cross-shaped plan with a series of yards carefully arranged to avoid harming existing trees.[21] Two dominant formal features, the circular parliament hall and

Plate 34. Sámi Parliament, Inari, Finland, exterior view. Photo by Mika Huisman, courtesy Halo Architects.

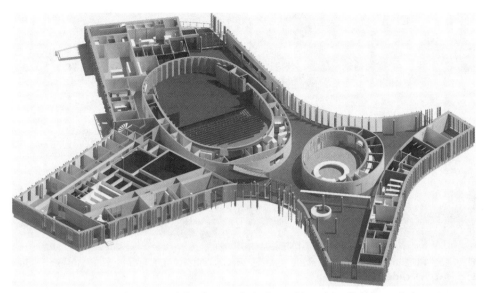

Figure 33.3. Sámi Parliament, Finland, extruded plan of interior, digital rendering. Courtesy HALO Architects.

auditorium, are integrated into a multifunctional complex including a film center, education center, music center, library, multipurpose hall, and a restaurant, plus several support spaces such as recording and video-editing studios, classrooms, archive spaces, offices, and conference rooms.[22] The facilities required by a typical civic program have been expanded to accommodate the ten organizations housed in the complex. The building structure is of concrete, cast in situ to form the two cylindrical drums of the circular halls, with concrete post and beam construction carrying the floor slabs and walls. The vertical timber façade, which extends the full height of the building up to the eaves, is clad in spruce, its austerity reflective of mainstream Scandinavian architecture and evocative of Scandinavian modernism.[23] The curvaceous interior walls are clad in treated pine boards applied horizontally, in a sensibility reminiscent of a musical instrument or hand-crafted object.[24]

Rather than a formal resemblance to any traditional architecture, the architects have focused on surface textures to convey cultural specificity. The building's smooth interior encased in a rough exterior is evocative of Sámi *duodji* or handcraft. The auditorium is oval-shaped, shaped like a traditional *kiisa* or wooden chest, while the assembly hall resembles a *risku*, a rounded piece of jewelery. Architect Lauri Louekari observes that the main inspiration is artifacts, not architecture; these associated objects are on display in a cabinet in the lobby.[25] Their rounded shapes, which make them easy to carry in the nomadic tradition, are translated into the curvaceous geometries of the assembly halls.

The more obvious connection to nomadic journeys across the northern landscape are in the circulation routes that circle the exterior wall, "as if between a precipice and the landscape opening out beyond," writes Louekari.[26] The combination of civic and cultural programs in the Finnish Sámi Parliament highlights the absence of politics in other cultural facilities designed for Aboriginal populations, or the lack of cultural specificity in the European democratic parliamentary model. The example also proves that the architecture of democratic government can be fashioned to respect the cultural specificity of a previously marginalized minority. Undoubtedly all parliamentary complexes have evolved through

Figure 33.4. **Sámi Parliament, Finland, interior view, auditorium. Photo by Mika Huisman, courtesy HALO Architects.**

forms and associations that are culturally inscribed. Democratic government even in Scandinavia is rarely housed in a culturally neutral building as it upholds the highly individuated property rights of mainstream European societies. The Sámi response combines parliament, community, and cultural center undeterred by modernist angst. The civic rights endorsed by the parliament are seen as substantiating land ownership for a vibrant cultural collective fully invested in identitarian and ontological relationships.

NOTES

1. Arctic Centre, "The Sámi Parliament—Samediggi," available at http://www.arcticcentre.org/EN/RESEARCH/Arctic-research-in-Finland/Institutions/Associations-and-offices/Sami-parliament.

2. Thanks to Hans Murman at Murman Arckitecter, Janne Laukka at HALO Architects, and Merete Haukedal at Stein Halvorson Ltd. for providing information on the architecture. Thanks also to Marie Enoksson, Sámi Parliament, Kiruna; Anders Henriksen, Sámi Parliament, Norway; and Anneli Länsman from Sámi Parliament, Finland, for reviewing our text.

3. Malin Rising and David MacDougall, "Sweden's Indigenous Sámi in Fight Against Miners," Associated Press, August 29, 2013.

4. United Nations Non-Governmental Liaison Service, "Implementing the UN Declaration on the Rights of Indigenous Peoples: What Role for Parliamentarians?" available at http://www.un-ngls.org/spip.php?page=article_s&id_article=3900.

5. Communication between author and Marie Enoksson, Sámi Parliament, Sweden, in November 2013.

6. Joar Nango, "The Sámi Building Tradition: A Complex Picture," *Northern Experiments: The Barents Urban Survey*, available at http://www.northernexperiments.net/index.php?/saami-building/.

7. Joar Nango, "The Sámi Building Tradition."

8. Henry Miles, "Parliamentary Prescience," *Architectural Review*, April 1, 2001, 49–53.

9. This section is based on communications and data provided by Halvorson Architects.

10. Stein Halvorsen Arkitekter, "Parliament for the Sámi People," *ArchDaily*, February 8, 2009, available at http://www.archdaily.com/5489/parliament-for-the-Sámi-people-sh-arkitekter.

11. Stein Halvorsen Arkitekter, "Parliament for the Sámi People."

12. Ibid.

13. Miles, "Parliamentary Prescience."

14. Ibid.

15. Ibid.

16. News in English, "Sámi Parliament Hit By Rotting Wood," available at http://www.newsineng lish.no/2012/08/15/sami-parliament-hit-by-rotting-wood/.

17. Open Buildings, "New Sámi Parliament Building—Badjáneampi," available at http://openbuild ings.com/buildings/new-sami-parliment-building-badjneampi-profile-5359.

18. Sápmi, "The Sámi Parliament in Sweden," available at http://www.eng.samer.se/servlet/ GetDoc?meta_id=1103.

19. Communication between author and architectural firm Murman Arkitekter, November 2013.

20. Lauri Louekari, "Sámi Sitelines," available at http://www.fourthdoor.co.uk/unstructured/unstruc tured_6/sajos_sami_cultural_centre.php.

21. This section is based on communications and data provided by HALO Architects.

22. Communication between author and architect, September 13–23, 2013.

23. Louekari, "Sámi Sitelines."

24. Communication between author and architect, September 13–23, 2013.

25. Louekari, "Sámi Sitelines."

26. Ibid.

34

Shung Ye Museum of Formosan Aborigines, Taipei, Taiwan

Location: 282, Sec. 2 Chih-shan Rd, Shih-lin, Taipei, 11143, Taiwan
Date: 1994–1996
Client: Lin Ching-fu, Nai Aung Lin Cultural Foundation
Communities: Saisiat, Atayal, Tsou, Bunun, Amis, Rukai, Puyuma, Paiwan, Yami, Thao, Kavalan, Truku, Sakiyaza, and Sediq
Architect: Kao Erh Pan
Chairman: Lin Ching-fu
Director: Eric H. Y. Yu
Structural Engineering: Zhongli Engineering Consultants
Construction: Fuchu General Contractor
Interior Design: Hisamitsu Shigeo
Exhibition Design (retrofitted in 2004): Nomura Design and Engineering, Japan
Site Area: 364.1 square meters (Building Area 129.9 square meters)
Cost: approximately $7.5 million

A rare example of an Asian metropolitan museum, purpose-designed for an Aboriginal collection, the Shung Ye Museum of Formosan Aborigines is located in the Waishuangsi section of Taipei (Plate 35).[1] It is unique in Asia because of its specific Aboriginal focus. Ethnographic museums elsewhere in Asia, including many in Taiwan, tend to explore culture broadly, or are conceived as theme parks for tourist interest. In contrast, the Shung Ye Museum is clearly an institution that houses a modern collection in a modernist architecture alluding to Taiwan's Aboriginal cultures. It is a museum devoted to Taiwan's Aboriginal histories, cultures, and artifacts.

BACKGROUND

Taiwan's Aboriginal communities are descendants of Austronesian peoples who arrived in Taiwan over sixty thousand years ago. Nine of the nineteen tribes still remaining on the island: the Saisiat, Atayal, Tsou, Bunun, Amis, Rukai, Puyuma, Paiwan, and Yami have distinct and

Plate 35. Shung Ye Museum of Formosan Aborigines, Taipei, Taiwan, exterior view. Photo courtesy Shung Ye Museum of Formosan Aborigines.

relatively well-preserved cultures.[2] They reside in the central mountain ranges and eastern coastal areas of the island. Their architectural, cultural, and material heritage is in tangible form. The Thao, Kavalan, Truku, Sakiyaza, and Sediq tribes have been formally recognized more recently, and the acknowledgment of Indigenous communities in Taiwan is an evolving political process.[3] In Taiwan, Indigenous identities are linked to a complex postcolonial politics resulting from multiple histories of colonization, from imperial histories of land alienation and dispossession to assimilation and indigenization in recent times.

Han Chinese settlers initially came to the island known then in Europe as Formosa during the seventeenth century, as plantation workers for the Dutch East India Company. The Qing Empire ousted the Dutch, and Formosa was governed as a Chinese province well into the nineteenth century. The development of museums did not commence until the island was ceded to the Japanese in 1895 after the Qing were defeated in the first Sino-Japanese War. Japanese anthropologists initially studied Taiwan's Indigenous tribes to support the imperial goal of assimilating and governing the island's population.[4] Twenty-three museums established by the Japanese became vehicles for ideological change.[5] Their objectives were the scientific investigation of the colony's resources, economic expansion, Japanese tourism, and education of the colonized. Japanese rule continued until 1944. Following Japanese defeat in World War II, the island was once again brought under mainland Chinese rule. By then, however, the revolutionary Kuomintang (KMT) had overthrown the Qing dynasty. They ruled on the mainland from 1928 during the turbulent years of the civil war.

Following their defeat by the Communist Party of China, the KMT fled to Taiwan in 1949.[6] The KMT brought with them two million refugees from China, many of them associated with the ousted government, military, and commercial leaders. The KMT consolidated their position on the island under martial law. Museum policy was defined by the "Chinese Cultural Renaissance Movement," which strove to build cultural legitimacy for the KMT.[7] The National Palace Museum built in 1956 was the recipient of some of the most prized collections from the Palace Museum in Beijing, moved there for their protection during the Chinese Cultural Revolution (1966–1976). It is believed to be the largest collection of ancient Chinese artifacts and artworks in the world. The National Palace Museum was symbolic of the custodianship of the ancient Chinese heritage to which the KMT felt they were the rightful heirs.[8] From then on, with US economic and military aid, Taiwan—renamed the Republic of China—entered an era of capital-driven economic growth and political tension with its Communist neighbor. The 1970s and 1980s saw incipient democratization and changes in cultural policy. Martial law was lifted in Taiwan in 1987.

The culture of Taiwan is produced against this turbulent political history and resultant shifting cultural demographic. Lin Chia-Hui links emergent communitarianism to the social indigenization of the 1980s and the codification of Cultural Heritage Preservation policies under the Council of Cultural Affairs.[9] Wang Sung Shan describes a "new museum movement" shaped by political, economic, and academic influences as well as popular participation.[10] The 1990s in particular was a period when the Taiwanese independence movement challenged the one-China policy.[11] Taiwanization and de-Sinicization became political goals. Immigrant/settler and Indigenous identities were drawn into a plural national culture, distinct from Taiwan's Han-dominated neighbor across the Straits. The persistence of Indigenous cultures served a national purpose, distinguishing Taiwan culturally from mainland China. Indigenous nations (or *yuanzhu minzu*) were written into the 1997 revisions of the Taiwan–Republic of China Constitution, and a Basic Law on Indigenous Nations was passed in 2005.[12] Hai Ren, who studies the evolving exhibition culture at the National Museum of Natural Science in Taichung (built in 1981), argues that a national Aboriginal culture was produced during that decade.[13] Practices of consuming culture and knowledge production were instrumentalized through a range of institutions, museums, theaters, and theme parks that assimilated Aboriginal peoples into the Taiwanese nation space.[14] The Community Development Cultural Policy of 1994 saw the exponential growth of local and private museums.

Many scholars attribute the resurgent interest in Aboriginal cultural authenticity among Taiwanese to these transnational political pressures. They point out that a number of Indigenous museums were built in Taiwan during this period, including the Wulai Atayal Museum in Taipei County, the Ketagalan Cultural Museum in Taipei's Beitou District, and the Taiwan Indigenous Peoples Culture Park, which is operated by the Council of Indigenous Peoples Culture Park Area Management Bureau in Pingtung.[15] While the provocation may be political, and the funding may arise through immigrant capital, the recognition of Indigenous cultures has been of increasing benefit to Taiwan's Indigenous peoples.

The Shung Ye Museum of Formosan Aborigines is dedicated to the study of local Aboriginal peoples. The Museum is located diagonally across from the National Palace Museum, the most important museum in the capital, illustrating the original distinction between national and Indigenous cultures. However, the Shung Ye Museum is not a national institution burdened by political agendas; it is a private metropolitan museum, and unique in this regard.

HISTORY OF THE MUSEUM

Conceived with the objective of creating mutual respect in a society dominated by Chinese immigrants, museum founder Lin Ching-fu's idea for the Museum was initiated in 1985 through a cultural and education foundation. The project, designed to commemorate his father, Lin Nai Aung, was an extension of the people-centered philosophy of the local Shun Ye Group, of which Lin Ching-fu was chairman and cofounder.[16] The architect commissioned for the project was Kao Erh Pan, from the first generation of post–World War II architects, whose education in Japan differentiated his approach from the US-educated generation that followed. Kao had previously designed Lin's residence Yue Li Vila, in which Lin's substantial collection of Formosan artifacts was originally stored. A shortage of storage space in that residence prompted the decision to create a purpose-designed facility.

The genesis of the Museum predated the political climate of the 1990s and was an early pioneer in this regard. The project endured almost a decade of delays while legislation governing the establishment of museums was formulated. The Museum's development recommenced in 1994 and was registered in 1996. At the time of its creation, the Museum's focus was new and original, and there was skepticism as to its viability and audience.[17] Yet Lin Ching-fu remained convinced that intercultural knowledge of this kind was essential, due to the political entanglements of the various communities. Jou Chuang, who has given a detailed account of this facility, describes it as stimulating ethnic fusion. He quotes Lin as saying,

> From the Qing Dynasty to the Japanese Occupation and even now, each ethnic group has borne contradictory feelings deep in their minds throughout the political and economic entanglements during all these years. We are all one as people of Taiwan. I am not an aborigine, but this is what I want to do for them—to help preserve the cultural assets that have been handed down from their ancestors and pass the torch intact to their offspring.[18]

Lin donated his collection of Aboriginal artifacts, collected over thirty years, to the Museum.

PROJECT DESCRIPTION

The Shung Ye Museum has an iconic form in a late modernist aesthetic. The museum form is derived from an Indigenous Formosan watchtower, which has its genesis in Austranesian stilt houses.[19] These towers are used to welcome fishermen returning home from the sea. The formal response evolved from consultations between Lin and Kao leading up to the commission, where the desire for an evocative architectural expression was expressed. The building's exposed concrete finishes and expressed structure stylistically allies the museum building with Brutalist architecture, evident in the architect's inspirations. Kao worked under the Japanese modernist architect Kunio Maekawa while studying in Japan. His Taipei Fine Arts Museum built in 1983 was influenced and strongly evocative of Le Corbusier's National Museum of Western Art in Tokyo, Japan (1957) and is regarded as following the Japanese Metabolist tradition. His success in designing the Taipei Fine Arts Museum won him the reputation sought after for the Shung Ye Museum commission.

The reinforced concrete structural system and use of a shear wall is rigorously modernist, an austere architecture that captures the spirit of the postwar decades. A curtain wall on the front of the building counters this heavy aesthetic, drawing light into the void behind it and highlighting the roof form. Shale, a material used in the construction of Indigenous cottages,

Figure 34.1.   Shung Ye Museum of Formosan Aborigines, details of sculptural art work at entrance. Photo by Frank Chen, authorized by Shung Ye Museum of Formosan Aborigines.

is used around the buildings base. Marble is used in the interior and in a bold expression of the Indigenous program that articulates the building's façade. A thirteen-meter high by one meter diameter white granite totem pole, intricately carved with Aboriginal motifs, is set at the center of the Museum's external façade.[20] The totem pole is the work of non-Aboriginal artist Kuo Ching-Chi. The design on the lintel was created by the Formosan artist Sakuliu Pavavalung from the Paiwan tribe, and is titled "Glory." The interior organization of the Museum was modeled on the National Museum of Ethnography in Japan (1977).

The Museum is organized thematically across its four levels, and its permanent displays were designed and retrofitted by a Japanese exhibition specialist company, Nomura Design and Engineering in 2004. The use of 3-D animated film displays depicting Taiwan's Indigenous communities draw on technologies of new museology that target a broader youthful audience. Upon entering the main foyer, the visitor encounters a map on transparent glass that links Formosan Aboriginal groups to Austranesian peoples by illustrating their common languages, cultural practices, customs, and cultivation methods. A large, circular display featuring a digital map and screen located at the center of the lobby identifies the distribution of Taiwan's Indigenous tribes and villages.[21]

EXHIBITION SPACES

The major exhibit on the entrance level, themed "Man and Nature," introduces the diverse Indigenous tribes and their cultures using life-sized cutouts.[22] These are contrasted with contemporary photographs of Indigenous peoples. At the rear of the hall is a stone sculpture of Paiwan and a Yami (Tao) fishing boat symbolizing the mountainous and coastal lands of the tribes.

The second floor is devoted to "Lifestyles" and "Implements, Tools and Weapons," and includes models of traditional dwellings. In addition to the material culture on display—which includes pottery, musical instruments, rattan baskets, carvings, hunting weapons, fishing gear, and millet wine-making vessels—are architectural features, including a Yami ancestral post, a model of a hearth found in an Ami dwelling, and a *Tsou kuba* or men's meeting hall. The display is supported by filmic displays on building and craftsmanship.

The third floor, devoted to "Clothing, Ornaments and Culture," displays the intricately patterned clothing of the various tribes. The Museum's textile collection is particularly rich. Indigenous weaving is described and depicted. The "Beliefs and Ceremonies" exhibit in the basement of the building holds ritual objects related to animism, ancestral worship, and head hunting. The social and religious meanings and functions of these objects are explained using historic photographs. The basement also includes prehistoric artifacts.

Social contact, cultural awareness, and Indigenous representation are facilitated through special temporary exhibitions. A designated individual, group, or organization is selected, and current Indigenous issues and practices—including artwork, craft, photography, clothing, and cultural festivals—are displayed during the spring and autumn seasons. Village culture is showcased in winter months in cooperation with a specific Indigenous village. The Museum's objective is that "through these special exhibitions it is hoped that Taiwan's indigenous peoples can be given a voice in an urban setting and hold onto the right to interpret their culture."[23]

Lin's collection forms part of a broader archive of 1866 artifacts, including 1673 artifacts from the different tribes and a donation of 193 photographic plates taken by Torri Ryuzo from the University of Tokyo.[24] The "Ethnology" collection includes costume and clothes, textile and ornaments, livelihood tools, ceremonial instruments, and handicrafts. There is also an art collection of local Taiwanese artists. A temperature-controlled preservation room has been designed to house the artifacts with Vietnamese cypress interiors and storing cabinets of American aromatic cedar.[25]

RECEPTION

The pedagogical initiatives of the Museum are many, targeting school groups, teachers, and researchers. Summer activities including cultural story tours, animated films, and an Indigenous village classroom are designed specifically for children. In addition to the conventional lecture series, the Museum invites Indigenous artisans to demonstrate Indigenous craft making and everyday creative practices. The Museum publishes reports and exhibition catalogues, monographs, and research papers. However, due to its private ownership, the Museum cannot compete with public institutions in terms of scale, resources, and exhibits. Visits are largely organized through schools or institutes for educational purposes.[26]

The Shung Ye Museum has several successful outreach programs. It has a mission to retrieve historical archives and works both with local and international academic institutions.[27] The Museum sponsors a budget for several international universities to archive and research Formosan Aboriginal communities.[28]

NOTES

1. Thanks to Annie Chen from the Shang Ye Museum of Formosan Aborigines for providing information and photographs of the building. Much of the information on the collection in this account is summarized from the Museum website. Thanks also to Ted Chen and Lin Chia-Hui, who assisted in accessing and translating material, and Frank Chen for photographs of the displays, details, and interior.

2. Stephanie Ho, "Travel in Taiwan: Museums," available at http://www.sinica.edu.tw/tit/museums/1294_shung-ye.html.

3. Shung Ye Museum of Formosan Aborigines, "Introduction to the Museum," available at http://www.museum.org.tw/SYMM_en/01.htm.

4. Scott Simon, "Writing Indigeneity in Taiwan," in *Re-Writing Culture in Taiwan*, eds. Fang-long Shih, Stuart Thompson, and Paul François Tremlett (London and New York: Routledge, 2009), 56; Edward Vickers, "Re-Writing Museums in Taiwan," in *Re-Writing Culture in Taiwan*, eds. Shih, Thompson, and Tremlett, 75.

5. Yui-tan Chang, "The History and Identity of Taiwan's Museums: A Brief Review," in eds. Chang Yui-tan and Suzanne MacLeod, *Building Identity: The Making of National Museums and Identity Politics* (Taipei: National Museum of History, 2012), 185.

6. Formosa was renamed Taiwan in 1949.

7. Chang, "The History and Identity of Taiwan's Museums," 186.

8. Vickers, "Re-Writing museums in Taiwan," 77.

9. Chia-hui Lin, "Museumisation and Communitarianism in Post-Martial Law Taiwan," in *Building Identity: The Making of National Museums and Identity Politics*, eds. Chang Yui-tan and Suzanne MacLeod (Taipei: National Museum of History, 2012), 171–72.

10. Wan Sung Shan, *Cha I To Yang Hsing Yu Po Wu Kuan* (Difference, Multiformity and Museum) (Taipei: Tas Hsiang, 2003), 22–23 (cited by Chia-hui Lin in *Museumisation and Communitarianism* at 178).

11. The One China Policy under the consensus of 1992 agrees that China and Taiwan are inalienable and that there is only one sovereign state, but it disagrees on which government is legitimately in charge.

12. Scott Simon, "Paths to Autonomy: Aboriginality and the Nation in Taiwan," in *The Margins of Becoming: Identity and Culture in Taiwan*, eds. C. Storm and M. Harrison (Weisbaden: Harrassowitz, 2006), 221–40.

13. Hai Ren, "Economies of Culture: Theme Parks, Museums and Capital Accumulation in China, Hong Kong and Taiwan," PhD dissertation submitted to the Department of Anthropology at the University of Washington, 1998, 144.

14. Ren, "Economies of Culture," 159.

15. Cindy Sui, "A Blast from the Past But Who Is Listening?" *Taipei Times*, June 25, 2009.

16. Communication on the architect-client relationship based on research by Lin Chia-Hui. See Trade Asia, "Shung Ye Trading Co Ltd.," available at http://www.etradeasia.com/ company_detail/142886/0/SHUNG_YE_TRADING_CO__LTD_-.html.

17. Jou Chuang, "Shung Ye Museum of Formosan Aborigines Passes the Torch of Indigenous Culture," +culture.tw.*Taiwan*, March 22, 2013, available at http://www.culture.tw/ index.php?option=com_content&task=view&id=2367&Itemid=157#plurk.

18. Chuang, "Shung Ye Museum of Formosan Aborigines."

19. Architect, "Shung Ye Museum of Formosan Aborigines," *Architect* 8 (1994), 140–45. This article includes an interview with Kao done by Ding róng sheng and Hú chù pèi, titled "Reshaping the Primitive Form of a Place: An Interview with Kao Erh Pan." The information on the Museum's architecture included in this section was translated from this article by Lin Chia-Hui.

20. *Shung Ye Museum of Formosan Aborigines Guidebook* (Taipei: Shung Ye Museum of Formosan Aborigines, 2011), 8.

21. Shung Ye Museum of Formosan Aborigines, "Permanent Exhibitions," available at http://www.museum.org.tw/symm_en/031.htm. This section is based on the website.

22. Shung Ye Museum of Formosan Aborigines, "Permanent Exhibitions."

23. Shung Ye Museum of Formosan Aborigines, "Exhibition," available at http://www.museum.org
.tw/SYMM_en/02.htm.

24. Shung Ye Museum of Formosan Aborigines, "Collection," available at http://www.museum.org
.tw/SYMM_en/03.htm.

25. Shung Ye Museum of Formosan Aborigines, "Collection."

26. Based on notes by Lin Chia-Hui.

27. Chuang, "Shung Ye Museum of Formosan Aborigines."

28. Ibid.

35

Tiagarra Aboriginal Cultural Centre and Museum, Devonport, Tasmania, Australia

Location: Bluff Road, Devonport, Tasmania
Date: 1976
Client: Devonport City Council
Operation: Six Rivers Aboriginal Corporation (SRAC) (since 1995)
SRAC Chair: Aboriginal Elder Paul Docking
Architect: Albert A. Freak Associates
Construction Supervisor: Ray Barker

Located on Tasmania's northern coastline in Devonport, the home of the vehicle ferry to and from Melbourne, the Mersey Bluff provides not only a prominent and significant Indigenous cultural area but also a modern-day recreational foreshore area.[1] With a fringe parkland, the Tiagarra Aboriginal Centre sits among several facilities, including Devonport's main beachfront and Surf Lifesaving Club, Mersey Bluff Lighthouse, a small caravan park, the Bass Straight Maritime Museum, numerous sporting grounds, and the original Devonport cemetery.[2]

Tiagarra, designed by architect Albert A. Freak Associates, is an interpretation center housing more than three thousand artifacts and eighteen displays that interpret the traditional living patterns, management of resources and the environment, and coastal habitation and trading economies of the Tasmanian Aboriginal peoples.[3] Its main purpose has also been the preservation of and visitor education regarding the prehistoric sites in the area, including tool scatters and a midden site. Although based on a museological program with a pedagogical purpose, it bears the attributes of a regional "keeping place" linked to significant heritage sites. It takes its Aboriginal name *Tiagarra* after the Bruny Island term meaning "to keep."

BACKGROUND

Prompted by the archaeologically significant petroglyphs on the site, a local heritage group—including Peter Sims, fellow of the Australian Institute of Aboriginal and Torres Strait Islander Studies and expert on Tasmanian motif sites—put forward the proposal for a cultural center to the Devonport Council in 1975. Sims was part of the Historic Scientific Advisory Committee

Figure 35.1. Tiagarra Aboriginal Cultural Centre and Museum, exterior view. Photo by Janet McGaw, 2013.

that drafted the Tasmanian Relic Act of 1975 and continues to lobby for acknowledgment of Indigenous heritage and identification of sites. The Committee works to highlight issues of heritage, vandalism, and management, and the need to care for resources related to these heritage sites.[4] He observes that the exposed rocks at Mersey Bluff, with 270 markings first reported by Europeans in 1923, identify the site as probably the most extensive for Tasmanian xenoliths.[5] Figures of the now-extinct Tasmanian emu and the abalone shell are clearly evident, although some scholars dispute their anthropogenic origin.[6] Sims takes the view that the popularity of the site in fact "inspires ongoing debate about Tasmanian rock art, its meaning and preservation." He comments:

> The process of Tasmanian Aboriginal people re-discovering and re-connecting with these remnants of an unusually specialised and nomadic way of life, based on hunting seals and land mammals and the gathering of shellfish is still in its early stages.[7]

In 1976, the Mersey Leven Aboriginal Corporation and the Commonwealth Department of Employment, Education, Training and Youth Affairs supported the venture for establishing a cultural center. The facility was built by the Devonport Council and was only the second facility in the nation to display Aboriginal artifacts, with little or no direct input from the broad Tasmanian Aboriginal community at that time. Tiagarra was opened in 1976 by the then governor of South Australia, Pastor Douglas Nicholls, with a public address by Michael Mansell, then State Secretary of the Aboriginal Information Service Tasmania (later the Tasmanian Aboriginal Commission). The facility was leased for twenty years by the Mersey Leven Aboriginal Corporation (now Six Rivers Aboriginal Corporation or SRAC) in 1995. At that time, the corporation took on a brief to represent the local community as well as Tasmania's wider Indigenous community. Due to this broadened perspective and extensive collection, the Centre has always needed

Figure 35.2.   Petroglyph resembling an abalone shell from the area near Mersey Bluff. Photo by Janet McGaw, 2013.

supportive funding and has never been a self-sustaining operation, whether under the management of the local Devonport Council or the relevant Aboriginal corporation. Its evolution and transformation reciprocates the involvement of different stakeholder groups, providing an instructive example of the changing face of "keeping places" with increasing regard for Indigenous heritage and greater involvement of the Indigenous community.

PROJECT DESCRIPTION

The architecture of the Tiagarra Aboriginal Centre is said to resemble Tasmanian Aboriginal dwellings of the island's northwest. Tasmanian architect Albert A. Freak completed the War Memorial Swimming Centre at Devonport in 1972. His design for Tiagarra continues the tradition of Tasmanian hardwood construction in its structure. Initially modeled on anthropological or history museums of an earlier era, the displays included dioramas and cabinets of artifacts where visitors were given information leaflets on the various exhibits. Postcontact histories of dispossession were not included.[8] However, with increasing tourist interest and additional funding, the facility was refashioned as an interpretive center in 2004.[9]

The inclusion of contemporary histories has altered the focus of the Centre from the archaeological past to the living present. Two large murals donated by Tasmanian artist Max Angus, famous for his watercolor renderings of the island's landscapes, convey this shift. The mural *Changing Life of Tribal Tasmanian Aborigines* document the sealers, land competition, symbols of European life and its institutions, including law, church, jailors, and punishment, the Black War of 1839, and the removal of a group of Tasmanian Aborigines to Wybalenna on Flinders Island. In the 1990s, the Centre was reconceived as a place where Aboriginal Tasmanians could meet, hold workshops and events, and keep and pass on cultural practices such as shell necklace work, basket weaving, bush foods, and medicines.[10] A gift shop sells books, souvenirs, and local Aboriginal arts and crafts. Increasing involvement by the local Aboriginal community since 1995 reflects the changing focus of Tiagarra away from a museum and toward an interpretive, functioning cultural center.

RECEPTION

Under the terms of the lease, Tiagarra is to be operated by the SRAC until 2015, under its chairperson and Elder, Paul Docking.[11] The center is currently only open for prebooked group tours, predominantly of school groups seeking to fulfill the national education curriculum requirements to include Aboriginal and Torres Straits Islander cultures. Recent events at the center included the launch of the book *Grease and Ochre* by Riawunna Elder Aunty Patsy Cameron as part of NAIDOC Week celebrations on July 5, 2012.[12] The building was a recipient of the State/Territory Award Certificate at the Australian Reconciliation Convention in 1997.[13]

The SRAC has recently reviewed the operations and is currently in negotiations with the Council to secure a future for the facility beyond 2015 when the lease expires. The Corporation is lobbying the Council to agree to engage with a broader range of stakeholders who have the experience, expertise, and small-museum knowledge in order to access the resources to develop a long-term future plan for Tiagarra. These stakeholders include the Department of Education, Heritage Tasmania, Arts Tasmania, and Tasmanian Museums and Art Galleries.

NOTES

1. Thanks to David Gough for providing information on Tiagarra in 2012. Thanks also to Paul Docking and Michelle Pearce for subsequent information and for facilitating a visit by Janet McGaw to the site in 2013. Thanks also to Paul Docking for notes on the write-up included here.

2. Gweneth Newman Leigh, "Coastal Communities," *Architecture AU*, May 11, 2012, available at http://architectureau.com/articles/coastal-communities/.

3. Tourism Tasmania, "Tiagarra Aboriginal Cultural Centre," available at http://www.discovertasmania.com/attraction/tiagarraaboriginalculturecentreandmuseum (link no longer active, last accessed July 13, 2012). Communication with David Gough, 2012.

4. Peter Sims, "Indigenous Heritage Law Reform," submission to Heritage Division, Department of the Environment, Water, Heritage and the Arts, Canberra, October 25, 2009, available at https://www.environment.gov.au/system/files/pages/080619b8-678d-4d4a-905a-a287b0ab0fb7/files/peter-c-sims-oam.pdf.

5. Peter Sims, "No Reprieve for Tasmanian Rock Art," *Arts* 2, no. 4 (2013): 194, available at http://www.mdpi.com/2076-0752/2/4/182/htm.

6. Sims, "No Reprieve for Tasmanian Rock Art," 195.

7. Ibid., 194–95, 197.

8. Bronwyn Batten, "From Prehistory to History: Shared Perspectives in Australian Heritage Interpretation," PhD thesis submitted in the Department of Indigenous Studies at Macquarie University in 2005, 72–80. Available at http://hdl.handle.net/1959.14/445.

9. Batten, "From Prehistory to History."

10. Communication with David Gough, 2012.

11. Batten, "From Prehistory to History."

12. Bronwyn Purvis, "Carrying Place with You," ABC Open, available at http://open.abc.net.au/posts/tags/aunty%20patsy%20cameron.

13. Heather Zeppel, "Aboriginal Tourism in Australia: A Research Bibliography," Co-Operative Research Centre for Sustainable Tourism Research Report Series: Report 2, 1999, available at http://www.crctourism.com.au/wms/upload/resources/bookshop/Aboriginal%20Tourism%20in%20Australia.PDF.

36

Tjapukai Aboriginal Cultural Park, Caravonica, Queensland, Australia

Location: Cairns Western Arterial Road, Caravonica, Queensland
Date: 1989 (redevelopment 2013–2014)
Owner: Indigenous Business Australia
Architect: Toland Shiraishi Architects Pty. Ltd. (Hiromi Shiraishi and Robert Toland)
Project Managers: Jones Lang LaSalle
Structural Engineer: Colefax Rodgers Consulting Engineers Pty. Ltd.
Service Engineers: William Sales Partnership Buildings Pty. Ltd.
Principal Certifying Authority: Knisco Development Solutions
Interpretation: Tjapukai Content Committee and Story Inc.
Area: 25 acres
Cost: approximately $850,000 (redevelopment: approximately $12 million)
Chief Executive Officer: Geoff Olson

Situated on a twenty-five-acre property in Caravonica, near Cairns in northern Queensland, the Tjapukai Aboriginal Cultural Park is the largest Indigenous cultural park in Australia, and has evolved from a dance theater into a major cultural tourism venue.[1] The Indigenous community represented is the Djabugay people, who live in the rain forest north of Cairns, including the communities of Oak Forest, Mantaka, Korowra, Koah, and Mona Mona. *Tjapukai* means "rain forest" in Djabugay language.[2] The Park's programmatic brief arises out of its revised mission, vision, and conceptual structure agreed by the Indigenous Business Australia (IBA) board in 2011 to respond to substantial changes in international and domestic tourism behavior since the tourism "heyday" of the late 1990s.

The Park complex draws together several spatial practices of dance, tourism, and cultural display, housed in a tentlike, tensile membrane structure reminiscent of traveling performances. The Park's history originated with the Tjakupai dance troupe. The troupe grew to be a national and internationally acclaimed theatre group, and due to this success was able to develop a specific site for performance purposes. Their performances were spatialized in a cultural center, with seven separate arenas for interactive demonstrations and cultural performances. These arenas include the History Theatre, the Creation Theatre, and the Dance Theatre, as well as a cultural village, a two-hundred-seat restaurant, and other dining and retail areas. Themes explored across the Park include the creation myths of the Djabugay and their interaction with the European world. The use of new audiovisual technologies, such as holographic images, offers a sophisticated translation of the troupe's theatrical performances.

The Park is essentially conceived for non-Indigenous audiences and serves both pedagogical and commercial objectives. In the cultural village, visitors participate in activities such as learning to throw spears and boomerangs. Since 2002, an evening show and banquet offer visitors the opportunity to participate in a *corroboree* (the term *corroboree* was used by European colonizers to describe Indigenous ceremonies). The introduction of the evening show has created distinct experiences of Tjapukai by day and by night. The park also offers venues for hire for a range of activities from conferences to weddings. The park is wholly owned by the IBA, a federal government agency.

Projects such as Tjapukai need to develop Indigenous cultural awareness without resorting to stereotypes, as well as offer sophisticated cultural interpretations as entertainment. Balancing these different pedagogical goals can be challenging. However, when compared with museum environments, theatrical performances provide dynamic opportunities for social display, and increasingly, museums, too, produce spectacular effects. For example, the video screens featuring Aboriginal dancers at the National Museum of Australia's Gallery of First Australians exemplify the ceremonial significance of the welcoming dance.[3] Although these two different programs, the museum and open-air theater, build cultural awareness at two ends of the spatial spectrum, they borrow certain attributes from each other so as to extend their reach. The museums featured in this book are incorporating new place-making strategies, while Tjapukai is transitioning to a more permanent tourism venue.

BACKGROUND

The Tjapukai Dance Theatre began life in the basement of the Kuranda Shopping Centre in 1987 under the management of theater artists Don and Judy Freeman (from the United States and Canada, respectively). The Freemans' partners included David and Cindy Hudson and five local Djabugay men: Willie Brim, Alby Baird, Wayne Nicols, Irwin Riley, Neville Hobler, and Dion Riley.[4] Their original production was a one-hour play that sought to portray the spirit of the *Bama* or "people of the rain forest." Many of the dancers were from Djabugay country. Following the performance of this production at World Expo '88 in Brisbane, they moved into a purpose-built theater in Kuranda in 1989, which cost approximately $750,000 to build. During the next seventeen years, the troupe toured internationally, visiting France, New Zealand, the United States, Korea, Japan, Singapore, Austria, Canada, Guam, and Taiwan. It won over two hundred accolades, many for Australian tourism. The troupe represented Australia at later World Expositions in Japan and Korea, featured in the Commonwealth Games in Canada in 1994, and entered the *Guinness Book of World Records* as Australia's longest-running stage show. Queen Elizabeth and Prince Philip visited the troupe in 2002. Five dancers from Tjapukai were involved in the bid to bring the 2018 Commonwealth Games to the Gold Coast.[5]

PROJECT DESCRIPTION

The $12 million Tjapukai redevelopment commenced in March 2013 and was completed in December 2014. It aimed to expand Tjapukai into a national venue conceived around the

Figure 36.1.   Tjapukai Aboriginal Cultural Park, previous structure. Photo courtesy Tjapukai Aboriginal Cultural Park.

theme "Gateway to Indigenous Australia: Seeing Nature through Our Eyes."[6] Sydney's Toland Architectural Design Partners was awarded the redevelopment contract in 2011 following their success in a design competition for the project. Their winning entry was designed in collaboration with an interpretive design company, Trigger (Plate 36).

Toland has worked collaboratively with Aboriginal communities across Australia, including on projects at Kamay Botany Bay National Park in Kurnell, New South Wales.[7] The firm was also engaged as design consultant on the extensive Ngarluma Yindjibarndi Cultural Complex in the Pilbara in Western Australia (see chapter 27). For Tjapukai, Toland prepared a clear mission, vision, conceptual structure, and feasibility proposal completed and approved by the IBA in 2011, to which funds were then committed. The fundamental reason for redevelopment was that since its inception in the 1990s, Tjapukai had not evolved to match the changing needs of its audiences. Moreover, the redevelopment had to be carefully planned to allow the ongoing functioning of Tjapukai at a number of alternative areas on the grounds while the core facilities were being reconstructed.

The theme of nature is directly drawn from the experience of the rain forest in Djabugay country. While the design is contemporary, projecting the renewal and vitality of Djabugay culture by incorporating environmentally sustainable design principles and modern aesthetics, formal concepts have been abstracted from traditional Indigenous associations and everyday practices. The high ceiling of the main building defines a socially interactive space containing two theaters. The circular volumes of the first is inspired by a "dilly bag," a traditional carry bag woven from pandanus leaves and the egg of the cassowary, a large flightless bird native to the local rain forest. The curved walls of the second high-tech amphitheater are designed for three-dimensional projection. The New Zealand interpretive designers, Story Inc., created the show.

The redevelopment was also planned to connect previously isolated facilities within the Tjapukai site, opening them up to new functions. The objective is a multifunctional build-

Plate 36. Tjapukai Aboriginal Cultural Park, Caravonica, Queensland, Australia, main entry design. Courtesy Toland Shiraishi Architects.

ing capable of housing conferences, private functions, educational programs, and a visual arts space. The intention is to create a harmonious environment for interactions between locals and international visitors. This is supported by a purpose-designed industrial interior of salvaged and recycled building materials that can be adapted to suit varied needs. Toland describes this approach as representing a "global trend" and satisfying Tjapukai and the IBA's entrepreneurial objectives.[8]

The redevelopment expands Tjapukai with the inclusion of a number of services, including cultural interpretation by Story Inc., so as to present visitors with a renewed Indigenous perspective. A range of new visitor experiences spanning "Day," "Night," and new ways of representing culture are being developed by the team at Tjapukai. The cultural village, including the dance theater, the boomerang- and spear-throwing fields, and activity huts, and the main building, including the kitchen and restaurant, has also been redeveloped. Australian creative media company Cummins Ross is rebranding Tjapukai for international tourism.[9]

RECEPTION

As one of the first experiments in Aboriginal cultural tourism, Tjapukai Aboriginal Cultural Park treads the fragile boundary between cultural product and tourist commodity, which reflects the tension faced by Indigenous cultural centers elsewhere in Australia. Programmatically, the activities presently on offer are replicated in many national venues. The project represents a scale of production that, while originating in everyday practices of teaching and storytelling, reproduces these activities for audience consumption. While similar criticisms to those raised against theme park environments may be relevant in this example, the benefits are considerable. The park has attracted over three million visitors since opening and has injected more than approximately $25 million to the local Aboriginal community in wages, royalties, and the purchase and commissioning of art and artifacts.[10] It is the largest private employer of Indigenous people in Cairns, and has developed into a major business enterprise employing forty-two Indigenous staff in a workforce of seventy-seven persons.[11] The Park also provides work for a wider spectrum of artists, craftsmen, tour guides, and coach drivers from the local community. An innovative employment strategy includes programs of recruitment, skill enhancement, career development, and cross-cultural awareness targeting both Indigenous and non-Indigenous employees. This program has been incorporated into Tjakupai's workplace practices following an agreement with the federal Department of Employment, Education and Training. The success of Tjakupai has inspired Aboriginal dance groups elsewhere in Australia and created new jobs for Aboriginal people in the tourism industry.[12] The park also enabled the non-Indigenous Freeman Productions to establish a financially successful cultural tourism business in Queensland.

The redevelopment of Tjapukai further challenges the model of Indigenous cultural facilities as the Park is reconfigured into a more sophisticated entertainment venue along metropolitan lines. The program now presents a hybrid of mainstream civic cultural facilities and cultural activity centers associated with nature reserves. As the programmatic content is formalized, the architecture of the Park has had to undergo a similar transformation to accommodate the changing demands of Tjakupai's cosmopolitan audience. These changes give the organization a new degree of permanence and visibility that was achieved in the past through visitor numbers. The decades-long transition from informal ephemeral practices to formal civic engagements demonstrates the growing performative reach of Aboriginal cultural facilities and consequent national opportunities and pressures.

NOTES

1. Thanks to Hiromi Shiraishi, Neil Anderson, Robert Toland, and Mary Aston at Toland Architects and Geoff Olson at Tjapukai for comments on this section. Thanks also to Louise Biddle at IBA.

2. Tjapukai Aboriginal Cultural Park, "Tjapukai 25 Years On," available at http://www.tjapukai .com.au/tjapukai-the-culture/tjapukai-25-years-on/. Much of the information included in this chapter is sourced from this website.

3. See chapter 2, Australian Institute of Aboriginal and Torres Strait Islander Studies and the National Museum of Australia, Canberra, Australia.

4. Tjapukai Aboriginal Cultural Park, "Tjapukai 25 Years On."

5. The Cairns Post, "Tjapukai Dancers Help Gold Coast's 2018 Commonwealth Games Bid," November 2, 2011, available at http://www.cairns.com.au/article/2011/10/28/188495_local-news.html.

6. Communication with architect, Hiromi Shiraishi, November 2013.

7. On the Kamay Botany Bay National Park, see Toland Trigger, "Kamay Botany Bay La Perouse Headland & Bare Island Draft Interpretation, Landscape & Architectural Plan Public Exhibition," available at http://www.environment.nsw.gov.au/resources/planmanagement/ draft/KamayBotanyBay DraftIP.pdf.

8. Communication with architect, Hiromi Shiraishi, November 2013.

9. Tjapukai Aboriginal Cultural Park, "Tjapukai to Begin $12m Redevelopment," media release dated January 31, 2013, available at http://www.tjapukai.com.au/wp-content/uploads/2011/03/MEDIA -RELEASE-Tjapukai-Redevelopment.pdf.

10. Cairns Local Tourism Network, "Tjapukai Celebrates 25th Anniversary and Redevelopment 2012," *Cairns Today,* available at http://www.trinitybeach.org/trinitybeach/attractions.2/tjapukai -aboriginal-cultural-park.745/.

11. Cairns Local Tourism Network, "Tjapukai Celebrates 25th Anniversary and Redevelopment 2012."

12. Freeman Productions, "Tjapukai Aboriginal Cultural Park," available at http://www.freemanpro ductions.com.au/tjapukai.html (accessed October 30, 2013).

37

Tjulyuru Cultural and Civic Centre, Warburton Aboriginal Community, Western Australia, Australia

Location: Great Central Road, Warburton, Western Australia
Date: 2000
Communities: Ngaanyatjarra people of the Western Desert
Architect: Insideout Architects
Engineer: SKM Townsville
Builder: Sitzler Brothers
Cost: approximately $1.8 million
Funding: Ngaanyatjarra Council, Shire of Ngaanyatjarraku and the Aboriginal Torres Strait Islander Commission

The Tjulyuru Cultural and Civic Centre is located in the remote Ngaanyatjarra region around Warburton in southeast Western Australia. Warburton is situated approximately 1,500 kilometers from Perth by road, in a desert area bounded by the Gibson Desert to the northwest and the Great Victoria Desert to the southeast. The Ngaanyatjarra area spans a vast expanse of 159,948 square kilometers and has approximately two thousand Aboriginal inhabitants living across eleven communities.[1] The Shire of Ngaanyatjarraku formally owns the Tjulyuru building.

PROJECT DESCRIPTION

A civic and cultural hub for visitors and locals alike, Tjulyuru is a long, low building that stands on a low prominence in the rust-red desert sand of the Great Plate Central Road (Plate 37). Constructed of concrete blockwork that has been rendered a rich yellow ochre, the building is composed of two colonnaded wings that embrace an open courtyard. One wing accommodates two exhibition areas; the other contains the gallery shop and a café, as well as the community administration center. The upward tilting verandas that surround the courtyard are supported by blockwork piers that provide shaded places in which to gather.

Designed to reflect both the landscape of the Central Desert and the Ngaanyatjarra people, the building makes numerous references to Ngaanyatjarra culture and society without incorporating any of the motifs that are characteristically used to denote Aboriginality in

Plate 37.   Tjulyuru Cultural and Civic Centre, Warburton Aboriginal Community, Western Australia in its setting. Photo by Mike Gillam, courtesy Insideout Architects.

architecture, such as curvilinear forms or references to ancestral beings—elements the clients and steering committee explicitly stated they did not want.[2] Rather, the vivid colors and materials of the Ngaanyatjarra landscape are referenced throughout the building. Rust-red sand and creek pebbles form the aggregate in the polished concrete floors, while red earth, shrubs, and grasses form an organic corridor through the site. Locally made art, including glass panels and sculptures, adorns the interiors of the building. There are numerous ways to access the building, with many doors connecting the inside to the outside. As Shaneen Fantin points out, the building

> was specifically designed to support and encourage existing Aboriginal living practices, as well as kin-related Aboriginal etiquette and respect for the layering of Aboriginal knowledge systems. The former manifests in a flexibility of space which avoids a linear progression through the architecture enabling easy entry and exit, and the latter in preventing unwanted intrusion into particular parts of the centre through the layering of spaces from public to private or secular to secret.[3]

CONSULTATION PROCESS

Insideout Architects was commissioned to design the center in 1998. The practice set up in Warburton for the duration of the design, documentations, and construction stages. Insideout was also responsible for the interior design and project management. Community consultation and collaboration was an important part of this process, with senior custodians and young people of all eleven Ngaanyatjarra communities involved. Construction in one of the most remote places in Australia proved challenging, and a number of logistical hurdles and cultural issues had to be negotiated. Notwithstanding these difficulties, however, the project was completed within budget and nine weeks early.

OBJECTIVES

After a decade of planning and extensive community consultation, the Center was designed to provide the Ngaanyatjarra people with an opportunity to strengthen their culture and encourage its understanding among the wider national and global community. Opened in October 2000 by the then premier of Western Australia, Richard Court, the Tjulyuru Cultural and Civic Centre is not simply an exhibition and performance venue but has become the central facility serving the people of the Ngaanyatjarra region. The Center accommodates the local government for the region, the Ngaanyatjarra Council, and provides many community services and facilities for locals and tourists alike. Still, its most noteworthy feature is the extensive Tjulyuru Regional Arts Gallery, a purpose-built art gallery that houses the nationally significant Warburton Arts Collection. The Collection contains over three hundred works, making it the world's largest collection of community owned and controlled Aboriginal art. The collection, which has grown since the Warburton Arts Project was established in 1990, has toured globally and offers visitors a rare insight into the complexities of the Ngaanyatjarra world. The collection includes acrylic paintings, described as "rich tapestry-like canvases,"[4] as well as rock art projects, art glass, sound recordings, and festival production. Commenting on the success of the Tjulyuru Cultural and Civic Centre, Nicholas Rothwell points out:

> One finds, too, that rarest thing in the cloistered spaces of a museum environment—artists at work, wandering up and down their gallery, considering and examining their masterpieces, touching them, singing to them, taking in the odd splendour of their surroundings, the freshness of the filtered-air environment contrasting with the blazing sunshine, the ochre soil and dusty Spinifex visible outside.[5]

Not only does the building showcase the culture of the Ngaanyatjarra people, it also serves as a space of mediation between the Ngaanyatjarra and the outside world.[6] The Center offers an opportunity for Ngaanyatjarra people to engage visitors in their own environment.

RECEPTION

Tjulyuru serves as a cultural focus for the surrounding communities and visitors to the area alike. It represents a significant step in the journey toward Aboriginal self-determination in Australia's Central Desert region. It is intended that tourism and art-based ventures will help buoy the region's economic development, provide greater employment opportunities, and, in doing so, further strengthen Ngaanyatajrra culture. In 2001, Tjulyuru won a number of Royal Australian Institute of Architects awards, including the Tracy Memorial Award, the Commercial Award, and a Commendation in the Environment Award.

NOTES

1. Thanks to Tania Dennis of Insideout Architects for communications on this project. Thanks to the client group for permissions from Shire of Ngaanyatjarraku president, Mr. (John) Damian McLean, and councillors Lalla West, Preston Thomas, and Cyril Simms. Original draft by Carolynne Baker.

2. Shaneen Fantin, "Aboriginal Identities in Architecture," *Architecture Australia* 92, no. 5 (September/October 2003): 85.

3. Fantin, "Aboriginal Identities in Architecture," 86–87.

4. Ibid., 86–87.

5. Nicholas Rothwell, "Dreamtime Comes True," *Weekend Australian*, February 10, 2001.

6. Rothwell, "Dreamtime Comes True."

38

Uluru-Kata Tjuta Cultural Centre, Northern Territory, Australia

Date: 1990–1995
Location: Uluru (formerly known as Ayers Rock), Northern Territory, Australia
Client: Mutitjulu Community and Australian Nature Conservation Agency
Architect: Gregory Burgess Architects
Project Team: Gregory Burgess, Peter Ryan, Steve Duddy, Ian Khoo, Phillip Bigg, Robert Lock, Anna Lindstad, Alvyn Williams, and Thomas Kinloch
Environmental Designer: Sonja Peters and Form Australia
Landscape Designers: Kevin Taylor and Kate Cullity
Engineers: P. J. Ytyrup
Service Engineer: W. O. Ross
Tourist Consultant: David Western
Funding: Federal and Northern Territory Governments
Cost: approximately $4.7 million

Located on a remote site in the Northern Territory, 450 kilometers west of Alice Springs, Uluru is the Pitjantjatjara name for a sandstone inselberg formerly known as Ayers Rock. Uluru and Kata Tjuta form two series of bornhardts (domed rocks) that rise out of the vast expanse of the Uluru-Kata Tjuta National Park, which covers a total area of 1,326 square kilometers.[1] These iconic sites attract four hundred thousand visitors per year. The traditional owners of Uluru, the Anangu, have used the cultural center and its program to assert their rights to the land and reinscribe the site as an Aboriginal cultural space.[2] The Centre educates *Minga* or visitors into Anangu ways, mediating their perceptions and behaviors of the landscape within a shared cultural ethos (Plate 38).[3]

BACKGROUND

The Anangu comprise the Pitjantjara and Yankunytjatjara of the western central desert. The relationship the Anangu have with Uluru is complex and highly integrated with their self-identification. The site is sacred, etched into their life-world through creation stories, ancestral

262

Plate 38.   Uluru-Kata Tjuta Cultural Centre, Northern Territory, Australia, aerial view. Photo by John Gollings, courtesy Gregory Burgess Architects.

sites, and detailed knowledge of the flora and fauna that form a moral ethical structure known as *Tjukurpa* or Law.[4] *Tjukurpa* governs daily life and is learned by walking the country and learning the oral tradition.[5]

The history of Uluru as an Australian national icon began with its declaration as a national park in 1958. With the creation of the Ayers Rock and Mount Olga National Park as a tourist space, the Northern Territory Reserve Board attempted to resettle the Anangu outside the park's borders. "Ayers Rock" became a highly popular tourist destination. The Anangu struggle for rights to manage the land within the Ayers Rock and Mount Olga Park lasted until 1983.[6] Ownership of Uluru was partially returned to the local Pitjantjatjara Aboriginal community in 1985, with the settlement of a ninety-nine-year lease of joint management with the National Parks and Wildlife Agency. The management plan of 1986 included a proposal for an Aboriginal cultural center.

The Uluru-Kata Tjuta Cultural Centre may be regarded as an effort by the Anangu to assert their renewed authority by translating their perspective to settler and tourist audiences. It was framed as place of meaningful cultural exchange, a new interpretive space in relation to the story of the park and of Anangu culture and a contact zone or interface between the Anangu and tourism.[7]

The Cultural Centre also legitimized and gave visibility to the Anangu presence in the park. A small community of Anangu, the Mutitjulu, established themselves east of the rock as caretakers of Uluru. Increasing tourism prompted the relocation of tourist facilities immediately adjacent to the rock to the Yulara Tourist Centre, eighteen kilometers from Uluru, where a larger community dependent on tourism developed. The Mutitjulu were awarded an annual rental payment of AUD$150,000, being approximately 25 percent of park entrance fees.[8] The joint partnership in managing the park was intended to reap benefits for the Anangu in training, opportunities, and income via the tourism economy.

Contestations over the spatio-temporal occupation of Uluru revealed a struggle between the conflicting prerogatives of the Mutitjulu custodians of Uluru and metropolitan tourists. The revision of the park as an Aboriginal space included regulation of the tourist industry and media, with heightened efforts at discouraging the popular tourist climb of the rock. However, such measures were met with resistance by tourist authorities. Following its declaration as a world heritage site in 1994, annual visitor numbers to Uluru rose; there were over four hundred thousand visitors in the year 2000.[9] Increased tourism exacerbated the conflict over the cultural disrespect shown the Anangu by tourists climbing the rock. The Cultural Centre aimed to bridge these differences in perspective.

PROJECT DESCRIPTION

Australian architect Paul Pholeros developed the initial brief in 1990; twenty-five architects competed for the project. Gregory Burgess, who had completed the Brambuk Cultural Centre at Halls Gap that same year, was awarded the commission.

Burgess, who follows the anthroposophy of Rudolf Steiner, focused on housing a field of activities rather than proposing formal or aesthetic solutions.[10] He stresses the need to be sensitized to the fluid interchange of mythical, spatial, and material ways of knowing, and observes this of any culture he designs for, including his own.[11] Exemplary strategies adopted in the design include a collaborative process, whereby the community is able to lay claim to the design. The consultation process involved the two client groups—the Mutitjulu community and the Australian Nature Conservation Agency—and a team of professionals, including Burgess, display designer Sonja Peters, and landscape architects Kevin Taylor and Kate Cullity.[12] A work studio and drop-in space was organized in the Mutitjulu Community Centre where the team spent a three-and-a-half-week period familiarizing themselves with the stories and ways of the community and the *Tjukurpa*. Such efforts at integration into community life were aimed at building trust and showing respect to the traditional owners. The consultation process to be followed was documented in the brief.

The Anangu brought their stories to the first consultation meeting around an aerial map of Uluru, dotting the entire perimeter of the site with events from the *Tjukurpa*. Knowledge was gendered, and designated Mutitjulu female Elders carried the knowledge back and forth between the community and the workshop.[13] The story of a battle between *Liru*, the poisonous snake, and *Kunya*, the carpet snake, which gave rise to specific features on one side of the rock, was depicted in a painting by Barbara Tjikatu and Nipper Winmati to illustrate the convergence of the snakes upon Uluru.[14] The women identified a dead, desert oak surrounded by young oaks as representing metamorphozed warriors of the Liru clan.[15] The Elders then sketched the building plan, program, and movement through the buildings repeatedly on the sand. Movement through the Centre was further spatialized in a painting by Nellie Patterson, which showed how the patterns within the building might serve to divert visitors, forcing them to engage with its content.[16]

The concept of careful spatial choreography and control was necessary to reflect the scale of the landscape. Landscape architect Kevin Taylor has described the design strategies of locating the car and bus parks at a distance from the building and creating a series of winding paths through a landscape island around the center in order to prompt visitors to pause and listen to the landscape.[17]

Burgess designed two undulating structures, poised as though in battle around a central courtyard drawing on the metaphor of the snakes *Liru* and *Kunya*. This generative image is evoked by the dimly lit, tunnel-like entrance to the southern building, where roof members follow a skeletal pattern. As described by Michael Tawa, the arrival sequence was designed to take the visitor from the car park past the *Inma* ground where dances are held to enter the *Tjukurpa* space where the law is recounted through various media, art, ceramics, and audio-visuals.[18] The arrival sequence would then broaden to describe male and female aspects of Anangu culture and lead on to the second major space in the sequence, the *Nintiringkunpai*, a pentagonal space where the joint management of the park between Anangu and Australian National Travel Association is explained.[19] The *Maruku* arts and crafts gallery, the third major space, sells handcrafts from sixteen Anangu communities, and Anangu work on handcrafts below a *wiltja* (semicircular branch and bark shelter) in the yard. The northern building houses the *Minkiku*—the exhibition, performance, and meeting space—and related stores and services, while the *Inma* dancing ground to the west is arranged around the dead desert oak. A private courtyard and a larger area against the southward face of Uluru create a pattern of clearings around the built form. The snake metaphor is continued in the skeletal roof structure with its "peeling skin," a "carapace" or "crust" of copper and blood-wood shingles.

Technologies used in construction—which Tawa describes as "bush technology"—had to be developed specifically for the building.[20] The only representation of a local building tradition is in the *wiltja*. There was a deliberate use of rustic and unsophisticated materials, including adobe bricks, earthen floors, hardwood tree-trunks stripped of their bark, and radially sawn timbers, exemplifying Burgess's expression of the moral economy of the Anangu who tend to not expend energy in overrefining objects.[21] The connections between wooden members were

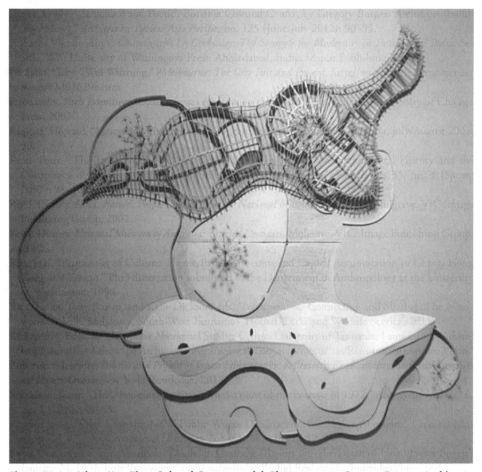

Figure 38.1.   Uluru-Kata Tjuta Cultural Centre, model. Photo courtesy Gregory Burgess Architects.

made in deliberately provisional ways, where jointing is not seamless, nailheads are visible, and beams are trussed together.[22] This aesthetic has won several awards for the building, including the 2004 Royal Australian Institute of Architects Gold Medal for Burgess.

However, postoccupation studies suggest that the building has had limited success in delivering opportunities for the Mutitjulu and other Anangu communities, and has become a building solely for metropolitan visitors.[23] Undoubtedly the Cultural Centre has been instrumental in changing tourist attitudes toward Uluru and the National Park, and serves as an anchor in the Anangu struggle to permanently close the arduous climb.[24] Yet the permanent closure of the climb, under discussion since September 2010, is dependent on the development of adequate alternative visitor experiences to cater to tourists. The Centre no longer facilitates the many social interactions for which it was originally designed.

RECEPTION

The Uluru-Kata Tjuta Cultural Centre was the recipient of several awards, including a High Commendation in the Royal Australian Institute of Architects Sir Zelman Cowan Award for

Figure 38.2. Uluru-Kata Tjuta Cultural Centre, interior. Photo Trevor Mein, courtesy Gregory Burgess Architects.

Public Buildings National Award in 1996; the Kenneth F. Brown Asia Pacific Culture and Architecture Award in 1998; a special mention in the Australian Cultural Studies National Awards in 1997; and the Royal Australian Institute of Architects (NT) New Institutional Building and Peoples' Choice Awards in 2004.

NOTES

1. Thanks to Gregory Burgess at Gregory Burgess Architects for providing architectural details and Grace Moore at Uluru Media for consulting with the community. A large part of this content is based on a detailed presentation made by Gregory Burgess at a workshop organized by Graham Brawn at the University of Melbourne on March 17, 2010.

2. The official population number of Anangu in 2000 was 385. John Taylor, "Anangu Population Dynamics and Future Growth in Uluru-Kata Tjuta National Park: Discussion Paper," Centre for Aboriginal Economic Policy Research at the Australian National University, 2001, available at http://caepr.anu.edu.au/Publications/DP/2001DP211.php.

3. *Minga* means non-Aboriginal tourist, but it is used in reference to tourists who opt to climb Uluru against the wishes of the Anangu.

4. Lisa Findley, *Building Change: Architecture, Politics and Cultural Agency* (London and New York: Routledge, 2005), 88.

5. Michael Tawa, "Liru and Kunya," *Architecture Australia* (March/April 1996): 50.

6. Findley, *Building Change*, 93.

7. Jillian Walliss, "The Right to Land versus the Right to Landscape: Uluru-Kata Tjuta National Park, Australia," in *The Right to Landscape: Contesting Landscape and Human Rights,* eds. Shelley Egoz,

Jala Makhzoumie, and Gloria Pungetti (UK and USA: Ashgate, 2011), 160; in reference to Uluru-Kata Tjuta Board of Management, *Uluru (Ayers Rock-Mount Olga) National Park: Plan of Management* (Canberra: Commonwealth of Australia), 1986.

8. Walliss, "The Right to Land," 156.

9. Commonwealth Department of the Environment, "History of the Park," available at http://www.environment.gov.au/topics/national-parks/uluru-kata-tjuta-national-park/culture-and-history/history-park.

10. Findley, *Building Change*, 96–97.

11. Based on a presentation made by Gregory Burgess on his design method at a workshop organized by Graham Brawn at the University of Melbourne on March 17, 2010.

12. Gregory Burgess Architects: Sonja Peter, Environmental Designer; Kevin Taylor and Kate Cullity, Landscape Designers; David Western, Tourist Consultant; and Anthony Prowse and Associates, Quantity Surveyors, "Uluru National Park Cultural Centre: Project Brief and Concept Design," brief prepared for the Mutitjulu Community and Australian National Parks and Wildlife Service, October 1990.

13. *Tjamiwa* and "Nipper" are identified as bringing the ideas of the men to the forum, while Nellie Patterson represented the women's ideas. Findley, *Building Change*, 98.

14. Ibid., 101.

15. Gregory Burgess, "The Uluru-Kata Tjuta Cultural Centre," *Architect Victoria* (January/February 1998): 20.

16. Burgess et al., "Uluru National Park Cultural Centre," 4.

17. Kevin Taylor, "Uluru-Kata Tjuta Cultural Centre," *Landscape Australia* 23, no. 1 (2001): 27.

18. Tawa, "Liru and Kunya," 50, 54.

19. Ibid., 50.

20. Ibid., 54.

21. Findley, *Building Change*, 108–9.

22. Ibid., 108–9.

23. Kim Dovey, "Seeing Uluru," *Thresholds* 21 (2000): 60–65.

24. Findley, *Building Change*, 83. Outback Australia Travel Secrets, "Travel Guide: Climbing Ayers Rock/Uluru," available at http://www.outback-australia-travel-secrets.com/climbing-ayers-rock-uluru.html.

39

Wilcannia Health Service, Wilcannia, New South Wales, Australia[1]

Location: Ross Street, Wilcannia, New South Wales
Date: 2002
Client: Department of Health (New South Wales Far West Area Health Service) and NSW Health
Community: Wilcannia Community Working Party
Architect and Design Director: Dillon Kombumerri
Architect Team: Kevin O'Brien, John Moschatos, and Phil Senior
Project Manager: Greg Poulsen, GHD
Landscape Architect: Nicole Thompson, Government Architect's Office, NSW
Structural/Civil Consultant: Vijay Badwhar, Government Architect's Office, NSW
Builder: Andrew Lahey, Lahey Constructions
Interior Designer: Alison Page, Merrima Aboriginal Design Unit, Government Architect's Office, NSW
Funding: NSW Health
Cost: approximately $1.6 million

The River Darling was made by *Ngatji*, an ancestral serpent, that wriggled its course while traveling across the land. Its name is Barka, and the people of Wilcannia are Barkinji or "river-people." Barka remains a resource of spiritual and physical sustenance; a place of recreation and ceremony; a refuge from the township, mission, or station; a marker of the seasons; a gauge of the health of country; and a link in the intricately woven narratives of other river stories and other river peoples.

BACKGROUND

In 1878, Cyril Blacket won a competition to build a hospital in Wilcannia, on the edge of town, overlooking a bend in the Darling. Blacket's hospital, completed in 1879, was built of locally quarried, white quartzite sandstone to a symmetrical cruciform plan. It featured central

Figure 39.1.   Wilcannia Health Service, exterior view. Photo by Brett Boardman, courtesy Merrima.

consulting rooms and male and female wards on either side of the cruciform. Oriented north toward the township, away from the Darling, its major function was servicing the needs of riverboat traffic passing Wilcannia, known as "Queen City of the West" and the third largest Australian shipping port of the late 1800s.

Run along strict lines of exclusion and control, the hospital became, for the Barkinji, a "sick place" where people needing treatment were incarcerated, "out of sight and out of mind," out the back, away from community and country. In spite of this sorry history, Barkinji experiences have built the hospital and grounds into cultural memory, replete with stories and recollections of birth, sickness, and death. Rather than erase these memories, the community was keen to preserve the site and buildings as remembered, to respect family associations and affinities developed over the years, and to reconnect this renewed site of healing with the river.

CONSULTATION PROCESS

In 1998, the Merrima Aboriginal Design Unit of the NSW Government Architect's Office won a tender to redevelop the hospital. Numerous additions had made the facility unsuitable for the current health needs of the community. Merrima's brief was to provide an integrated multipurpose health center, combining social services, community health, and respite accommodation. The design team's input was extensive. They developed and presented seven design options and attended twelve site visits, of which six were under construction. The project was facilitated by the Barkinji Community Reference Group with the Wilcannia Community Working Party, chaired by William Bates and made up of twenty-nine members drawn from hospital staff, Indigenous Elders, and community representatives. The architectural team met with the Working Party on a regular basis and sought the endorsement of concepts and the selection of the preferred design. The architects presented 2-D and 3-D material and models to help explain the design, and an open public meeting was arranged to showcase the preferred design chosen by the Working Party.

PROJECT DESCRIPTION

The first design move was to clear the hospital building of ad-hoc extensions and retrieve the original Blacket structure. The internal fit-out carefully left intact several original features that could not be restored and incorporated—such as coffered corrugated metal and timber ceilings in the female and male wards, masonry flues, and dormer window surrounds. These are now concealed behind plasterboard ceilings in case of more substantial future restoration. The restoration, including work done by the community under traineeship programs, focused on stone walls and repointing, reroofing, and plumbing, painting, and landscaping. This has returned the building and grounds to something of their original aspect. Where more complete restoration proved unviable, elements were stabilized and finished in a simple way. Overall, the impression is of a patchwork, registering the marks of incremental modification. Rather than crystallizing an originary past, this restorative practice implies an ongoing future, with many opportunities for capacity building, trainee projects, and community involvement.

The current operation focuses on primary health care, emergency, outpatients, and respite care. There are initiatives for community-based education, outreach, home visitation, and follow-up health maintenance—including a teleconferencing facility for families to communicate with others recuperating elsewhere.

The building combines locally made mud bricks for both internal and external walls, corrugated metal and fiber cement wall sheeting, timber wall and roof framing and timber screens, concrete slab on ground, and corrugated roof sheeting. It provides a multipurpose health facility accommodating overnight stay, minor medical procedures, and community health programs. The upgraded facility has greatly improved the attendance for medical treatments and child immunizations, as well as pre- and postnatal checkups.

Outside, the artist Badger Bates has made three paving slabs showing *Ngatji*, the river goanna, and the *Parntuu* codfish. In Badger's designs, all characters point away from the hospital, toward the community, to indicate that people are welcome—but also that returning home, to be with family and country, is the best way to health.

The design by Merrima reorganizes hospital functions between the National Trust–listed Blacket building, a new linear wing facing the Barka, and a reception area between the two. The original hospital contains administration offices, ancillary spaces, and consulting rooms. The new wing provides respite rooms to the east, a lounge and nurses' station near reception, emergency outpatients adjacent to the ambulance bay, as well as staff facilities, kitchen, laundry, and storage to the west. Circulation is by way of a central spine, with plenty of daylight, controlled solar access, cross ventilation, and a system of retaining winter solar energy through pitched metal linings oriented north. For practical and cultural reasons, the mortuary facility is located at the far western end of the new wing, where access can be more discrete. Expressed as a separate mass, it is hinged northward, and incorporates a stepped and screened external terrace that allows families to gather privately and pay their respects (Plate 39).

The new wing is angled away from the Blacket building so as to open up an entry space and better address the Barka. It works in conjunction with the hospital and a stone outbuilding on the southeast to form a sheltered, sunny courtyard. The plan's articulation in two contiguous sections contributes much to the ensemble. The building hovers above a stabilized berm, turning with the river to reinforce landform and contour. The two sections are given individual orientations to the river, while the plan shape contains and protects the site to the north. This avoids a relentless and imposing wall on the river side; the buildings recede and don't impose themselves on the landscape.

Plate 39. Wilcannia Health Service, Wilcannia, New South Wales, Australia, veranda. Photo by Brett Boardman, courtesy Merrima.

The reception distributes circulation south to the new structure, north to the old building, and east-west to sheltered courtyard and landscaped areas. As a place of orientation and passage, with many openings and ways through, it contests the formalism and hierarchical symmetry of the original building and site layout. Likewise, and with the greatest respect, the old building is reinhabited and returned informally to the river. It turns away from itself, into a more democratic site of access and egress, gathering and dispersing, engagement and disengagement. Literally turned inside out, it becomes reconciled to what it had forgotten, and in the process, is reconstructed and renewed.

Spatial moves in the design also have metaphorical value. Shifts in the building plan and form take up organic alignments. The angled, cross-sectional profile appears to bellow or expand outward. The architecture is made to be sensitive to the gestures and motions of place. Architect Dillon Kombumerri has spoken of the animate character of the buildings: that they appear to breathe, to be alive; that they evoke skin, gill, fin, and lung; that they arc and spread like limbs and wings; that they are clad to read like armature and carapace; that they frame and register time changing by casting shadows onto their own surfaces and onto the ground.

CONTRIBUTION

Merrima's original contribution is less a new building than a new way of reading and capitalizing on the potential of what is already there. The perimeter of Blacket's building, together with several outbuildings and sheds, provides a framework for simple interventions. The new buildings use these to help zone the site and create a layered and sequenced organization. External spaces are as important as internal rooms. In some cases, internal spaces read as external—in the western corridor, for example, where a combination of the cross-sectional profile, splayed upper walls of the southern sequence of rooms, and natural light create the impression of a shaded street lined with discrete, small-scaled buildings. In this way, the inside is turned inside out and returned to country—that is, to an outside that had always been there.

This is Merrima's proposition: that architecture might consist primarily in how the in-between is conceived, shaped, furnished, and opened up to inhabitation. New spaces are made between buildings, between river and town, between turn-of-the-century and contemporary health practices. Site planning, including the relationships between old and new buildings, provides opportunities for places that could be later spliced and tucked into recesses as needs change. Now that the buildings and site belong to the river, they harbor a way of being close to place and country—protecting and making room for memory and for stories. In this way, architecture "works." It contributes to cultural sustainment by reconciling person and place, community and country. Its function is not disembodied or abstracted from the sociocultural but grounded in it. Rather than being isolated, objectified, aestheticized, or monumentalized, architecture exists primarily as a site of cultural practice—and its success is judged inasmuch as it affords and promotes this practice.

RECEPTION

The Wilcannia Health Service project has received several awards, including the award for Environmental Commitment in the Public and Commercial Buildings Category of the Australian Timber Awards in 2003; the "Gold" Award in the New South Wales Premier's Awards for Services to Regional and Rural New South Wales; the Royal Australian Institute of Architects' Cecil Blackett Award for Rural Building; and a Major Award in the National Trust Awards.

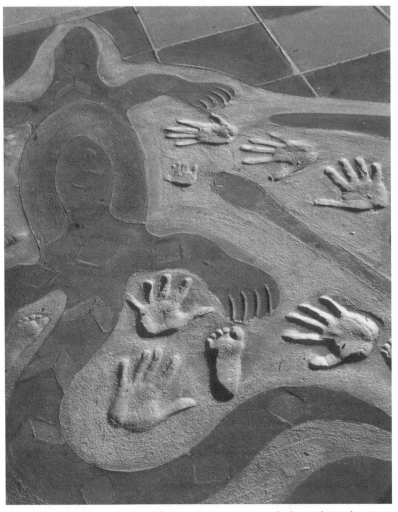

Figure 39.2. Wilcannia Health Service, pavement design. Photo by Brett Boardman, courtesy Merrima.

Text by Professor Michael Tawa of the Faculty of Architecture, Design and Planning
at the University of Sydney. Chapter published previously as Michael Tawa,
"Wilcannia Health Service," *Architecture Australia* 19, no. 4
(July/August 2002): 70–76. Available at architectureau.com.

NOTE

1. http://architectureau.com/articles/wilcannia-health-service/. Thanks to Dillon Kombumerri for feedback on this article as originally published.

40

Worn Gundidj, Tower Hill, Victoria, Australia

Location: Tower Hill Reserve near Warrnambool
Date: 1962–1969
Client: Public Works Department, Victoria
Builder: Warnambool Construction
Architect: Robin Boyd (1919–1971)
Cost: approximately $47,460

Worn Gundidj is an early example of a design for a natural history center in a revegetated landscape. Revegetation was the central focus of the Tower Hill Wildlife Reserve project. Tower Hill, an inactive volcano, lies between Warrnambool and Port Fairy in western Victoria in the Victorian Volcanic Plain bioregion. The ecology of the region is cinder cone woodland, less than 3 percent of which has survived pastoral clearing.[1] The traditional owners of the area are the Koroitgundidj people. Both the Tower Hill Wildlife Reserve and Worn Gundidj, originally named the Tower Hill Natural History Centre, are listed on the Victorian heritage register. Although not strictly an Indigenous cultural center, the project suggests a claim made through intervention in the landscape. The nearest Indigenous community is at Framlingham, to the northeast of Warrnambool.

BACKGROUND

European pastoralists cleared much of the vegetation in the Tower Hill area by the 1850s. In 1866 the inner rim of the volcanic crater was reserved for public recreation under the management of the Tower Hill Acclimatisation Society (1866–1869), which formed to introduce exotic plants and animals into the area. The Tower Hill area was declared a state forest in 1873, and it became the first national park in Victoria in 1892.[2] However, clearing of native vegetation, cattle grazing, and quarrying persisted within the bounds of the park until the 1930s under the management of the Koroit Council.

The Warrnambool Field Naturalist Club began initial attempts at revegetation in 1958, a few years prior to the construction of the Tower Hill Visitor Centre. The revegetation project

275

Figure 40.1.   Tower Hill Reserve. Photo by author, 2011.

was based on an 1855 painting by Eugene von Guérard, a Viennese painter of the German Romantic tradition (1811–1901) who had come as a prospector to the Victorian goldfields.[3] James Dawson of Kangatong near Warrnambool commissioned Von Guérard's painting of Tower Hill. The microscopic detailing of the painting, which included individual plant species, formed the basis of the initial revegetation of Tower Hill. Australian cultural historian Tim Bonyhady observes that although absolute veracity of the painting's depiction of native species could not be determined, it "became the most powerful testimony to how Tower Hill had been degraded by European settlement—and a template of how it would come into its own again."[4] As a result, plants not native to the area were introduced through initial attempts at revegetation.[5] Extensive historical and ecological research has subsequently been undertaken, and non-native species have been replaced by native species. Von Guérard's painting was located at the Visitor Centre for six years, and then was moved to the Warrnambool Art Gallery. Tower Hill remains a subject for landscape painting.[6]

In 1961, Tower Hill was declared a State Wildlife Reserve, and the revegetation project begun by the Warrnambool Field Naturalist Club was taken over by the Fisheries and Wildlife Division of the Victorian Ministry for Conservation. The revegetation project, cited as the first of its kind in Victoria, provided the model for the Landcare Australia movement of the late 1980s.[7] In a grassroots effort involving schoolchildren, field naturalists, game hunters, and other volunteers, exotic species were removed and over forty thousand native trees were planted throughout the Reserve. Between 1964 and 1985, eight native mammal and bird species specific to the area were successfully reintroduced, including the eastern gray kangaroo, the short-beaked echidna, the emu, the Cape Barren goose, the magpie goose, the sugar glider,

Figure 40.2. Worn Gundidj Visitor Centre, exterior view. Photo courtesy John Gollings.

the common brushtail possum, and the koala. The agile antechinus was reintroduced in 1995. The wetlands and grasslands of the Tower Hill Reserve now support 150 species of birds, and the koala population has reached such levels that there is a population control program underway.[8] A volunteer organization called Friends of Tower Hill was formed in 1993, and Parks Victoria has managed the Reserve since 1997.

The commission for the Tower Hill Natural History Centre in 1962 coincided with the creation of the Wildlife Reserve. The intention was to educate visitors on the restoration of the environment, and to draw attention to "the destruction and reconstruction of wildlife habitat and demonstrate historical relics."[9] *The Age* newspaper described it as an ultramodern facility and set the estimated cost of approximately $29,700, and predicted that it would become one of the biggest tourist attractions in Victoria.[10] The push for conservation of the area was prompted by reductions in game bird numbers due to hunting. Game bird hunting continues in the surrounds.[11]

Prominent Melbourne architect Robin Boyd (1919–1971) was selected for the project due to his involvement in the conservation movement and dedication to an Australian identity in architecture. Boyd was well known for his critical writings, his response to the natural environment, and development of a distinctively Australian modernism. His design of the Tower Hill Centre is regarded as a successful exemplar of this approach.[12] Boyd's inspiration for the design was drawn from the volcanic island hilltops, which gave the Centre its circular form and sloping roof with an open internal space and central hollow stone column.[13]

The central column is crowned by a skylight, creating a space reminiscent of the volcano crater. The outer wall of the glazed pavilion is constructed with timber and has a stone skirt up to cill level. The roof is supported by the central column and has deep eaves with radially arranged and laminated timber rafters. The building houses interpretive displays and publications, including a print of the von Guérard painting. The Reserve has a bird hide and picnic

Figure 40.3. Worn Gundidj Visitor Centre, interior column. Photo courtesy John Gollings.

facilities, and there are five self-guided walks that follow different ecological themes: the Peak Climb (orientation and geology), the Lava Tongue Boardwalk (wetlands and wildlife), the Hat Island Habitat Track (revegetation), the Whurrong Walk (wetlands and habitat), and the Journey to the Last Volcano (geology and wildlife).[14]

RECEPTION

The Worn Gundidj Aboriginal Co-Operative was established in 1992 and managed a Community Development Employment Project until 2007. In 2002, Worn Gundidj entered into a Commercial Services Agreement with Parks Victoria to provide visitation experiences, tourist information, and saleable items at Tower Hill Wildlife Reserve, and the Visitor Centre was renamed Worn Gundidj. The Co-Operative has ties with Warrnambool City Council, Moyne Shire Council, Koroit Traders and Tourism Association, Shipwreck Coast Tourism, Friends of Tower Hill, Deakin University, and South West TAFE. Aboriginal art and craft is sold at the Worn Gundidj Cultural Centre, and the community conducts guided tours. Horticulture is the Co-Operative's primary area of business and employment, and it manages a commercial nursery.[15]

Several intellectual and ethical questions are raised by the Tower Hill project, only one of which is the appropriation of a European painterly eye as the inspiration for landscape regeneration. Boyd did not acknowledge Indigenous building traditions, although he commented on the use of a circular plan to mitigate the impact of an artificial form in a natural landscape.[16] The structure, including its use of stone, is certainly reminiscent of Aboriginal stone shelters in the western districts of Victoria. The connection, however, was made much later via a different project inspired by the Natural History Centre, designed by Boyd's partner Frederick Romberg at Shepparton. Romberg's Bangerang Cultural Centre adopts a very similar circular form (see chapter 3). Aboriginal stakeholder Sandy Atkinson prompted the design of Bangerang. Upon seeing Boyd's circular design at Tower Hill, Atkinson recognized its symbolic resonance for Aboriginal communities. Atkinson approached Boyd's partner, Fredrick Romberg, who accordingly designed Bangerang in a similar circular form.

NOTES

1. The Tower Hill website offers a detailed history of the project from which much of the information in this chapter is drawn. See Worn Gundidj Enterprises, "History and Heritage," available at http://www.towerhill.org.au/index.php/about-reserve/history.

2. Victorian Heritage Register, "Tower Hill State Game Reserve," available at http://vhd.heritage council.vic.gov.au/places/14278/download-report.

3. Warrnambool Art Gallery, "The Artists: Eugene von Guérard," available at http://www.artists footsteps.com/html/vonGuerard_TowerHill.htm. See also National Gallery of Victoria, "Eugene von Guérard," available at http://www.ngv.vic.gov.au/explore/ collection/artist/1647/.

4. Tim Bonyhady, *The Colonial Earth* (Melbourne: Melbourne University Press, 2000), 358.

5. WG Enterprises, "Worn Gundidj," available at http://www.worngundidj.org.au/.

6. Bonyhady, *The Colonial Earth*, 363.

7. Worn Gundidj Enterprises, "History and Heritage."

8. Ibid.

9. "National History Island," *The Age*, October 31, 1967.

10. "National History Island."

11. Victorian Heritage Register, "Tower Hill State Game Reserve." For a detailed study of the financial problems related to the project, see Bonyhady, *The Colonial Earth*, 361–66.

12. Geoffrey Serle, *Robin Boyd: A Life* (Melbourne: Melbourne University Press, 1995), 262–63.

13. Victorian Heritage Register, "Tower Hill State Game Reserve."

14. Parks Victoria, "Tower Hill Future Directions Strategy: Final Report August 2002," available at http://parkweb.vic.gov.au/__data/assets/pdf_file/0019/313444/Tower-Hill-Future-Directions -Strategy.pdf.

15. Rural Industries Research and Development Corporation, "Outback Spirit Bushfoods: A Learning Model in Marketing and Supply Chain Management," January 2007, available at https://rirdc .infoservices.com.au/downloads/06-037.pdf.

16. Robin Boyd, *Living in Australia* (Melbourne: Thames and Hudson, 2013), 122, 164–65.

41

Yagan Memorial Park, Belhus, Western Australia, Australia

Location: West Swan Road, Belhus, Upper Swan, Western Australia
Date: 2008–2010
Clients: Derbal Yerrigan Committee for the Reburial of Yagan's Kaat, the City of Swan, and the Department of Indigenous Affairs, Western Australia
Community: Nyoongar community
Art Consultant: Artsource (senior consultant Jenny Kerr; consultancy and employment manager Beverley Iles)
Artists: Nyoongar artists Peter Farmer, Sandra Hill, and Kylie Ricks with non-Indigenous ceramic artist Jenny Dawson
Construction: Ctech Engineering (Marc Abonnel) and Rammed Earth WA (Roman Antoniuk)
Landscape Architect: City of Swan (Wendy Seymour)
Cost: approximately $126,000

The Yagan Memorial Park in the Perth suburb of Belhus in Upper Swan exemplifies the challenge of maintaining Indigenous presence in a settler community—in this case a suburban region of Perth known for wineries and related tourism.[1] The Park is a built landscape that claims the site for commemoration and commands a view of the traditional lands of the Nyoongar. Its situation on the side of a hill leading off from the freeway makes arrival at this park a deliberate choice. The Yagan Memorial Park is a powerful demonstration of how art, landscape, and built elements may combine in articulating traumatic histories and initiating reconciliatory practices. Conceived as a place for reflection, with benches located between sinuous, rammed-earth walls, the site itself is not immediately visible to passers-by. The invitation to enter is instead signaled by an artistic interpretation of scarred trees that flank the entrance to a meandering path. As symbols of prior occupation, scarred trees are often the only traces of Indigenous presence in settler areas, and their representation prepares the visitor for other lost and recovered traces symbolized by this space.

Figure 41.1. Yagan Memorial Park, space for reflection. Photo by the author, 2013.

Figure 41.2. Yagan Memorial Park, entrance showing scarred tree sculptures by Indigenous artists, Peter Farmer and Kylie Ricks. Photo by author, 2013.

BACKGROUND

The Park commemorates a violent history of colonial encounter, massacre, removal of Indigenous remains, and their subsequent repatriation. Early contact between settlers and Nyoongar were initially amicable; however, relations quickly deteriorated. The area occupied by the colonists was of great economic and ceremonial significance to the Nyoongar community, and at least 178 incidences of violence between European settlers and the local Nyoongar peoples were recorded between 1826 and 1852.[2] By 1864, disease, violence, and the loss of food-gathering sites had further decimated the local people.[3]

There is a strong history of Indigenous resistance in the Perth area, and the Nyoongar produced strong leaders, including Midgegooroo, and later, his son Yagan, a Whadjuk Nyoongar man who became a renowned patriot for the Nyoongar community.[4] Yagan initially attempted to promote cordial relations with the European settlers, but he later played an active role in hostile encounters and was described as refusing to acknowledge the legitimacy of white power.[5] A bounty was placed on Yagan's head when he was held responsible for several European deaths. The records suggested that these murders were reprisals for the murders of his father, brother, and uncle, a form of vengeance demanded under Nyoongar law.[6] Yagan was captured in 1832 and imprisoned at the Round House Prison in Fremantle. He was later exiled to Carnac Island along with two other Nyoongar prisoners.[7] The three prisoners escaped after six weeks; however, Yagan was subsequently shot dead by the brothers William and James Keats in 1833. Yagan's fellow escapees killed William Keats, while James escaped along the Canning River and later claimed the bounty on Yagan's head.[8] Yagan's remains were notoriously dismembered after his murder.[9] His back, which bore tribal markings, was skinned, and his body beheaded. Yagan's head or *kaat* was preserved by smoking and transported to England for study and display at the Liverpool Museum, and subsequently buried in England at the Everton Cemetery in 1964. Following a sustained campaign led by Nyoongar Elder and descendant of Yagan Ken Colbung, Yagan's remains were exhumed and repatriated in 1997.[10]

At the time of Yagan's death in 1833, there were fears of an Aboriginal uprising in the Swan River settlement.[11] This tension was believed to have prompted the Pinjarra Massacre in October 1834, when at least fifteen and probably closer to eighty Nyoongar were murdered by a mounted force of police, soldiers, and settlers near Pinjarra.[12] The Pinjarra Massacre site is not formally acknowledged, and traditional owners have been refused permission to install an interpretation of the massacre at the site.[13]

The story of Yagan's *kaat* and associated violence resonates even today with troubling outcomes. In nearby Perth, a form of symbolic violence has been wrought upon Robert Hitchcock's 1984 sculpture *Yagan*, included in the "Art City" walking tour that highlights some key pieces of public art within the city.[14] Several of the pieces make reference to the lost fauna of the Swan River Coastal plain, erased by the development of the city. In 1984, Hitchcock was commissioned to produce a bronze sculpture of Yagan, which was installed on Heirisson Island. In that same year, Yagan's statue was infamously beheaded multiple times in an act of vandalism. Indigenous writer Archie Weller wrote a story in response to the repeated desecration of the Yagan statue titled "Confessions of a Headhunter," which was adapted into a short film in 2000. The film's protagonists make their way through Perth's parklands and public space beheading the colonial statues of the city as a political response to the beheading of both Yagan and his statue.

PROJECT DESCRIPTION

The Yagan Memorial Park was designed collaboratively by Indigenous and other artists and landscape architects at the City of Swan. The Park was the outcome of a long community campaign initiated by the Derbal Yerrigan Committee, which formed in 1997 to agitate for the reburial of Yagan's *kaat* and was ultimately supported by the Department of Indigenous Affairs and the City of Swan.[15] *Derbal Yerrigan* means "Swan River" in local language. As Nyoongar Elder and chair of the Derbal Yerrigan Committee Richard Wilkes explained of the need for repatriation, "(i) is very important, because I believe that, spiritually, once we rebury Yagan's *kaat* into the ground then his spirit will become one again and the spirit of Yagan will rise up in and amongst us. I believe, too, that the leaders will evolve within the Nyoongar people in the same way that he was."[16] Elders consulted on the project included Wilkes and Albert Corunna, who oversaw the appropriate repatriation and reburial of Yagan's *kaat*. Following forensic investigations, in 2008 the site was selected as the most appropriate and was vested with the Aboriginal Affairs Planning Authority.[17] The project was developed over a two-year period and was opened in 2010 by Western Australian premier Colin Barnett following a private traditional Nyoongar burial ceremony.[18]

The reburial site and commemorative park is located near where Yagan's *kaat* was severed from his body, a place identified by forensic archaeologist Richard Wright as the most likely location for Yagan's remains.[19] Art consultants Artsource, the peak membership body for visual artists in Western Australia, managed the collaborative public art component, working closely with Indigenous artists.[20] The project had three components: the entrance, the entry passage with interpretive artworks, and the wall where Yagan's *kaat* is interred. Following a call for expressions of interest by the City of Swan, the Department of Aboriginal Affairs, and Nyoongar Elders, a number of artists presented their work. Nyoongar artists Peter Farmer and Kylie Ricks were selected to work on the entrance scarred-tree sculptures and the curvilinear rammed-earth walls, while Nyoongar artist Sandra Hill and non-Indigenous ceramic artist Jenny Dawson were commissioned to produce the interpretive artworks. These artworks tell the story of the life and death of Yagan.[21] The three elements come together in an integrated landscape with clear thresholds, pathways, and places for reflection orienting visitors away from the road toward the river. A number of artists, Indigenous artist-helpers, and other experts assisted in the process.[22] The artists were also commissioned to create Yagan's gravesite.

The project took two years from conception to completion, with the construction taking eight months and the interpretive artwork taking around eight to nine weeks. The City of Swan employed Indigenous horticultural trainees in preparing, planting, and fencing the site through a DYC-endorsed heritage training program.[23] The artists were also involved in lengthy consultations with Elders of the Nyoongar community via the Derbal Yerrigan Committee. The proposal for a visual story held immediate appeal for the Elders. The power of visual and spatial praxis, in comparison to the written and textual representations habitually used in heritage sites, is convincingly illustrated through this project. Symbolic and totemic forms are invoked. The curvilinear walls are evocative of *Waugal*, the river serpent, moving in and out of the land. The use of rammed earth evokes geological strata. Yet the space itself and the practice of commemoration remain open to interpretation in contemporary terms.

The intention of the Park was not only to provide a site for Nyoongar commemoration but also to educate the community at large. As artist Sandra Hill observed of the project, "(v)isual art is a powerful weapon against racism and discrimination."[24] She further observed that "Yagan was a heroic Nyoongar leader, and his death was tragic and wasteful. Had he lived he may have negotiated a different, more equitable future for the Nyoongar. Following his loss, black-white relations dissolved into frontier wars."[25] She further insisted that the story is important not only for the Nyoongar people, who number approximately thirty-five thousand, but for all Western Australians.

Other artists involved in the project reiterate these sentiments. Peter Farmer, whose grandparents and great-grandparents lived near the site during the early twentieth century, has a strong affinity with the area and the Swan River people; he notes that both he and artist Kylie Ricks share an ancestor, born in King's Park.[26] Such deep associations with place and community enabled the understanding and maintenance of strict cultural protocols for the creation of artworks. For example, the male scarred tree at the entrance was designed by Farmer to represent the Nyoongar shield, while the female tree designed by Ricks represents the *coolamon* or carrying vessel. Since traditionally women collected more than 75 percent of the food, the women's scarred tree is larger. The inspiration for the trees came from a midden site opposite the park, where human skeletal remains over thirty-seven thousand years old have been unearthed; scarred trees stand on that site. Farmer was also consulted on the design of the landscape walls. The use of white symbolizes the Swan River, and the designs on the outside were made to look like the shield.

Visitors entering the site are deliberately channeled through a narrow passage built of rammed-earth walls—a mixture of earth, concrete, and red gravel—which are inlaid with hand-painted and silkscreen-printed porcelain tiles by Sandra Hill and Jenny Dawson (Plate 40). Hill

Plate 40.   Yagan Memorial Park, Belhus, Western Australia, passageway with interpretive story. Photo by author, 2013.

notes that the narrow passage was intended to arrest the visitor, to make them pause and learn the story of Yagan. The narrow eastern edge of each wall is decorated with an image of the Nyoongar moieties, the *wardang* or crow and the *manitch* or white cockatoo. Life before white settlement is depicted on the river-side wall, and the violent dispossession that brought death, poverty, and disease to the Nyoongar is depicted on the road-side wall. Although the height of the walls had to be reduced in accordance with public liability considerations, they still achieve the purpose of focusing the visitor and conveying a somber sensibility. Forced to pause and learn the story of what happened to the people of the Swan Valley, visitors are taught respect for the commemorative space.

The story of Yagan, including the scene of his death, effectively captures the decline of Indigenous culture following white settlement. The scenes of the timeline were painted on handmade clay tiles, fired several times, and covered with three layers of glaze. A complex technique was used to include archival and heritage images in the walls. Digital technology was used to create screen prints with a limited color palette of black and white on white porcelain tiles. These were combined with hand-drawn designs, and vibrant bands of blue and brown were used for emphasis. The tiles are high-fired stoneware, made durable for external weather conditions, with the painted surface melted into the body of the clay. The tiles are large and had to be handled carefully during installation—with some difficulty, observes Hill, because the walls were not planar surfaces. Five to six artist helpers participated in underpainting the tiles, and others assisted in holding them up as they were fixed to the wall. Ceramic artist Jenny Dawson, who collaborated with Hill, is an expert in ceramic techniques.

Figure 41.3. Yagan Memorial Park, hand-painted and silkscreen-printed porcelain tiles by artists Sandra Hill and Jenny Dawson depicting the conflict between European and Aboriginal peoples. Photo by author, 2013.

Moving beyond the time tunnel, the wall theme continues deeper into the landscape, channeling and orienting visitors to the view. The curvilinear wall blocks the view of the freeway and was designed so as not to disrupt existing landscaping features, such as large rocks and foliage on the site. Peter Farmer worked with Roman Antonuik and the contractor Rammed Earth WA Pty. Ltd. on the freeform monolithic walls, selecting the ochre pigmentation for the bands along the wall. The size and character of the rammed-earth wall makes it seem like a landscape feature, while the color ochre has long been associated with traditional ceremonies.[27] The contemplative space is arranged with timber benches oriented toward the view. The lighter band of color inserted in the wall represents the Swan River, respected by the Nyoongar as "the giver of life." These patterns etched in the wall are also inspired by the carvings found on shields depicting lineage and totems that "imbue such objects with power for use in ceremony and dance."[28]

RECEPTION

There had been speculation that the Yagan Memorial Park would be further expanded to include a Nyoongar cultural center or museum.[29] However, this seems less likely at present, as a cultural consultation process has begun at the nearby former Pryton and Lockridge reserves site known as Korndin Kulluch or Place of Reconciliation, which includes a recommendation for a Centre for Cultural Learning or a Nyoongar Museum for the fostering of cultural connections and knowledge between Elders and the youth of the Nyoongar community.[30] The project area is particularly significant, not only as the site of the former Swan Valley Nyoongar Community Camp but also due to its connection to Bennett Brook, which is believed to be the resting place of the *Waugal*.[31]

Landscape projects such as the Yagan Memorial Park encourage a form of spatial practice associated with storytelling, where communication is not dependent on interpretive signage. The absence of a textual explanation at the Yagan Memorial Park is its strength. Visitors who encounter the Park must take the trouble to research the history while being taught alternative Indigenous ways of knowing a place. Sensorial experiences precede other forms of knowing. Such strategies are particularly useful in representing contested and violent histories where heritage remains vulnerable to deliberate acts of erasure.

NOTES

1. Thanks to Ron Bradfield, Beverley Iles, Peter Farmer, and Jenny Dawson for comments on this account and to Sandra Hill for a lengthy discussion of the interpretive artwork. The project was supported by a number of organizations including the Department of Indigenous Affairs, Lotterywest, and the Western Australian State Government; John Brinkman, Department of Indigenous Affairs Midland Partners; Derbal Yerrigan Committee for the Reburial of Yagan's Kaat; and Department of Indigenous Affairs.

2. Jane M. Jacobs, *Edge of Empire: Postcolonialism and the City* (London and New York: Routledge, 1996), 107.

3. George Seddon and David Ravine, *A City and Its Setting: Images of Perth, Western Australia* (Fremantle: Fremantle Arts Centre Press, 1986), 110.

4. Seddon and Ravine, *A City and Its Setting*, 90.

5. S. Hallam and L. Tilbrook, *Aborigines of the Southwest Region, 1829–1840* (Perth: UWA Press, 1990), 333, cited by South West Aboriginal Land & Sea Council, "Yagan," *Kaartdijin Nyoongar: Nyoongar Knowledge*, available at http://www.noongarculture.org.au/ yagan/?searched=yes.

6. Jens Korff, "Perth's Aboriginal History," Creative Spirits, available at http://www.creativespirits .info/australia/western-australia/perth/perths-aboriginal-history.

7. N. Green, *Broken Spears: Aborigines and Europeans in the Southwest of Australia* (Perth: Focus Education Services, 1984), 79. Also Hallam and Tilbrook, *Aborigines of the Southwest Region*, 333.

8. Monument Australia, "Yagan Memorial Park," available at http://monumentaustralia.org.au/ themes/people/indigenous/display/93059-yagan-memorial-park.

9. Seddon and Ravine, *A City and Its Setting*, 90.

10. Monument Australia, "Yagan Memoral Park"; and Hannah McGlade, "The Repatriation of Ya-gan: A Story of Manufacturing Dissent," *Law Text Culture*, no. 4 (1998): 245–55, 245.

11. Korff, *Perth's Aboriginal History.*

12. Seddon and Ravine, *A City and Its Setting*, 94.

13. Pinjarra Massacre Site, 2011, "The Site Tour," available at http://www.pinjarramassacresite.com/ content/tour-audio/ (link no longer active, last accessed December 15, 2012).

14. Experience Perth, "Public Art Walks," available at http://www.experienceperth.com/things-to -see-and-do/arts-and-culture/public-art-walks.

15. Monument Australia, "Yagan Memorial Park."

16. Nyanda Smith, "The Yagan Memorial Park: A Site of Significance," *Artsource Newsletter*, August 2010; Department of Aboriginal Affairs, "Yagan Memorial Park Newsletter, February 2010" available at http://www.daa.wa.gov.au/Documents/News/Yagan%20Memorial%20Park/YMP_Newsletter_Feb24 .pdf (link no longer active, last accessed November 28, 2013).

17. Department of Aboriginal Affairs, "Yagan Memorial Park Newsletter."

18. Monument Australia, "Yagan Memorial Park."

19. Derbal Yerrigan Committee, "Yagan Memorial Park Newsletter: February 2010," available at http://www.dia.wa.gov.au/Documents/News/Yagan%20Memorial%20Park/YMP_Newsletter_Feb24 .pdf, 3 (link no longer active, last accessed December 12, 2012).

20. Artsource website, http://www.artsource.net.au/About-Us#sthash.2GXvJ905.dpuf (accessed October 23, 2013).

21. Artsource, "Yagan Memorial Park," available at http://www.artsource.net.au/Consulting/client -services/Public-Art-Procurement/Yagan-Memorial-Park.

22. Others include Rob Cripwell, Labyrinth Mosaics; Jason Hirst, artist; Peter Zuvela, photographer; Tony Pankiw, metal fabricator; Laurel Nannup, Tracie Pushman, and Ellen McFetridge, studio assistants; Jenny Dawson, Peter Zuvela, Ivan Zuvela, and Viktor Eszenyi, installation team.

23. Derbal Yerrigan Committee, "Yagan Memorial Park Newsletter."

24. Telephone conversation between the author and Sandra Hill, November 2013.

25. Telephone conversation between the author and Sandra Hill, November 2013.

26. Email communication with Peter Farmer, November 2013.

27. Thanks to Beverley Iles for the information in this section.

28. Thanks to Beverley Iles.

29. Korff, *Perth's Aboriginal History.*

30. Western Australian Planning Commission, "Draft Pyrton-Lockridge Reserves Cultural Consulta-tion Report 2012", 4, available at http://www.finance.wa.gov.au/cms/uploadedFiles/ Building_Manage ment_and_Works/Policy/Cultural%20Consultation%20Report%20web.pdf?n=9898.

31. Department of Finance, "Korndin Kulluch: A Place of Reconciliation," available at http://www .finance.wa.gov.au/cms/content.aspx?id=15860%20.

Glossary of Terms

AIATSIS Australian Institute of Aboriginal and Torres Strait Islander Studies
CAIRNS Centre for American Indian Research and Native Studies
CMHR Canadian Museum for Human Rights
CRC Cultural Resources Center
EXPO International Exposition
IBA Indigenous Business Australia
KMT Kuomintang
MOA Museum of Anthropology
NAIDOC *National Aboriginal and Islander Day Observance Committee*
NCIE National Centre of Indigenous Excellence
NMA National Museum of Australia
NMAI National Museum of the American Indian
ROC Republic of China
TAFE Technical and Further Education
VTOLG Victorian Traditional Owners Land Justice Group

Bibliography

Aboriginal Tent Embassy. 40th Anniversary website (link no longer active, last accessed October 7, 2013).

Aird, Michael. *Brisbane Blacks*. Southport, Queensland: Keeaira Press, 2001.

American Indian Community House [The]. *Community Bulletin* 24, no. I (Summer 2009).

Amery, Rob, and Georgina Yambo Williams. "Reclaiming through Renaming: The Reinstatement of Kaurna Toponyms in Adelaide and the Adelaide Plains." In *The Land Is a Map: Place-Names of Indigenous Origin in Australia*, edited by L. Hercus, F. Hodges, and J. Simpson, chapter 18, 255–76. Canberra: Pandanus Books in association with Pacific Linguistics, 2002.

Anderson, Margaret. "Comment: Oh What a Tangled Web . . . Politics, History and Museums." *Australian Historical Studies* 119 (2002): 179–85.

Anonymous. "Institutions, The National Museum of Ethnology." *Current Anthropology* 16, no. 2 (June 1975): 182.

Anonymous. "News and Views: Top Award for Tourist Spot." *Building Construction Materials and Equipment (BCME)* 36:43, no. 265 (1995): 13.

Anonymous. "Nk'mip Desert Cultural Centre, Governor General's Medal Winner." *Canadian Architect*, May 2008. http://www.canadianarchitect.com/news/nk-mip-desert-cultural-centre/1000222881/?type=Print%20Archives.

Anonymous. "Project Review: Gone Troppo: Kakadu Information Centre." *Architectural and Interior Specifier* 3, no. 4 (1994): 26–29.

Anonymous. "Sense of Place." *Commercial Design Trends* 21, no. 15 (2005): 82–87.

Anonymous. "Shung Ye Museum of Formosan Aborigines." *Architect* (Taiwan) no. 8 (1994): 140–45.

Aronczyk, Melissa, and Miranda Brady. "Crowdsourcing as Consultation: Branding History at Canada's Museum of Civilization (Part I)." *antenna*, December 18, 2012. http://blog.commarts.wisc.edu/2012/12/18/crowdsourcing-as-consultation-branding-history-at-canadas-museum-of-civilization-part-i/.

Austin, Mike. "The Tjibaou Culture Centre in New Caledonia." In M. J. Oswald and R. J. Moore (Eds.), *Re-Framing Architecture: Theory, Science and Myth*, 25–29. Sydney: Archadia Press, 2000.

Austin, Mike. "The Tjibaou Culture Centre." *Pander* 8 (Winter 1999). http://www.thepander.co.nz/architecture/maustin8.php#note3.

Australian Broadcasting Commission. "Mission Voices." http://www.abc.net.au/missionvoices/cummeragunja/voices_of_cummerangunja/default.htm (link no longer active, accessed July 2, 2012).

Australian Government, Department of Environment. "National Heritage Places, Brewarrina Aboriginal Fish Traps (Baiame's Ngunnhu)." *National Heritage List*. http://www.environment.gov.au/node/19636.

Australian Government, Department of Environment. "World Heritage Places, Tasmanian Wilderness." http://www.environment.gov.au/node/19816.

Australian Indigenous Art Commission. Musée du Quai Branly, Australian_Indigenous_Art_Commission.pdf.

Batten, Bronwyn. "From Prehistory to History: Shared Perspectives in Australian Heritage Interpretation." PhD Thesis, Macquarie University, Division of Society, Culture, Media and Philosophy, Warawara Department of Indigenous Studies, 2005. Australasian Digital Theses Program, http://hdl.handle.net/1959.14/445, Section 2: 72–80.

Bensa, Alban. "Piano Nouméa." *L'Architecture d'aujourd'hui* 308 (December 1996): 44–57.

Best, Ysola. "Brady, Donald (Don) (1927–1984)." *Australian Dictionary of Biography*. http://adb.anu.edu.au/biography/brady-donald-don-12246.

Blasselle, Agnès, and Anna Guarneri. "The Opening of the Musée du Quai Branly: Valuing/Displaying the 'Other' in Post-Colonial France." Humanity in Action. http://www.humanityinaction.org/knowledgebase/200-the-opening-of-the-musee-du-quai-branly-valuing-displaying-the-other-in-post-colonial-france.

Blue Spruce, Duane, ed. *Spirit of a Native Place: Building the National Museum of the American Indian*. Washington, DC: Smithsonian, National Museum of the American Indian, 2004.

Blue Spruce, Duane, and Tanya Thrasher, eds. *The Land Has Memory*. Washington, DC: Smithsonian, National Museum of the American Indian, 2008.

Bonyhady, Tim. *The Colonial Earth*. Melbourne: Melbourne University Press, 2000.

Boyd, Robin. *Living in Australia*. Melbourne: Thames and Hudson, 2013.

Bozic-Vrbancic, Senka. "One Nation, Two Peoples, Many Cultures: Exhibiting Identity at Te Papa Tongerewa." *Journal of the Polynesian Society* 112, no. 3 (2003): 295–313.

Breen, Shayne, and Dyan Summers, eds. *Aboriginal Connections with Launceston*. Launceston City Council, 2006.

Brown, Deidre. "Respecting Experience." In *Jasmax*, edited by Stephen Stratford, 170–73. Auckland: New Zealand Architectural Publications Trust, 2007.

Burgess, Gregory. "Gregory Burgess: Brambuk Living Cultural Centre." *A + U: Architecture and Urbanism* 320 (May 1997): 112–17.

Burgess, Gregory. "The Uluru-Kata Tjuta Cultural Centre." *Architect Victoria* (January/February 1998): 20–21.

Burrinja Cultural Centre. "Building Community through the Arts." Undated brochure available at the facility during 2011–2012.

Butts, David. "Māori and Museums: The Politics of Indigenous Recognition," chapter 17, 225–43. In *Museums, Society, Inequality*, edited by Richard Sandell. London; New York: Routledge, 2002.

Cameron, Patsy. *Grease and Ochre: The Blending of Two Cultures at the Colonial Sea Frontier*. Launceston: Fuller Bookshop, 2011.

Casey, Maryrose. "Disturbing Performances of Race and Nation: King Bungaree, John Noble and Jimmy Clements." *International Journal of Critical Indigenous Studies* 2, no. 2 (2009): 25–35.

Chang, Yui-tan. "The History and Identity of Taiwan's Museums: A Brief Review." In *Building Identity, The Making of National Museums and Identity Politics*, edited by Chang Yui-tan and Suzanne MacLeod, 185–88. Taipei: National Museum of History, 2012.

Clark, Ian. "Brambuk Koori Living Cultural Centre—Budja Budja, Hall's Gap, Victoria—Taking a Journey through Time." *Agora* 26, no. 4 (1991): 10–12.

Clifford, James. *Routes: Travel and Translation in the Late Twentieth Century*. Cambridge, MA: Harvard University Press, 1997.

Cobb, Amanda. "Interview with W. Richard West, Director, National Museum of the American Indian." *American Indian Quarterly* 29, nos. 3 and 4 (Summer and Fall 2005): 517–37.

Cobb, Amanda. "The National Museum of the American Indian: Sharing the Gift." *American Indian Quarterly* 29, nos. 3 and 4 (Summer and Fall 2005): 361–83.

Commonwealth of Australia. *A New Agenda for Multicultural Australia*. Canberra, December 1999. http://www.immi.gov.au/ media/publications/multicultural/pdf_doc/agenda/agenda.pdf.

Commonwealth of Australia. *Review of the National Museum of Australia, Its Exhibitions and Public Programs*. A Report to the Council of the National Museum of Australia, July 2003.

Cook, Nigel, and John Hunt. "Nationalistic Expression." *Architecture New Zealand* (November/December 1990): 18–23.

Cooper, Karen Coody, and Nicolasa I. Sandova, eds. *Living Homes for Cultural Expression: North American Native Perspectives on Creating Community Museums*. Washington, DC: NMAI Editions, Smithsonian Institution, 2006.

Cvoro, Uros. "Monument to Anti-Monumentality: The Space of the National Museum of Australia." *Museum and Society* 4, no. 3 (November 2006): 116–28.

Davidson, Jim. "Brambuk, Capital of Gariwerd in Victoria's Grampian Ranges." *Australian Society* 10, no. 12 (December 1991): 32–35.

Dean, Bec. "Where Goes the Neighbourhood?" In *There Goes the Neighbourhood: Redfern and the Politics of Urban Space*, edited by Zanny Begg and Keg De Souza, 8–9. Sydney: Breakdown Press, 2009.

Dean, David, and Peter E. Rider. "Museums, Nation and Political History in the Australian National Museum and the Canadian Museum of Civilization." *Museum and Society* 3, no. 1(March 2005): 35–50.

Department of Aboriginal Affairs. "Yagan Memorial Park Newsletter, February 2010." http://www.daa.wa.gov.au/Documents/News/Yagan%20Memorial%20Park/.

Department of Finance. "Korndin Kulluch: A Place of Reconciliation." http://www.finance.wa.gov.au/cms/content.aspx?id=15860%20.

Department of Immigration and Border Protection. "A Multicultural Australia." https://www.dss.gov.au/our-responsibilities/settlement-and-multicultural-affairs/publications.

Department of Indigenous Affairs. "Roebourne Report: Issues, Current Responses and Strategies for Consideration," July 2009. http://www.daa.wa.gov.au/Documents/ReportsPublications/Roebourne%20Report%202009%20(FINAL)%20-%20Department%20of%20Indigenous%20Affairs.pdf (link no longer active, last accessed November 27, 2013).

Derbal Yerrigan Committee. "Yagan Memorial Park Newsletter: February 2010." http://www.dia.wa.gov.au/Documents/News/Yagan%20Memorial%20Park/YMP_Newsletter_Feb24.pdf, 3 (link no longer active, last accessed December 12, 2012).

Desert Knowledge Australia. "The Gascoyne Aboriginal Heritage and Cultural Centre." DKA ppt. http://www.desertknowledgeaustralia.wikispaces.com/file/view/DKA+Part+1.ppt. (link no longer active, last accessed December 19, 2013)

Desert Knowledge Australia. http://www.desertknowledgeaustralia.wikispaces.com/file/view/DKA+Part+1.ppt (link no longer active, last accessed December 19, 2013).

Dovey, Kim. "Architecture about Aborigines." *Architecture Australia* 85, no. 4 (July/August, 1996): 98–103.

Dovey, Kim. "Architecture for the Aborigines." *Architecture Australia* 85, no. 4 (July/August 1996): 98–103.

Dovey, Kim. "Continuing Cultural Tensions Are Evident in Stage One of the Galina Beek Living Cultural Centre at Healesville, Victoria–by Anthony Styant-Browne." *Architecture Australia* 85, no. 5 (September/October 1996): 72–75.

Dovey, Kim. "Seeing Uluru." *Thresholds* 21 (2000): 60–65.

Dow, Coral. "Aboriginal Tent Embassy: Icon or Eyesore?" Chronology (Australia Department of the Parliamentary Library. Information and Research Services) no. 3, 1999–2000. Social Policy Group, April 4, 2000. www.aph.gov.au/library/pubs/chron/845 1999-2000/2000chr03.htm.

Drew, Philip. *Leaves of Iron*. North Ryde, NSW: Angus and Robertson, 1993.

Drew, Philip. *Touch the Earth Lightly: Glenn Murcutt in His Own Words*. Sydney: Duffy and Snellgrove, 1999.

Dysart, Dinah, ed. *Edge of the Trees: A Sculptural Installation by Janet Laurence and Fiona Foley*. Sydney: Historic Houses Trust of NSW, 2000.

East Gippsland Shire Council, *Nowa Nowa District 5 Year Community Plan 2004–2009*; East Gippsland Shire Council, *Nowa Nowa Community Plan 2012–2016*. http://www.eastgippsland.vic.gov.au/Plans _and_Projects/Community_Planning/Nowa_Nowa_and_District.

Edmunds, Mary. *A Good Life: Human Rights and Encounters with Modernity*. Canberra: Australian National University Press, 2013.

Edquist, Harriet, ed. *Frederick Romberg, The Architecture of Migration, 1938–1975*. Melbourne: RMIT University Press, 2000.

Emmett, Peter. "What Is This Place?" In *Edge of the Trees: A Sculptural Installation by Janet Laurence and Fiona Foley*, edited by Dinah Dysart, 23. Sydney: Historic Houses Trust of NSW, 2000.

Fantin, Shaneen. "Aboriginal Identities in Architecture." *Architecture Australia* 92, no. 5 (September/ October 2003): 8487.

Ferguson, Susan. Brambuk Cultural Centre, 04, Architectural resource package, http://www.brambuk .com.au/assets/pdf/brambukspecs.pdf.

Findley, Lisa. *Building Change: Architecture, Politics and Cultural Agency*. London; New York: Routledge, 2005.

Fleras, Augie. "Politicizing Identity: Ethno-Politics in White Settler Dominions." In *Indigenising Peoples' Rights in Australia, Canada and New Zealand*, edited by Paul Havemann, 187–234. Auckland: Oxford University Press, 1999.

Flew, Terry. "Beyond Ad-Hocery: Defining Creative Industries." Paper presented at the Second International Conference on Cultural Policy Research, Wellington, 2002, 181–92.

Foley, Gary. "Black Power in Redfern." In *There Goes the Neighbourhood: Redfern and the Politics of Urban Space*, edited by Zanny Begg and Keg De Souza, 12–21. Sydney: Breakdown Press, 2009.

Fortmeyer, Russell. "In Canada, a Rammed-Earth Wall for the Ages." *Architectural Record*, March 2008. http://archrecord.construction.com/tech/technicalities/0803technicalities.asp.

France Diplomatie. "Dossiers: Official Statement—The Quai Branly Museum: A New Institution Engaged in the Dialogue of Cultures and Civilizations." http://www.diplomatie.gouv.fr/en/france_159/ discovering-france_2005/france-from-to-z_1978/culture_1979/the-musee-du-quai-branly_5035.html.

French, Ann. "Setting Standards: Te Papa Kaihautu." *Architecture New Zealand* (February 1998): 69–72.

Fromonot, Françoise. *Glenn Murcutt: Buildings + Projects 1962–2003*. London: Thames and Hudson, 2003.

Giddens, Anthony. *Modernity and Self-Identity*. Cambridge, UK: Polity Press, 1991.

Goad, Philip. *Troppo Architects*. Singapore: Periplus Editions, 2005.

Go-Sam, Carroll. "Fabricating Blackness: Aboriginal Identity Constructs in the Production and Authorisation of Architecture." In Proceedings of the XXVIIIth International Conference of the Society of Architectural Historians, Australia and New Zealand 2011, *Audience*, edited by Antony Moulis and Deborah van der Plaat, 1–27. http://espace.library.uq.edu.au/view/UQ:245276.

Graburn, Nelson. "Multiculturalism, Museums and Tourism in Japan." In *Multiculturalism in the New Japan: Crossing the Boundaries Within*, edited by Nelson H. Graburn, John Ertl, and R. Kenji Tierney, 218–40. Oxford; New York: Berghahn Books, 2008.

Green, C., and R. Painter. *A Survey for Aboriginal Values at Cox Bight and Melaleuca in the Southwest Conservation Area*. Unpublished report to the Parks and Wildlife Service, Tasmania, 1997.

Green, Neville. *Broken Spears: Aborigines and Europeans in the Southwest of Australia*. Perth, WA: Focus Education Services, 1984.

Gregory Burgess Architects, Sonja Peter, Environmental Designer, Kevin Taylor and Kate Cullity, Landscape Designers, David Western, Tourist Consultant and Anthony Prowse and Associates, Quantity Surveyors. "Uluru National Park Cultural Centre: Project Brief and Concept Design." Brief prepared for the Mutitjulu Community and Australian National Parks and Wildlife Service, October 1990.

Hage, Ghassan. *White Nation: Fantasies of White Supremacy in a Multicultural Society*. Annandale, NSW: Pluto Press, 1998.

Hallam, S., and L. Tilbrook. *Aborigines of the Southwest Region, 1829–1840*. Perth, WA: UWA Press, 1990.

Harris, Mark. "Mapping Australian Postcolonial Landscapes: From Resistance to Reconciliation." *Law Text Culture* no. 7 (2003): 71–97.

Harrison, Fiona. "Not Nothing: Shades of Public Space." *Journal of Australian Studies* 27, no. 76 (2003): 35–43.

Hawthorn, Audrey. *A Labour of Love: The Making of the Museum of Anthropology, UBC, The First Three Decades, 1947–76*. Vancouver: UBC, Museum of Anthropology, 1993.

Heidegger, M. *Being and Time*. Translated by J. Macquarrie and E. S. Robinson. Oxford: Blackwell Publishers, 1962.

Helstren, Linda Lizut. "Museum Survivance: Vizenor Before and After Repatriation." In *Gerald Vizenor: Texts and Contexts*, edited by Deborah L. Madsen and A. Robert Lee, 231–48. Albuquerque, NM: University of New Mexico Press, 2010.

Hinkson, Melinda. *Aboriginal Sydney: A Guide to Important Places of the Past and Present*. Canberra, ACT: Aboriginal Studies Press, 2001.

Hourston, Laura. *Museum Builders II*. Chichester; Hoboken, NJ: Wiley-Academy, 2004.

Howard, John, The Hon. "The Liberal Tradition: The Beliefs and Values which Guide the Federal Government." Melbourne: Sir Robert Menzies Lecture Trust, Monash University, 1996.

Iglauer, Edith. *Seven Stones: A Portrait of Arthur Erickson, Architect*. Vancouver: Museum of Anthropology, University of British Columbia, 1972.

Jacknis, Ira. "A New Thing?: The NMAI in Historical and Institutional Perspective." *American Indian Quarterly* 30, nos. 3 and 4 (Summer and Fall 2006): 511–542.

Jackson, Daryl. "The Kevin Borland Timber in Architecture Award." *Architect* (October 1995): 9–12.

Jacobs, Jane M. *Edge of Empire: Postcolonialism and the City*. London; New York: Routledge, 1996.

Johnson, Roger. "Brambuk Living Cultural Centre." *Architecture Australia* 79, no. 10 (November 1990): 26–28.

Jones, Rhys. "Ordering the Landscape." In *Seeing the First Australians*, edited by Ian Donaldson, 181–209. Sydney: Allen and Unwin, 1985.

Josefsen, Eva. "The Saami and the National Parliaments: Channels for Political Influence, Inter-Parliamentary Union and UNDP." http://www.ipu.org/splz-e/chiapas10/saami.pdf.

Jury Citation. "Awards 1990: Institutional New." *Architect Victoria* (September 1990): 10–12.

Kaino, Lorna. "What Difference Does a Museum Make? Te Papa's Contribution to the New Zealand Economy." *Media International, Australia*, no. 117 (November 2005): 31–42.

Kaurna Tappa Iri Reconciliation Working Group. "KITRA Kaurna Tappa Iri Regional Agreement, Heritage Culture and Business Development 2005–2008." University of Adelaide, 2005.

Kepel, Gilles. *Banlieu de la Republique: Société, politique et religion à Clichy-sous-Bois et Montfermeil* (Suburbs of the Republic: Society, Politics and Religion in Clichy-sous-Bois and Montfermeil). Paris: Gallimard Editions, 2012.

King, Lisa. "Speaking Sovereignty and Communicating Change: Rhetorical Sovereignty and the Inaugural Exhibits at the NMAI." *American Indian Quarterly* 35, no. 1 (Winter 2011): 75–103.

Kirke, P. *The Shelter of Law: Designing with Communities for a Culture of Natural Justice*. Perth: Friend Books, 2009.

Koizumi, Junji. "Transformation of the Public Image of Anthropology: The Case of Japan." Paper presented at the European Association of Social Anthropologists (EASA) 9th Biennial Conference, University of Bristol, United Kingdom, September 21, 2006. http://www.ram-wan.net/documents/05_e _Journal/journal-3/8-koizumi.pdf.

Koleth, Elsa. "Multiculturalism: A Review of Australian Policy Statements and Recent Debates in Australia and Overseas." Social Policy Section, Parliament of Australia, Research Paper no. 6, 2010–2011, October 8, 2010. http://www.aph.gov.au/About_Parliament/Parliamentary_Departments/Parliamentary_Library/pubs/rp/rp1011/11rp06.

Koolhaas, Rem, and Hans Ulrich Obrist. *Project Japan: Metabolism Talks*. Koln: Tachen, 2011.

Kurokawa, Kisho. *Kisho Kurokawa: Abstract Symbolism.* Milano: L'Arcaedizioni, 1996.

Kurokawa, Kisho. *Kisho Kurokawa Architect and Associates: Selected and Current Works.* Mulgrave, VIC: Images Publishing Group, 2000.

Kurokawa, Kisho. *Kisho Kurokawa: From Metabolism to Symbiosis.* London: Academy Editions; New York: St. Martin's Press, 1992.

Lake Tyers Aboriginal Trust. *Lake Tyers Aboriginal Trust Conservation Management Plan.* http://www .laketyersaboriginaltrust.com.au/index.php?option=com_content&view=article&id=12&Itemid=19.

Laurence, Janet, and Fiona Foley. "The Artists' Submission." In *Edge of the Trees: A Sculptural Installation by Janet Laurence and Fiona Foley,* edited by Dinah Dysart, 49. Sydney: Historic Houses Trust of NSW, 2000.

Lehman, Greg. *Aboriginal Interpretation of the Tasmanian Wilderness World Heritage Area: Report to the Parks and Wildlife Service, Tasmania.* Hobart: Tasmanian Aboriginal Land Council, 1995.

Leigh, Gweneth Newman. "Coastal Communities." *Architecture AU,* May 11, 2012. http://architec tureau.com/articles/coastal-communities/.

Leslie, Tim. "The History of the Aboriginal Tent Embassy." Australian Broadcasting Corporation, January 27, 2012.

Lin, Chia-hui, "Museumisation and Communitarianism in Post-Martial Law Taiwan." In *Building Identity, The Making of National Museums and Identity Politics,* edited by Chang Yui-tan and Suzanne MacLeod, 171–84. Taipei: National Museum of History, 2012.

Lin, Zongjie. *Kenzo Tange and the Metabolist Movement: Urban Utopias of Modern Japan.* Routledge: Oxon, New York, 2010.

Local Government Association of South Australia and Government of South Australia. *Examples of Working Together in South Australia, Government of South Australia.* https://www.lga.sa.gov.au/ webdata/resources/files/Examples_of_Working_Together_in_SA___Page_1_9___LGA_OLG___ Nov_2000_pdf1.pdf.

Lochert, Mathilde. "Mediating Aboriginal Architecture." *Transition* 54–55 (1997): 8–19.

Lopez, Mark. *The Origins of Multiculturalism in Australian Politics 1945–1975.* Carlton South: Melbourne University Press, 2000.

Louekari, Lauri. "Sámi Sitelines." Unstructured 6. First published in *ARK, the Finnish Architecture Review* and translated by Frank Betke. http://www.fourthdoor.co.uk/unstructured/unstructured_6/ sajos_Sámi_cultural_centre.php.

Lujan, James. "A Museum of the Indian, Not for the Indian." *American Indian Quarterly* 29, nos. 3 and 4 (Summer and Fall 2005): 510–16.

Malnar, Joy Monice, and Frank Vodvarka. *New Architecture on Indigenous Lands.* Minneapolis, MN: University of Minnesota Press, 2013.

Malone, Gavin. "Ways of Belonging: Reconciliation and Adelaide's Public Space Indigenous Cultural Markers." *Geographical Research* 45, no. 2 (2007): 158–66.

Margie West and Art Gallery of the Northern Territory, eds. *Yalangbara, Art of the Djang'kawu.* Darwin: Museum and Art Gallery of Northern Territory, 2008.

Mathews, Janet. "Language Elicitation from Bourke, NSW, and some SA Language Material." Sound recorded in 1968. Australian Institute of Aboriginal and Torres Strait Islander Studies online collections. http://www.aiatsis.gov.au/collections/using-collection/search-collection.

McGaw, Janet, and Cliff Chang. "Melbourne's Hidden Waterways: Revealing Williams Creek." *Double Dialogues* 13 (Summer 2010). http://www.doubledialogues.com/article/melbournes-hidden-water ways-revealing-williams-creek/.

McGaw, Janet, and Anoma Pieris. *Assembling the Centre: Architecture for Indigenous Cultures, Australia and Beyond.* Abingdon, Oxon; New York: Routledge, 2015.

McGlade, Hannah. "The Repatriation of Yagan: A Story of Manufacturing Dissent." *Law Text Culture,* no. 4 (1998): 245–55.

Memmott, Paul. *Gunyah, Goondie + Wurley: The Aboriginal Architecture of Australia.* Brisbane: University of Queensland Press, 2007.

Memmott, Paul, and Joseph Reser. "Design Concepts and Processes for Public Aboriginal Architecture." *PaPER 55–56*, Cairns: Aboriginal Environments Research Centre, Department of Architecture, University of Queensland and Department of Psychology, James Cook University), 69–86.

Message, Kylie. "Contested Sites of Identity and the Cult of the New: The Centre Culturel Tjibaou and the Constitution of Culture in New Caledonia." *reCollections: Journal of the National Museum of Australia* 1, no. 1 (March 2006): 7–28.

Message, Kylie. "Culture, Citizenship and Australian Multiculturalism: The Contest Over Identity Formation at the National Museum of Australia." *Humanities Research* 15, no. 2 (2009): 23–48.

Miles, Henry. "Parliamentary Prescience." *Architectural Review*, April 1, 2001, 49–53.

Minister for Local Government and Aboriginal and Torres Strait Islander Partnerships. *Annual Highlights Report for Queensland's Discrete Indigenous Communities July 2009–June 2010.* http://www.cabinet.qld .gov.au/documents/2010/nov/ highlight%20report%20for%20qld%20indigenous%20communities/ Attachments/full-report.pdf.

Muldoon, Paul, and Andrew Schaap. "Aboriginal Sovereignty and the Politics of Reconciliation: The Constituent Power of the Aboriginal Embassy in Australia." *Environment and Planning D: Society and Space* 30, no. 3 (2012): 534–50.

Murphy, Bernice. "Centre Culturel Tjibaou: A Museum and Arts Center Redefining New Caledonia's Cultural Future." *Humanities Research* 9, no. 1 (2002): 77–90.

Murphy, Phin, and Tim Hart. "Riawunna: The Living Landscape Expressed through the Living Culture—Full Project Report." The Australian Institute of Landscape Architects. http://www.aila.org.au/ projects/tas/Riawunna/Riawunna3.htm.

Nango, Joar. "The Sámi Building Tradition: A Complex Picture (2009)." *Northern Experiments: The Barents Urban Survey.* http://www.northernexperiments.net/index.php?/saami-building/.

National Museum of Ethnology. "'Modernologio' Now: Kon Wajiro's Science of the Present." http:// www.minpaku.ac.jp/english/museum/exhibition/special/20120426kon/ exhibition.

National Museum of Ethnology. "Museum Survey and Guide 2014." http://www.minpaku.ac.jp/sites/ default/files/english/aboutus/youran/pdf/youran2014_en03.pdf.

Native Universe and Museums in the Twenty-First Century [The]: The Significance of the Museum of the American Indian. Washington, DC: NMAI Editions, Smithsonian Institution, 2005.

Naumann, Peter. "Naturally in Paris." *Architecture Australia* 95, no. 5 (September 2006): 88–95.

Neale, Margo. "Lin Onus (tribute)." *Artlink*, no. 1 (2000). http://www.artlink.com.au/articles/1394/ lin-onus/.

Ngurra Kuju Walyja—One Country One People—Stories from the Canning Stock Route. Melbourne, VIC: Macmillan Art Publishing, 2011.

Nichols, John. "Karijini Architectural Design Awards Submission." http://www.dec.wa.gov.au/content/ view/391/1270 (link no longer active, last accessed May 20, 2012).

Ningla A-Na (Hungry for Our Land). Produced and directed by Alessandro Cavadini. Melbourne: Australian Film Institute, 1972.

Office of Environment and Heritage, NSW Government. "Brewarrina Aboriginal Mission Site." http:// www.environment.nsw.gov.au/heritageapp/ ViewHeritageItemDetails.aspx?ID=5053415.

Office of Multicultural Affairs. *National Agenda for a Multicultural Australia.* Canberra: Australian Government Publishing Service, July 1989.

Page, Allison Joy. "19.5. Gurung Gunya: A New Dwelling." In *The Oxford Companion to Aboriginal Art and Culture,* edited by Sylvia Kleinert and Margo Neale, 423–26. Oxford; New York: Oxford University Press, 2000.

Parks and Wildlife Service Tasmania. "Evaluation Report 2013: Needwonnee Aboriginal Walk, Melaleuca." http://www.parks.tas.gov.au/file.aspx?id=31714.

Pieris, Anoma. *JCY: The Architecture of Jones Coulter Young.* Balmain, NSW: Pesaro Publishing, 2005.

Pitts, Angela. "Dreaming the Block." *Architecture Australia* 97, no. 5 (September/October 2008): 105–11.

Plomley, N. J. B., ed. *Friendly Mission: The Tasmanian Journals and Papers of George Augustus Robinson, 1829–1834* (2nd edition). Launceston: Tasmanian Historical Research Association, 2008.

Potter, Emily. "'Structural and Poetic': Burrinja Cultural Centre, by Gregory Burgess Architects (building review)." *Architecture Review Asia Pacific*, no. 125 (June/July 2012): 90–95.

Prakash, Vikramaditya. *Chandigarh's Le Corbusier: The Struggle for Modernity in Postcolonial India*. Seattle, WA: University of Washington Press; Ahmedabad, India: Mapin Publishing, 2002.

Presland, Gary. "Woi Wurrung." *eMelbourne: The City Past and Present*. http://www.emelbourne.net.au/ biogs/EM01629b.htm.

Price, Sally. *Paris Primitive: Jacques Chirac's Museum on the Quai Branly*. Chicago: University of Chicago Press, 2007.

Raggatt, Howard. "Letters and Fixes: Howard Raggatt Replies." *Architecture Australia*, July/August 2001, 96.

Read, Peter. "The Truth which Will Set Us All Free: National Reconciliation, Oral History and the Conspiracy of Silence." International conference, keynote address. *Oral History* 35, no. 1 (Spring 2007): 98–106.

Reed, Dimity. *Land, Nation, People: Stories from the National Museum of Australia*. Mulgrave, VIC: Image Publishing Group, 2002.

Reed, Dimity. *National Museum of Australia: Tangled Destinies*. Mulgrave, VIC: Image Publishing Group, 2002.

Ren, Hai. "Economies of Culture: Theme Parks, Museums and Capital Accumulation in China, Hong Kong and Taiwan." PhD dissertation submitted to the Department of Anthropology at the University of Washington, 1998.

Rice, Fiona, Tony Brown, and Kylie Dickson, eds. "Needwonnee: Connecting and Sharing: The Needwonnee Walk, Melaleuca, South-West Tasmania." Hobart: Parks and Wildlife Service, 2011.

Richardson, Edwina. "Riawunna Aboriginal Studies Centre, University of Tasmania, Launceston." Australian Institute of Landscape Architects. http://www.aila.org.au/projects/ tas/Riawunna/Riawunna2.htm.

Robertson, Jennifer. *Politics and Pitfalls of Japan Ethnography: Reflexivity, Responsibility, and Anthropological Ethics*. Oxon; New York: Routledge, 2013.

Robinson, Scott. "The Aboriginal Embassy: An Account of the Protests of 1972." *Aboriginal History* 18, no. 1 (1994): 49–63.

Rowe, David. "Olga Kosterin: NSW Public Works Department: Brewarrina Aboriginal Cultural Museum." *A + U: Architecture and Urbanism* 265 (October 1992): 12–19.

Royal Commission into Aboriginal Deaths in Custody. "Report into the Death of Lloyd James Boney," January 24, 1991. http://www.austlii.edu.au/au/other/IndigLRes/ rciadic/individual/brm_ljb/.

Royal Commission into Aboriginal Deaths in Custody. "Report of the Inquiry into the Death of John Peter Pat: Introduction," April 1991. http://www.austlii.edu.au/au/other/IndigLRes/rciadic/individual/brm_jpp/2.html.

Ryan, Lyndall. *The Aboriginal Tasmanians*. Brisbane: University of Queensland Press, 1981.

Sandell, Richard. *Museums, Society, Inequality*. London; New York: Routledge, 2002.

Sauvage, Alexandra. "Narratives of Colonisation: The Musée du Quai Branly in Context." *reCollections: Journal of the National Museum of Australia* 2, no. 2 (September 2007). http://recollections.nma.gov .au/issues/vol_2_no2/papers/ narratives_of_colonisation/.

Scott, Trevor. "Letters and Fixes: NMA, AIATSIS and Consultation." *Architecture Australia* 90, no. 4 (July/August 2001), 96.

Seddon, George, and David Ravine. *A City and Its Setting: Images of Perth, Western Australia*. Fremantle, WA: Fremantle Arts Centre Press, 1986.

Serle, Geoffrey. *Robin Boyd: A Life*. Melbourne: Melbourne University Press, 1995.

Shung Ye Museum of Formosan Aborigines Guidebook. Taipei: Shung Ye Museum of Formosan Aborigines, 2011.

Siddle, Richard M. *Race, Resistance and the Ainu of Japan*. Abingdon, Oxon; New York: Routledge, 2012.

Simon, Scott. "Paths to Autonomy: Aboriginality and the Nation in Taiwan." In *The Margins of Becoming: Identity and Culture in Taiwan*, edited by C. Storm and M. Harrison, 221–40. Weisbaden: Harrassowitz, 2006.

Simon, Scott. "Writing Indigeneity in Taiwan." In *Re-Writing Culture in Taiwan*, edited by Fang-long Shih, Stuart Thompson, and Paul François Tremlett, 50–68. London; New York: Routledge, 2009.

Sims, Peter. "Indigenous Heritage Law Reform." Submission to Heritage Division, Department of the Environment, Water, Heritage and the Arts, Canberra, October 25, 2009. https://www.environment.gov.au/system/files/pages/080619b8-678d-4d4a-905a-a287b0ab0fb7/files/peter-c-sims-oam.pdf.

Sims, Peter. "No Reprieve for Tasmanian Rock Art." *Arts* (special issue Rock Art) 2, no. 4 (2013): 182–224. doi:10.3390/arts2040182.

Smith, Nyanda. "The Yagan Memorial Park–A Site of Significance." *Artsource Newsletter*, August 2010.

Spark, Ceridwen. "Brambuk Living Cultural Centre: Indigenous Culture and the Production of Place." *Tourist Studies* 2, no. 1 (2002): 23–42.

Spence, Rory. "Brambuk Living Cultural Centre." *The Architectural Review* 184, no. 1100 (October 1988): 88–90.

Stead, Naomi. "The Semblance of Populism: National Museum of Australia (building review)." *Journal of Architecture* 9 (Autumn 2004): 385–96.

Stein Halvorsen Arkitekter. "Parliament for the Sámi People." *ArchDaily*, February 8, 2009. http://www.archdaily.com/5489/parliament-for-the-Sámi-people-sh-arkitekter.

Strakosch, Elizabeth. "Counter Monuments and Nation-Building in Australia." *Peace Review: A Journal of Social Justice* 22 (2010): 268–75.

Strakosch, Elizabeth. "The Political Complexies of 'New Memorials': Victims and Perpetrators Sharing Space in the Australian Capital." Presented at a Workshop on "Memorials and Museums," Berlin Roundtables, Memory Politics: Education, Memorials and Mass Media, October 21–26, 2009. Irmgard Coninx Stiftung, http://www.irmgard-coninx-stiftung.de/index.php?id=190, 7p (accessed January 30, 2012).

Styant-Browne, Tony. "Work for Aboriginal Communities." *Architect Victoria* (Winter 2001), 8–9.

Sykes, Roberta. *Black Power in Australia: Bobbie Sykes versus Senator Neville T. Bonner*, edited by Ann Turner and Neville Bonner. South Yarra, VIC: Heinemann Educational Australia, 1975.

Tawa, Michael. "Liru and Kunya." *Architecture Australia* (March/April 1996): 48–55.

Taylor, Jennifer. "A Rapport with the Setting." *Landscape Architecture* 80 (August 1990): 56–57.

Taylor, John. "Anangu Population Dynamics and Future Growth in Uluru-Kata Tjuta National Park." Discussion Paper 211, Centre for Aboriginal Economic Policy Research, Australian National University, 2001. http://caepr.anu.edu.au/Publications/DP/2001DP211.php.

Taylor, Kevin. "Uluru-Kata Tjuta Cultural Centre." *Landscape Australia* 23, no. 1 (2001): 26–29.

Thakre, Peeroj. "Earth and Sky." *Canadian Architect* 52, no. 3 (March 2007): 27–30.

Tindale, Norman. Tribal Boundaries in Aboriginal Australia (map). Canberra: Australian National University Press, 1974.

Tramposch, William. "Te Papa: An Invitation for Redefinition." *Museum International* 50, no. 3 (1998): 28–32.

Trigger, Toland. "Kamay Botany Bay La Perouse Headland and Bare Island Draft Interpretation, Landscape and Architectural Plan Public Exhibition." http://www.environment.nsw.gov.au/resources/planmanagement/ draft/KamayBotanyBayDraftIP.pdf.

Turgeon, Laurier, and Elise Dubuc. "Ethnology Museums: New Challenges and New Directions." *Ethnologies* 24, no. 2 (2002). http://www.celat.ulaval.ca/acef/242a.htm.

Turner, Caroline. "Linking the Past and Future: Cultural Exchanges and Cross-Cultural Engagements in Four Asian Museums." *Humanities Research* 9, no. 1 (2002): 13–28.

Tyrrell, Mark. "National Centre for Indigenous Excellence." *Landscape Architecture Australia* 127 (August 2010): 42–46. http://architectureau.com/articles/national-centre-for-indigenous-excellence/.

Umesao, Tadao. *An Ecological View of History: Japanese Civilization in the World Context*, translated by Beth Cary, Rosanna: Trans Pacific Press, 2003 (original publication in Japanese, 1967).

Umesao, Tadao. *The Art of Intellectual Production* (originally published in 1969; not translated into English).

United Nations Non-Governmental Liaison Service. "Implementing the UN Declaration on the Rights of Indigenous Peoples: What Role for Parliamentarians?" http://www.un-ngls.org/spip .php?page=article_s&id_article=3900.

Vernon, Christopher. "Axial Occupation." *Architecture Australia* 91, no. 5 (September/October 2002): 84–90.

Vernon, Christopher. "Canberra: Where Landscape Is Pre-Eminent." In *Planning Twentieth-Century Capital Cities*, edited by David Gordon, 130–49. London; New York: Routledge, 2006.

Vernon, Christopher. "The Aboriginal Tent Embassy." *Architecture Australia* 91, no. 6 (November/ December 2002): 36.

Vickers, Edward. "Re-Writing Museums in Taiwan." In *Re-Writing Culture in Taiwan*, edited by Fang-long Shih, Stuart Thompson, and Paul François Tremlett, 69–101. London; New York: Routledge, 2009.

Victorian Aboriginal Community Controlled Health Organisation, "Communities Working for Health and Well-Being: Success Stories from the Aboriginal Community Controlled Health Sector in Victoria," July 2007. http://www.lowitja.org.au/.../ VACCHO-Successes-Booklet-hi-res-screen.pdf.

Victorian Heritage Database place details. "Bangerang Cultural Centre." Report published October 28, 2013. http://vhd.heritage.vic.gov.au/reports/ report_place/13104.

Vizenor, Gerald, ed. *Manifest Manners: Narratives on Postindian Survivance*. Lincoln, NE: University of Nebraska Press, 1999.

Vizenor, Gerald, ed. *Survivance: Narratives of Native Presence*. Lincoln, NE: University of Nebraska Press, 2008.

Walker, Paul. "Culture." In Greig Crysler, Stephen Cairns, and Hilde Heynen, *The SAGE Handbook of Architectural Theory*, 369–82. London: Sage, 2012.

Walliss, Jillian. "The Right to Land versus the Right to Landscape: Uluru-Kata Tjuta National Park, Australia." In *The Right to Landscape: Contesting Landscape and Human Rights*, eds. Shelley Egoz, Jala Makhzoumie, and Gloria Pungetti, 153–65. Farnham, UK, Burlington, VT: Ashgate, 2011.

Walsh, Andrea N. *Nk'Mip Chronicles, Art from the Inkameep Day School*. Osoyoos, BC: Osoyoos Museum Society and Osoyoos Indian Band, 2005.

Wan Sung Shan, *Cha I To Yang Hsing Yu Po Wu Kuan* (Difference, Multiformity and Museum). Tas Hsiang, Taipei, 2003.

Ware, SueAnne. "Radar Competition, Section 2, Reconciling This Place." *Architecture Australia* 90, no. 5 (September/October 2001): 36–40.

Waterson, Roxana. *The Living House: An Anthropology of Architecture in Southeast Asia*. Singapore; Oxford; New York: Oxford University Press, 1990.

Weller, Richard. "Weaving the Axis." *Landscape Australia*, 20, no. 1 (February/March/April, 1998): 10–17.

West Jr., W. Richard. "As Long as We Keep Dancing: A Brief Personal History." In *Spirit of a Native Place: Building the National Museum of the American Indian*, edited by Duane Blue Spruce, 47–65. Washington, DC: Smithsonian, National Museum of the American Indian, 2004.

West, W. Richard. "A New Idea of Ourselves: The Changing Presentation of the American Indian." In *The Changing Presentation of the American Indian: Museums and Native Cultures*, edited with an introduction by W. Richard West, 7–13. Seattle: National Museum of the American Indian/Smithsonian Institution with University of Washington Press, 2000.

Western Australian Planning Commission. "Draft Pyrton-Lockridge Reserves Cultural Consultation Report 2012." http://www.finance.wa.gov.au/cms/uploadedFiles/ Building_Management_and_Works/ Policy/Cultural%20Consultation%20Report%20web.pdf?n=9898.

Wigley, Mark. *The Architecture of Deconstruction: Derrida's Haunt*. Cambridge, MA: MIT Press, 1993.

Williams, Georgina Yambo. "Sustainable Cultures and Creating New Cultures for Sustainability." Paper given at the Regional Institute Conference on Sustaining our Communities, Adelaide, March 3–6, 2002. http://www.regional.org.au/au/ soc/2002/5/williams.htm.

Wines, James. "Conclusion: Turning over a New Leaf." In James Wines, *Green Architecture*, 226–37. Los Angeles: Taschen, 2000.

Winkel, Margarita. "Academic Traditions, Urban Dynamics, and Colonial Threat: The Rise of Ethnography in Early Modern Japan." In *Anthropology and Colonialism in Asia and Oceania*, edited by Jan van Bremen and Akitoshi Shimizu, 40–64. Richmond, UK: Curzon Press.

YMP_Newsletter_Feb24.pdf (link no longer active, last accessed November 28, 2013).

Zeppel, Heather. "Aboriginal Tourism in Australia: A Research Bibliography." Co-Operative Research Centre for Sustainable Tourism Research Report Series: Report 2, 1999. http://www.crctourism.com.au/wms/upload/resources/bookshop/Aboriginal%20Tourism%20in%20Australia.PDF.

About the Editors and Contributors

Anoma Pieris is an associate professor at the Melbourne School of Design, University of Melbourne. She is an architectural historian by training with a specialist focus on South and Southeast Asian architecture. Her interdisciplinary approach draws on history, anthropology, and geography with an additional interest in gender studies. Anoma's publications include: *Architecture and Nationalism in Sri Lanka: The Trouser under the Cloth* (2012) and *Hidden Hands and Divided Landscapes: A Penal History of Singapore's Plural Society* (2009). Anoma is coauthor with Janet McGaw of the book *Assembling the Centre: Architecture for Indigenous Cultures: Australia and Beyond* (2015). She was also the lead author with four others on *Indigenous Place: Contemporary Buildings, Landmarks and Places of Significance in South East Australia and Beyond* (2014).

Michael Tawa is professor of architecture and director of the Masters of Architecture at the University of Sydney. He has taught architectural theory and design at the University of NSW, the University of South Australia, and Newcastle University (UK). He has been visiting professor at the École des Hautes Études en Sciences Sociales, Paris; Carleton University, Ottawa, and Newcastle University (UK). He has worked on engagement projects with Indigenous communities at Patjarr, Warburton Ranges, Urapuntja, Broken Hill, Wilcannia, and Bourke. Michael's recent publications include *Agencies of the Frame: Tectonic Strategies in Cinema and Architecture* and *Theorizing the Project: A Thematic Approach to Architectural Design*.

Dr. Elizabeth Grant is an architectural anthropologist and academic at the University of Adelaide. She overlays the fields of architecture and anthropology to conceptualize and frame the design and use of Indigenous spaces and places from interdisciplinary perspectives. Elizabeth has worked as a consultant on national and international architectural projects to ensure that the needs of and aspirations of Indigenous users are incorporated, and her work has led to major changes in the way prisons, courts, and other environments are designed for Indigenous users.